Moya Longsta

The Fiction of Albert Camus

A Complex Simplicity

PETER LANG

Oxford · Bern · Berlin · Bruxelles · Frankfurt am Main · New York · Wien

Bibliographic information published by Die Deutsche Bibliothek
Die Deutsche Bibliothek lists this publication in the Deutsche
Nationalbibliografie; detailed bibliographic data is available on the
Internet at ‹http://dnb.ddb.de›.

British Library and Library of Congress Cataloguing-in-Publication Data:
A catalogue record for this book is available from *The British Library*,
Great Britain, and from *The Library of Congress*, USA

ISSN 1422-9005
ISBN 3-03910-304-0
US-ISBN 0-8204-7229-8

© Peter Lang AG, International Academic Publishers, Bern 2007
Hochfeldstrasse 32, Postfach 746, CH-3000 Bern 9, Switzerland
info@peterlang.com, www.peterlang.com, www.peterlang.net

All rights reserved.
All parts of this publication are protected by copyright.
Any utilisation outside the strict limits of the copyright law, without
the permission of the publisher, is forbidden and liable to prosecution.
This applies in particular to reproductions, translations, microfilming,
and storage and processing in electronic retrieval systems.

Printed in Germany

To the memory of my parents, Jack and May Laverty,
and for Richard, Stephen and Peter

Contents

Acknowledgements		9
Abbreviations		11
Introduction	Sisyphus' Stone	13
Chapter I	The Gods of Happiness. *La Mort heureuse*	47
Chapter II	A Happy Life and a Happy Death. *L'Étranger*	73
Chapter III	Voices in a Time of Plague. *La Peste*	113
Chapter IV	A Sojourn in the Circles of Hell. *La Chute*	161
Chapter V	The Landscapes of Solitude. *L'Exil et le Royaume*	197
Chapter VI	Sailing to Ithaca. *Le Premier homme*	239
Conclusion	Adam's Tale Retold	273
Bibliography		287
Index		297

Acknowledgements

My heartfelt thanks go first of all to my husband Richard, without whose patience and hard work this volume would never have emerged in all its printed and finished glory from my personal computer, which seems to have an endless variety of little quirks, reserved for me alone. I also have a large debt of gratitude to my friend and colleague Professor Graham Gargett, of the University of Ulster, for his meticulous proof-reading of this long text, and his helpful suggestions. My thanks go to Dr Graham Speake of Peter Lang AG and Dr Peter Collier, my Series Editor, for their help, encouragement and suggestions, and to Mr Alan Mauro for his advice concerning the problems of presentation. Mr Frank Reynolds and the staff of the library of the University of Ulster have been unfailingly ready to oblige and inform, and to them also I am most grateful.

I am indebted to the publishing house of Gallimard for permission to quote from the works of Camus.as published in the Pleiade editions of *Essais* and *Théâtre, Récits, Nouvelles*, also from *Carnets I, II*, and *III, La Mort heureuse* (in *Cahiers Albert Camus I*), *Le Premier homme*, and *Albert Camus/Jean Grenier: Correspondance 1932–1960*. Penguin Books kindly gave me permission to quote from their English translations of the novels and short stories, *A Happy Death, The Outsider, The Plague, The Fall, Exile and the Kingdom,* and *The First Man*, also from their edition of *Selected Essays, The Myth of Sisyphus*, and *The Rebel*. Some of the material in Chapter II had appeared in an earlier form in *The French Review*, vol. 64, no.1, October 1990, and my thanks go to the editor of that journal for permission to re-use it.

Abbreviations

Camus

In the Pléiade collection (Paris, Gallimard):

Essais	*Essais*, 1965 (Achevé d'imprimer 2000)
TRN	*Théâtre, Récits, Nouvelles*, 1962 (achevé d'imprimer 1999)

Page numbers for references to *L'Étranger, La Peste, La Chute*, and the short stories of *L'Exil et le Royaume*, are to this Pléiade edition.

Other works:

Carnets I	*Carnets mai 1935–février 1942*, Gallimard, 1962
Carnets I	*Carnets janvier 1942–mars 1951*, Gallimard, 1964
Carnets III	*Carnets III mars 1951–décembre 1959*, Gallimard, 1989
Corr.AC/JG	*Albert Camus / Jean Grenier: Correspondance 1932–1960. Avertissement et notes par Marguerite Dobrenn*, NRF, Gallimard, 1981
MH	*(La Mort heureuse). Cahiers Albert Camus I : La mort heureuse. Introduction et notes de Jean Sarocchi*, NRF, Gallimard, 1971
Mythe	*Le Mythe de Sisyphe* (in *Essais*)
PH	*Le Premier homme*, Gallimard, 1994

Pascal

Pasc.	*Blaise Pascal. Œuvres complètes* (Pléiade edition, achevé d'imprimer 1969)

Camus: English translations

Exile	*Exile and the Kingdom*, trans. by Justin O'Brien, Penguin, 1983
Fall	*The Fall*, trans. by Justin O'Brien, Penguin, 2000
FM	*The First Man*, trans. by David Hapgood, Penguin, 1996
HD	*A Happy Death*, trans. by Richard Howard, Penguin, 1971
Myth	*The Myth of Sisyphus*, trans. by Justin O'Brien, Penguin, 2005
OS	*The Outsider*, trans. by Joseph Laredo, Penguin, 2000
Plague	*The Plague*, trans. by Stuart Gilbert, Penguin, 2001
Rebel	*The Rebel*, trans. by Antony Bower, Penguin, 1962
SE	*Selected Essays and Notebook*, ed. and trans. by Philip Thody, Penguin, 1979

A Note on the Translations

All French quotations in the main body of the text are translated into English in the footnotes, in which initial page references are to the French text, while references following the translated version are to the Penguin editions of the texts, where such exist. It is hoped that this will be helpful to non-French speakers. Other translations are my own. French quotations in the footnotes are not translated, since they are for illustration or additional information only. Where French critics are quoted in English in the body of the text I have added 'tr.' ('translated') to the page reference.

Introduction
Sisyphus' Stone

> *Juger que la vie vaut ou ne vaut pas la peine d'être vécue, c'est répondre à la question fondamentale de la philosophie.*
> Camus, Le Mythe de Sisyphe

> *'Oh, despair I understand. I know despair too, Sancho. Not final despair, of course.'*
> *'Mine isn't final either, Father. Or I wouldn't be sitting here on the ground beside you.'*
> *'Where would you be?'*
> *'I would be buried in unconsecrated ground, like other suicides.'*
> Graham Green, Monsieur Quixote

At the Edinburgh Festival of 2002, in a literary debate with Richard Holloway, the former Scottish Episcopalian bishop of Edinburgh, the avowedly atheist writer Philip Pullman forthrightly criticised modern fiction for failing in what it should be doing: 'It has unlimited potential to explore all sorts of metaphysical and moral questions', he said, adding that these questions dealt with issues of good and evil, death, paradise and hell. If a novel did not deal with death, he regarded it as 'trivial'. 'You can't leave morality out [of a novel]', he is reported as saying, 'unless your work is so stupid and trivial and so worthless that [nobody] would want to read it anyway.'[1] Camus certainly cannot be accused of triviality on any of these counts. In 1944, in his introduction to the 'Maxims' of the eighteenth-century moralist Chamfort, he would write the following:

---

1   See *The Guardian*, Monday, 12 August 2002, p.9.

> Nos plus grands moralistes ne sont pas des faiseurs de maximes, ce sont des romanciers. Qu'est-ce qu'un moraliste en effet? Disons seulement que c'est un homme qui a la passion du coeur humain.[2]

His fiction belongs to the great French classical tradition of *moralistes*, writers of aphorisms, maxims, and character *vignettes*, such as La Bruyère or La Rochefoucauld, and authors in the deeply serious tradition of Madame de Lafayette, of whom he was a profound admirer.

Camus was greatly admired for his seriousness of moral purpose by the generation which had experienced the horrors of the second world war, had become acquainted with the universe of the concentration camps, and been forced to reflect upon the human condition at its most bleak and chaotic. He fell out of favour however with the Left after the publication of *L'Homme révolté* (*The Rebel*) in 1951, in which he refused the totalitarianism and the labour camps of Soviet Russia as forcefully as he condemned the politics of capitalism. For Sartre and his circle, this represented a sell-out to the forces of reaction, and Camus was ferociously attacked in print by those whom he had regarded as friends and comrades-in-arms. Even before the publication of *L'Homme révolté*, he had made his position clear in *Ni Victimes ni Bourreaux* (*Neither Victims nor Executioners*), a collection of articles which had appeared in the journal *Combat* on 19 November 1946 and the following days, provoking a public controversy with Emmanuel D'Astier de la Vigerie, a politician with Communist sympathies. In reply to D'Astier's attacks, Camus wrote:

> Les camps faisaient partie de l'appareil d'État, en Allemagne. Ils font partie de l'appareil d'État, en Russie soviétique, vous ne pouvez l'ignorer. Dans ce dernier cas, ils sont justifiés, paraît-il, par la nécessité historique [...] Il n'y a pas de raison au monde, historique ou non, progressive ou réactionnaire, qui puisse me faire accepter le fait concentrationnaire.[3]

---

2   *Essais*, p.1099. 'Introduction aux "Maximes" de Chamfort', originally published in the collection *Incidences*, Monaco, 1944. 'Our greatest moralists are not writers of maxims, they are novelists. What is a moralist, in fact? Let us just say that it is a man who is passionately interested in the human heart.'

3   *Essais*, p.365. *Deuxième réponse à Emmanuel Astier de la Vigerie*, originally published in *La Gauche*, October 1948. 'The camps were part of the apparatus

The bitter political controversy marked the author and his work deeply. As for his literary reputation, after his death in 1960 it began to dip, his search for values was derided as 'boy-scoutism', his claim to any sort of philosophical weight denied, while his fiction and drama were superceded by the more radical experiments of the writers of the 'nouveau roman', such as Natalie Sarraute or Alain Robbe-Grillet, and the theatre of Beckett, Ionesco, and others. It is true that the political and ethical questions he raises are not focussed on the issues which came to the fore in the decade following his death: gender, race, sexuality, but his defence of dissent, of 'difference', of the individual, and his espousal of what a recent critic calls 'rebellious politics', should not be underestimated as a contribution to modern and indeed 'postmodern' thinking.[4] His popularity among the general educated reading public has never wavered, his novels, *L'Étranger* (*The Outsider*, also translated as *The Stranger*), *La Peste* (*The Plague*), *La Chute* (*The Fall*), as well as his other fictional writings, have been endlessly reprinted, read, and commented upon, inspiring fresh critical approaches in every succeeding generation. His major plays too, *Caligula*, *Le Malentendu* (*The Misunderstanding*), *Les Justes* (*The Just*), still continue to be played and to be studied. Over six million copies of *L'Étranger* have been printed in French alone, without counting the translations into some forty other languages.[5]

Today the simplistic view of Albert Camus has been recognised as shallow. His reputation has regained the ground which had come under attack. Colloquia, seminars and critics study with renewed enthusiasm everything he ever wrote, fiction, drama, essays, political journalism, also the *Carnets* (*Notebooks*), covering the years from 1935 until his death in January 1960, and which are not so much diaries as jottings inspired by his reading, ideas for his own work,

---

of the State in Germany. They are part of the apparatus of the State in Soviet Russia, as you cannot help but know. In the latter case, they are supposedly justified by historical necessity [...] No reason in the world, be it historical or not, progressive or reactionary, can induce me to accept the existence of the concentration camps.'

4 On these points, see Isaac, in particular chapter 7: 'Rebellious Politics Reconsidered', pp.227–59.
5 See Pingaud, p.214.

aphorisms and reflections of all kinds, outline plans for the fiction and dramas, short draft passages. Critical attention has been particularly focussed on his later output, the profoundly ironic and perplexing *La Chute*, the short narratives collected under the title of *L'Exil et le Royaume* (*Exile and the Kingdom*), the thinly disguised autobiography, *Le Premier homme* (*The First Man*), unfinished at the time of his fatal accident, and so never reaching its final transformation into the great novel Camus had intended it to become. Debate is alive and well: feminists argue about his attitude to women, critics such as Weyembergh defend his position as a thinker, others, such as Guérin, take issue with the political readings (those of Edward Said or Harold Bloom, for example) which view him as a French Algerian writing for a French audience and incapable of looking critically at the colonial perspective, while Algerian writers such as Abdelkader Djemai can salute him and acclaim *L'Étranger* as a masterpiece.[6]

All critics agree that the first published novel, *L'Étranger*, is *un livre classique*, a novel in the French classical tradition. Jottings in the *Carnets* show how profound was Camus's immersion in that tradition. He regarded himself and his contemporaries as its inheritors under a new dispensation, considering, for example, that 'du point de vue d'un nouveau classicisme', *La Peste* should be considered as 'la première tentation de mise en forme d'une passion collective'.[7] He identified at the centre of French classical literature a 'certain obstinacy', a single-mindedness which is the mainstay of its ideal of simplicity.[8] It schools us for life precisely because it is a disciplined art, a lesson in style, a masterclass for living. All of this he sees exemplified in the purity of line of the first great French novel, Madame de Lafayette's *La Princesse de Clèves*, whose 'simplicity' resides essentially, he says, in the 'obstinacy' with which Madame de Lafayette conveys throughout the peripeteia the central theme of the destructive power of love, and in

6   Djemai makes the remark in Dubois, 1995, p.200. For relevant publications of other authors quoted in this paragraph, see bibliography.
7   *Carnets II*, p.175. 'From the point of view of a new classicism, the first attempt to depict a collective passion.'
8   *L'Intelligence et l'échafaud*, *TRN*, p.1896: 'En art, un idéal de simplicité demande toujours la fixité de l'intention. On peut mettre ainsi au centre du roman français une certaine obstination.'

the 'magnificent' portrayal of restrained yet 'virile' passion in M. de Clèves.[9] He sees the same single-mindedness in Stendhal ('the litanies of energy'), in De Sade ('obstinacy in sin'), and in Proust ('an heroic ascesis').[10]

The obstinacy of Camus's œuvre can be located in the dogged search for a way of living which will affirm the dignity of the individual and explore the nature of happiness in a world without transcendental meaning, one in which man is at once a stranger and a child, like the stranger murdered by his own mother in *Le Malentendu*. Man is both child of nature and its victim, the game of life has no other end than death, and it is 'la mort qui donne au jeu et à l'héroïsme son vrai sens', the young Camus wrote in his *Carnets* in March 1936.[11] In the end, he added in May of that year, there is only one recourse:

> Ne pas perdre son temps. Rechercher l'expérience extrême dans la solitude. Épurer le jeu par la conquête de soi-même – la sachant absurde. Conciliation du sage hindou et du héros occidental.[12]

Calm acceptance or heroic defiance are the only dignified attitudes in the face of the situation to which Camus applies the term 'the Absurd', and which is the dichotomy between the senselessness of the world and the craving of man as a rational being, *homo sapiens*, to make sense of it. Camus said that his work would be a series of stages on the road to a 'perfection without reward'. *L'Étranger* and *Le Mythe de*

---

9   *Carnets II*, p.61. Note on *La Princesse de Clèves*: 'Sa simplicité réelle est dans sa conception de l'amour: Pour Mme. de Lafayette, l'amour est un péril […].' On the portrayal of Monsieur de Clèves's passion for his wife: 'Magnifique. C'est la pudeur de nos grands siècles. Elle est virile. Mais elle n'est pas sécheresse.'
10 *TRN*, p.1902, 'L'Intelligence et l'échafaud'.
11 *Carnets I*, p.29. 'It is death which confers their true sense upon this game and upon heroism.' One could compare this with Imbert's comment (p.579) on Stendhal's concept of heroism: 'Julien devient le héros stendhalien par excellence, celui qui fonde sa dignité sur sa manière d'envisager la mort.'
12 *Carnets I*, p.39. 'Let's not waste time. Let's seek extreme experience in solitude. Refine the game by victory over oneself, while realising that it is absurd. Reconcile the Hindu sage and the hero of Western tradition.'

Sisyphe are the 'point zéro' on this road, while *La Peste* marks a progression towards a deeper complexity.[13]

L'Étranger, taking shape at the same time as *Le Malentendu*, already possesses a classical harmony of structure and style, a simplicity and unity of theme, which Camus in the *Carnets* defines as 'la nudité de l'homme en face de l'absurde'.[14] The spare sentence-structures of the novel, consisting of a main clause only, or a main clause and subordinate followed by a full stop, lend all the greater force to the few astonishing lyrical passages which convey emotional climaxes. Yet for all its 'nudity', it is the most enigmatic and complex of novels, and therein lies its fascination.[15] Its simplicity is achieved through constant effort, the self-imposed discipline of the great tradition. We need only compare the style with that of its predecessor *La Mort heureuse* (*A Happy Death*), of which it was a transformation, or again with the last, unfinished work, *Le Premier homme*, in which we have what is stylistically still a draft, and whose long verbose passages would no doubt have been reworked or excised in places, and the structure tightened. Comparison has been made with the drafts of *Madame Bovary*.[16] For Camus as for Flaubert, simplicity comes to laborious birth from complexity.

Stendhal, a writer much read and pondered by Camus[17] (and himself also a great admirer of Madame de Lafayette's *La Princesse de Clèves*), once famously described the novel as a mirror carried by a traveller journeying along a road, reflecting now the mud of the gutter,

---

13   *Carnets II*, p.31: 'Cette œuvre comptera autant de formes que d'étapes sur le chemin d'une perfection sans récompense. *L'Étranger* est le point zéro. Id. *Le Mythe*. *La Peste* est un progrès, non du zéro vers l'infini, mais vers une complexité plus profonde qui reste à définir.'

14   *Carnets II*, p.36. 'The nudity of man confronted with the Absurd.'

15   See the opening remarks of Pingaud.

16   For a discussion of the style of *L'Étranger* and *Le Premier homme*, see Dubois (1995), pp.178–232: '*Le premier homme*: le roman inachevé d'Albert Camus', and the following 'Table ronde' discussion, in which Michel Maillard makes the comparison with Flaubert, as seen in the drafts of *Madame Bovary* (p.202).

17   In the three volumes of the *Carnets*, there are twenty-three references to Stendhal, including quotations from his *Journal*, and from *La Vie de Henry Brulard*, *De l'amour*, *La Vie de Rossini*, *La Chartreuse de Parme*, *Le Rouge et le Noir*, *Les Chroniques italiennes*.

and now the clear blue of the heavens.[18] The analogy was intended somewhat disingenuously to establish a claim to total objectivity and to be a disclaimer of any moral or immoral subtext. Any analysis of Stendhal's novels will, however, reveal an underlying moral, political and social seriousness conveyed by a Swiftian irony which lays bare the hypocrisies of the age. Stendhal's *Le Rouge et le Noir* aspires to be a 'chronicle' of the times, as, on one level, does Camus's *La Peste*, which is also 'une chronique', but Camus's fiction, be it in the form of 'chronicle', journal, monologue or *récit*, operates also, and perhaps principally, on another plane, that of parable.

Camus, writing about his plays, had given notice that 'psychology', and 'ingenious anecdotes and intriguing situations' were not what interested him as an author; since genuine drama deals with 'human destiny in its entirety, its simplicity and its grandeur'.[19] For him, Sophocles is a greater tragic dramatist than Euripides, because the epicentre of his tragedy is the loss of the essential balance in the moral universe, while Euripides displaces the focal point towards the individual and psychology, which is 'the decadence of tragedy'.[20] The same perspective, without any doubt, was also Camus's concept of his own fiction. Unlike Stendhal's walker, who is on a level with other passers-by and with the scenes and incidents he observes, the solitary Sisyphus of Camus's *Mythe* views the world from a height and from a distance. The questions he raises concern the human condition itself, and however simple and grand man's fate may be, the most innocent of investigations will lead to the discovery of ever greater complexities along the roadway.

For Stendhal's traveller, the journey itself is the source of interest, there are no signposts to his destination, no clue as to whether it

---

18 *Le Rouge et le Noir*, Part 2, chap. XIX. 'Un roman est un miroir qui se promène sur une grande route. Tantôt il reflète à vos yeux l'azur des cieux, tantôt la fange des bourbiers de la route.' See also the epigraph to Part 1, chap. XIII: 'Un roman, c'est un miroir qu'on promène le long du chemin.'

19 *TRN*, p.1835, note for the performance of *Les Justes* by the Comédie de l'Est (1955): great drama presents 'le destin humain tout entier dans ce qu'il a de simple et grand [...] La "psychologie", en tout cas, les anecdotes ingénieuses et les situations piquantes [...] me laissent indifférent en tant qu'auteur.'

20 *TRN*, see p.1707, in 'Sur l'avenir de la tragédie'.

be heaven, hell, or the country dreamed of by the *philosophes* of the Enlightenment and ruled over by the goddess Reason. Stendhal's agnosticism and somewhat elitist political scepticism (his Republicanism was of a distinctly snobbish variety) can well be taken as the antecedent of the radical disbelief of the generation of Sartre and Camus, while his dictum that, in the absence of God, His Prime Minister, *le hasard*, rules the world adequately enough, sits well with the notion of an 'absurd' or senseless universe in which life is a mere accident whose course is at the mercy of irrational forces. Ironic, agnostic, concerned: the affinities between Stendhal and Camus have been remarked upon by a number of critics, and the plight of Julien Sorel in the death cell or that of Meursault facing his execution obliges the reader to address questions concerning values and mortality. However, while Stendhal's concern (like Swift's) arises primarily from indignation at the injustices of a hypocritical society, Camus's fictional work is driven above all by the search for meaning in a universe rendered meaningless by the transcience of all things and the universality of death.

Stendhal is a social critic, Camus ponders the philosophers who have dwelt upon man's fate. 'On ne pense que par images. Si tu veux être philosophe, écris des romans', Camus wrote in early 1936, at the age of twenty-two.[21] Characters become representative of us all, taking on mythical status. Meursault is the Outsider, the Stranger, the Innocent in a hostile world, a Christ-figure, an Adam thrown out of the garden of Eden, a sacrificial victim, a scapegoat. The interpretations, sometimes proffered by Camus himself, sometimes by critics and commentators, are many. The universe is a forest of polysemic symbols, in which the fierce sun becomes the figure of life, or of death, of the hostility of nature, of fertility, or of paternity and the oppressive values of patriarchy, while the sea is an image of eternity, of maternity, life-giving, or liberating, or threatening, as the context may dictate, and a plague represents death, war, also the irrationality of the universe, and the mystery of evil.

---

21   *Carnets I*, p.23. 'We can only think in images. If you want to be a philosopher, write novels.'

While sharing the initial position of Sartre and the atheist existentialists, and denying the existence of any higher meaning in creation, Camus repeatedly refused to be classed among them. He did not share Sartre's extreme individualistic existentialism, the pessimistic denial of an essential, shared human nature.[22] Already as early as 1946, in an essay on French existentialism, Hannah Arendt considered the concept of the 'absurdity' (meaninglessness) of existence and the refusal of bourgeois values to be the only common ground between Sartre and Camus. The latter himself did not wish to subscribe to a system, affirming in 1945:

> Je ne suis pas un philosophe. Je ne crois pas assez à la raison pour croire à un système. Ce qui m'intéresse, c'est de savoir *comment on peut se conduire quand on ne croit ni en Dieu ni en la raison*.[23]

In his *Carnets* in 1946, he repeated the affirmation:

> Je n'ai pas envie d'être un génie philosophique. Je n'ai même pas envie d'être un génie du tout, ayant déjà assez de mal à être un homme.[24]

Camus is, as Quilliot remarks, not a philosopher but a moralist.[25] Maurice Weyembergh makes a distinction between 'philosopher' and 'thinker', classifying Camus as the latter, and analysing his work principally in the light of three philosophers with whom he feels there is an affinity: Nietzsche, Hannah Arendt, and the American Richard Rorty.[26] Hannah Arendt, recalling Heidegger's affirmation that poetry and thinking (philosophising) are 'close neighbours', has defined a 'professional philosopher' as one who develops a system or a method for the understanding of the world, while for a 'thinker' the world

---

22   On this point and its political implications, see Isaac, Introduction, and *passim*.
23   Interview with the Swiss journal *Servir*, in 1945, quoted Quilliot, TRN, p.1937 (my italics). 'I am not a philosopher. I have insufficient belief in reason to believe in a system. What interests me is *to know how to behave*, when one believes neither in God nor in Reason' (my italics).
24   *Carnets II*, p.172. 'I have no desire to be a philosophical genius, nor indeed any kind of genius, finding it hard enough to be a human being.'
25   Quilliot's remark is in his commentary on *L'Homme révolté*, Essais, p.1611.
26   Weyembergh, see the discussion on p. 21.

reveals itself in images and metaphor. She considers, for example, the novel *La Nausée* (*Nausea*) to be Sartre's most important *philosophical* work. Philosophy is born, she writes, with Parmenides' poem of the journey to the gates of day and night, guided by the muse who reveals the unity of being, and with Plato's 'essentially poetic' allegory of the cave with its flickering reflections of the invisible. These are the two seminal myths, 'the two earliest, most famous [and] influential of all thought parables'.[27] Quoting Hannah Arendt, Weyembergh writes (p.21), 'The image multiplies the philosophy by ten'. While the image speaks to the heart, the abstractions of philosophy speak only to the head. To quote Pascal: 'The heart has its reasons which reason does not know.'[28] Or, as Camus remarks in *Le Mythe de Sisyphe*, dismissing scientific explanations of the world:

> Ainsi cette science qui devait tout m'apprendre finit dans l'hypothèse [...] Qu'avais-je besoin de tant d'efforts? La ligne douce de ces collines et la main du soir sur ce coeur agité m'en apprennent bien plus.[29]

There are indeed two seminal notions of the origins of 'thinking': on the one hand the 'admiring wonder' inspired by the beauty of the world, in which Plato found the source of all human reflection, and on the other, the confrontation with suffering and the problem of evil, which is the tragic matter of the Book of Job. The first infuses the Apollonian *happy, naïve, ironic, esthetic* intellectuality of the Greeks

---

27 See Arendt, *Thinking*, vol.I, p.108. The reference is to Heidegger's *Aus der Erfahrung des Denkens*, Berne, 1947. The subsequent reference to Sartre is in Section III, 15, p.147: 'Plato's Answer and Its Echoes'. In her Introduction (p.8), Arendt had already adduced Heidegger's view, adding that Aristotle 'was of the same opinion: poetry and philosophy somehow belong together'.

28 Pascal's *Pensées*, his great theological work, was unfinished at his death; its voluminous fragments were edited and published posthumously in 1670. References throughout this work are to the Pléiade edition of the *Œuvres complètes*, 1969, with numbering indicating pagination, not individual *Pensées*.

29 *Essais*, p.112. 'So that science which was to teach me everything ends up in a hypothesis [...] What need had I of so many efforts? The soft line of these hills and the hand of evening on this troubled heart teach me much more', *Myth*, p.18.

(to borrow the epithets chosen for it by Kierkegaard),[30] and the second the 'dread' or *Angst* of a Kierkegaard or a Dostoyevsky, both of whose entire works are, in the words of the Russian religious philosopher Shestov (1866–1938), 'variations on the theme of the Book of Job'.[31] For Kierkegaard, Shestov remarks (1969, p.31):

> The origin of philosophy is not *wonder*, as Plato and Aristotle taught, but *despair*. Human thought undergoes a complete transformation in despair and terror, discovering new powers which lead it to those sources of truth considered unimportant by other persons.

Kierkegaard called his philosophy 'existential' to mark his total opposition to the speculative philosophy of Hegel, which he saw as the 'tyranny' of rationalism with its iron 'laws of nature'.

Germaine Brée observes that what Camus could not accept in certain forms of existentialism was this primacy attributed to death-directed despair (or *anguish*), over positive and life-enhancing experience (1972, p.138). In September 1945, he sought to make his own position clear:

> Je n'ai pas beaucoup de goût pour la trop célèbre philosophie existentielle, et, pour tout dire, j'en crois les conclusions fausses.[32]

Again in November of that year he would repeat the disavowal:

> Non, je ne suis pas existentialiste [...] Sartre est existentialiste, et le seul livre d'idées que j'ai publié, le *Mythe de Sisyphe*, était dirigé contre les philosophes dits existentialistes.[33]

---

30 *The Sickness unto Death*, in *The Essential Kierkegaard* (pp.351–70), see p. 367.
31 Leo Shestov (1969), p.22. Shestov's name is written as *Chestov* in French editions of his work.
32 In *Combat*, September 1945; 'Le pessimisme et le courage', in *Essais*, p.312. 'The celebrated existential philosophy is not greatly to my taste, and, to tell the truth, I believe its conclusions to be false.'
33 Quoted in Quilliot's biographical notes, *TRN*, pp.xxxiii–iv. 'No, I am not an existentialist. Sartre is an existentialist, and the only philosophical work that I have published, *The Myth of Sisyphus*, was written against the "existentialist" philosophers.'

His whole effort was directed from the beginning to the discovery of an answer to the challenge of 'absurdity', to the justification of an existence devoid of transcendental meaning, and to proclaiming the triumph of a life-affirming significance in the face of mortality and contingency. The anguish of the existentialists is countered in his *Weltanschauung* by the celebratory rapture of the pre-Socratics, of a Nietzsche or a Gide.

While according them a profound respect, Camus refuses to make the leap into faith with Pascal, Kierkegaard or Dostoyevsky, considering it to be 'philosophical suicide'. He sees in the bleakness of Kafka's *The Trial* the perfect portrayal of existential despair, but refuses to 'renounce lucidity' and pursue the will-o'the-wisp of hope which glimmers at the end of *The Castle*.[34] The theistic existentialist philosophers such as Kierkegaard or Shestov 'embrace the God who devours them', he writes, having already protested that the onslaught on reason had never been so fierce as at present, the front line of the attack stretching 'from Jaspers to Heidegger, from Kierkegaard to Shestov, from the phenomenologists to Scheler'.[35] Resisting the powerful influence of these thinkers and writers, Camus looks back nostalgically to the lost paradise of the Greek world with its love of beauty and balance, especially that primal world of the pre-Socratics, bathed in the fresh joyful light of the beginnings of natural philosophy and scientific enquiry. 'Nous avons exilé la beauté, les Grecs ont pris les armes pour elle', he wrote in an essay of 1948, 'L'Exil d'Hélène', adding:

---

34   See the appendix to *Le Mythe de Sisyphe*, 'L'Espoir et l'Absurde dans l'œuvre de Franz Kafka', *Essais*, pp.199–211.
35   *Essais, Le Mythe de Sisyphe*, p.208: 'Ils embrassent le Dieu qui les dévore.' ibid., p.114: 'Mais jamais peut-être en aucun temps comme le nôtre, l'attaque contre la raison n'a été plus vive. [...] De Jaspers à Heidegger, de Kierkegaard à Chestov, des phénoménologues à Scheler [...] toute une famille d'esprits [...] [s'est] acharné[e] à barrer la voie royale de la raison et à retrouver les droits chemins de la vérité.' These philosophies are discussed in this first part of the *Mythe*, entitled 'Un raisonnement absurde'. See in particular the sub-sections entitled 'Les murs absurdes' (pp.105–18) and 'Le suicide philosophique', pp.119–35.

> La pensée grecque s'est toujours retranchée sur l'idée de limite. Elle n'a rien poussé à bout, ni le sacré ni la raison, parce qu'elle n'a rien nié, ni le sacré ni la raison. Elle a fait la part de tout, équilibrant l'ombre par la lumière.[36]

It was a difficult balance which he strove to achieve in his creative writing from one work to the next.

In his final year at school, the darkness of the pessimism of Pascal, of the Book of Job, or of Dostoyevsky, was counterbalanced by the 'lucidité stérile et conquérante et une négation obstinée de toute consolation surnaturelle',[37] which the adolescent Camus found in his enthusiastic reading of Nietzsche, a spirit imbued with the ideals of classical and pre-classical Greece, enamoured of the pre-Socratics, proclaiming the death of God and the utter abandonment of man in the universe. Shestov had already pointed out the paradoxical kinship which exists between Pascal's praise of a 'hard' God and Nietzsche's 'blasphemies'.[38] While the latter's view of the human predicament without God matches that of the theistic pessimists, his response is the radical negation of theirs. Through the cry of Zarathustra, quoted by Camus in *Le Mythe*, Nietzsche had proclaimed the absence of any eternal Will purposefully governing the universe.[39] He had thereby also drawn the 'extreme consequences' which Camus had postulated in *Le Mythe*, proclaiming not only the death of God, but also the absence of any pre-ordained values or rules governing behaviour. Camus

---

36 *Essais*, p.853. 'We have exiled beauty, the Greeks took up arms on its behalf [...] Greek thought always took its stand upon the idea of limit. It carried nothing to extremes, neither religion nor reason, because it denied nothing, neither reason nor religion. It gave everything its share, balancing light with shade', *SE*, p.136.
37 *Le Mythe de Sisyphe*, 'L'Espoir et l'absurde dans l'œuvre de Franz Kafka', in *Essais*, p.210. '[Nietzsche's] final message lies in a sterile and conquering lucidity and an obstinate negation of any supernatural consolation', *Myth*, p.133. For the young Camus's reading, see Quilliot's *Notes*, *Essais*, pp.1172–3.
38 See Shestov: *La Nuit de Gethsémani*, pp.50–1.
39 *Essais*, p.114. Camus quotes the cry of Zarathrustra as follows: 'Par hasard, c'est la plus vieille noblesse du monde. Je l'ai rendue à toutes les choses quand j'ai dit qu'au-dessus d'elles aucune volonté éternelle ne voulait.' He is quoting no doubt from memory, and he somewhat truncates the original, taken from the third part of 'Thus Spake Zarathustra', section 3: 'Before Sunrise'.

would write in 1950, 'Refuser toute signification au monde revient à supprimer tout jugement de valeur'.[40] The problem is the establishment of values. Sartre, in *L'Existentialisme est un humanisme*, had more prosaically set out the same lesson for a general public in 1945. Critics pointed out that the essay was a not altogether satisfactory attempt to propound a social ethic which would complement the conclusions of *L'Être et le Néant* (*Being and Nothingness*), in which Sartre had outlined a morality based on the total freedom of the individual to make his or her ethical choices.[41]

A progression from the individual ethical dilemma to the search for social values is evident not only in Sartre's work, but in Camus's *œuvre* also, Meursault the outsider being relayed in *La Peste* by the altruistic doctor-figure of Bernard Rieux. Camus would more than once quote the despairing cry of Dostoyevsky's Ivan Karamazov: if God is dead, 'Tout est permis!', but he goes on to affirm that:

> Il ne s'agit pas d'un cri de délivrance et de joie, mais d'une constatation amère [...] Tout est permis ne signifie pas que rien n'est défendu.[42]

Even more explicitly, in August 1938, he wrote in his *Carnets*:

> L'homme vraiment libre est celui qui, acceptant la mort comme telle, en accepte du même coup les conséquences – c'est-à-dire le renversement de toutes les valeurs traditionnelles de la vie. Le 'Tout est permis' d'Ivan Karamazov est la seule expression d'une liberté cohérente. Mais il faut aller au fond de la formule.[43]

---

40 In 'L'Énigme', *Essais*, p.865. 'Refusing [...] the world all meaning amounts to abolishing all value judgements', *SE*, p.145.
41 See, for example, Pilkington's article.
42 *Mythe*, in *Essais*, p.149. ' "Everything is permitted," exclaims Ivan Karamazov [...] It is not an outburst of relief or joy but rather a bitter acknowledgement of a fact [...] Everything is permitted does not mean that nothing is forbidden', *Myth*, p.65.
43 *Carnets I*, p.118. 'The truly free man is the one who, accepting death for what it is, accepts the consequences of that also, *i.e.* the overthrow of all the traditional values. Ivan Karamazov's "Everything is permitted" is the only logically consistent description of freedom. But the statement has to be thought through to the end.'

It is in the 'thinking through' that reason, rationality, has its limited role in a universe devoid of sense and purpose. Lucidity is the only recourse against the Absurd, to use the Kierkegaardian term which Camus adopted and adapted for his own position. 'The Absurd' and 'Absurdist', are terms much used and abused in student essays. Camus would later say that the much over-used word had finished up by annoying him.[44] Kierkegaard had used it in the sense of the (misquoted) dictum of Tertullian: 'Credo quia absurdum'. What the early Father of the Church and the 'Father of Existentialism' both mean by it, is that the essential tenet of Christianity, the notion of the Incarnation, is so incredible that no human myth-maker would have dared propose it for general acceptance, *ergo*, Truth being not only stranger but stronger than fiction, we must accept that it can only come from the source of Truth, from God himself. Camus's use of the term is different: 'Ce qui est absurde, c'est la confrontation de cet irrationnel et de ce désir éperdu de clarté dont l'appel résonne au plus profond de l'homme'.[45]

The 'Absurd Man' is one who has come to the conclusion that we live in an 'absurd' universe, *i.e.* one devoid of inherent meaning, but who nonetheless affirms the validity of reason within its own parameters. Camus recognises that reason, lucidity, is powerless to overturn the 'walls of the Absurd', which are our mortality, the transcience of all things, the unknowability and irreconcilable strangeness of the world around us. He affirms the limitations of our human reason to provide answers to the existential dilemma, but refuses to despair of it, regarding it as an efficient tool, indeed the only one we have, in its proper sphere, which is that of human experience.[46] The 'Absurd Man'

---

44 Interview in *Les Nouvelles littéraires*, 10 May 1951, in *Essais*, p.1342: 'Ce mot d' "Absurde" a eu une malheureuse fortune, et j'avoue qu'il en est venu à m'agacer.'
45 *Mythe*, 'Les Murs absurdes', in *Essais*, p.113. 'What is absurd is the confrontation of the irrational and the wild longing for clarity whose call echoes in the human heart', *Myth*, p.20.
46 *Mythe*, pp.124–5. 'Il est vain de nier absolument la raison. Elle a son ordre dans lequel elle est efficace. C'est justement celui de l'expérience humaine.' 'It is useless to negate reason absolutely. It has its order in which it is efficacious. It is properly that of human experience', *Myth*, p.34.

is also, in the fictional universe of Camus, always the First Man, an Adam alone in the world, without divine or human father, knowing no pre-ordained commandments or guidelines, who must start from the basic questions of the value of life and the appropriate ways of living it. *La vie, mode d'emploi.*

This fundamental standpoint is the philosophical keystone of *Le Mythe de Sisyphe*, whose theme is famously the question of whether life is worth living, given that, in the absence of a transcendental or religious dimension, its transcience robs it of any ultimate significance. Death, extinction, is what makes the world 'absurd' to the rational mind. As one critic writes, death 'is *the* source of meaninglessness in man's world' (McBride, p.5, author's italics). The 'pessimism concerning the human condition', as Camus would call it,[47] is that of the ancients lamenting the brevity of existence, of Hamlet pondering the option of suicide, of Macbeth or Lear, for whom life is a tale told by an idiot, signifying nothing, and if gods there be, they kill us for their sport.

The bleakness of the 'existentialist' writers and thinkers, their preoccupation with the 'hopelessness' of our mortal condition, goes far beyond the ironic vision of a nineteenth-century predecessor such as Stendhal. Wherever the Stendhalian traveller's path may lead, it is going *somewhere*, even if the walker does not know where that may be. His attitude towards the goal of his journey is agnostic, not nihilistic. He makes his way at his own pace, choosing his path, meeting other wanderers, and enjoying the opportunity for reflection and observation along the way. A little over a century later, by the early stages of the most horrific war in history, when Camus is publishing his first major work, *Le Mythe de Sisyphe*, the nature of the journey has changed, and the whole undertaking is altogether less agreeable. Sisyphus is not travelling along a road, but toiling day after day up a mountain, only to see the great boulder which he has pushed to the

---

47   *Essais*, p.374. In 'L'Incroyant et les Chrétiens', an address delivered in the Dominican friary of Latour Maubourg in 1948: 'Je dirai que pessimiste quant à la destinée humaine, je suis optimiste quant à l'homme.' Camus had made the same affirmation in his notebooks a couple of years earlier, see *Carnets II*, p.160.

summit go crashing right down to the foot of the hill again, so that the labour has to be endlessly repeated, to no ultimate purpose.

Sisyphus is not going anywhere, he eternally repeats the same laborious daily round. Where Stendhal's notion of time is linear, a road stretching ahead, that of Sisyphus is cyclical. For the hero of *Le Mythe*, as for the pre-Socratics so beloved of both Nietzsche and Camus, time is an *eternal return*, a wheel upon which the helpless and innocent individual spins round and round, his will being directed only to the acceptance of the world as it is, with all its beauty but also all the anguish of the human condition to which he finds himself so inexplicably condemned. In the eternal circle, the world of the 'absurd' hero, there is no starting point, no logic of cause and effect, no place for a unique event such as a Fall. Camus's early heroes, Mersault (*La Mort heureuse*) or Meursault (*L'Étranger*), are, like Sisyphus, innocents, because, for them, man himself is radically innocent.

The very sequence of Camus's titles retraces, in an anticlockwise movement, one could say, the circular path from death, *La Mort heureuse* of Mersault, to the birth of the New Adam, the First Man, *Le Premier homme*. The itinerary starts with the death of Zagreus and Mersault's brief sojourn in the Chénouan Garden of Eden, thence it winds on through Meursault's expulsion from the kingdom of happiness in *L'Étranger* (a loss revisited in *Exil et le Royaume*), to a trek across the bleak landscape of *La Peste*, a place of human wretchedness, before reaching the scene of *La Chute*, of the original Fall as preached by a cynical John the Baptist; the circle closes again with the birth of the First Man, 'né sur une terre sans aïeux et sans mémoire',[48] created in nobody's image and carrying no inherited burden of guilt (although he will discover his own, as we shall see).

A remark in the *Carnets* holds the seed of a whole crop of reflections on the question of human culpability or innocence:

---

48   PH, p.261, in the concluding paragraph. '[He had been] born in a land without forefathers and without memory', FM, p.220.

> L'esprit révolutionnaire refuse le péché originel. Ce faisant, il s'y enfonce. L'esprit grec n'y pense pas. Ce faisant, il y échappe.⁴⁹

Hannah Arendt has pointed out (Vol.2, pp.11–19) that the doctrine of original sin makes sense only in the linear concept of time, fundamental to the entire Christian theology of salvation. In his remarkable dissertation for his postgraduate diploma, a comparative study of the thought of Saint Augustine and that of the philosopher Plotinus, the twenty-two-year-old Camus had remarked:

> Pour Plotin, il n'est pas d'Histoire. Mais pour un Chrétien l'art ne suffit pas. Le monde se déroule suivant une mise-en-scène divine [...] Le coup de théâtre de l'Incarnation n'a aucun sens pour Plotin.⁵⁰

For the Greek philosopher, History does not exist, as the Greeks still believed in an eternal and cyclical world ('Les Grecs croyaient encore à un monde cyclique, éternel et nécessaire', ibid., p.1226). Pondering Nietzsche, more than twenty years later, in 1959, Camus wrote again in his *Carnets*: 'Le sens historique n'est qu'une théologie masquée'.⁵¹ This is, of course, a theology which Camus always refused.

The preoccupation with questions of culpability and innocence is nonetheless fundamental to his whole work. In him the nostalgia for the Arcadian innocence of Greece and the indignation of the revolutionary at the state of the world co-exist, sometimes uneasily. For the revolutionary, time, if not linear, cannot be a closed circle, but rather a series of revolutions spiralling upwards, and while refusing the notion of original sin, he has nonetheless to come to terms with history and

---

49   *Carnets II*, p.339. 'The revolutionary mind refuses the notion of original sin. In so doing, it becomes immersed in it. The Greek mind gives it no thought. In so doing, it escapes from it.'

50   *Essais*, pp.1271–2. 'For Plotinus, there is no History. But for the Christian, art is not enough. The world proceeds according to a divine scenario [...] The *coup de théâtre* of the Incarnation makes no sense to Plotinus.' The title of the dissertation was 'Métaphysique chrétienne et néoplatonisme', *Essais*, pp.1224–1313. It has been translated by J. McBride (1993, chapter VIII, pp.93–171). McBride's Chapter VII, entitled 'Christian Metaphysics and Neoplatonism' (pp.77–92), is a discussion of the work.

51   *Carnets III*, p.265. 'A sense of history is only a disguised theology.'

the human origins of social evils. It had taken the horrors of the second world war, the experience of the Occupation, and the nightmare of the concentration camps, to shake Camus's early belief in human innocence, turning the blamelessness of his fictional heroes Mersault or Meursault into the tortured irony of the hero of *La Chute*, with his 'immersion' in the notion of guilt. This, Camus would say, is the pit into which the revolutionary falls. He would concede in 1949 that

> en sommme, l'Évangile est réaliste [...] Il sait que l'homme ne peut pas être pur. Mais il peut faire l'effort de reconnaître son impureté, c'est-à-dire pardonner.[52]

Sisyphus, however, is still the Innocent. He knows that his toilsome and pointless mode of living is a punishment inflicted by the hostile gods of the universe for some mysterious fault, for which he does not feel any responsibility or guilt. Homer, Camus reminds us, had suggested that this hero's fault was to have overcome death, 'enchaîné la mort', while another tradition maintains that having obtained permission to leave the kingdom of the dead in order to visit his wife, he so loved the beauty of the world that he refused to return to Hades. Sisyphus is 'the Absurd hero', says Camus. His contempt for the gods, his hatred of death and his passion for life have brought upon him this terrible chastisement.[53] All he feels within himself, however, is his 'irreparable innocence.'[54] Nonetheless he comes to the optimistic conclusion that life is indeed worth living, even at this price. It is worth living because happiness is possible, indeed natural, within the given parameters. The walk down the mountain is the time for the reflection which Stendhal's traveller had enjoyed going along the roadway; it is

---

52 *Carnets II*, p.270. 'All in all, the Gospel is realistic. It knows that man cannot be pure. But he can make the effort to recognise his lack of purity, that is to say, he can forgive.'
53 *Essais*, p.196. 'On a compris que Sisyphe est le héros absurde. Il l'est autant par ses passions que par son tourment. Son mépris des dieux, sa haine de la mort et sa passion pour la vie, lui ont valu ce supplice indicible.'
54 *Mythe*, in *Essais*, p.137. 'On voudrait lui faire reconnaître sa culpabilité. Lui se sent innocent. À vrai dire, il ne sent que cela, son innocence irréparable.'

a privilege and a joy which compensates for every weary moment of the arduous ascent.

In Camus's parable, the Greek myth is the acount of Everyman's daily toil in a world devoid of ultimate meaning. Sisyphus is a simple but supremely obstinate hero. He will for ever refuse to be miserable, as he pushes his great boulder up the hill, for the struggle itself is his victory over his own weaknesses and over the malevolence of the forces ruling the universe. On his way down the mountain, hearing the myriad tiny voices which speak to him of the wonder of creation ('les mille petites voix émerveillées de la terre', p.197), he affirms that all is well. Sisyphus' happiness is heroic. Like the Nietzschean hero of the future, he is the one who possesses enough strength of Will to live without seeking any sense in phenomena, to exist in a world without meaning.[55]

The Sisyphean happy ending is not achievable without the travail on the way. All Camus's heroes suffer the shock of the encounter with unhappiness which marks the turning point in their lives. Mersault, in *La Mort heureuse*, sees its image in the squalor of his neighbour Cardona's life and room, and commits a murder rather than acquiesce in such a future. In *L'Étranger*, Meursault's life is transformed in an instant from innocence and happiness to unhappiness and culpability by the shooting on the beach. Carefree Oran is stricken by the Plague, Clamence's egoistic happiness in *La Chute* sinks beneath the waters of the Seine on the evening of the suicide of the unknown woman. The re-establishment of happiness is postulated upon an essential innocence ('purity of heart', as Zagreus terms it) and the courage to look unhappiness and death frankly in the face. It would seem thus to be reserved for those who demonstrate what in the language of moral theology used to be called *heroic virtue*, yet Mersault and Meursault, certainly neither saints nor heroes in the classical definition of the words, both achieve the happy ending which is a 'happy death'.

---

55   *Der Wille zur Macht*, 585A. 'Das genug Willenskraft besitzt, dass es des Sinnes in den Dingen entbehren kann [und] in einer sinnlosen Welt zu leben aushält.'

In what sense could Camus famously declare that Meursault is 'the only Christ we deserve'?[56] How can Patrice Mersault affirm his innocence? The narrator of *La Peste*, Dr Rieux, has no taste for either heroes or saints, what interests him is 'to be a man'. To which his friend Tarrou, who has confided that his desire is to know how to be a saint without God, replies that they are both in search of the same thing, but that it is Rieux who is the more ambitious.[57] In his *Carnets* for 1949, quoting the Catholic philosopher Jacques Maritain, Camus would clarify his understanding of 'sanctity':

> La sainteté aussi est une révolte: c'est refuser les choses telles qu'elles sont. C'est prendre sur soi le malheur du monde.[58]

Already in 1942, he had remarked that what he was seeking to explore in his work, that already written (*Le Mythe, L'Étranger, La Peste*) and that still to come, was ' a heroism without God', man standing alone, a sort of 'difficult march towards a sanctity based on negation' (i.e. negation of transcendance).

Camus admires in Christianity what he calls the *'superiority of example'*, that of Christ and his saints, a *style of life*.[59] Sisyphus is this hero without transcendence, this saint without God. The great lesson he offers is a *style*, a way of living, a persistence in the affirmation of the value of life itself, the only value on which he is required to

---

56 TRN, p.1928. In the *Préface* to the American edition of *L'Étranger* (January 1955), Camus described Meursault as 'le seul Christ que nous méritions'.

57 TRN, p.1427. 'En somme, dit Tarrou avec simplicité, ce qui m'intéresse, c'est de savoir comment on devient un saint. – Mais vous ne croyez pas en Dieu. – Justement. Peut-on être un saint sans Dieu, c'est le seul problème concret que je connaisse aujourd'hui.' [Rieux replies:] 'Je n'ai pas de goût, je crois, pour l'héroïsme et la sainteté. Ce qui m'intéresse, c'est d'être un homme.' [Tarrou:] – 'Oui, nous cherchons la même chose, mais je suis moins ambitieux.'

58 *Carnets II*, p.298. 'Sanctity also is a revolt, it is the refusal of things as they are. It means taking upon oneself the misery of the world.'

59 *Carnets II*, p.31. 'Qu'est-ce que je médite de plus grand que moi et que j'éprouve sans pouvoir le définir? Une sorte de marche difficile vers une sainteté de la négation – un héroïsme sans Dieu – l'homme pur enfin [...] Qu'est-ce qui fait la supériorité d'exemple (la seule) du christianisme? Le Christ et ses saints – la recherche d'un style de vie .'

decide. Emmanuel Mounier has pointed out that 'Daily effort, self-control, patience, perseverance, the whole vocabulary of asceticism constitutes the framework of *Le Mythe de Sisyphe*' (p.73, tr.). It is in these values that the style of Sisyphus and the style of Christ and the disciples overlap, Christ takes up the cross, Sisyphus pushes the stone.

Camus once described the transition from Hellenism to Christianity as 'the true and sole turning-point of history'.[60] The pre-1960 Europe in which he lived was not yet the radically post-Christian world of the late twentieth century. In an interview given in 1951, he remarked:

> La vérité, c'est que c'est un destin bien lourd que de naître sur une terre païenne en des temps chrétiens. C'est mon cas. Je me sens plus près des valeurs du monde antique que des chrétiennes.[61]

Which values does he mean? The stoicism of Sisyphus is not the only inspiration, there is in antiquity a rival *style* to such asceticism: the ecstatic worship of the great god Dionysus. Sisyphus is a hero, but Dionysus is a divinity, and one whom Camus fervently worships. He sees the greatness of the world of Greece in its passionate attachment to this earth and its beauty, a sun-drenched world full of warmth and light, physically, spiritually and intellectually. 'À cette heure', he had written in an essay published in 1937, 'tout mon royaume est de ce monde',[62] a direct challenge to Christ's affirmation before Pilate: '*My Kingdom is not of this world*'. *Auf dieser Erde stehen meine Freuden*, proclaims Goethe's Faust, another archetypal figure who increasingly fascinated Camus.[63] Pascal had urged the non-believer to wager upon eternal life, in comparison to which human existence is as nothing. Camus, as Henri Peyre has said (p.68), is the anti-Pascal in that he

---

60   *Carnets III*, p.342. 'Le passage de l'Hellénisme au Christianisme, véritable et seul tournant de l'histoire.'

61   *Essais*, p.1343. Interview in *Les Nouvelles Littéraires*, 10 May 1951. 'The truth is that it is a heavy fate to be born on pagan earth in a Christian era. That is the case with me. I feel closer to the values of the ancient world than to Christian values.'

62   'L'Envers et l'Endroit', *Essais*, p.49. 'At this moment my whole kingdom is of this world', *SE*, p.64.

63   'My joys are here on earth.' For Faust, see *Carnets III*, pp.110 and 130.

makes the opposite wager. 'Pascal, le plus grand de tous, hier et aujourd'hui' was Camus's tribute in his *Carnets* in 1955 to the great seventeenth-century apologist for Christianity. But he had already made his own position clear, prefacing the accolade with the remark that 'Je suis de ceux que Pascal bouleverse et ne convertit pas.'[64]

The title of Camus's collection of essays *L'Envers et l'Endroit* (which is also the title of the final essay), presents translation difficulties and has been rendered, not entirely satisfactorily, as *Betwixt and Between*, or *The Wrong Side and the Right Side*, but in fact it signifies the two aspects of the world, sun and shadow, joy and suffering, *both sides of the coin*. Camus refuses to ignore either:

> Entre cet endroit et cet envers du monde, je ne veux pas choisir […] Le grand courage, c'est encore de tenir les yeux ouverts sur la lumière comme sur la mort.[65]

The moment of which Camus speaks in his essay, the instant when 'all his kingdom' is of this world, is not high summer, but the eternal moment of a cold, bright January day, seen from the window of an adolescent's sickroom. Not a moment for physical indulgence, but for contemplation. For Camus, what theologians call the *beatific vision* is not contemplation of the glory of God in Paradise, but contemplation of the beauty of the world and its transcience, the sacred source of the *lacrimae rerum*.

Between classical and Christian Europe, Camus opts for the first. In Greek thought he discerned both a foreshadowing of Christianity and something which was a rejection of it *avant la lettre*. On 21 December 1957, he would declare:

> J'ai des préoccupations chrétiennes, mais ma nature est païenne […] Je me sens à l'aise chez les Grecs, et pas ceux de Platon: les pré-socratiques.[66]

---

64 *Carnets III*, p.177. 'I am among those immensely moved by Pascal, and not converted. Pascal, the greatest of all, yesterday and today.'
65 *Essais*, p.49. 'I do not want to choose between these two sides of the world […] Great courage still consists in gazing steadfastly at the light and on death', *SE*, p.64.

He was however, as Henri Peyre again points out (p.68), the sort of pagan to whom Christians should be indebted, the non-believer who has 'asked the right questions'. Indeed, Camus never ceased to ask those questions, starting with the writing of his post-graduate dissertation on Augustine and Plotinus, a highly personal document, revealing the preoccupations and the duality which would remain permanently at the heart of his work. He is at once both Plotinus *and* Saint Augustine, Plotinus in whose philosophy he sees 'un point de vue d'artiste', and Saint Augustine who is 'obsessed' by the problem of evil ('le problème du mal l'obsède') and 'poursuivi par l'idée de la mort [...] Grec par son besoin de cohérence, Chrétien par les inquiétudes de sa sensibilité'.[67]

In the opening essay of *L'Envers et l'Endroit*, entitled 'L'Ironie', an old woman, semi-paralysed and clinging to a cheap lead crucifix, is, in the narrator's opinion, plunged deep into the 'wretchedness of man in God' ('misère de l'homme en Dieu', *Essais*, p.16), an ironic allusion to Pascal's vision of the 'wretchedness of man *without* God'.[68] The final essay, which gives its title to the whole collection, opens with the anecdote of another aged woman, who, having come into a small inheritance, purchases in the cemetery a tomb of the kind current in Mediterranean countries since antiquity, a mini-mausoleum. She furnishes its interior with a *prie-Dieu*, and spends long hours there in meditation and prayer. The young Camus adamantly refuses this world-denying claustration, but his sickroom is in fact as much a place of solitude and contemplation as her vault, his contemplation of the natural world the pendant to her meditation on the hereafter.

---

66   See *Le Figaro littéraire*, 21 December 1957 (Quoted Quilliot, *Essais*, p.1615): 'I have Christian preoccupations, but my nature is pagan [...] I feel at home with the Greeks, not those of Plato, but the pre-Socratics.'
67   *Essais*, pp.1271. 'The pilosophy of Plotinus is an artist's point of view.' And ibid., pp.1294–5. 'But at the same time, [Augustine] is haunted by the idea of death [...] Greek in his need for logical consistency, Christian in the preoccupations of his sensibility.'
68   Pascal's defence of the Christian religion was to be built upon an analysis of human nature, as follows: '1. Partie. Misère de l'homme sans Dieu. 2. Partie. Félicité de l'homme avec Dieu'.

Camus refuses a Christianity hostile to pleasure and to nature, but at the same time the moral seriousness of Christian spirituality, rooted in an ascetic and compassionate affinity with the poor, was deeply attractive to him. He admired the rigorous and uncompromising ethic of Pascal and Augustine, telling an interviewer in 1948:

> Je réfléchirais avant de dire comme vous que la foi chrétienne est une démission. Peut-on écrire ce mot pour un saint Augustin ou un Pascal? [...] Ceci dit, je ne suis pas chrétien. Je suis né pauvre, sous un ciel heureux, dans une nature avec laquelle on sent un accord, non une hostilité [...] Je me sens un coeur grec.[69]

The Christian ideal is perfected for him in Francis of Assisi, who has 'Mediterranianised' it, making of what was 'interior and tormented' a 'hymn to nature and to simple joy'.[70] In the cloisters of Franciscan monasteries, be it at Genoa or Fiesole or Palma, he feels at peace. 'J'ai le sens du sacré, et je ne crois pas à la vie future, voilà tout', he would say to his interviewer Jean-Claude Brisville at the end of the fifties.[71] The tension between the ascetic and the hedonist, between the Hellenist and the Christian *styles of life*, shapes all of Camus's work, which is a quest to reconcile not only mortality and happiness, but to reclaim the state of innocence which entitles each of us to dwell in harmony with the Garden of Eden around us.

The two novels taking shape in Camus's mind at the same time as he was writing *Le Mythe de Sisyphe* were *La Mort heureuse* and *L'Étranger*. The first drama, *Caligula*, had been written in 1938,

---

69 *Essais*, p.380. 'I would reflect before saying, like you, that the Christian faith is a surrender. Can one apply such a term to saint Augustine or Pascal? [...] Having said that, I am not a Christian. I was born poor, under a happy sky, in a natural setting with which one feels harmony, not hostility [...] My heart is Greek.'

70 *Essais*, p.1323. 'François d'Assise [...] qui fait du christianisme, tout intérieur et tourmenté, un hymne à la nature et à la joie naïve.'

71 *Essais*, p.1923. 'I have the sense of the sacred, and I do not believe in a future life, that's all.' In Genoa (November 1954) he has a 'bref instant de bonheur' in the little cloister of San Matteo (*Carnets III*, p.136); in Palma, in 1937, he spends 'long hours' in the 'petit cloître gothique de San Francisco' ('Amour de vivre', in *L'Envers et l'Endroit*, *Essais*, p.43). On Fiesole, see *Carnets I*, 15 September 1937, pp.74–5, and *Noces* (*Essais*, p.84).

although it was not performed until 1945. Its earliest projected title was *Caligula ou le sens de la mort* (*Caligula or the Meaning of Death*).[72] The trio composed of the essay, the published novel and the drama constituted what the author has called 'the cycle of the Absurd', focussed on the irrationality of creation and the problem of our mortality. *La Mort heureuse* was not published in the author's lifetime, as he was dissatisfied with it, for reasons which will be looked at later, but its title is the key to the whole of Camus's work, and particularly to the enigmas of this 'cycle of the Absurd', obsessed with the apparently conflicting concepts of mortality and of happiness. The first part of the novel is entitled *Mort naturelle* (*Natural Death*), ironically enough, since the only death which actually occurs in it is a murder, while the second part is *La Mort consciente* (*Conscious Death*). These titles are somewhat enigmatic, but Camus gives hints elsewhere as to their significance. In his *Carnets*, in August 1938, he wrote: 'On conscious death, see Nietzsche, *The Twilight of the Idols*', adding a quotation:

> Sur la mort consciente, cf. Nietzsche. Crépuscule des Idoles, p. 203. Nietzsche: 'C'est aux âmes les plus spirituelles, en admettant qu'elles soient les plus courageuses, qu'il est donné de vivre les tragédies les plus douloureuses. Mais c'est bien pour cela qu'elles tiennent la vie en honneur, parce qu'elle leur oppose son plus grand antagonisme.'.[73]

Courage is the determination to look death directly in the face, to seek no palliative: 'Le vrai, le seul progrès de la civilisation [...] c'est de créer des morts conscientes', Camus wrote in his lyrical essay 'Le Vent à Djémila'.[74]

Jean Gassin, in his exhaustive psychoanlytic study of Camus's *œuvre*, affirms that 'the sole subject is death, death inflicted upon

---

72   *Carnets I*, p.43 (January 1937): 'Caligula ou le sens de la mort. 4 Actes.'
73   *Carnets I*, p. 119. 'On conscious death, cf. Nietzsche. Twilight of the Idols, Nietzsche: "It is to the most spiritual souls, allowing that they are the most courageous, that it is given to experience the most painful tragedies. But it is for that reason that they hold life in honour, because it shows them its greatest hostility.".'
74   In *Noces, Essais*, p.64. 'The true, the only progress of civilisation [...] lies in creating conscious deaths', *SE*, p.78.

another, or self-inflicted' (p.253, tr.). I would contend however, that death in itself is not the focus of Camus's philosophical reflection, which is rather the search for a truth which would reconcile the inevitability of demise and the desire for a state of joy here and now. Camus's preoccupation is therefore humanist, not religious, despite the sometimes religious references or overtones of his writing. Alain Robbe-Grillet, pointing out the anthropomorphism of Camus's images in *L'Étranger* (the 'blood-coloured' earth, the 'somnolent' headland, the 'panting' sea, and so on), concludes that the 'Absurd' is a form of 'tragic humanism' (1963, see pp.56–8). The 'natural' death recounted in the first part of *La Mort heureuse* is that of the protagonist Mersault's mother, who takes ten years to die of a horribly disfiguring and disabling disease. It is a death which Mersault ensures that his friend Zagreus will avoid, and it is the latter who chooses a 'conscious' death.

The first of all value judgements is that made by Sisyphus at the end of the essay: life is indeed worth living. Camus has pointed out that to eat, to nourish oneself, is in itself a value-judgement, since one is choosing to live.[75] Camus describes the notion of the 'absurdity' of the world and the human condition in it as a 'clearing of the decks' to make way for the unimpeded construction of a view of life from a starting point of 'methodical doubt' (echoes of Descartes's *Discourse on Method*), a position from which it is necessary to move forward.[76] If we conclude that life is worth living, how should we live it? If we accept that there is no sense or purpose in the universe, that all is contained within the short span we live out here, then we can take no

---

75 *Essais*, p.865, 'L'Énigme' (in *L'Été*). 'Vivre, et par exemple, se nourrir, est en soi un jugement de valeur. On choisit de durer dès l'instant où on ne se laisse pas mourir.' 'Living and eating, for example, is in itself a value judgement. You choose to stay alive [...]', *SE*, p.145.

76 *Essais*, p.1342–3. Interview in *Les Nouvelles littéraires*, 5 October 1951: 'Quand j'analysais le sentiment de l'Absurde dans le Mythe de Sisyphe, j'étais à la recherche d'une méthode et non d'une doctrine. Je pratiquais le doute méthodique. Je cherchais à faire cette "table rase" à partir de laquelle on peut commencer à construire. Si on pose que rien n'a de sens, alors il faut conclure à l'absurdité du monde. Mais rien n'a-t-il de sens? Je n'ai jamais pensé qu'on puisse rester sur cette position.'

values or rules as given.[77] This being so, all experiences must be regarded as equally valid and valuable and the 'Absurd ' hero will seek to live not in the best way possible, but to the fullest extent possible.[78] Fulfilment, therefore happiness, is not a matter of quality, but of quantity of experience. We shall see, in the light of subsequent works, that this must be taken as a *provisional* judgement, in the absence of the establishment of any hierarchy of values.

As icons of this 'absurdist' philosophy (taking care to warn us that these are not *models*, but merely *examples*, and moreover that 'un exemple n'est pas forcément un exemple à suivre' (*Essais*, p.150; 'an example is not necessarily an example to follow'), Camus proposes Don Juan, the Actor, and the Conqueror. As for the Actor and the Conqueror, we can understand well enough how they achieve fulfilment through their respectively vicarious or multifarious experience of lives and worlds. Don Juan is more problematic, until we realise that Camus's Don Juan is not a mere vulgar seducer, but rather a rebel, a protester against a non-existent divinity, a collector of intense amorous experience ('Pourquoi faudrait-il aimer rarement pour aimer beaucoup?[79] Rizzuto points out that this Don Juan is a rebel agains what Camus regarded as the living death of 'bourgeois' happiness: marriage and the 40-hour-a-week job. In his case, he writes (1998, p.31),

> each encounter is total. It then dies completely so it can be reborn, signifying that there is no sense of experience as a cumulative process, above all no marriage or fidelity, insofar as these reflect social commandments.

He is a man of honour who keeps his rendez-vous with the terrible Commander, a stoic Don Juan fully prepared to pay the price for every action, and whom Camus prefers to think of as ending his days in

77   *Mythe*, in *Essais*, pp.142–3. 'La croyance au sens de la vie suppose toujours une échelle de valeurs, un choix, nos préférences. La croyance à l'absurde, selon nos définitions, enseigne le contraire.'
78   ibid., p.143. 'Si j'admets que ma liberté n'a de sens que par rapport à son destin limité, alors je dois dire que ce qui compte n'est pas de vivre le mieux mais de vivre le plus. [...] Une fois pour toutes, les jugements de valeur sont écartés ici au profit des jugements de fait.'
79   ibid., p.152. 'Why should it be essential to love rarely in order to love much?', *Myth*, p.67.

seclusion in a convent set upon a hillside, paying homage to a God in whom he does not believe, looking out from the window of his cell, and lost in contemplation of some silent and magnificent Spanish plain. A Don Juan indeed who has the qualities of soldier and of poet. An *innocent* Don Juan, just as Sisyphus is innocent.

Sisyphus' happiness is in solitude and contemplation, and for Don Juan happiness is ultimately silence, awe, and emptiness. Camus takes issue with Stendhal (and after him Nietzsche), who had famously declared, in a footnote in his treatise *De l'amour*, that beauty was 'the promise of happiness':

> Le beau, dit Nietzsche, après Stendhal, est une promesse de bonheur. Mais s'il n'est pas le bonheur même, que peut-il promettre?[80]

For Stendhal the promise was that of the harmony of two souls, of passionate and perfect love. For Camus the answer is not to be found there. His protagonists are solitaries, they fear the bondage of love. Mersault, the hero of *La Mort heureuse*, leaves the house he shares with his three young women friends, and, when asked why, he replies, 'Je risquerais d'être aimé, et ça m'empêcherait d'être heureux.'[81]

The glorification of Don Juan's male erotic imperialism in *Le Mythe de Sisyphe* stands in a complex relationship to a denunciation of the tyranny of the sexual drive, expressed a number of times throughout the *Carnets*, for example, as early as 1942: 'La vie sexuelle a été donnée à l'homme pour le détourner peut-être de sa vraie voie', or again in 1953: 'Qui, d'un peu exigeant, pourrait jamais consentir du fond du coeur à cette tyrannie? Chasteté, ô liberté!'. This from the Camus who could declare: 'L'amour physique a toujours été lié pour moi à un sentiment irrésistible d'innocence et de joie.'[82]

---

80   *Carnets II*, p.60. 'Beauty, said Nietzsche, echoing Stendhal, is a promise of happiness. But if it is not itself happiness, what does it promise?' See Stendhal, *De l'Amour*, chap. XVII, p.41, Classiques Garnier, Paris, 1959.
81   *La Mort heureuse*, p.155. 'There's a risk of being loved [...] and that would keep me from being happy', *HD*, p.112.
82   *Carnets II*, p.49 and *Carnets III*, p.80 and p.274. Translations are as follows: 'Sex life has been given to man perhaps to turn him aside from his true path', 'Who, being in the least demanding of himself, could wholeheartedly consent to

The call to abstinence is inspired not by the traditional Christian view of the antagonism of flesh and spirit, but is rather in line with the received wisdom of classical antiquity, which considered any over-indulgence, whether sexual, alcoholic or other, not as a mark of masculinity but of weakness, destructive of the autonomy and unity of the personality. Like the gladiator or athlete preparing for the contest, Camus the artist sees periods of monk-like abstinence and solitude as essential to his vocation and his creativity:

> La sexualité ne mène à rien. Elle n'est pas immorale mais elle est improductive. [...] Mais seule la chasteté est liée à un progrès personnel.[83]

Don Juan's work of art, on the other hand, is no doubt his own life, total freedom and undiminished aristocracy of spirit crowning unlimited experience. Camus never abandoned the idea of writing a play about him. In later years, by 1954, the figures of Don Juan and Faust, the two great metaphysical rebels, had merged in his imagination, and he thought of writing a drama entitled *Don Juan Faust*, or *Don Faust*.[84] Would Don Juan have been confronted with questions which are totally absent from *Le Mythe*? Is Clamence, in *La Chute*, Don Juan's guilt-racked reincarnation in the world of the concentration camps?[85]

Happiness is anterior to experience. It is the young Camus who, in his early rhapsodic collection of essays, *Noces* (*Nuptials*), celebrates in ecstatic mode his union with the maternal, pagan earth, a rapture in which desire, eroticism and a primal and indestructible purity of heart co-exist. But, as one critic has pointed out, no doubts arise and no questions are asked in this Tipasa, this land blessed by the gods of earth, sky and sea, in which the individual consummates his mystic

---

this tyranny? Chastity, O liberty!', 'For me, physical love has always been bound up with an irresistible sentiment of innocence and joy'. See Rizzuto's analysis of this question (1998), pp. 59ff.

83 *Carnets II*, p.51. 'Sexuality leads to nothing. It is not immoral but it is unproductive.[...] Only chastity is linked to a personal progress', *SE*, p.265.

84 See *Carnets III*, pp.110 and 130.

85 See again Rizzuto (1998), pp.73–5, for a discussion of the question.

marriage, and there is 'no woman and no fall'.[86] But there will come a Fall, to plunge innocent Adam into the hell of the universe of the Holocaust, and the Other will intrude into this solipsistic world, whether as Woman or Arab or Brazilian ship's cook, and will implicitly demand a response. Neither Sisyphus' contemplation of the beauty of creation nor Don Juan's ardent and guilt-free serial *amours* will constitute a sufficient answer.

Yet Sisyphus is happy. Patrice Mersault will die a happy death. Meursault, in *L'Étranger*, facing imminent execution at the end of the novel, achieves a state of reconciliation with the natural world and of rapturous thanksgiving for the privilege of life, however short, which will make of his death a consummation accepted in joy. Happiness appears achievable even in the most extreme of conditions. But there is another death in the first novel, one which is neither accidental, natural nor joyful: the death of the wheelchair-bound Zagreus, who has made the opposite choice to Sisyphus. Zagreus has decided that his own life is no longer worth living, better to bow out and leave the means of running the race to someone more likely to win, someone endowed with youth, health, and a perfect body. Contemplation without action, mind without body, can never achieve that perfect union with the natural world which is the Camusian concept of happiness. 'Et vous, Mersault,' says Zagreus to his young friend and disciple, 'avec votre corps, votre seul devoir est de vivre et d'être heureux.'[87] But happiness ranges from the bovine to that of the mystic, and the statement is qualified before the lesson ends: the desire for happiness is, Zagreus affirms, the noblest aspiration in the human heart, but its realisation is reserved for the *pure in heart*.[88] 'Oui, il y a un bonheur plus haut où le bonheur paraît futile', as Camus would write.[89] What is

---

86   Rizzuto (1998), see p.7.
87   *MH*, p.70. 'And you, Mersault, with a body like yours, your one duty is to live and be happy', *HD*, p.44.
88   *MH*, p.76. 'L'exigence du bonheur me paraissait ce qu'il y a de plus noble au coeur de l'homme. À mes yeux, tout se justifiait par elle. *Un coeur pur* y suffisait' (my italics).
89   *Noces*, in *Essais*, p.86. 'Yes, there is a higher happiness where happiness seems trivial', *SE*, p.99.

this happiness? What is this purity of heart? What arduous road must Parsifal take to find the Holy Grail?

Camus's work is a search for answers to these questions, and he came to conceive of it as a series of three great 'cycles'. The first he called the 'cycle of the Absurd': man faced with his own mortality; the second is the 'cycle of Revolt': metaphysical and collective rebellion against the injustice of the human condition and the problem of evil; finally there was to be a third cycle, celebrating the attainment of measure, balance, and love, and which Camus had embarked upon with *Le Premier homme*, the novel unfinished when his life was so senselessly ended in a car crash on the road from Lourmarin to Paris in January 1960. He had classified these cycles as: 1. Le Mythe de Sisyphe (L'Absurde). – II. Le Mythe de Prométhée (Révolte). – III. Le Mythe de Némésis, Nemesis being for him the 'goddess of measure, fatal to all excess.'[90] At this final stage he seems to be taken up more and more with the idea of some sort of fusion of Christian and pagan values:

> Le monde marche vers le paganisme mais il rejette encore les valeurs païennes. Il faut les restaurer, paganiser la croyance, gréciser le Christ et l'équilibre revient.[91]

Camus believed, perhaps paradoxically, that the Greek worshippers of the gods of Tipasa could have accommodated Christianity more easily than the existentialism of his contemporaries:

> Les Grecs n'auraient rien compris à l'existentialisme – alors que, *malgré le scandale*, ils ont pu entrer dans le Christianisme. C'est que l'existentialisme ne suppose pas de *conduite*.[92]

---

90 See *Carnets II*, p.328 (1950), and *Carnets III*, p.78 (note), and p.187 (1956).
91 *Carnets III*, p. 220 (1958). 'The world is heading towards paganism, but it still rejects pagan values. They must be restored, we must paganise belief, Hellenise Christ, and balance will be re-established.'
92 *Carnets II*, p.116 (Camus's italics). 'The Greeks would have been baffled by existentialism, whereas, in spite of being *scandalised*, they were able to enter into Christianity. Existentialism, you see, postulates no rule of *conduct*.'

The Greek, like the Christian, seeks *a style de vie*, a way of living, and one moreover that is not valid solely for Arcadia or the garden of Eden. There is a 'Greece of light' and a 'Greece of darkness', a Greece which is 'pessimistic, deaf and tragic' ('Grèce pessimiste, sourde et tragique'), as the young Camus noted, both at the beginning and at the end of his diploma.[93] For all his unwavering rejection of the notion of a fallen human nature and his passionate conviction that the only kingdom to which we can aspire is indeed 'of this world', the two elements, the Christian at its most morally uncompromising, and the Greek at its most life-affirming, pervade all of his work, and give it both its depth and its complexity. Quilliot writes: 'Camus était à la fois étranger à l'esprit religieux et profondément marqué par l'inquiétude métaphysique.'[94] It is not surprising that he was fascinated not only by saint Augustine, but also by the sternness of Pascal, Augustine's great seventeenth-century disciple, in whom the philosopher Emmanuel Mounier has seen one of the 'fathers' of existentialism, insofar as he reaffirmed the Christian sense of the tragic in the human condition (Mounier, p.119). There are two defining vistas in Camus's journey: the view from the mountain which Sisyphus climbs, and the dark abyss along the edge of which Pascal walks.

In the conclusion of his dissertation on Saint Augustine and Plotinus, Camus had quoted Pascal:

> 'Les hommes, dit Pascal, ne pouvant guérir la mort, ils se sont avisés de n'y point penser.' Tout l'effort du Christianisme est de s'opposer à cette paresse du coeur.[95]

Camus's own effort, throughout his work, would also be to combat the 'laziness of the heart', to look upon life, death, and the world with an unflinching gaze, and to move from each perspective to the next, from the individual to the social, from the assumption of innocence to the

---

93 See *Essais*, p.1225 and p.1309.
94 *Essais*, p.1220. 'Camus was a stranger to the religious spirit and at the same time profoundly marked by metaphysical unease.'
95 *Essais*, p.1309. 'Not being able to find a cure for death, men have decided not to think about it. All the effort of Christianity is to combat this laziness of the heart.'

enigma of evil and guilt, and from the adolescent pursuit of happiness to the achievement of maturity. The fatal accident on the road from Lourmarin on 4 January 1960 cut short this odyssey, and what form the final vision would have taken we cannot know. He once wrote in his *Carnets*:

> Alors que dans la journée le vol des oiseaux paraît toujours sans but, le soir ils semblent toujours retrouver une destination. Ils volent vers quelque chose. Ainsi peut-être au soir de la vie... Y a-t-il un soir de la vie?[96]

No evening of life was given to him in which to find an answer to this riddle, but it is the question itself which is important, the perspectives to which, throughout his work, he wishes to direct our contemplation, the 'certain obstinacy' with which, like his admired classical authors, he leads us on towards the rendez-vous awaiting us,[97] and thereby so compellingly forbids our hearts to drift and founder in the sands of slothfulness.

---

96   *Carnets II*, p.98. 'While in the daytime birds always look as if they are flying about aimlessly, in the evening they always seem to find a destination again. They fly towards something. So it is perhaps in the evening of life... Is there an evening of life?' *SE*, p.271.

97   'L'Intelligence et l'échafaud', *TRN*, pp.1895–6: 'Leur seul souci semble être de mener imperturbablement leurs personnages au rendez-vous qui les attend.'

Chapter I
The Gods of Happiness. *La Mort heureuse*

> *O litus vita mihi dulcius, o mare! felix*
> *Cui licet ad terras ire subinde meas!*
> Petronius
>
> *Et chaque matin je rouvre mes yeux dans le paradis.*
> Claudel, *La Maison fermée*

It is in his happiness that Sisyphus is privileged beyond the lot of Everyman. After all, why should he not be happy? He is immortal, he has inexhaustible health and strength, enabling him day after day to push his boulder up the hill. If he is in fact a prisoner, he is in an open prison, one which affords the opportunity for both action and contemplation, the two conditions which constitute all the dignity of the human being. He has time to enjoy the beauty of the world from the top of his mountain. He has no responsibilities except to himself, therefore no worries. He is in fact very far removed from the crippled Zagreus of *La Mort heureuse*, or indeed the little urban employee whose life consists of

> lever, tramway, quatre heures de bureau ou d'usine, repas, tramway, quatre heures de travail, repas, sommeil, et lundi mardi mercredi jeudi vendredi et samedi sur le même rythme.[1]

The employee cannot look down from the mountain, Zagreus cannot walk up the hill.

Mortality, the relentless daily round, the silence of the universe, the futility of reason, it is these that are the 'walls of the Absurd'

---

1   *Mythe*, in *Essais*, pp.106–7. 'Rising, tram, four hours in the office or factory, meal, tram, four hours of work, meal, sleep and Monday, Tuesday, Wednesday, Thursday, Friday and Saturday, according to the same rhythm', *Myth*, p.11.

which imprison us,[2] the walls of Meursault's condemned cell, or of Zagreus's imprisoning house. Zagreus in his wheelchair lacks what makes Sisyphus' life worth living: his legs. Life is for Camus movement, action. Contemplation is a finality, not the whole of life, and on its own it is not enough, because

> il vient toujours un temps où il faut choisir entre la contemplation et l'action. Cela s'appelle devenir un homme.[3]

The Actor, the Conqueror, Don Juan are men of action; when that time is past, they contemplate death stoically as the price to be paid for the experience of life. Zagreus has been cheated of his happiness by the absurdity of an accident which has robbed him of his legs, but he too is now ready to accept death, for he has found a way of making death itself fruitful, in the handing on of the possibilty of happiness to his younger, healthy, god-like disciple, Mersault.

Unlike the monastic cell of Don Juan, the secular prison of the crippled Zagreus, the wheelchair and the house, cannot afford him the immense spiritual perspective over a majestic and silent plain. Denied both action and contemplation, he will acquiesce gracefully but sadly in his own extinction, bidding farewell to the world, as he closes that sixteenth-century guide to the life of urbane society, *The Courtier*, which rests upon his lap.[4] The pendant to this volume is the statuette

---

2   *Mythe*, pp.117–18: 'L'homme se trouve devant l'irrationnel. Il sent en lui son désir de bonheur et de raison. L'absurde naît de cette confrontation entre l'appel humain et le silence déraisonnable du monde.' Alfred de Vigny had already bitterly protested that man can only reply 'par un froid silence / Au silence éternel de la Divinité' ('Le Mont des Oliviers'). Quilliot (*Essais*, p.1174) underlines the parallel between the metaphysical revolt in Vigny's poetry and Camus's cry in a letter to his fiancée, Simone Hié (quoted *Essais*, p.1173): 'D'ailleurs la seule réponse qui nous sera faite sera un froid silence qui nous dressera contre Dieu et contre le monde.'

3   *Mythe*, p.165. 'There always comes a time when one must choose between contemplation and action. This is called becoming a man', *Myth*, p.84.

4   Camus seems to have confused Baldassare Castiglione and Baltasar Gracian. He ascribes *L'Homme de cour* to the latter, but it was the former who was the author of *Il Cortegiano* (1528), while Gracian was the author of numerous works on the art of living in polite society, such as *El Discreto* (1646) and *El Arte de la Prudencia* (1647).

of a little smiling Buddha, which Zagreus keeps upon his table. His final aspiration is to escape from the world and from the wheel of time. Herbert Lottman (p.74) notes that the twenty-year old Camus and his first wife, Simone Hié, had a little plaster Buddha on a desk in their house in Algiers, while the Indian writer and academic Villas Sarang (see p.55) has pointed out affinities in Camus's thought with ascetic Indian philosophies, and would even describe Meursault, in *L'Étranger*, with all his indifference to worldy satisfaction, his rejection of the idea of a personal God, and his near-monkish existence, as 'the only Buddha we deserve'.

Zagreus is an unwilling recluse, excluded from normal social intercourse. His plight is all the more ironic since his very name rings with Dionysian echoes.[5] The son of Zeus and Persephone, the Zagreus of Greek mythology was torn limb from limb as a child by the jealous Titans, and from his heart, preserved by Zeus, was born Dionysus. He is thus, like Sisyphus, a victim of the hostile forces of the universe, just as, in *La Mort heureuse*, Zagreus is the victim of the 'absurd', the unpredictable accident which robs him of his mobility. His immobility precludes him, in the eyes of the author of *Le Mythe de Sisyphe*, from attaining any degree of happiness.

Immobility, for the young Camus, means death in another form. Hence also his horror of old age, with its imprisoning physical infirmities, a horror so evident in his early essays, the very first of which ('L'Ironie') depicts a little old woman who had been always on the go and full of chat ('remuante et bavarde', p.15), and who now, paralysed all down her right side, sitting alone in her corner when the young go out in the evening, would be better off dead. The silent witness in the essay, a young man, judges hers to be the worst misery he has ever seen, and for a fleeting moment, feels for her an intense flash of hatred, which in truth is directed at the state of agedness itself. The

---

5   See Reichelberg (1983), p.74: the name evokes 'l'esprit dionysiaque qui insuffle tous les héros mythiques de la Grèce et des récits camusiens'. Germaine Brée (1972, p.66) sees in the figure of Zagreus the sign that 'the myth Camus has in mind is the Dionysian myth of the artist'. The cult of Dionysus was associated not only with orgiastic fertility celebrations, but also with the origins of comedy and tragedy, dance and music.

second portrait in this same essay is that of her elderly husband, also condemned 'to silence and solitude'(p.18). This is not the rich silence and solitude of Sisyphus or Don Juan, but the impoverishment and draining away of life, mental, affective, esthetic and physical. The old man is still able to wander painfully and slowly down the street, hungry for human contact, but in the end he too is alone, at a loss, having nothing, already dead ('seul, desemparé, nu, mort déjà', p.20). The same horror of 'les vieux' and their physical degeneration is evident in the second chapter of *La Mort heureuse*, where Mersault's friend Céleste, the *patron* of the restaurant (he will reappear in *L'Étranger*), mentions a friend who refuses to go anywhere except in the company of his son, his own elderly contemporaries (at fifty!) being too depressing (p.36).

Camus was well aware of the problems inherent in a philosophy which could lead to the devaluation of the life of the socially, physically or mentally disadvantaged. From the beginning of his career as a journalist in his native Algeria, his record as a champion of the underdog, the weak, the exploited is irreproachable. He knew well enough that Sartre's affirmation (and that of the Existentialists), that a man is the sum of his actions, leaves little room for appreciation of the value of the unfortunate:

> Selon nos existentialistes, tout homme est responsable de ce qu'il est. Ce qui explique la disparition totale de la compasson dans leur univers de vieillards agressifs. Pourtant ils prétendent lutter contre l'injustice sociale [...] Alors? Le mutilé, la laide, le timide?[6]

Nonetheless, truly imprisoned in his truncated body, as Meursault, in *L'Étranger*, will later imagine himself imprisoned in the trunk of a hollow tree, Zagreus has been trapped for years in a living death before he meets Patrice Mersault, whom he indirectly solicits to put an end to this intolerable situation. He has taken all necessary steps to shield his protégé from the consequences of the action, also to provide

---

6   *Carnets III*, p.113. 'According to our existentialists, every individual is responsible for what he is. This explains the total disappearance of compassion in their universe of aggressive old men. And yet they claim to be fighting against social injustice [...] What about those who are handicapped, ugly, shy?'

for those who have been employed in his service, and, significantly, to leave a bequest for the improvement of the conditions in which 'those condemned to death' are held. Is he not himself the archetypal condemned prisoner?[7]

The image of the prisoner in the condemned cell has been seminal in French literature since Pascal formulated it in his *Pensées*. When writing his post-graduate dissertation, the young Camus had quoted the famous passage:

> Qu'on imagine un nombre d'hommes dans les chaînes, et tous condamnés à mort, dont les uns étaient chaque jour égorgés à la vue des autres, ceux qui restent voient leur propre condition dans celle de leurs semblables, et, se regardant avec douleur et sans espérance, attendent leur tour. Cest l'image de la condition des hommes.[8]

In his *Carnets*, in 1936, among plans for six 'stories', we already find one to be entitled 'The Story of the Man Condemned to Death' ('Histoire du Condamné à Mort', *Carnets I*, p.26.). Sartre, at the time of the publication of *L'Étranger*, was the first to point to Pascal as a forerunner of Camus.[9]

Zagreus sees no point in waiting for the death sentence to be carried out, when he could make a gift of the happy life of which he has been cheated to the young healthy Mersault, provided only that the latter prove himself 'worthy' of it. Mersault has the physical attributes to join the happy few; lying asleep athwart his bed, he resembles some 'solitary and stubborn god' thrown into an alien world (*Un dieu solitaire et têtu, jeté endormi dans un monde étranger*, p.57). His very name resonates with the sun and the sea (*mer* and *sol*). As Dionysus

---

[7] The prison image, as has been pointed out by a number of commentators, goes back to Sir Thomas More (*A Dialogue of Comfort against Tribulation*), or even to Plato's cave and to St. Paul. See Brombert (1975), Quilliot (1970).

[8] Pascal, *Pensées*; quoted by Camus, *Essais*, p.1235. 'Imagine a number of men in chains, all condemned to death, and of whom several are slain each day in full view of the others; those who remain see their own condition in that of their fellows, and, looking sorrowfully and hopelessly at each other, await their turn. This is the image of the human condition.'

[9] See Sartre, 1947, also translated as 'An explication of *L'Étranger*'; in Germaine Brée (ed.), 1962.

was born of the heart of the mythological Zagreus, so the young god in Mersault will be brought to life through the heart of the crippled Zagreus, who instils in him the gospel of happiness as the supreme goal: 'L'exigence du bonheur me paraissait ce qu'il y a de plus noble au coeur de l'homme'.[10] What value judgement lurks in the phrase? Zagreus frankly admits that he himself has not hesitated before criminality in order to amass the fortune necessary to his happiness. Indeed, he affirms that he would have stopped at nothing, the nobility of the aspiration validating the route to be taken: 'À mes yeux, tout se justifiait par elle. *Un coeur pur* y suffisait'.

The happiness that Zagreus so prizes consists in a life of 'solitude and ardour' ('la vie [...] dans la solitude et l'ardeur', p.77). The qualities that he will demand in the seeker after happiness are Nietzschean will and energy, the same qualities that, before Nietzsche, Stendhal had ascribed to his heroes. Stendhalian too is a recognition that happiness depends upon freedom of action and that such freedom requires financial independence.[11] Zagreus affirms:

> On ne peut être heureux sans argent [...] J'ai remarqué que chez certains êtres d'élite il y a une sorte de snobisme spirituel à croire que l'argent n'est pas nécessaire au bonheur. C'est bête, c'est faux, et dans une certaine mesure, c'est lâche.

All that is necessary is

> la volonté du bonheur. Seulement il faut du temps pour être heureux. Beaucoup de temps. [...] Avoir de l'argent, c'est avoir du temps [...] Être ou devenir riche, c'est avoir du temps pour être heureux quand on est *digne de l'être.*[12]

10   p.76 (both quotations in this paragraph; my italics). 'The craving for happiness seemed to me the noblest thing in man's heart.' The quote continues (see the end of the paragraph): 'In my eyes, that justified everything. *A pure heart* was enough', *HD*, p.49 (my italics).

11   This is the motivation behind Julien Sorel's ambition and struggle to rise in society: without position and money, he will never be free to achieve the great things of which he dreams. Stendhal's letters to his sister Pauline insist upon the need for her to make a wealthy marriage.

12   pp.75–6 (my italics). 'You can't be happy without money [...] I've noticed that there's a kind of spiritual snobbery in certain "superior beings" who think that money isn't necessary for happiness. Which is stupid, which is false, and to a

The last phrase is of course another value judgement allied to the notion of the 'pure in heart'.

Zagreus's death is, from the victim's point of view, an assisted suicide. But why should he need assistance? He has the use of his arms, a pistol within reach, and indeed Mersault leaves the body in a position which allows the death to be explained easily as self-inflicted. Zagreus however will not kill himself, for, despite the humiliations of his body, he admits that he would accept even worse afflictions, such as blindness or inability to speak:

> J'accepterais pis encore, aveugle, muet, tout ce que vous voudrez, pourvu seulement que je sente dans mon ventre cette flamme sombre et ardente qui est moi et moi vivant. Je ne songerais qu'à remercier la vie pour m'avoir permis de brûler encore.[13]

But for a worthy successor he will allow the flame to be put out, or rather he will pass on the flame of a life worth living to the next generation. He is both mentor and father-figure to Mersault, in whom can be discerned the ideal son. Endowed with physical beauty, health, and intelligence, only his strength of character remains to be demonstrated. The truth is that Zagreus's indirect invitation is a challenge, the test which Mersault must pass to prove himself deserving of the chance which Zagreus is offering him to 'live and be happy' ('Votre seul devoir est de vivre et d'être heureux', p.70).

While the first part of the novel, in which Mersault kills Zagreus, is paradoxically entitled 'Natural Death', the second, in which his own death is a return to the state of a 'stone among the stones', a graceful glide into oblivion, into 'the worlds where all is still',[14] is sub-titled 'Conscious Death'. The preoccupations behind this phrase are those of the young Camus, who, in his early essay 'Le Vent à Djémila' ('The

certain degree cowardly [...] [You only need] the will to happiness. Only it takes time to be happy. A lot of time [...] To be or to become rich is to have time to be happy, if you *deserve it*', HD, pp.48–9 (my italics).

13   p.70. 'I'd accept even worse – blind, dumb, anything, as long as I feel in my body that dark fire that is me, me alive. The only thing that would occur to me would be to thank life for letting me burn on', HD, pp.43–4.
14   p.204: 'Et pierre parmi les pierres, il retourna dans la joie de son coeur à la vérité des mondes immobiles.'

Wind at Djémila'), as the sun sinks behind the ancient ruins and the wind sweeps around him, feels himself to be engaged in a 'stern tête-à-tête with death', metamorphosing into a 'stone among the stones' (that phrase already), in communion with the 'beating heart of the world'. A calm and 'arid' lucidity in the face of death, which he proudly claims as the clear-headedness of youth, refusal of supernatural consolation, regret for the passing of the beauty of the world, these are the lessons he takes from 'the solitude and the silence of the dead city'. The only real progress of civilisation is, he writes, 'to create conscious deaths'.[15]

Weyembergh justifies the sub-title of the second part of the novel by regarding as deliberately suicidal Mersault's decision to live to the full a demanding physical life, choosing to expose himself to sea and sun, in spite of indications of an undermined state of health and the warnings of his friends.[16] One could also say that Mersault is fully aware to the very end of the process of dying, and accepts it with joy. 'Conscious death' would appear to apply at least equally, however, to the death of Zagreus, in spite of the sub-title of the early part of the novel. Weyembergh and Quilliot both point to a reference in Camus's *Carnets* in August 1938: 'Sur la mort consciente, cf. Nietzsche, *Crépuscule des Idoles*, p.203'.[17] In the passage to which Camus refers, Nietzsche talks of the *duty* of the doctor to terminate life which has lost dignity, and of suicide as a means of 'dying proudly' ('*auf eine stolze Art*'). In facilitating such a procedure, Zagreus chooses his 'conscious death' and thereby, we are to understand, dies in dignity, while Patrice becomes the Nietzschean doctor, putting an end to the life of a Sisyphus for whom there is no longer any joy in carrying the heavy burden. Yet Camus's underlying unease with this role for his hero is clear in the purgatory which he makes him undergo in his expiatory

---

15 'Le Vent à Djémila' was composed sometime between 1937 and 1939. See *Essais*, pp.60–6, in particular p.62: 'Et sa fugitive étreinte me donnait, pierre parmi les pierres, la solitude d'une colonne'. Also p.64: 'Le vrai, le seul progrès de la civilisation [...] c'est de créer des morts conscientes.'
16 See *MH*, pp.156 and 180, and Weyembergh, op.cit., pp.77–8.
17 *Carnets I*, p.119. 'On conscious death, cf. Nietzsche, *The Twilight of the Idols.*' See also Quilliot, *Essais*, p.1352, note 7 to p.64.

flight from the paradise of North Africa to the dismal wasteland of Middle Europe and the bleak hotel room of Prague.

In the second part of the novel, when Mersault is established in his haven of Chenoua, he finds his *alter ego* in the local doctor, but in spite of his urge to confide in this friend, he is unable to recount the death of Zagreus, fearing that his motives might be judged mercenary. Moreover he cannot bear the thought that a part of himself should pass judgement on another ('Il lui semblait insupportable qu'une partie de lui jugeât l'autre', p.184). There is then a 'part of himself' which he fears to look at, the reader must conclude. Is it, as he supposes, to do with money, or rather with the fact that his act has put him on the side of death? He has given Zagreus no encouragement to live, no assistance in that direction. On the contrary, he has merely expressed his own life-denying despair, on that dark, wet, dismal Sunday afternoon:

> J'ai envie de me marier, de me suicider, ou de m'abonner à 'L'Illustration'. Un geste désespéré, quoi.[18]

The empty Sunday afternoon will reappear in *L'Étranger*, an image of the futility and disappearance of religious hope, but the chronicler of *La Peste* will be another Dr Bernard, this time Dr Bernard Rieux, whose life is dedicated to the fight against the forces of despair and death, and to the life-giving care of even the most wretched of his patients.

Mersault is challenged to be a Gidean or Nietzschean hero, beyond good and evil, one who is prepared to step outside the rules which apply to the generality of men, to risk all. 'C'est un beau risque à prendre' (p.79; 'It's a fine risk to take'), he remarks near the end of the key conversation with his mentor. Camus, echoing Nietzsche, had already proclaimed the right to happiness in his early essays: 'Il n'y a pas de honte à être heureux'.[19] His French and Latin teacher remembered that, in his final school year, Nietzsche was 'the Law and the

---

18   p.68. 'I feel like getting married, or committing suicide, or else subscribing to *L'Illustration*. Something desperate, you know', *HD*, p.42.
19   In *Noces*, *Essais*, p.58. 'There is no shame in being happy', *SE*, p.72. See also *Essais*, p.1348, Quilliot's note 9 to p.58.

Prophets for him'.[20] Later he would come to see the dangers lurking in this prophet's thought, pointing out that 'the old dream' of Nietzsche had been transformed into the messianism of the Communists,[21] whose totalitarian ideal he always opposed, despite having briefly joined the party in 1934. As for Gide, Camus had read *Les Nourritures Terrestres* at the age of seventeen, and at eighteen he wrote to his mentor Jean Grenier: 'Mon goût pour Gide redouble en lisant son *Journal* [...] Je continue aussi à le préférer à tout autre écrivain.'[22] However, in a text of 1951, he would make clear that, in spite of his immense admiration, he never took Gide as a spiritual or intellectual mentor, but regarded him as the exemplar of an artist, 'le gardien, fils du roi, qui veillait aux portes d'un jardin où je voulais vivre'.[23]

Zagreus has found a way to be the begetter of a son worthy to enter the Gidean or Nietzschean elite for whom happiness is attained on a spiritual and aesthetic level reached only by those who, like Sisyphus, are able to climb the mountain, to be heroes. Heroism, for Camus as for Stendhal, is associated with height. Patrice too will climb a mountain before he dies, reaching the acme of his heroism, of his happiness, the fullness of friendship, on Mount Chenoua with his three young women friends, after which his health declines. At the beginning of 1936, Camus had drawn in his *Carnets* a diagram or map, showing progression from the starting points of 'Absurdity' and 'Lucidity' to the state of 'Saint', on the one hand (Tarrou, in *La Peste*, will seek to be 'a saint without God'), and on the other hand, the path to action and Socialism, but behind each lie 'the heroic values' (see *Carnets I*, p.23). These Nietzschean heroic values are formulated by Don Juan, in *Le Mythe de Sisyphe*, and also in notes which Camus was making in 1939, just as he was finishing *L'Étranger*, for a play he was planning, in which a key episode would be a conversation between the

---

20   Quoted in Quilliot's notes in *Essais*, pp.1172–3: 'Nietzsche était alors pour lui la loi et les prophètes. Il le citait à tout propos et même hors de propos.'
21   Letter of 20 September 1943 to Francis Ponge, quoted Quilliot, *Essais*, p.1566.
22   *Corr.AC/JG*, p.11 (20 May 1932): 'My taste for Gide has doubled on reading his *Journal* [...] I still prefer him to any other writer.'
23   'Rencontres avec André Gide', in *Essais*, p.1118. 'The model of the artist, the king's son, who kept watch over the gates of the garden in which I wanted to live', *SE*, p.175.

Don and a Franciscan brother. Don Juan declares that he believes in only three things: courage, intelligence, and women. When reminded of the Christian values of charity and love (of neighbour), he replies that he knows only tenderness and generosity, the 'virile forms of these female virtues.'[24]

'Nous ne voulons pas de n'importe quel héros', Camus would write after the war, in 1946. 'Les raisons de l'héroïsme sont plus importantes que l'héroïsme lui-même.'[25] Memories of the fascist striking of heroic attitudes made such a *caveat* imperative. Camus was aware also of the apparent contradiction between his attachment to the poor and the humble, and the notion of an elite, albeit a moral elite. In the important preface which he composed in 1953–4 to his early collection of essays entitled *L'Envers et l'Endroit* (written in 1935–6), he protests that his answer to the charge of elitism and 'aristocracy', is precisely in these essays, in their passionate tribute to his origins:

> Une mère silencieuse, la pauvreté, la lumière sur les oliviers d'Italie, l'amour solitaire et peuplé, tout ce qui témoigne, à mes propres yeux, de la vérité.

As to the concept of 'honour',

> notre monde tient ce mot [honneur] pour obscène; aristocrate fait partie des injures littéraires et philosophiques. Je ne suis pas aristocrate, ma réponse tient dans ce livre: voici les miens, mes maîtres, ma lignée; voici, par eux, ce qui me réunit à tous. Et cependant, oui, j'ai besoin d'honneur, parce que je ne suis pas assez grand pour m'en passer![26]

---

24 *Carnets I*, pp. 214–15. 'Don Juan. – Je crois au courage, à l'intelligence, et aux femmes.[...] *Le père* – [...] Il s'agit seulement de deux sentiments que vous vous obstinez à méconnaître : la charité et l'amour. *Don Juan.* – Je ne connais que la tendresse et la générosité qui sont les formes viriles de ces vertus femelles.'

25 *Carnets II*, 189–90. 'We don't want just any hero. The motivations of heroism are more important than heroism itself.'

26 Preface to *L'Envers et l'Endroit*, in *Essais*, p.10 and p.11. 'A silent mother, poverty, the light on the olive trees of Italy, the populated loneliness of love, everything that in my own eyes bears witness to the truth', *SE*, p.23; 'But our society finds this word [honour] obscene; 'aristocrat' is a literary and philosophical insult. I am not an aristocrat, my reply is contained in this book: here are my people, my masters, my race; here is what, through them, links me with

'J'ai de l'honneur', says Don Juan to the dread Commander, in *Le Mythe*, 'et je remplis ma promesse parce que je suis chevalier.'[27] But honour, while being the supreme aristocratic virtue, is also a universal human value; the 'poor district' of Algiers has its honour code too:

> On a sa morale, et bien particulière. On ne 'manque' pas à sa mère. On fait respecter sa femme dans les rues. On a des égards pour la femme enceinte. On ne tombe pas à deux sur un adversaire, parce que 'ça fait vilain'. Pour qui n'observe pas ces commandements élémentaires, 'il n'est pas un homme', et l'affaire est réglée. Ceci me paraît juste et fort.[28]

The murder of Zagreus is a duty which Mersault imposes upon himself. Zagreus's death then imposes a subsequent debt of honour: that of attaining the happiness for which the willing victim has made the supreme sacrifice. Drained by the effort which he has made, Mersault returns to to his room and falls exhausted into a long sleep, a small death which marks the end of one life and the beginning of another

The new life begins, however, not with a plunge into enjoyment, but with a process of ascetic purification: the journey across the sea (the purifying waters of baptism?) and thence to the cold, wet, and alien wastelands of Central Europe and the purgatory of Prague. 'Il n'y a pas de plaisir à voyager', Camus wrote in his *Carnets* at the beginning of 1936,

> j'y verrais plutôt une ascèse. [...] Le loisir nous écarte de nous-même comme le divertissement de Pascal éloigne de Dieu. Le voyage [...] nous y ramène.[29]

---

everyone. And yet I do need honour, because I am not big enough to be able to do without it!', *SE*, pp.24–5.
27 *Mythe*, pp.153–4. 'I have honour,and I am keeping my promise because I am a knight', *Myth*, p.69.
28 'L'Été à Alger', *Essais*, p.72. 'You "don't let your mother down". You see to it that your wife is respected in the street. You show consideration to pregnant women. You don't attack an enemy two to one, because "that's 'dirty'". If anyone fails to observe these elementary rules, "He's not a man", and that's all there is to it. That seems to me just and strong', *SE*, p.86.
29 *Carnets I*, p. 26. 'There is no pleasure in travel. I would regard it rather as an asceticism. [...] Pleasure separates us from ourselves as Pascal's *divertissement* [distraction] separates from God. A journey [...] brings us back.'

The discomforts of travel are a mortification of the flesh, concentrating our minds on higher things! Although Mersault's first objective is financial independence, his joys are not those which can be purchased; not for him the life of high society, of luxury hotels, glittering casinos, or millionaire's yachts. True freedom vanishes with an excess of wealth, as Camus had always known. In the Preface for the Pléiade edition of his early essays, he writes:

> Je suis avare de cette liberté qui disparaît avec l'excès des biens. Le plus grand des luxes n'a jamais cessé de coïncider pour moi avec un certain dénuement.[30]

Mersault is no more a vulgar hedonist than was Sisyphus.

Mersault's is a journey to find an inner unity, to cease to be 'separated from [himself]'. In Prague he lodges in a miserable boarding-house and eats in cheap cafés, not at all the style of one who has just acquired a fortune. Even his god-like appearance has suffered: he is ill-shaven, unkempt, in his eyes the look of a nervous animal (p.99). The sojourn in hell ends with the nightmare experience of coming upon a murdered corpse lying in the street, round which a crazed figure is ritualistically and drunkenly dancing. Is this latter the murderer? a friend? friend *and* murderer? How and by whom the victim has been murdered is not stated in the text, but the incident is actually a reminiscence of an experience in Algiers which had evidently marked Camus profoundly, and which he describes in a text of 1934, 'Les Voix du quartier pauvre'.[31] This text explains that the victim had been shot by a café owner after he had kicked the latter's pregnant wife. The man dancing around him is his friend. Both had been drunk. The same incident will be recounted in *Le Premier homme* (p.128).

For Mersault the scene remains enigmatic, he asks no questions, sees only a pool of blood in which the head lies, an image which obsesses him until, in his hotel room, he sees the gaping wound, imagines putting his fingers into it. Is the scene a savage caricature of the previous murder scene? The head of the corpse has fallen to the left,

---

30   *Essais*, p.7. 'I cling like a miser to that liberty which immediately disappears with the arrival of excess wealth. For me the highest luxury has always included a certain bareness', *SE*, p.20.
31   The relevant passage is reproduced in Sarocchi's note on p.224.

shattered by a bullet, just as Zagreus's head, with its gaping wound, had fallen to the left. The oneiric silence of both episodes, the contrast between the horror of the scene and the normality of the world beyond, the butcher's van sounding its horn outside Zagreus's villa, the distant noise of the traffic passing in Prague, intensify the alienation from reality and the repeat episode brings Mersault to the brink of madness ('Il y avait là [...] une minute d'équilibre, passé laquelle il semblait à Mersault que tout s'écroulerait dans la folie', p.108). Traumatised, he finally collapses in a flood of tears in his hotel room, and thus begins his purging and resurrection.

The fever which he has suffered since the murder leaves him on the return journey, when he arrives as far south as Vienna. The sight of women, flowers, frivolity and luxury transposes him from the nightmare that was Prague to the light-hearted dream-world of 'la ville la moins naturelle du monde'.[32] After Vienna, Zagreus ceases to haunt him: 'Pas une seule fois depuis Vienne il n'avait songé à Zagreus.'[33] The joyful artificiality of Vienna is only a short-term remedy, his lasting recovery will be effected in the light and life of the warm south. Arriving in Italy, he enters again the promised land of Mediterranean sun, sea, flowers and women, and crossing the sea from Genoa to Algiers, he realises that 'il avait à construire son bonheur et *sa justification*'.[34] Weyembergh has pointed out that Camus describes, in a lecture entitled *L'Artiste et son temps*, how Nietzsche also, 'crushed and exalted' after the break with his mistress, Lou Salomé, reflecting on the enormous *œuvre* he had still to undertake, walked by night upon the heights above the gulf of Genoa and found strength in contemplating the flames devouring the great bundles of leaves and branches which he had collected.[35] Weyembergh also points to Mersault's description of his secret past life as his *œuvre*, when deciding not to disclose it to Dr Bernard, and comments: 'the word

---

32   p.118. 'The least natural city in the world', *HD*, p.83.
33   p.125. 'Not once since Vienna had he thought of Zagreus', *HD*, p.90.
34   p.122 (my italics). 'He had to create his happiness and his *justification*', *HD*, p.87 (my italics).
35   The lecture was delivered on 14 December 1957, in Upsala, after Camus had received the Nobel prize. See Weyembergh, p.79.

œuvre is of prime significance: Patrice is both the artist and his own artistic creation'.[36] For Mersault, as for Nietzsche, the achievement of happiness is a work of art, a duty, a moral striving:

> Étendu sur le pont, il comprenait qu'il ne fallait pas s'endormir mais veiller, veiller contre les amis, contre le confort de l'âme et du corps.[37]

As, filled with joy, he sails into the welcoming bay of Algiers, he is again the Innocent, reassured that his vocation, and his obligation, is to be happy.[38]

Happiness for Mersault is inseparable from solitude. He allows himself an interlude of friendship in the 'House above the World' on the hillside overlooking the bay of Algiers, which he shares with his three young women friends, Catherine, Claire and Rose. Again the lifestyle is simple, frugal even, and their friendship reaches the moment of sacralisation on the last evening which they spend together on the terrace of the house, each lost in his or her own solitude, in contemplation of the night and the stars, in each heart a mixture of joy and melancholy: 'Cette double leçon qui mène à la mort heureuse'.[39] The midnight dew falls upon them like a baptism, and the episode ends with the transfiguration of Patrice Mersault upon this mountain:

> Patrice lève le bras vers la nuit, entraîne dans son élan des gerbes d'étoiles, l'eau du ciel battue par son bras et Alger à ses pieds.[40]

The acolyte is now consecrated and ready to embark upon his priesthood. The next morning he sets out to find his hermitage in the desert.

---

36 Weyembergh writes on p.80: 'Le mot *œuvre* est capital: Patrice est à la fois l'artiste et son propre œuvre.' He refers to p.181.
37 p.122. 'Stretched out on the deck, he realised that there could be no question of sleeping but that he must stay awake, must remain conscious despite friends, despite the comfort of body and soul', *HD*, p.87.
38 'Innocent, bouleversé par la joie, il comprit enfin qu'il était fait pour le bonheur', *HD*, p.125.
39 p.147. 'That double lesson which leads to the happy death', *HD*, p.108.
40 p.148. 'Patrice raised an arm toward the night, sweeping sheaves of stars in his gesture, the sea of the heavens stirred by his arm and all Algiers at his feet', *HD*, p.108.

In Chenoua, within view of the ancient Greek ruins of Tipasa, Mersault establishes himself in another house upon a height, from which he makes the final difficult ascent to the fulfilment of his vocation. Tipasa is the sacred place of harmony between man and nature, the dwelling place of the ancient divinities of happiness, as Camus had already proclaimed it to be in 1937, in the opening sentence of his essay 'Noces à Tipasa':

> Au printemps, Tipasa est habitée par les dieux, et les dieux parlent dans le soleil et l'odeur des absinthes.[41]

Here if anywhere, one can fulfil one's duty to be happy. After a long day of solitude and contemplation in Tipasa, Camus, in this youthful essay, has the emotional experience of a state which, 'en certaines circonstances, nous fait un devoir d'être heureux'.[42]

Mersault provides himself with a wife, Lucienne (a solitary young woman, bereft of family), but on condition that she reside in Algiers, coming to Chenoua only when sent for. He agrees to marry her if she so wishes and in fact does so, but when she later complains that he does not love her, he replies that he had never said he did ('Mais je ne te l'ai jamais dit, mon petit', p.161). She will become Marie in the next novel, *L'Étranger*. Significantly, she is not one of the three friends with whom he shares the house: friendship, love, and marriage are separate things for him. Friendship and intermittent companionship are what suits Mersault, not *le grand amour* (nor, indeed any sort of normal married life). His life is disciplined: his 'strange happiness' is conditional upon early rising, regular sea-bathing and careful attention to health.[43] It is very much the dream life of an intellectual who is still mentally an adolescent.

Through a friendship with the local doctor, whom we know only as Dr Bernard, Patrice participates in a rather lordly capacity in the life

---

41   *Essais*, p.55. 'In spring Tipasa is inhabited by the gods and the gods speak in the sun and the scent of absinthe leaves', *SE*, p.69.
42   *Essais*, p.60. 'The intense fulfilment of a condition which, in certain circumstances, makes it our duty to be happy', *SE*, p.74.
43   p.167. 'Le bonheur singulier qu'il recherchait trouvait ses conditions dans des levers matinaux, des bains réguliers, et une hygiène consciente.'

of the village. Bernard too lives an essentially solitary life, his wife being 'almost mute'. Another acquaintance is the elderly one-armed fisherman Pérez, a man of companionable silences, whose name will be given to the friend of Meursault's mother, Thomas Pérez, in *L'Étranger* (and we have already met, in the first part of *La Mort heureuse*, a certain Jean Pérez, who has died of tuberculosis and overstrenuous love-making with his wife!). Here, as in *L'Étranger*, Pérez can be seen as a shadowy father-figure (*père/Pérez*), an avatar of Zagreus, like him disabled, although this time it is an arm which is missing. He takes Mersault fishing, cooks the fish for him and feeds him after the expeditions. Throughout his *œuvre* Camus searches for the father he never knew,[44] a search to which the last, unfinished novel, *Le Premier homme*, is dedicated. From another angle, the two friendships, with the doctor and the fisherman, represent the human ideal proposed throughout Camus's works, they are icons of the healer and the humble.

The apprenticeship of silence and solitude is difficult. The arduous effort necessary to the achievement of happiness is compared in the narrative to the task of a sculptor,[45] and Mersault realises that his ambition is the creation of a work of art. But it is as a writer, not a sculptor, that Camus had conceived the character. In 1936, he had made a note in his *Carnets*, in which Patrice tells Catherine that he has found his vocation and that his great novel will be *the story of the man condemned to death* (my italics).[46] After a final ascent of the mountain with his three friends, he becomes ill, and feels the need to confide in Bernard, in the way that the artist feels compelled to communicate:

---

44   His father was wounded in the battle of the Marne, and died in the hospital of St.-Brieuc (Brittany), on 14 October 1914. Albert Camus was not yet a year old.
45   pp.169–70. 'De même qu'il faut savoir s'arrêter en art, qu'un moment vient toujours où une sculpture ne doit plus être touchée [...] de même il faut un minimum d'inintelligence pour parfaire une vie dans le bonheur.'
46   *Carnets I*, p.25. 'IIIe. Partie (tout au présent). Chap. I. '– Catherine, dit Patrice, je sais que maintenant je vais écrire. Histoire du condamné à mort. Je suis rendu à ma véritable fonction qui est d'écrire.' See also p.26.

> comme l'artiste, après avoir longstemps caressé et édifié son œuvre, éprouve un jour la nécessité de la mettre au jour et de communiquer enfin avec les hommes.[47]

Is he about to recount to Bernard the death of Zagreus? In the end he says nothing, since Bernard has admitted that the one case in which he is capable of contempt is that of an individual motivated by self-interest or the taste for money.[48] Alone, Mersault makes an examination of conscience, and concludes that he does not come into this category, that his action has been revolt against the injustices of birth and social conditions, against the curse which condemns the poor 'to end in dire poverty lives begun in dire poverty'.[49] Nonetheless, he will not risk submitting to Bernard's judgement, for he sees in his friend a sort of *alter ego*, as we have noted previously. When we look at his justification, we see that it has nothing to do with compassion for Zagreus, and all to do with his own refusal of disadvantage, disguised as a general concern. He cannot submit to his friend's judgement because there is a part of *himself* which he refuses to scrutinise.

The affinity appears at first glance unexpected, the two men have different concepts of happiness. Bernard has spent years in Indochina, feels exiled in this remote place, hankers after a life of action, 'ablaze and marvellous', and declares that he loves life too much to be satisfied with nature ('J'aime trop la vie pour me satisfaire de la nature', p.183). Nonetheless he represents a concept of happiness parallel with and equally valid to that of Mersault, but explored neither here nor in Camus's other work, except perhaps negatively in Jean-Baptiste Clamence in *La Chute*. He is the Adventurer (possibly combined with Don Juan) to Mersault's Artist. But the Adventurer and the Artist are twin spirits in the heroism of the Absurd.

---

47 p.181. 'It was the way an artist, after carefully moulding and caressing his work, at last feels the need to show it, to communicate with men', *HD*, p.135.
48 pp.183–4. '– Êtes-vous capable d'avoir du mépris pour un homme? […] – C'est assez simple, il me semble. Dans tous les cas où il serait poussé par l'intérêt ou le goût de l'argent.'
49 p.184. 'Cette malédiction sordide et révoltante selon laquelle les pauvres finissent dans la misère la vie qu'ils ont commencée dans la misère.'

One can of course see the symbol of the price to be paid for Mersault's action in the decline of his own health, which significantly is heralded by the three sneezes which unexpectedly rack him as he walks away from Zagreus's villa, carrying the suitcase with the money which is to be the source of his freedom and happiness. The sneezing is the first sympton of the disease which will bring him to an early grave. Three sneezes announce Mersault's death, three notes are played upon the flute of the Arab recumbent upon the beach in *L'Étranger*, five pistol shots end Meursault's innocence and happiness in that novel. Numbers, as in any parable, are heavy with significance. Did not the cock crow three times to awaken the conscience of Saint Peter? But this is in no way a conventional morality tale. Mersault is a puritanical devotee of the cult of a very difficult happiness, which in his case comes close to resembling a religious vocation. He kills Zagreus not in order to become rich, but in order to fulfil his duty to himself, to realise the god-like potential within (reflected in his physical appearance), to perfect the work of art which is a human destiny, to achieve that spiritual state of happiness which is the obligation and the birthright of the 'pure in heart'.

Within the world of the literary construct, Mersault is innocent because he acts in obedience not to the desire for luxury or for money for its own sake, but in revolt against the enemy of human dignity and happiness, against the squalor and injustice of poverty, exhibited at its most distressing in the episode of his visit to the filthy, stinking room in which the cooper Cardona lives alone, like a neglected animal. Cardona's degeneration dates from the death of his mother. He is a solitary, unable to form relationships, 'sourd, à demi-muet, méchant et brutal'.[50] Even his sister has found him impossible to live with, and abandoned him.[51] He is a terrifying warning of what Mersault could become, for Mersault also (like Meursault in the next novel) has with-

---

50   p.86. 'Deaf, half-dumb, a mean and violent man', *HD*, p.55.
51   He is a negative image of Camus's uncle Étienne Sintès, his mother's brother, also a cooper, of whom Camus was in fact very fond. Étienne figures largely in *Le Premier homme*, with his deafness, his limited speech, his outbursts of anger, his jealous affection for his sister, and his good looks. His mother adored him. Camus's images are always double, never simple.

drawn into one-room living after the death of his mother (a pattern which provides material for a great number of Freudian interpretations of the novels). In Cardona and in the squalor in which he lives, Mersault sees the future, and he refuses it:

> Dans la chambre sordide où cet homme respirait à force [...] il fermait les yeux sur le désespoir qui pour la première fois depuis longtemps montait en lui comme une mer. Devant le malheur et la solitude, son coeur aujourd'hui disait 'Non'. Et dans la grande détresse qui l'emplissait, Mersault sentait bien que sa révolte était la seule chose vraie en lui et que le reste était misère et complaisance.[52]

The next day Mersault kills Zagreus.

Camus is obsessed with problems of innocence and guilt, of injustice (metaphysical, social and political) and revolt, and wrestles with them throughout his drama and fiction. The 'Innocent Murderers' are Mersault, Meursault, or, in the political arena, the Russian revolutionaries of 1905 who are the 'meurtriers délicats' of *L'Homme révolté* (1951), while the most attractive figure among them, the poet Kaliayev, is the hero of the play *Les Justes* (1950). Designated by 'the Organisation' to assassinate the Grand Duke, Kaliayev makes no attempt to escape capture after the event, and goes fervently to a martyr's death (but who is a martyr and who is a terrorist?). Camus sees a nobility in these revolutionaries who are willing to pay for a life with their own lives. Mersault, too, pays for the life he has taken through the early end of his own life. His death is not a punishment, it is a balance, an immanent justice, which is an essential component of the pattern of the fiction.

Mersault allows himself no regrets, no feelings of guilt, and his innocence is insisted upon by the invisible and omniscient narrator:

---

52 p.88. 'In the miserable room where there there was scarcely enough air to breathe [...] he closed his eyes on the despair which rose within him like a tide for the first time in a long while. Today, in the face of abjection and solitude, his heart said "No". And in the great distress that washed over him, Mersault realised that his rebellion was the only authentic thing in him and that everything elsewhere was misery and submisson', *HD*, p.60.

> Dans l'innocence de son coeur, il acceptait ce ciel vert et cette terre mouillée d'amour avec le même tremblement de passion et de désir que lorsqu'il avait tué Zagreus dans l'innocence de son cœur.⁵³

When death at last comes, after a midnight bathe 'in the solitude and the silence of the night', he is determined to meet it with full consciousness, and he thinks one last time of Zagreus:

> Il se prenait d'un amour violent et fraternel pour cet homme dont il s'était senti si loin, et il comprenait qu'à le tuer il avait consommé avec lui des noces qui les liaient à jamais [...] Et dans l'immobilité même de Zagreus en face de la mort, il retrouvait l'image secrète et dure de sa propre vie.⁵⁴

Death is union, union with the Other, union with the eternal and the unchanging. His duty accomplished, Mersault can return to the earth:

> [Il] avait rempli son rôle, avait parfait l'unique devoir de l'homme qui est seulement d'être heureux.[...] Et pierre parmi les pierres, il retourna dans la joie de son coeur à la vérité des mondes immobiles.⁵⁵

Weyembergh (pp.80–1) has commented upon the appearance at this point of the father-figure, the lame fisherman Pérez, erect in his boat and rowing past in the sunset as Patrice lies dying. The image is heavy with symbolism. Pérez is at once Charon and a Zagreus who has vanquished his disability; he is also a father who restores to the maternal sea the little fishes which he catches, with the words: 'Go find your mother' ('*Va chez ta mère*', p.171). Patrice will be united in death with father and mother, with Zagreus whose life he has taken and

---

53   p.186. 'In the innocence of his heart, Mersault accepted this green sky and this love-soaked earth with the same thrill of passion and desire as when he had killed Zagreus in the innocence of his heart', *HD*, p.140.
54   p.201. 'He was overcome by a violent and fraternal love for this man from whom he had felt so far and he realised by killing him he had consummated a union which bound them together for ever [...] And in Zagreus' very immobility confronting death, he encountered the secret image of his own life', *HD*, p.152.
55   p.202 and p.204. 'For he had played his part, fashioned his role, perfected man's one duty, which is only to be happy', *HD*, p.153; 'And stone among the stones, he returned in the joy of his heart to the truth of the motionless worlds', *HD*, p.155.

vicariously lived, and with the eternal truth of the inanimate and unchanging universe.

La Mort heureuse is a first, very juvenile and unsatisfactory attempt to wrestle in a novel with the questions of happiness, friendship, innocence and revolt which will from then on inform every element of Camus's writing: essays, fiction, drama, political journalism, controversies, speeches and lectures. Mersault, in revolt against his lot, deciding to rid himself of the crippling burden of Sisyphus's stone, will become Meursault, who, in *L'Étranger*, has resigned himself to acceptance of the dreary round and asks no more than to find his happiness in what lies within his immediate reach. The trigger which is deliberately pulled to kill Zagreus will be pressed once more as in a trance to kill the Arab on the beach. Mersault will contemplate the world from a height, looking down at the vistas lying below the houses of Algiers or Chenoua, literally exalted in his aesthetic and spiritual solitude, while Meursault will be obliged to look upwards from his prison cell, separated from the world and from happiness by the absurdity of the universe and the inhumanity of a justice system which is no justice.

The god-like Mersault is transformed into the inconspicuous Meursault. It is however the latter who will truly die a 'conscious death', whereas Mersault fades away in an aura of poetry and melancholy. Marthe, who had been Zagreus' lover before Mersault's, and whom he takes as mistress out of vanity, and Lucienne, whom he indifferently consents to marry, will coalesce into the touching figure of Marie in the later novel. But the most astonishing transformation is that of the friend who is the instigator or cause of the central act in both lives: Zagreus will become Sintès. Zagreus has transgressed the law and yet kept intact a nobility of character which enables him to accept death in order to allow his friend to live to the full; Sintès is a violent petty criminal, exploitative of those with whom he comes in contact. In each case the nobility or baseness of the concept of happiness defines the man. Sintès's aims are entirely selfish and unsavoury. The paternal, self-sacrificial act of Zagreus brings his friend ultimately to his death, but a natural death which is fraternal union with the world, and which is blessed by the symbols of both the paternal and the maternal. Meursault's unnatural death, on the other hand, society's revenge, is the result of his indulgent inertia towards Sintès. It is his ultimate isolation from his fellow human beings, who, at least in his imagination, will appear only as spectators at the end, greeting him with 'cries of hatred'. Mersault's death is a mystical expiation of the death of Zagreus, but also an image of the bond of comprehension and friendship. He dies with Lucienne at his bedside and in the friendship of Dr Bernard. But to neither does he dare confide the secret of the death of Zagreus, thereby reducing these relationships to something closer to the level of acquaintanceships. Both Mersault and Meursault achieve, through suffering and effort, union with the natural world, but human relationships depend upon qualities of innocence and aspiration which Camus would never cease to reflect upon.

The improbability of the crime, and the even greater improbability of Mersault's spiritual rise and continuance in a state of prelapsarian innocence thereafter, are weaknesses of the novel. No doubt the moralist Camus felt slurping beneath his feet this swamp on which he was trying to build a coherent fictional structure. The novel becomes a series of episodes, risks being bogged down in a morass of thinly adapted autobiographical reminiscences. Camus had not, as Bernard Pingaud remarks (see pp.59ff.), as yet found his 'voice', a disciplined utterance, communicating as much by silence at by what is said. By the end of 1938, he would be able at last to define it: the true work of art, he declared, is 'that which says less' ('La véritable œuvre d'art est celle qui dit moins', *Carnets I*, p.127). The rhetoric and lyricism of the apprentice novelist, which fail to convince in *La Mort heureuse*, are replaced by the linguistic miminalism of *L'Étranger*, allowing the reader to reflect for himself upon the complexities behind the simplicity of the narrative, and reserving the register of image and metaphor for the intensely dramatic portrayal of emotional crisis. The heroic aura of Mersault vanishes to reveal the unpretentious Meursault. The third-person narrative, with its rhetoric and omniscient narrator, is replaced by a first-person narrative, with all the enigmas of the narrative voice, the questions of reliability and the conundrums of what is left unsaid. Light is cast however upon the enigmas of Meursault's personality, and therefore the meaning of the novel, if we understand how Camus had conceived this first fictional hero.

Sisyphus is a solitary hero. Mersault, and indeed later Meursault, are self-absorbed protagonists. They do not unreservedly share their lives with any other human being, despite Mersault's friendship with Dr Bernard, his part-time marriage with Lucienne, and the sacralisation of his friendship with the three young women in the House above the World. In the universe of Don Juan, with its male virtues, 'la bonté cède la place à la générosité, la tendresse au silence viril, la communion au courage solitaire'.[56] For Mersault and Meursault relationships with the natural world are union and redemption, but human relationships are either sidelined or fatal. Mersault is united with Zagreus only in death. How is innocence to be understood and maintained in the human context, and to what degree is happiness dependent upon it? Is there never any shame in being happy? These are not the problems raised in the 'cycle of the Absurd', nor in *La Mort heureuse*, and they have to wait. Camus adheres to what one may call a unity of preoccupation which is no less rigid than the unity of action in French classical theatre. In *Le Mythe*, as in *La Mort heureuse*, and in *L'Étranger*, the question is rigorously how to reconcile mortality and happiness.

By 1939, Camus's thoughts were turning away from the happy Sisyphus to a more complex figure who had been in his mind from 1936 at least: the prisoner in the condemned cell who refuses the consolations of religion, the innocent victim of a vindictive judicial system and the hostile forces of the 'Absurd'.[57] The victim of the gods, Sisyphus, will become Meursault, 'the only Christ that we deserve' as Camus would later describe him, and the search for the resolution of the questions of meaning and values, guilt and innocence,

---

56 *Mythe*, in *Essais*, p.153. 'Kindness yields to generosity, affection to virile silence, and communion to solitary courage', *Myth*, p.69.

57 Patrice Mersault intends to write the story of the man condemned to death: 'Je lui envoie le prêtre pour l'affaiblir tous les jours', *Carnets I*, p.25. The notes in *Carnets I* concerning *La Mort heureuse* disappear at the beginning of 1939. Notes for April and June 1937 take up the theme of the condemned man and the prisoner who refuses religious consolation and 'meurt sans une phrase'. (pp.49–50). In autumn 1938 two notes seem to anounce *L'Étranger*: the œuvre d'art which 'dit moins', and the opening phrases of the novel: 'Aujourd'hui maman est morte [...]' (pp.127 and 129).

happiness and fulfilment, will take the artist on an arduous journey *à rebours* from death to birth and rebirth, from *La Mort heureuse* to *Le Premier homme*, from the innocence of Mersault via the innocence of the Meursault/Christ-figure, through the valley of the shadow of death and the penitential waters of the Jordan/Amsterdam, to the *innocence regained* of Adam/Everyman in the Eden of the humble and the poor 'in spirit'.

Chapter II
A Happy Life and a Happy Death. *L'Étranger*

> *Pour que soit possible une œuvre absurde, il faut que l'intelligence sous sa forme la plus lucide soit mêlée. Mais il faut en même temps qu'elle n'y paraisse point, sinon comme l'intelligence qui ordonne.*
> Camus, Le Mythe de Sisyphe
>
> *Camus is more often cryptic than simplistic.*
> Germaine Brée, Camus and Sartre

The happiness of Mersault in *La Mort heureuse* is that of the devotee of a Nietzschean ideal, the strenuous achievement of perfect harmony between mind, body and the natural world in all the glory of sun and sea. But Mersault's body is vanquished by what it adores, the price of his happiness is brevity of life. He resembles the hero of Balzac's novel *La Peau de chagrin*, who comes into possession of a miraculous shagreen cloth which grants every wish, but shrinks each time. When it disappears, Raphaël will die, and duly does so, in ecstacy, in the arms of his mistress.

From *La Mort heureuse* to *L'Étranger*, the central question remains identical: how is one to live in such a way as to die happy? While Mersault, the hero of the first work, pursues the Nietzschean ideal of rapture and perfect harmony of mind, body and nature, Meursault's project is more modest, it is simply the avoidance of unhappiness, a life lived quietly and in total adherence to what he perceives as the truth about himself, about the world around him, and about the human condition. Camus would later declare (somewhat controversially) that Meursault is a Christ-figure, 'the only Christ we deserve'.[1] With a touch of hyperbole, he can be seen as Christ-like in his

---

1   TRN, p.1929: '– le seul Christ que nous méritions'. (Preface to the American edition, January 1955).

poverty, in his rejection of worldly measures of success (career, money), his refusal to condemn others, his determination to live and die by the truth as he understands it. But what he is in fact is the non-believing inheritor of the ascetic legacy of Saint Augustine, whose treatise on *The Happy Life* is listed in the bibliography of Camus's dissertation.[2] What should a man desire in order to be happy? Why can a man achieve his desire and still not attain happiness? How is one to live a happy life in the perspective of death? For Augustine the pursuit of happiness is the pursuit of God, who is Truth, for Meursault also the pursuit of happiness is the pursuit of truth, but 'a truth which is still negative, the truth of being and feeling', as Camus would later affirm,[3] the modest truth which is limited to what the individual can know about himself and his own responses to the world, human and natural, around him. In his honesty will lie his essential innocence.

L'Étranger is at a deep level an exploration of the relationship between happiness, innocence, and man's fate. The famous opening phrase, 'Aujourd'hui maman est morte' (p.1127; 'Today *maman* died'), is the starting point for a reflection upon death in all its forms: natural death, violent death, or death inflicted in the name of some political or social abstraction. 'Le président m'a dit dans une forme bizarre', says Meursault, 'que j'aurais la tête tranchée sur une place publique au nom du peuple français.'[4] Meursault's paraphrase of the death sentence, literally 'I would have my head cut off', shocks by its bluntness and underlying irony. It is often not sufficiently pointed out that the novel is also a protest against capital punishment, Camus being a passionate abolitionist. Death is the consequence of guilt, as judges, politicians and theologians see it. But who is guilty? The question raises social, moral and metaphysical debates.

---

2   *De beata vita*, see *Essais*, p.1312. For a discussion of this point, see McBride, chapter III, 'St. Augustine: The Place of Happiness', pp.25–40.
3   See Camus's *Préface* to the American edition of the novel, reprinted in *TRN*, pp.1928–9: 'Une passion profonde [...] l'anime, la passion de l'absolu et de la vérité [...] Il s'agit d'une vérité encore négative, la vérité d'être et de sentir.'
4   p.1201. 'The judge told me in a peculiar way that I would be decapitated in a public square in the name of the French people', *OS*, p.103.

The story is simple, but the complex preoccupations of the novel are best formulated in a set of four propositons, composed of two antithetical pairs, which can be set out as follows:

1a) Men die and they are not happy. This is the proposition of Caligula, in the play of that name, which forms the third element of the 'cycle of the Absurd', along with *Le Mythe* and *L'Étranger*. The mad emperor had been in Camus's mind since 1937, he had written the play in 1938, but it was not performed until 1945;

1b) Men die and they are happy (*La Mort heureuse*);

2a) Men die and they are guilty (the view of the presiding judge and the court in *L'Étranger*);

2b) Men die and they are innocent (the passionate conviction of Mersault and Meursault).

Which of these propositions will stand the test of the condemned cell? What is guilt, what is innocence, and how are they related to happiness in the life of the 'Absurd' hero, who steadfastly refuses to hope for any life beyond the present one? Meursault's refusal is implicit from the beginning, in his account of his mother's death and funeral, and then explicit in his interviews with the examining magistrate and with the chaplain:

> 'N'avez-vous donc aucun espoir, et vivez-vous avec la pensée que vous allez mourir tout entier?' – 'Oui,' ai-je répondu.[5]

This is the starting and finishing point, the '*point zéro*'.

In 1946, Sartre would demand, in *L'Existentialisme est un humanisme*, that those who hold a 'consistently atheistic position' draw the logical conclusions from it. He went on to maintain that the primary question for the bourgeois 'humanist' (whom he provocatively classified as a hypocrite, *un salaud*) is that of the basis of his values in the absence of God. If He does not exist, what values exist without Him? How can one kick away the pedestal and hope that the statues of all the Virtues will remain hanging in mid-air? In 1945, Camus had already posed the question:

---

5   *TNR*, p.1208. ' "Have you really no hope at all and do you believe that you are to die outright?" "Yes," I replied', *OS*, p.112.

> Il s'agit de savoir pour nous si l'homme, sans le secours de l'éternel ou de la pensée rationaliste, peut créer à lui seul ses propres valeurs.[6]

At the outset, Meursault makes no value judgements, but simply tries to get through life with as little pain as possible, while also trying to inflict as little pain as possible. The swing from this state of *avoidance* of unhappiness and harm (it can hardly be stated in such positive terms as 'happiness' and 'innocence') to the loss of freedom (therefore unhappiness) and status of murderer (therefore guilt) forces Meursault at last to ponder the essential value judgement as to whether his own life has been, and is, worth living. Rachel Bespaloff writes: 'Camus's thought is contained in a single question: What value abides in the eyes of the man condemned to death who refuses the consolation of the supernatural?' (p.92).

We can vary the formulations of the four propositions to give two antithetical triangular structures, with death as the master angle governing the two others: death / happiness / innocence, and death / unhappiness / guilt. The relationship of death to happiness and innocence (as already highlighted in *La Mort heureuse*) is transformed into the reverse relationship (death / unhappiness / guilt) by the five pistol shots at the centre of *L'Étranger*, one for each point of the pentagram which is the symbol, buried in our subconscious, of the human body with its head and outstretched limbs, the body of the Arab spread-eagled upon the sand.[7] Or should we think of the five wounds of Christ upon the cross, the ultimate innocent victim? In July 1939, Camus had made a somewhat cryptic note of an image which must

---

6 In 'Le Pessimisme et le Courage', originally published in *Combat*, Sept. 1945, see *Essais*, p.312. 'We need to know if man, without recourse to the eternal or to rationalist thought, can create his values on his own.' Also in that year, in the essay *Remarque sur la révolte*, we find the same question: 'L'homme peut-t-il, à lui seul et sans le secours de l'éternel, créer ses propres valeurs?' *Essais*, p.1696.

7 See Jung, vol. II, p.219: 'According to the old view, five is the number of the natural ("hylican") man, whose outstretched limbs form, with the head, a pentagram.'

have impressed itself upon his mind: 'Sur la plage, l'homme, les bras en croix, *crucifié* au soleil' (my italics).[8]

Assassin, executioner, Christ-killer, *Monsieur l'Antéchrist* in the half-in-joke, wholly-in-earnest raillery of the examining judge who is scandalised by the accused's lack of religion, Meursault becomes in the eyes of society, whose voice is that of the state prosecutor, simply a monster. It is in the court scenes that the novel departs most clearly from the plausibility of 'realism', soaring into parable, with the prosecutor heaping all possible guilt upon the accused, declaring him morally guilty of matricide, capable of patricide, devoid of any shred of humanity, until the stature of the insignificant Meursault is aggrandised into that of the archetypal criminal.[9] Already in one of the earliest reviews of the novel, in July 1942, Marcel Arland had ascribed the vehemence of the prosecutor and judge to their instinctive recognition in Meursault of all the common human failings and weaknesses hidden within themselves, a subconscious complex of culpability which we all suppress: 'Ce coupable latent en chacun de nous et que nous voulons ignorer à jamais.'[10]

Thus having created a victim, Meursault becomes himself a victim, a scapegoat, taking upon himself the burden of *fault* and *misfortune* ('*faute*' and '*malheur*' in the text), and becoming 'the only Christ that we deserve'.[11] He is a mirror image of Christ, whose death is established by the last of the five wounds, the lance-thrust through the heart, while of Meursault's five revolver shots it is the first which

---

8   *Carnets I*, p.161. 'On the beach, the man, his arms outstretched, *crucified* in the sunshine.'
9   See the closing speech for the prosecution, especially pp.1197–8; also Pingaud, p.45, and Girard.
10 Marcel Arland, in *Comœdia*, 11 July 1942, pp.1–2; quoted Pingaud, pp.154–6. 'This latent transgressor in each one of us which we desire to shut out of our minds for ever.'
11 Morot-Sir points to a previous comment of Camus which casts some light upon the Meursault/Christ analogy: 'Meursault est UN CHRIST QUE NOUS POURRIONS ÊTRE.' (Camus's capitals). Interview reported in the Japanese paper *Asahi*, 15 January 1952, and re-translated into French in *Revue des Lettres Modernes: Albert Camus 14*, p.160. See Morot-Sir, pp.7–26. Ingrid di Meglio points out (p.16) that Meursault's death saves only himself; there is no 'vicariat', as in Christology.

extinguishes life and transforms the innocent into the executioner. The four subsequent bullets fired into the prostrate body can be seen as a Jungian quaternity, constituting the emprisoning walls of the *Absurd* in which we are all trapped, and which Camus had described in *Le Mythe de Sisyphe*. Jung assures us that quaternities appear 'in times of psychic disorientation' (which admirably fits Meursault's state of mind at the moment of the murder), adding that 'they are not inventions of the conscious mind, but are spontaneous products of the unconscious' (vol. 8, p.457).

The four walls of the prison-cell into which Meursault will be flung are those of Pascal's prisoner awaiting execution. Having made his appearance as Zagreus in Camus's first novel and preferred death, the Prisoner will now, in his reincarnation as Meursault, narrate the sojourn in that place of suffering and unhappiness where, as Dante tells us, all hope is abandoned, and to which the name given is Hell. Meursault experiences his metamorphosis into an assassin as the destruction of an *equilibrium*, a force which swings him round from his happiness to face 'la porte du malheur' (p.1168; 'the door of unhappiness'). Once over that threshold, he must find a way out of the four walls of the prison of his unhappiness, effacing fault and unhappiness, and re-establishing happiness and innocence in a triumphant and liberating relationship with mortality itself.

In this metaphysical perspective, it is tempting to see the 'three notes' of the Arab's reed-pipe in the pivotal scene as the reflection of this final, eternal triangle, given the context of silence, stillness, the suspension of time ('Il y avait déjà deux heures que la journée n'avançait plus') and the tranquillity of both Arabs, who 'avaient l'air tout à fait calmes et presque contents'.[12] Jung notes the affinities of the number three with the soul, the spiritual, and Patrick McCarthy has suggested that both the Arabs and Meursault's mother may possess 'along with their psychological and political associations, religious elements before which Meursault recoils' (1988, p.84). Another critic has noted that the Arabs are reclining before a spring, symbol of the spiritual life, and suggests that they are 'the defenders and guardians'

---

12 p.1167 and p.1165. 'For two hours now the day had stood still', *OS*, p.59; 'They seemed quite calm and almost contented', ibid., p.56.

of archaic values to which Meursault has no access (Montgomery, 1997, see p.179).

We note also the curiously melodious voice of the nurse present at Meursault's mother's funeral, the *infirmière déléguée*. With her long, bony face ('son visage osseux et long', p.1135), she is clearly an avatar of the figure of Death personified previously in the Arab nurse who had kept a vigil in the morgue, her face eaten away by cancer beneath the white, mummy-like bandaging. Hearing that melodious voice, the siren-like seduction of death, Meursault had concluded that there was no way out ('Il n'y avait pas d'issue', p.1137), no evading our mortal condition, no transcendental hope, yet death itself has its sweetness as well as its horror. It is a duality, like the two nurses. And is not the musicality of the voice also that of the 'three notes' of the reed-pipe? Meursault, purged of evil and emptied of hope ('purgé du mal, vidé d'espoir', p.1211), attains a final peace before his execution which is an experience of immanence and timelessness. Camus would write in 1954:

> Je lis souvent que je suis athée, j'entends parler de mon athéisme. Or ces mots ne me disent rien, ils n'ont pas de sens pour moi. Je ne crois pas à Dieu *et* je ne suis pas athée. (Camus's italics).[13]

The novel's fascination lies in the complexity and harmony of its patterns, which extend beyond the 'parallelism of the two parts' in which Camus himself declared that the whole sense of the work was contained.[14] Narratologists see Camus faced with a 'paradoxical tension between *absurdity* and *rational narration*'[15] which has to be resolved on the aesthetic level. However the rational narration has not only to cope with the portrayal of *absurdité*, but also with that of the quest for significance and for values in a meaningless universe, and in

---

13 1 November 1954, *Carnets III*, p.128 'I often read that I am an atheist. These words mean nothing to me, they make no sense. I don't believe in God *and* I am not an atheist.'
14 *Carnets II*, p.30: 'Le sens du livre tient exactement dans le parallélisme des deux parties.'
15 The phrase is from Noyer-Weidner (tr.), in Gay-Crosier (ed., 1980), pp.72–86.

that endeavour every detail of the narration fits into an aesthetic pattern which engenders meaning.

The first problem is that of preserving innocence and happiness in an existence constantly threatened by the irrational, the second is the confrontation with *unhappiness* and *fault* in the perspective of personal extinction. Significantly, Meursault is known to us only by a surname which evokes concepts of life, death and the pursuit of happiness (the sea, the sun, the mother, the earth, death, a leap): *Mer/Soleil, Meurt/Sol, Meurt/Saut, Mère/Sol.*[16] He is minimally individualised, which is not to say that he is not an individual, but, as in the *cliché négatif* ('photographic negative') of which Camus speaks (see below) his individual traits are dark, not highlighted. In the words of Viggiani 'the novel is a parable and must be so interpreted' (p.879). To support my own reading of the text, it is necessary to show that Meursault is intelligent enough to understand the problem which he is required to solve; also that he is representative enough of us all to confer general validity upon his solution, if he finds one; then to analyse the key concepts of happiness and innocence, since the success or failure of the enterprise is measured in terms of these goals, and they alone emerge as conferring value upon existence; and finally to analyse the degree and nature of Meursault's failure or success.

Meursault's intellect has been thoroughly debated by critics, some of whom have regarded him as 'a person of low intelligence', or, albeit intelligent, a rudimentary being, or 'an absurd man who doesn't even reason'.[17] On the other hand, it must be (and has been) noted that Meursault has been a student, forced to give up his studies not because

---

16   Le Hir observes that between *La Mort heureuse* and *L'Étranger* Mersault has become Meursault (the first syllable thus changing the resonance from life to death, from the sea (*la mer*) to dying (*il meurt*). Gassin points out (seee p.39) the homophone *mer/mère*, and the closely related *mort*, 'une "mer heureuse" est donc aussi bien une "mère heureuse" qu'une "mort heureuse".' See also Viggiani's discussion of the nomenclature of characters, p.873. The idea of a 'leap into death' (*Meurt/Saut*) is suggested by Rizzuto (1981, see p.28). The relationship *Mère/Sol* and hence of the mother to the earth is my own suggestion.

17   See Cruickshank, p.159, Quilliot (1970), p.98, and more recently, Chabot, p.107.

of any failure, but because of his poverty.[18] Already in 1963, Rousset had pointed out that a first-person narration is 'the interpretation of oneself by oneself', and requires, as a preliminary, a splitting of the consciousness into observer and observed (see p.52), and recent criticism generally sees in Meursault an intelligent and reflective mind from the outset of the narrative. Rizzuto (1981, p.24) has remarked that what we have before us in the novel is a 'coherent and cogently structured narrative' behind which there lies 'a lucid intelligence and a purpose'. It is necessary to keep in mind Camus's own clue to the enigma, writing in his *Carnets* of 1942:

> Meursault n'affirme jamais rien. Et je n'en ai donné qu'un cliché négatif. Rien ne pouvait vous faire préjuger de son attitude profonde, sinon justement le dernier chapitre.[19]

His 'extreme indifference' however continues to puzzle, and one critic remarks that, while it seems to be the 'zero degree of awareness', it is offset by an exact observation of external facts. He adds that Meursault is moreover able to express himself in two styles of language, the 'neutral style' and the 'lyrical style', while at the end of the last chapter he suddenly reveals himself to have a command of 'dialectical style', ascribed to a progressive awakening of awareness (Noyer-Weidner, see p.83). Numerous critics have spoken of such a coming to awareness. However, a command of a dialectical skill cannot merely be the result of increased awareness any more than the ability to express oneself felicitously in three different styles. *Le style, c'est l'homme.*

What is often overlooked in discussions of Meursault's intelligence is that Camus has created a protagonist with the gifts of a writer, and at times of a poet. As one critic says, he can be viewed from this angle as Meursault-Camus-The Artist (Morot-Sir, see p.25).

---

18 Castex (p.69) points out that the mention of Meursault's studies was deliberately inserted into the narrative by Camus after the drafting of the first manuscript 'pour dissiper toute équivoque sur le personnage.'

19 *Carnets II*, p.33. 'Meursault never affirms anything. And I have given only a photographic negative of him. Nothing could allow you to surmise his deeper attitude, except precisely the last chapter.'

Castex remarks that Camus, after the end of his studies, had done everything to avoid the kind of career and life that Meursault has accepted. Meursault is not Camus, but he is the man Camus *could have* become (Castex, see pp.73–4). We have already seen in *La Mort heureuse* that Mersault, the *onlie begetter* of Meursault, is essentially an artist, and that Camus had, in his early notes and outlines, made his protagonist plan a novel to be entitled *Histoire du condamné à mort*.[20] Barrier pointed out in 1962 that in *L'Étranger*, the conversational turns of phrase and deliberate impressions of platitude conceal stylistic devices of elegance.[21] McCarthy has noted the attributes of poetry: 'Natural forces, the sun, sea, sand and rocks, are personified' (1988, p.20). Physical sensations are at first noted, but then turn into a flood of independent images. In this respect, it matters not to the argument about Meursault as artist whether what we have in front of us is a diary, memoirs, the transcript of a recorded voice, or even an inner monologue.[22]

Having the gifts of a writer and a poet, Meursault is naturally an observer in the first instance. Indeed he passes a whole Sunday afternoon and evening observing from his window the passers-by in the street below and the changing spectacle of the sky until the first stars come out. Pratt's view (p.16) that Meursault is a 'contemplative' would account for his passivity and also, as the same critic has pointed out, for the irony which we detect in his observations: 'the contemplative mind is naturally inclined to irony'. 'Toute mon œuvre est ironique', Camus wrote in 1950.[23] For Jean Sarocchi also, Meursault is a

---

20   See Chapter I, note 46. *The Story of the Man Condemned to Death.*
21   Critics who deny Meursault's intelligence or see him as only gradually coming to awareness disregard these elements. Rabaté, for example, states categorically that Meursault is neither poet nor writer, on the grounds that neither hidden intent nor purposeful structuring on the part of the narrator is discernable (see pp.100–3). The absence of intent is debatable, and in any case would not show that Meursault is necessarily bereft of the gifts of the writer or poet, nor of intelligence.
22   For a discussion of whether the narrative is a *journal* or a *récit oral*, see Tacca's article, as also the discussion following the article.
23   *Carnets II*, p.317. 'All my work is ironic.'

supreme ironist, while at the same time a contemplative whose ultimate silence in his cell has the quality of that of the great mystics.[24]

If we accept that Meursault has an ironic intelligence (capable moreover of detecting the irony of others),[25] the satirical or indeed comic aspect of certain situations becomes totally apparent. The examining magistrate's reasons for belief in God are rendered puerile by a reductive reporting of his discourse and the portrayal of his *unreasonable* waving of the crucifix across the table, like some latter-day inquisitor (the implied image is also important, as a critique of the whole justice system). 'À vrai dire, je l'avais très mal suivi dans son raisonnement', comments Meursault modestly,[26] but the reader has already concluded that there is no reasoning, no argument to follow.

Implicitly criticized throughout Part II is the lack of reason of the 'reasoners', the examining magistrate, the defence lawyer, the whole courtroom. Brian Fitch remarks, comparing the activity of the lawyers to that of writers and readers of novels, that 'the operative criterion is not that of truth but of verisimilitude' (1982, p.53). Patrick McCarthy sees them portrayed as writers of bad novels, creating a puppet character, totally coherent and lacking in freedom (1988, p.69), while Eisenzweig remarks that, like the journalists, the lawyers do not reflect reality but create a fiction (p.88). A friendly journalist remarks to Meursault, that the press has hyped up his case a bit, it being the silly season ('Vous savez, nous avons monté un peu votre affaire', p.1185). Morot-Sir has pointed out (pp.10–12) that the questions raised in the novel about justice go far beyond the debate about capital punishment and concern the whole of the justice system, including the prison régime and the pressures of social prejudice, remaining as relevant today as when the work was written.

---

24   See pp.211–2 of the discussion at the end of the proceedings of the Amiens conference of 1992, in *Albert Camus 16*.
25   p.1192. 'Puis [le procureur] a dit *avec quelque ironie* qu'il ne voudrait pas insister sur une situation délicate' (my italics). 'Then in a slightly ironic tone [the prosecutor] said that he didn't wish to dwell on such a delicate matter', *OS*, p.90.
26   p.1175. 'To tell the truth, I hadn't followed his argument at all well', *OS*, p.68.

The irony is close to that of *Candide*, whatever Camus may have objected to Sartre's comparison.²⁷ Meursault cannot, as a reasonable, ordinary citizen, much less as an outsider and an innocent, understand why it is necessary to appoint a lawyer to argue such a straightforward case as his. The magistrate's answer is not an explanation, but a simple assertion, 'Si vous ne choisissez pas d'avocat, nous en désignerons un d'office.'²⁸ The irony beneath the seeming innocence of Meursault's reply, 'J'ai trouvé qu'il était très commode que la justice se chargeât de ces détails', goes unnoticed by the magistrate, who, in best Pangloss fashion, as Meursault remarks,

> m'a approuvé et *a conclu* que la loi était bien faite. Au début je ne l'ai pas pris au sérieux (my italics).²⁹

However, it is precisely that which you do not take seriously which is most dangerous. Thus, as Meursault says later, one should never play games. 'Il ne faut jamais jouer' (p.1182).

Nobody in the course of the trial considers Meursault to be unintelligent. 'Cet homme, messieurs, cet homme est intelligent', says the prosecutor, basing his opinion on Meursault's replies, his use of language. 'Il connait la valeur des mots.'³⁰ Meursault accepts this expert assessment, reflecting somewhat ironically that he cannot quite see 'comment les qualités d'un homme ordinaire pouvaient devenir des

---

27 Sartre (1947) described *L'Étranger* as 'très proche d'un conte de Voltaire'. Vigée, in his Foreword to Reichelberg (p.11), writes that Camus had personally declared to him that this reading was totally wrong: 'Loin de situer ses écrits dans la tradition nihiliste classique issue de *Candide*, Camus voyait dans *L'Étranger* comme dans *La Chute* une étape de la reconquête du sens.' Deguy points out that Sartre's comparison is meant as anything but a compliment, and that in reducing the novel to a philosophical sketch he is guilty of a certain 'mauvaise foi' (in *Albert Camus 16*, see pp.75–9).
28 p.1171. 'If you don't choose a lawyer yourself, we'll appoint one for you automatically', *OS*, p.63.
29 p.1171. 'I thought it most convenient that the legal system should take care of such details [...] He agreed and said it showed how well the law worked. At first I didn't take him seriously', *OS*, p.63.
30 p.1196. ' This man is intelligent [...] He knows the value of words', *OS*, p.97.

charges écrasantes contre un coupable'.[31] Both an 'intelligent man' and an 'ordinary man', he is representative of us all, with his faults and mistakes, if such they are. 'The only Christ that we deserve', he becomes a fusion of Adam and Christ, endowed with mythical stature in his reconciliation with man's fate and place in nature at the novel's end.[32]

Nathalie Sarraute sees both despair and lucidity in Meursault and considers him to be 'an example, perhaps a lesson' (p.59). He is neither a moron nor a monster. If he were to be considered psychologically abnormal, he could be neither example nor lesson. I do not therefore propose to discuss psychological interpretations such as that of Leites, who diagnoses a personality disorder expressed finally in 'an oral scoptophilic and sadomasochistic ectasy bordering on panic' (p.264). As already noted, Camus, writing about his theatre, had affirmed that what interested him was not the individual psyche, but the human condition in all its entirety, simplicity and grandeur.[33] Meursault repeatedly affirms his typicality. When he first meets his lawyer, he would like to assert that he was 'absolutely like everybody else' ('J'étais comme tout le monde, absolument comme tout le monde', p.1173). *Un Homme comme les autres* (*A Man Like Any Other*) was in fact a subtitle which Camus had pondered (Quilliot's notes, p.1916). *The Stranger* (in many respects, my preferred translation of the title), is, paradoxically, Everyman. He is none other than Adam, a Stranger in an absurd and incomprehensible universe.

Nevertheless, this ordinary intelligent person is an enigma, at least to the reader. He does not appear strange to those around him before the murder, but they do not have the privilege, as does the reader,

---

31   p.1196. 'I couldn't understand how the qualities of an ordinary man could be used as damning evidence of guilt', *OS*, p.97.

32   See, for example, Crochet, who views Meursault as a fusion of the figures of Adam, Oedipus and Christ. Viggiani (see p.870) had already pointed out the Oedipal analogy. More recently, one critic has compared him to Job, standing at the point where a new order (in Meursault's case, post-Christian) is about to replace the old, and as the representative of the new, suffering persecution from a society which sees its values questioned and its unity threatened. (N. Sjursen in *Albert Camus 16*, pp.123–35).

33   *TRN*, p.1835. 'le destin humain tout entier dans ce qu'il a de simple et grand.'

of being privy to his thoughts or reflections (at least to an edited version of them). When, like Marie, they approach near enough to gain some insight into his mind, they too are perplexed. For his own part, he sees his reactions as those of any normal person, even when the 'normal' person is clearly shocked by them. Such is the reaction of the young clerk of the court writing the transcript of the interrogation with the examining magistrate when Meursault replies (with apparent lack of appropriate intensity) that he had loved his mother 'just like everybody else does' ('comme tout le monde', p.1174). This is the third time in four paragraphs that Meursault uses this phrase ('like everybody else') in reference to himself. The same sort of apparently unemotional phrase had shocked Marie:

> Elle a voulu savoir alors si je l'aimais. J'ai répondu comme je l'avais déjà fait une fois, que cela ne signifiait rien mais que sans doute je ne l'aimais pas.[34]

Shocking in both responses is what critics see as 'indifference' or lack of awareness, but which in fact is a wary *rationality*, a puritanical refusal to endorse the use of an undefined (undefinable?) concept (*'love'*), which is at the same time a defence against the pain of loss and an endeavour to rationalise the irrational. It is the indifference of the Stoics. Hannah Arendt, paraphrasing Epictetus, sums up the teaching of Stoicism as follows: 'Be stonelike and you will be invulnerable'.[35] A stone feels no pain, is indifferent to hurt or insult. Patrice Mersault, we remember, had become 'stone among the stones', and returned 'in the joy of his heart' to the worlds where all is still.

One critic had already detected, at the time the novel was published, the 'anaesthetic' effect of Meursault's apparent indifference. Quoting Meursault's reply when questioned as to whether putting his mother into a home had pained him personally ('J'ai répondu que ni maman ni moi n'attendions plus rien l'un de l'autre, ni d'ailleurs de

---

[34]   p.1156. 'She then wanted to know if I loved her. I replied as I had done once already, that it didn't mean anything but that I probably didn't', *OS*, p.44.

[35]   Arendt, *Vol. 2: Willing*, p.79. The paraphrase is of Epictetus' doctrine of *apatheia*, in the *Discourses*.

personne'),[36] he sees this 'cruel resignation' as covering up a desolating sense of abandonment, the inexpressible pain of not being in a position (for reasons of poverty) to honour and look after one's mother, a terrible resentment against both social inequalities and immanent injustice.[37] Yet none of this finds expression in the first-person narrative, a form which normally privileges the revelation of the inner being.

Meursault, says Bernard Pingaud, is 'not a man without reactions. He is a man who conceals his reactions' (p.93, tr.). He seems determined, in the words of Yeats's epitaph, to 'cast a cold eye on life, on death', and the result is, as Castex has said, that his problem becomes that of his relationships with others.[38] Whether the repression of affectivity is deliberate or rooted in the subconscious is unclear. The vital clue to Meursault's personality thus concealed, the reader becomes all the more intrigued. The response which so startles the clerk of the court is itself eminently rational, in that if Meursault is, as he feels himself to be, 'like everybody else' it follows, syllogistically, that he must love his mother 'like everybody else'. However, the phrase is meaningless, since Meursault cannot *know* how other men love their mothers. In the area of the emotions, every man is an island, and logic or reason alone cannot bridge the gap between individuals.

Meursault moreover is a curious contemplative who refuses to contemplate *himself*, having made himself a stranger to his own inner being. He will tell the lawyer after his arrest that he had rather lost the habit of introspection ('J'avais un peu perdu l'habitude de m'interroger', p.1172). But the corollary of that statement must be that he had once had the habit of looking inwards, just as he had once been a

---

36 p.1188. 'He asked me if it had been a personal sacrifice for me and I replied that neither mother nor I expected anything more of each other, or in fact of anyone else', *OS*, p.85.

37 'Ce terrible abandon, cette atonie désespérée cachent des sentiments positifs très simples et très colorés : la douleur inexplicable d'être hors d'état d'honorer sa mère, le ressentiment aigu contre l'injustice des hommes... et des dieux', Fieschi, in the *Nouvelle Revue Française*, September 1942. Quoted Pingaud, p.168.

38 Castex (1965) p.30: 'Le problème psychologique central de *L'Étranger*: celui des rapports du héros avec autrui.'

student. The mirror on his table is now yellowed, incapable of giving a clear reflection of the onlooker. He looks out onto the street or up into the sky but does not explore his own house, having shut down all but one room, in which restricted space he lives since the departure of his mother.

When does he begin to shut down the areas of self-questioning and introspection in his mind? It seems obvious that the decision to abandon the greater part of the flat, which had been homely 'when *maman* was there' ('Il était commode quand maman était là', p.1139), corresponds to a decision to block out certain mental activities. Without *maman* the flat is no longer comfortable, nor is life. It is no longer *homely*, and the occupant becomes a stranger in his own house, a stranger to himself in fact. There are whole areas which evoke a sense of loss. For three years since her departure for the nursing home Meursault's mother has been as good as dead to him, for what is death but separation and silence? Meursault never enquires about the immediate cause of his mother's death, because death eludes explanation. It is what renders all else meaningless. Meursault refuses to look upon his dead mother, or to contemplate even the approach of death, old age, which appears grotesque to him in the blinding and unnatural light of the morgue. He flees from that whole nightmarish experience back to the reassuring urban environment of Algiers, the new Adam who is the child of nature only on sunny weekends.

Camus had affirmed that the sense of the novel was contained in the final scene with the prison chaplain, whose culmination is Meursault's passionate and angry affirmation of non-belief and of the finality of death. Camus goes on to excoriate those who mistake a negative attitude for 'giving up' rather than a deliberate *choice*, and affirms that there is no other possible way of life for a man deprived of God, and 'all men are so deprived'.[39] Meursault's outburst (he has the full range of emotions after all, anger, fear, panic, and, as we will see, love), the

---

39   See *Carnets II*, pp.29–30: 'Avec l'aumônier, mon Étranger ne se justifie pas. Il se met en colère, c'est très différent.' Also pp.30–1: 'Critiques sur *L'Étranger* […] Imbéciles qui croyez que la négation est un abandon quand elle est un choix […] Il n'y a pas d'autre vie possible pour un homme privé de Dieu – et tous les hommes le sont.'

violent refusal to 'waste [his] time with God' ('Je ne voulais pas perdre [mon temps] avec Dieu', p.1210), is clearly the revelation of a conviction long held and intellectually and emotionally adhered to. He cannot conceive that his mother could ever have wished to 'waste [her] time with God' either, declaring that she had never in her life given a thought to religion ('Maman, sans être athée, n'avait jamais pensé de son vivant à la religion', p.1129). This rash statement merely demonstrates the strength of Meursault's desire to be united in spirit with his mother, his abhorrence of anything separating him from her, his recoiling therefore, as McCarthy (1988) has suggested, at the possibility of a spiritual dimension to her life which he cannot share. His 'J'ai pensé à maman', at the very end of the novel, his final conviction that he now shares her feeling of liberation in the face of death, is both a reaffirmation and a reclamation of community of spirit between himself and a mother for whom love is too deep to be expressed, either in words or in tears.

Meursault is Sisyphus only to a limited degree, but he is, as entirely as he can make himself, the 'Absurd Man', as defined by Camus in his essay: the individual who has consciously concluded that life is without any superior sense or purpose, and who seeks a rational and human way of living in that context. Interestingly, the narrator of *L'Étranger* uses the term 'absurd' only once, when, at the end of the novel, in the middle of his passionate outburst against the chaplain, he proclaims vehemently the supreme value of 'cette vie absurde que j'avais menée'.[40] As the critic Frantz Favre has pointed out, the adjective cannot here be taken in its everyday sense ('ridiculous'), nor, in the midst of such an emotional outpouring, as an irony. Meursault has just proclaimed that he has been right, always right, in living in one way rather than another, in doing this rather than that, in other words, his style of life has been a deliberate choice. He has seen the absurdity of life in the sense in which Sisyphus had seen it, and his choice has been to try to get through with as little pain as possible, hence the suppression of the emotions and the emphasis on periods of sleep.

Meursault being an unbeliever, Sunday has no religious connotations, but is merely another empty day. Death and emptiness (which

---

40   p.1210. 'this absurd life I'd been leading', *OS*, p.115.

Meursault perceives as '*ennui*'), and his determination to ignore both, as well as the meaninglessness of the passage of time, are summed up at the end of that same second chapter of the first part of the novel:

> J'ai pensé que c'était toujours un dimanche de tiré, que maman était maintenant enterrée, que j'allais reprendre mon travail et que, somme toute, il n'y avait rien de changé.[41]

It is in this chapter, in which precisely nothing happens, that Meursault reveals most about his mental attitudes, about his defence against anguish and his relief at successfully *killing* time. One strategy for so doing is sleep, as Meursault frankly acknowledges in prison, where he sleeps even more excessively than he had done in his flat.

Life, as we have seen in *Le Mythe de Sisyphe* is absurd in the sense that it has no meaning, and its unpredictability is simply an aspect of its meaninglessness. The murder which Meursault will commit will be the result of an unlucky chance: if he had not taken the revolver away from Raymond, precisely to prevent a crime, he would not have been carrying it when he unexpectedly met up again with the Arabs, and the crime would not have been committed. There is no rhyme or reason to it. Crime, accident, error, or simply *misfortune* (as Meursault's friend Céleste will describe it)? In a completely irrational world, one devoid of intent, value judgements make no sense. Above all, they cannot be traced back to some First Cause, or some ethic based upon the concept of 'Natural Law', but can only be arrived at existentially.

Meursault's unformulated values are certainly not materialistic. His rejection of ambition, his refusal to judge, his frugal way of life could be confused with the ideal of the Beatitudes. He is indeed one of the 'poor in spirit', but the source of this attitude is a profound pessimism at the antipodes of Christian optimism. Since the great enemy time takes all away, he limits all his joys and desires to that which involves no permanent commitment and whose loss he has schooled

---

41 p. 1142. 'I realized that I'd managed to get through another Sunday, that mother was now buried, that I was going back to work and that, after all, nothing had changed', *OS*, p.28.

himself to view with equanimity.[42] Thus while deriving joy from Marie and indeed counting '[her] laughter and [her] dresses' ('le rire et les robes de Marie', p.1199), among the simplest and the most lasting of his joys, he convinces himself that nothing binds them to each other once the physical bond has been removed, and that if she were dead, she would no longer mean anything to him.[43] Is this a manifestation of a Don Juan complex?[44] Meursault's existence is far removed from the Don Juanesque pursuit of pleasure in multiplicity. His attitude is rather fear of loss. One critic points out that when, in his prison cell, he receives Marie's letter telling him that she will no longer be allowed to visit him, his imprisonment becomes psychologically irremediable, his link with life itself is broken, and her absence 'opens the way to death'.[45]

Nguyen Van Huy distinguishes three different sorts of happiness in Camus's work, of which the first is the physical joy which results from union with the world of the senses, the others being the 'humanist' joy in solidarity with one's fellow man, and the 'metaphysical' joy in the union with spiritual values. Meursault's expectations are limited to the first of these, but in fact he deludes himself, for the physical and the spiritual are not so easily separated in human happiness. Among the 'simplest and most lasting' of his joys, as well as delight in Marie's laughter and her dresses, are 'des odeurs d'été, le quartier que

---

42 Champigny (see pp.70 ff.) places Meursault among the Epicureans, who distinguished between three sorts of desires: the natural and necessary, the natural and unnecessary, and those which were neither natural nor necessary (e.g. ambition or vanity), the avoidance of which was wisdom. Mounier notes the asceticism of Camus's doctrine as expounded in *Le Mythe de Sisyphe* (see pp.67 ff). Pratt (p.15) sees Meursault as a disciple of the Greek philosophers such as Plotinus (on whom, as noted, he had written his post-graduate dissertation).
43 pp.1206–7. 'En dehors de nos deux corps maintenant séparés, rien ne nous liait et ne nous rappelait l'un à l'autre. À partir de ce moment, d'ailleurs [*i.e.* should she die], le souvenir de Marie m'aurait été indifférent. Morte, elle ne m'intéressait plus.'
44 On Marie, Meursault, and Don Juan, see Rizzuto (1998), pp.27–9.
45 Montgomery, p.158, quoting *TRN*, p.1177: 'De ce jour-là, j'ai senti que j'étais chez moi dans ma cellule et que ma vie s'y arrêtait.'

j'aimais, un certain ciel du soir'.[46] Simplicity of heart, tenderness, joy in the beauty of the world, reflection, empathy, pathos, these are not physical phenomena. The Lucienne of *La Mort heureuse* now becomes Marie, a unique, precious person, drawn with a heartbreaking pathos in all her fragile beauty, which is intimated and never described. She is particularly touching in the visit to the prison and in her appearance in court, in the despair which she cannot express and her tears which she cannot hold back. When asked, in an interview with J.-C. Brisville, not long before he died, which were his favourite characters, Camus named three: Marie and Céleste, from *L'Étranger*, and Dora, the heroine of his drama *Les Justes*.[47] Meursault seeks no other conquest than Marie, complies with her wishes, even to the point of agreeing to marry her, and when he finally confronts imminent death in the encounter with the prison chaplain, it is her face that he passionately desires to see, ablaze with the 'colour of the sun and the flame of desire'.[48]

The deep-rooted emotions which reason cannot for ever suppress explode here as elsewhere in the ardent imagery: desire, grief, anger, the sense of tragic bewilderment or fatality. Don Juan looses his invulnerability as soon as the feminine Other acquires a name: Marie. And what a name! Not Helen of Troy, not Faust's Gretchen, but the *Ewig-Weibliches* as symbol both of innocent young womanhood and of maternal devotion, Mary in her glory, traditionally identified with the *Woman clothed with the Sun* of the Apocalypse. Roland Barthes (1970) had analysed the sun-imagery in the three key episodes of the novel (the funeral, the murder on the beach, and the courtroom scenes), but here it is none other than Marie who is metamorphosed into the Sun-Divinity, symbol of life itself.

Happiness at its minimal point, which is all that Meursault seeks from life, is merely the avoidance of its opposite, unhappiness, or

---

46   p.1199. '– my simplest and most lasting pleasures: the smells of summer, the part of town that I loved, the sky on certain evenings, Marie's dresses and the way she laughed', *OS*, p.101.
47   'Réponses à Jean-Claude. Brisville', *Essais*, see p.1922.
48   p.1209: 'Ce visage avait la couleur du soleil et la flamme du désir: c'était celui de Marie.'

misfortune (the French word *malheur* signifies both). Happiness is dependent upon not only the avoidance of one's own misfortune, but the avoidance of causing unhappiness to any other individual (why this should be so is is implicit but not examined in this novel). Innocence, 'doing no harm', is therefore the basic requirement. Loss of innocence is not guilt, not a 'sin', but rather a *malheur*, a misfortune, an accident. *Malheur* is of course a term devoid of moral connotations. While sin implies the thwarting of some divine purpose, *malheur* or *misfortune* is a collision with the irrational universe. Meursault will tell the chaplain that the notion of sin is meaningless for him ('Je lui ai dit que je ne savais pas ce qu'était un péché', p.1208), and Céleste, when asked what he thinks of Meursault's crime, will tell the court that for him it is *un malheur* (p.1191).

Camus himself, in *Le Mythe de Sisyphe*, had already rejected the notion of sin and guilt. The 'Absurd Man' refuses these essentially theological/moral categories because he wishes to act only in accordance with what he fully comprehends:

> Il ne veut faire justement que ce qu'il comprend bien. On lui assure que c'est péché d'orgueil, mais il n'entend pas la notion de péché [...] On voudrait lui faire reconnaître sa culpabilité. Lui se sent innocent. À vrai dire, il ne sent que cela, son innocence irréparable.[49]

Meursault makes a distinction between 'sin' and 'guilt', and recognises himself as 'guilty' only in the sense that the court has declared him so.[50] Yet all of Camus's work is obsessed with the idea of a judgement and of judges, of fault and loss of innocence; there is in *L'Étranger* 'a real fixation with judgement which recurs in *La Peste* and of course in *La Chute*', writes Bernard Pingaud (p.36, tr.). Meursault's innocent eye, to which the proceedings taking place in court

---

49 *Mythe, Essais*, p.137. 'Indeed, he does not want to do anything but what he fully understands. He is assured that this is the sin of pride, but he does not understand the notion of sin [...] An attempt is made to get him to admit his guilt. He feels innocent. To tell the truth, that is all he feels – his irreparable innocence', *Myth*, p.51.
50 pp.1208–9: 'Je lui ai dit que je ne savais pas ce qu'était un péché. On m'avait seulement appris que j'étais un coupable.'

appear incomprehensible, is no different from that of Kafka's Joseph K. in *The Trial*, a work which Camus regarded as the perfect example of the 'absurdist' novel and of which he wrote:

> Rien n'y manque, ni la révolte inexprimée [...] ni le désespoir lucide et muet [...] ni cette étonnante liberté d'allure que les personnages du roman respirent jusqu'à la mort finale.[51]

Meursault too exhibits this astonishing freedom, in his refusal to conform to the expectations of the court, to deny the truth of his own experience. Joseph K., the commercial traveller, who, like Meursault, is 'like everbody else',[52] is an innocent victim, and Meursault too, despite the murder, appears as the victim of hostile forces, be they metaphysical, physical, or social. He rejects the notion of moral culpability, but from the first pages of the novel he betrays a curious unease, a defensiveness, a fear of being found in the wrong. How is the individual to avoid that collision with the irrationality of the universe which results in the loss of innocence? As he remarks in his account of his Sunday in the flat, one is always in some way to blame: 'De toute façon, on est toujours un peu fautif' (p.1139). It is in the same account that he first mentions hand-washing. He is a compulsive hand-washer, making us think of other hand-washers such as Pontius Pilate or Lady Macbeth. 'Wash away my iniquities and cleanse me from my sins', says the priest as he washes his hands in the ancient ritual which precedes the most solemn moment of the Mass. Desire for purification is the most obvious impulse in Meursault's obsession, but purification from what?

Uri Eisenzweig notes that Meursault washes his hands on that Sunday after cutting out and pasting into an exercise-book a newspaper advertisement for Kruschen salts. The critic interprets the action as a sign that 'writing is dirty, in *L'Étranger*', indeed, even worse, it is

---

51   *Mythe*, 'L'Espoir et l'Absurde dans Kafka', *Essais*, p.205. 'Nothing is lacking, neither the unexpressed revolt [...] nor lucid and mute despair [...] nor that amazing freedom of manner which the characters of the novel exemplify until their ultimate death', *Myth*, pp.125–6.

52   ibid., *Essais*, p.204. 'C'est un Européen moyen. Il [Joseph K.] est comme tout le monde.'

excremental (see p.20). For Eisenzweig the domain of the written is the sphere of the paternal values rejected by Meursault, that of the law, judges, police, of secular and religious authorities, whose ultimate representative is the prison chaplain. Is that an over-interpretation? We may remark that newsprint is dirty literally as well as metaphorically and that washing one's hand after handling it is a normal activity. As to the Kruschen salts advertisement, it can be seen as an ironic comment on the derisory aspects of human nature, the excremental side of existence, rarely mentioned but undermining all our self-importance. Meursault puts it among his collection of items which amuse him in the papers. Or is the 'excremental' in fact the world of politics and history, and the handwashing on this occasion a symbol of disengagement? Meursault's imperviousness to political events has been underlined by Pingaud. It must also be noted, however, that his total indifference to the political landscape is very far removed from Camus's own passionate involvement in social justice and world events. He is, says Pingaud, a 'negative' hero, uninterested in the war in Spain, the rise of totalitarianism or the lot of the Arab community. Pingaud's conclusion is that 'history is absent from the novel' (p.23). Is this withdrawal conscious or unconscious, a self-defence or a self-absorption? Washing his hands each time he leaves the office, Meursault also signals his disinvolvement from the world of work; it is a symbolic act of purification that prepares a return to a more natural existence. 'À propos, connaissez-vous la Grèce?' Clamence will ask in *La Chute*,

> Non? Tant mieux. Qu'y ferions-nous, je vous le demande? Il y faut des coeurs purs [...] Avant de nous présenter dans les îles grecques, il faudrait nous laver longuement.[53]

Critics analysing Meursault's responsibility for events point to his dealings with Raymond, or, echoing the strictures of his neighbours, comment on his treatment of his mother. They consider that he disregarded natural prudence in returning to the beach, or even argue

---

53 *TNR*, pp.1525–6. 'By the way, do you know Greece? No? So much the better. There it requires pure hearts [...] Before appearing in the Greek islands, we should have to wash at length', *Fall*, pp.72–3.

that he was subconsciously choosing death rather than commitment and domesticity (reflected in the Masson couple) in the impending marriage to Marie. His predecessor Mersault had, after all, considered marriage to be the equivalent of suicide; it is 'un geste désespéré, quoi?'. Political readings, from Conor Cruise O'Brien to Emmet Parker or Edward Said, deconstruct the French/Arab relationship in the colonial context of Algeria. Germaine Brée takes issue with O'Brien in defence of Camus (1972, pp.151–3 and pp.212ff.), while Patrick McCarthy (1988) considers that 'Meursault kills the Arab because he is threatened by a brother-rival whose claim to Algeria is greater than his own' (p.54).

Other interpretations also abound. According to Pratt, Meursault's fault is in returning to the beach; he seems to 'yield to the temptation of transcendance, to the desire to surpass the material conditions of life' (see p.81). Reichelberg writes similarly, that he should have resisted the 'deceitful invitation of the noonday sun', that wisdom required him to accept certain limits (see p.80). Le Hir suggests that Meursault's real fault lies in having put his mother into a home; he is reproached three times for this, by the director of the home, by Salamano, and by the tribunal (see p.45). Psychoanalytic interpretations are best represented by Gassin, who sees the murder of the Arab as a symbolic attack on the mother; the hero must choose 'annihilation *in* the mother' or 'annihilation *of* the mother' (author's italics; see p.214). Rizzuto (1981) considers that Meursault's self-centered nature cannot face the impending marriage: 'with this fact in mind, Meursault proceeds to make his choice and kill the Arab'; he has a death-wish, preferring 'shade and repose' to involvement in a community (pp.19–20).

There is however a more radical *hubris* in Meursault, which consists in the attempt to parry the 'absurdity' of existence by refusing importance to all that lies beyond the immediate, all that is outside the control of the mind (mortality, affectivity), and in the cultivation of an ironic detachment, together with a refusal of all value-judgements. The root of this detachment is fear of loss, of pain, of death itself, hence Meursault's reflexes are at all times defensive. He deliberately aims low in life (the best way to avoid disappointment), so low in fact that he shoots a man already prostrate on the ground.

The avoidance of value-judgements, together with the stifling of affectivity, underlie the downgrading of relationships of love (Marie) or friendship. Anyone can be Meursault's friend, and he passively accepts the sleazy and violent Sintès as his 'pal': 'J'ai dit que ça m'était égal',[54] is his comment. Sintès's deeply unpleasant account of his violent relationship with his Arab mistress does not lead to any revulsion on Meursault's part. When Sintès asks what Meursault thinks of the story, he replies that he hasn't really thought about it, but 'it's interesting' ('J'ai répondu qu je n'en pensais rien, mais que c'était intéressant', p.1147). Implicitly Meursault regards all language, whether oral or written, as suspect (hence the refusal to subscribe to vocabulary such as 'love'), and therefore bases no judgements upon it. What is more ominous is that this refusal of judgement leads him in this instance to disregard both justice and truth. To please Sintès, 'parce que je n'avais pas de raison de ne pas le contenter',[55] he writes the letter which lures the Arab girl back to another beating, and subsequently accompanies the aggressor to the police station in order to testify that Raymond had been provoked by the unfaithfulness of his mistress, an allegation for which Meursault has no evidence other than Sintès's unreliable word. Certain critics see in Sintès's treatment of the Arab girl an image of 'the historical rape inflicted on Algerian Muslims by the settler population in general'.[56] Meursault can therefore be viewed as complicit in this crime also. At the very least he perverts the course of justice in order to show solidarity with a violent French Algerian.

But there is also a deeper, more complex pattern underlying this episode, and the seed of Meursault's own fate is sown in it. As one critic has pointed out, in writing the letter, he substitutes himself for Sintès, and the episode constitutes the sealing of a kind of blood brotherhood.[57] In line with such an interpretation, it could also be

54   p.1146; 'I said I didn't mind', *OS*, p.33.
55   p.1148; 'because I had no reason not to please him', *OS*, p.36.
56   See Hargreaves, pp.101–12. Hargreaves gives an account of the views of commentators such as the French historian Pierre Nora, the Algerian Minister of Education after independence, Ahmed Taleb Ibrahimi, and later Conor Cruise O'Brien. The quotation is from p.108.
57   Jones (1992), p.123, n.2. Jones notes Sintès's account of having beaten the girl until she bled, and of having punched her brother so that his face was covered

claimed that the meal which Meursault shares with Sintès has a quasi-sacramental nature. The object is certainly a shared communion, a degree of male bonding: '[Il] m'a dit qu'entre hommes on se comprenait toujours',[58] but the ceremony is sacrilegious, its turpitude reflected in the dirty room, the unmade bed, the dirty bandage which Sintès wraps around his hand, and it requires a human victim: the Arab girl. The theme of blood, so prominent in this episode, foreshadows the blood drawn on the beach, that of the bloodied face of the Arab punched by Sintès, that of Sintès slashed in the arm and mouth by the Arab's knife, and that of Meursault's victim (pp.1164–5).

When Meursault leaves Sintès's flat, having accepted to become a kind of *alter Sintès*, he finds himself in the obscurity of the landing and the stairwell from which there rises a dark, dank whiff of air, 'un souffle obscure et humide'. The darkness, the dankness, the sinister stairwell, certainly suggest a spiritual abyss, a moral nadir, and Meursault finds himself paralysed, deafened by the blood pounding in his head.[59] The only external sound is the muffled whine of Salamano's maltreated dog. Salamano and his dog are chained together in a relationship which for one means subjugation, and on the part of the other is characterised by violence and injustice. It has been variously interpreted,[60] but it is not unreasonable to see in it a pessimistic image of the relationship between the French and Arab populations of Algeria, which must have weighed upon Camus's conscious and subconscious mind at least since the days of his investigative journalism for *Alger Républicain*, in the immediate pre-war period. Rather than taking the view of those critics who accuse Camus of having a blinkered *pied-noir* point of view, I would suggest that the ill-treatment of the Arabs in the novel, the humiliation and beating of the woman, the murder of the man on the beach, the poverty of the Arab population,

   in blood, also Sintès's own injured right hand, which he covers with a dirty bandage, and the blood-sausage (*boudin*) which he shares with Meursault.
58 p.1148. '[He] said that we men always understood one another', *OS*, p.36.
59 p.1149. 'Des profondeurs de la cage d'escalier montait un souffle obscur et humide. Je n'entendais que les coups de mon sang qui bourdonnait à mes oreilles. Je suis resté immobile.'
60 Notably by Pichon-Rivière and Baranger, who suggest that, in Meursault's subconscious, the dog is a mother-substitute.

their preponderance in the overcrowded prison population, the evident 'outsider' status they occupy in their own land, the denial of a voice, add up to a very serious indictment of the relationship between the dominant European population and the indigenous people. 'Camus's Arabs may well be the unlikely heroes of the novel, and their silence could conceal more things to admire than to despise', writes a recent critic (Rigaud, p.191).

That Meursault does not reflect upon the situation and treatment of the Arabs as unjust or abnormal simply makes the indictment all the more damning. We are by implication invited to see his attitudes simply as those of a representative French Algerian living in modest circumstances, neither consciously racist nor committed to any political ideology. The dog's whine, muffled and behind closed doors, is a protest in advance against the violence to be suffered by the Arab woman, the coming murder of the Arab on the beach, and a denunciation of the part Meursault has accepted for himself on the side of injustice. It is not only Salamano whose hands are now dirty.[61]

The oppressive enclosed space, the dank current of midnight air, the pounding of the blood in the head, the immobility, will find their obverse imagery in the the endless beach, the blazing midday sun, and that moment, on the day of the murder, when Meursault returns to the beach hut and, instead of ascending the stairs (no longer the dark stairwell), which would bring him out of the sphere of violence and into the company of the women, lacks the will or the strength to make the effort. His head pounding again, this time with the sun, he is momentarily immobile in the blinding light beating down from above ('la tête retentissante de soleil […] la pluie aveuglante qui descendait du soleil', p.1166), before returning to the beach and to his destiny. A destiny which is the outcome of his failure to make a judgement about the situation. 'Rester ici ou partir, cela revenait au même', is the reflection with which he sets his foot upon the path to catastrophe.[62] The malign influence of the dark, dank breath of disaster yet to come,

---

61   The Hispanicised name sounds, to the French reader, like 'dirty hand' ('sale main').
62   p.1166. 'Whether I stayed there or moved, it would come to the same thing', *OS*, p.58.

which had passed over him on that evening above the stairwell, will not be dispelled until the very end of the novel, when, in the great outburst of passionate rejection of the pleas of the chaplain, he proclaims the advent of another 'dark breath', one which sweeps over him from the future years which he will now never live, sweeping away in its path the dark, the guilt and the unhappiness, and bringing salvation in the revelation that life itself is the great, the only privilege (p.1210). After this catharsis, Meursault is at last reconciled with his own death, with the natural world, and returned to the state of grace of his innocence and happiness.

In view of Meursault's dealings with Sintès, in what sense can Camus claim for him a 'passion for truth'? Camus went on (as we have seen at the beginning of this chapter) to define his 'truth': it is 'une vérité encore négative, la vérité d'être et de sentir' ('a truth which is still negative, the truth of being and feeling'). For such a truth, Meursault is prepared to face the death-sentence, alienating court and jury by his non-conformity with their concept of what is 'normal' in this sphere of attitudes and emotions. However, this 'negative', solipsistic truth is an inadequate foundation on which to build relationships, and in his refusal to go beyond it, to attempt to understand and appreciate the Other at his or her true value, Meursault devalues his relationships and falls from grace. It is his failure to evaluate friendship on the basis of truth and justice which has been at the source of his complaisance towards Sintès, of his involvement in the other's violent quarrel, and which leads directly to a murder which he commits in Sintès's place, with Sintès's revolver, and on a beach where he would not have been without Sintès's 'friendship'.

The novel can be seen as a demonstration of the impossibility of living *without* value-judgements. The problem is also that Meursault does not have enough faith in the truth of his feelings to base any course of action upon them. The relationship with Marie is incomplete, because Meursault never seeks a communion at a level beyond the physical, despite a depth of feeling which has far greater potential. His fastidiousness in his account of Sintès's squalid flat is clearly discernable, however he does not translate it into moral fastidiousness. Unfortunately for him.

The only relationship in which from the beginning Meursault recognises a dimension beyond the physical is, of course, that with his mother. It is a communion very deeply felt when he looks upon the countryside at her funeral, and which overpowers him at the end of the novel when he awakens to the night stars and breathes in the scents of night, earth and salt ('des odeurs de nuit, de terre et de sel', p.1211). However, his decision to send her away is based not upon this communion, but (perhaps necessarily) on a rational response to a difficult situation: the lack of money to have her cared for at home. The voice of the heart has had to be silenced. Significantly, the rational explanation is formulated initially not by Meursault but by the *directeur* of the home who speaks what McCarthy (1988, p.17) calls 'the language of authority', *i.e.* that of political or economic power, domains in which the heart has no place.

Meursault gives a clue to other, deeper levels of possible motivation with his startlingly lucid aphorism that 'tous les êtres sains avaient plus ou moins souhaité la mort de ceux qu'ils aimaient'.[63] It is simply a rational formulation of the fact that within every 'normal person' lies a voice demanding the right to enjoy to the full the intoxicating gift of life, untrammelled by bonds of love or responsibility. It is the temptation which had seduced Mersault in the first novel. The aphorism shocks because it leaves unsaid an equally important truth: within those who are truly 'normal' and mentally healthy the voice of love speaks even louder. Meursault has had to bow to the constraints of his poverty, send his mother away, and he has rationalised away as far as possible the pain, yet he cannot escape the protest of the deeper inner voice which takes the form of an irrational, vague but obsessive guilt-complex. Had he been compelled by circumstance, or had he yielded to the worst, unspoken temptation, that of freedom? The sympathetic reader may exonerate him, but he himself cannot disentangle the motivations, and introspection is torment, hence he ceases to look into himself.

His mother's tears at the separation are ascribed to habit, *l'habitude* (p.1128), thus again banishing affectivity. Is this not an example

---

63 p.1172. 'To a certain extent all normal people sometimes wished their loved ones were dead', *OS*, p.65.

of *mauvaise foi* on Meursault's part, an attempt to evade the pain of causing pain? Or an apologia in support of his innocence in the matter? Moreover, in spite of his conscious refusal to evaluate or to pass judgement, he does in fact do both here: he assesses the inner life of another human being (as he also does when affirming that 'Maman, sans être athée, n'avait jamais pensé de son vivant à la religion'),[64] and effectively sentences his mother to await her death in a form of imprisonment, because she is silent and in spite of her tears. There is deep irony in the fact that society does the same to him: he is judged in the name of reason and condemned because of his silence and because he does not shed tears.

The second part of the novel offers Meursault both a reflection of the ideal relationship with his mother and of the débacle which has come about through his ill-defined fault. The first is the prison visit of the little old woman to her son. They sit in silence, gazing intently at each other: 'Le seul îlot de silence était à côté de moi dans ce petit jeune homme et cette vieille qui se regardaient'.[65] Meursault had on the contrary averted his eyes from his mother's gaze. The second sign is the scrap of newspaper with the story of the returned Czechoslovakian traveller: a son deserts his mother, becomes a stranger to her, cannot re-establish the relationship and must die. The Orestes-Clytemnestra relationship is reversed: the mother kills the son. Or is the latter transferring the burden of guilt onto his victim?

Both incidents are recounted in Chapter 2 of Part II of the novel, which is a clear pendant to the second chapter of Part I. Meursault's refusal to explore his abode in Part I is replaced by the impossibility of exploring anything beyond the walls of the prison cell in Part II. The

---

64   p.1129. 'Though she wasn't an atheist, mother had never given a thought to religion in her life', *OS*, p.12.

65   p.1179. 'The only oasis of silence was just next to me where the young man and the little old lady were gazing at each other', *OS*, p.74. Although the young man addresses his mother, like Meursault, as 'maman', the couple seems to be Arab. Marie is surrounded by Arab visitors, and the Arabs talk in low voices, intimately, while the Europeans feel obliged to shout (p.1178, *OS*, p.72). This detail, and the portrayal of the ideal mother/son relationship in an Arab couple, indicates a high regard on Camus's part for Arab spirituality. The lack of any ethnic label, however, bestows universality on the two figures.

cell itself replaces the flat: 'J'ai senti que j'étais chez moi dans ma cellule'.[66] It is no longer merely an image of Meursault's own life, but of the human condition. The cell is not only an image of our mortal condition, but also, like the monk's cell, a place of reflection on man's fate, a place of meditation raised to the level of poetry or religion, as the case may be. The cell offers Meursault glimpses of sea and sky, images of eternity, in place of the street life which he had contemplated from the balcony of the flat. It is a contemplation which now demands effort and intensity; he perceives the object of his longing, the sea, only when he is 'agrippé aux barreaux, [son] visage tendu vers la lumière'.[67]

He is now obliged to look upwards or inwards. The yellowed mirror of the flat, from which Meursault's image had been absent, is replaced by the tin dish in which he sees himself: 'Il m'a semblé que mon image restait sérieuse alors même que j'essayais de lui sourire'.[68] In the depths of the dish, levels of his being which he had previously refused to contemplate look out at him, while the exteriorisation of his personality, the voice with which he has been speaking until now, reveals his previous estrangement from his own inner self. As he had not visited his mother, so Marie now cannot visit him.[69] The advertisement for Kruschen salts is replaced by the item in the scrap of old newspaper, the ironic view of human nature by the tragic aspects of the human predicament, which Meursault can no longer regard with mere amusement. This time he makes a value-judgement and draws a moral lesson: 'De toute façon, je trouvais que le voyageur l'avait un peu mérité et qu'il ne faut jamais jouer'.[70] 'Man may become *homo ludens* or he may create new moral values', as Patrick McCarthy remarks, commenting on *Le Mythe de Sisyphe* (1988, p.85).

---

66   p.1177. 'I felt that my cell was my home', *OS*, p.71.
67   p.1177. '– clinging to the bars, [his] face straining towards the light', *OS*, p.72.
68   p.1183. 'My reflection seemed to stay serious even when I tried to smile at it', *OS*, p.79.
69   Various critics have seen in Marie an avatar of the mother-figure. See, for example, Gassin.
70   p.1182. 'Anyway, I decided that the traveller had deserved it really and that you should never play around', *OS*, p.78.

Zagreus, the substitute father-figure, had had to die in order to provide Mersault with the means of freedom, Meursault's mother has had to go into the home in order that her son might be free to lead his life. The parental generation must make way for the young. Is this the deepest, original *malheur*, the ultimate source of the guilt-complex? In an ironic reversal of the natural order, it is the traveller's mother, the parental figure in *Le Malentendu*, who unknowingly kills the son (or helps to kill him). Meursault passes judgement on the traveller, thus condemning the son and exonerating the mother. It is a double condemnation, that of the son who fails to communicate with his mother, a failure to find words, and that of the individual who plays games with words, a failure to ascribe adequate importance to the truth, the fatal error in Meursault's relationship with Sintès.

Truth for Meursault is, as we have seen, an instinct, 'the truth of being and feeling'. Not until the final encounter with the chaplain, will he pass judgement on a fellow human being, and then it comes from his innermost self: 'Qu'importait que Raymond fût mon copain autant que Céleste qui *valait mieux que lui*?' (my italics).[71] How has he recognised Céleste's worth? He has recognised it in his own spontaneous reaction to this friend's pathetic and loyal attempt to stand by him at the trial: 'C'est la première fois de ma vie que j'ai eu envie d'embrasser un homme'.[72] The intelligence as well as the emotions, head and heart together, are necessary to such recognition. Reduced to its basic propositions, Camus's morality has been denigrated as simplistic or naïve, but its simplicity is arrived at through an intellectual asceticism, a disciplined effort to find answers within the human heart to questions not asked by psychologists but by philosophers. Céleste is a better man than Raymond Sintès, because Céleste is an innocent (as his very name implies) and all his actions show him to be so, while Raymond (whose name rhymes with *démon*) knows only violence, lies and the exploitation of others. Meursault will deny to the end that anything matters except the miraculous privilege of life itself, but if the

---

71 p.1211. 'What did it matter that Raymond was just as much my mate as Céleste who was *worth more than him*?' *OS*, p.116 (my italics).
72 p.1191. 'It was the first time in my life that I'd ever wanted to kiss a man', *OS*, pp.89–90.

value of life consists in the measure of happiness it affords, the fact is that Sintès has destroyed Meursault's happiness and that Céleste offers the only cure for the alienation and unhappiness of the Stranger, the Outsider, which is the recognition of kinship with one's fellow human beings and of their goodwill.

Values extrapolated from an intuitively recognised truth thus gain a hold in Meursault's universe, and are disregarded at the cost of happiness. But the value of life itself has first to be established, its transcience overcome. Meursault's greatest problem, right to the final scene with the chaplain, is that of making sense of time:

> Du fond de mon avenir [...] un souffle obscur remontait vers moi à travers des années qui n'étaient pas encore venues et ce souffle égalisait sur son passage tout ce qu'on me proposait alors dans les années pas plus réelles que je vivais.[73]

This dark breath blowing 'from the depths of [his] future' levels everything in the 'unreal years' that he is living, robbing them of meaning, because they are years in which *today* relentlessly becomes *yesterday*:

> Aujourd'hui maman est morte. Ou peut-être hier, je ne sais pas [...] Cela ne veut rien dire.[74]

In the long months of prison, the whole question had been to *kill time* ('tuer le temps', p.1181).Totally deprived of all that Pascal calls *divertissement* (distraction) and forced to contemplate the human condition in its starkest terms, he tries to live through the experience in two ways. First he denies that it is unbearable:

> J'ai souvent pensé alors que si l'on m'avait fait vivre dans un tronc d'arbre sec, sans autre occupation que de regarder la fleur du ciel au-dessus de ma tête, je

---

73   p.1210. 'From the depths of my future [...] I'd felt a vague breath drifting towards me across all the years that were still to come, and on its way this breath had evened out everything that was then being proposed to me in the equally unreal years I was living through', *OS*, p.115.
74   p.1127. 'Mother died today. Or maybe yesterday, I don't know [...] That doesn't mean anything', *OS*, p.9.

m'y serais peu à peu habitué. J'aurais attendu des passages d'oiseaux ou des rencontres de nuages.⁷⁵

The despair of Zagreus is thus rescinded. Secondly Meursault has recourse to memory, not to affective memories of pleasant past experiences or of people, but to a long catalogue of objects in his room, an attempt to make an inventory, to bring intellectual order into chaos, to enumerate (p.1181). Jung again remarks that 'Number helps more than anything else to bring order into the chaos of appearances [...] It may well be the most primitive element of order in the human mind' (vol 8, p. 456).

The purpose of both strategies is to validate survival at the rock-bottom point at which a human being is still human, to affirm that life is still worth living even in the absence of all freedom of choice and activity. The conclusion seems to be positive in the case of both procedures, since the infinite variety and richness of the world, either of nature or of the humblest objects, is such that

> un homme qui n'aurait vécu qu'un seul jour pourrait sans peine vivre cent ans dans une prison. Il aurait assez de souvenirs pour ne pas s'ennuyer.⁷⁶

The hyperbole of these affirmations is undermined however by the melancholy of the closing phrase of that section of the novel, as Meursault contemplates his 'serious and sad' reflection in the tin dish, by the fading light coming through the tiny window above him: 'Personne ne peut imaginer ce que sont les soirs dans les prisons.'⁷⁷ Is Pascal right after all? The third technique which Meursault adopts is in fact an admission of defeat. He sleeps up to eighteen hours a day, leaving him 'six hours to kill' ('Il me restait alors six heures à tuer', p.1182). Oblivion is preferred to consciousness, and killing time is a form of temporary suicide.

---

75 p.1180. 'I often thought in those days that even if I'd been made to live in a hollow tree trunk, with nothing to do but look up at the bit of sky overhead, I'd gradually have got used to it. I'd have looked forward to seeing birds fly past or clouds run together', *OS*, p.75.
76 p.1182. 'A man who'd only lived for a day could easily live for a hundred years in a prison. He'd have enough memories not to get bored', *OS*, p.77.
77 p.1183. 'No one can imagine what the evenings in prisons are like', *OS*, p.79.

This despair is however not the last word. Having fled from the confrontation with death in the first chapter, having ironically become the agent of death himself, having sought to *kill time* as an expedient, Meursault is finally obliged to confront his own death and to face his own fear. At last he discovers that the only important question is to reconcile life with death, to make sense of mortality:

> Comment n'avais-je pas vu que rien n'était plus important qu'une exécution capitale et que, en somme, c'était la seule chose vraiment intéressante pour un homme![78]

He wrestles with the angel of death and emerges triumphant. The priest, who offers the ultimate evasion, is forced to flee. Most importantly, Meursault refuses the image of the divine *liberator*, of whom Pascal writes in a letter to his sister:

> Nous devons nous considérer comme des criminels dans une prison toute remplie des images de leur libérateur et des instructions nécessaires pour sortir de la servitude.[79]

The chaplain begs Meursault to see this image, but the only image that he wishes to see, as he passionately declares, is that of Marie's face lighting up the gloom of the cell. From involuntary executioner Meursault has become victim, but paradoxically also a victor for whom death has lost its sting. In finding the expression of his suffering, Meursault finds at last his catharsis and redemption. The outpouring of words *purges* him of his anguish, and his reconciliation finds expression in that marvellous final paragraph of the novel in which the burning hostile sun is replaced by the warm peaceful night, flowing into him like a tide from the sea. Goethe's Torquato Tasso had already discovered the unifying and redemptive power of language:

---

78   p.1203. 'I don't know how I hadn't realized before that nothing was more important than executions and that, in actual fact, they were the only thing a man could really be interested in!' *OS*, p.106.

79   *Pasc.* p.483: 'Lettre de Pascal et de sa soeur Jacqueline à Madame Périer, leur soeur', 1 April 1648: 'We must regard ourselves as criminals in a prison filled with images of their liberator and with the instructions for emerging from our servitude.'

> Und wenn der Mensch in seiner Qual verstummt,
> Gab mir ein Gott zu sagen, wie ich leide.[80]

When language reaches a certain intensity it is both catharsis and salvation, but, as Barthes remarked, it is 'never innocent', (1972, p.16, tr.), since the intentionality of the author directs all linguistic choice. J. McCann, for example, has pointed out that Camus's 'non-literary' text is as much 'mediated by interpretation' as any 'literary' alternative. 'La gachette a cédé', for instance, ('The trigger gave way'), absolves Meursault from responsibility and is 'not a statement of fact but an interpretation' (p.56). Throughout the work, the perfect tense, pertaining to oral language, gives the immediacy of speech and replaces the literary French past historic, previously the norm in narrative texts. The first-person singular narrator and the use of the present and perfect tenses hugely intensify the emotional charge at climactic points (as here) or, on the contrary, convey detachment or ironic distance.

The emotions, which make of the individual an island, also build the bridges which allow us to meet. The battle Meursault wages to overcome his fear and to reason himself into an acceptance of his fate makes him fully one of us, inspires our sympathy, fear, and pity. The chaplain is the first to weep for him: '[Il] m'a regardé un moment en silence. Il avait les yeux pleins de larmes. Il s'est détourné et il a disparu'.[81] Already at the end of the trial, in the perspective of death, signals of fraternity have surrounded Meursault. Paradoxically, these emanate from the very representatives of the society which condemns him, the lawyer, the policemen, who try wordlessly to show consideration:

> Il m'a semblé alors reconnaître le sentiment que je lisais sur tous les visages. Je crois bien que c'était de la considération. Les gendarmes étaient très doux avec moi. L'avocat a posé sa main sur mon poignet.[82]

80   'And although man suffers in silence, / A god has given me the gift of expressing my pain.'
81   p.1211. 'He looked at me for a moment in silence. His eyes were full of tears. Then he turned away and disappeared', *OS*, p.116.
82   p.1201. 'And I think I recognized the expression that I could see on every face. I think it was one of respect. The policemen were very gentle with me. The lawyer placed his hand on my wrist', *OS*, p.103.

Just as it is the emotions which build the bridges between men, so too Meursault's own powerful instinctive reaction to the prospect of annihilation invalidates all possible intellectual argument against the value of living. Try as he will to reason himself out of his fear of death, to loosen voluntarily his grip on life, he knows by his own passionate emotional response that life is infinitely precious and that all arguments diminishing its value are specious. He repeats the old world-weary clichés to himself:

> Mais tout le monde sait que la vie ne vaut pas la peine d'être vécue. Dans le fond, je n'ignorais pas que mourir à trente ans ou à soixante-dix ans importe peu [...] Rien n'était plus clair en somme.[83]

But all of these reasonings are in vain, because, at the very thought of the possibility of living a little longer, he experiences

> ce bond terrible que je sentais en moi à la pensée de vingt ans de vie à venir. [...] cet élan du sang et du corps qui me piquait les yeux d'une joie insensée.[84]

The heart has its reasons which reason does not know, as Pascal had said. Meursault is no longer able to suppress the inner voice crying out to live, and when it finally bursts from him in an explosion of joy and anger ('avec des bondissements de joie et de colère', p.1210) he finally attains the great truth that life itself is the privilege and that everyone is privileged: 'Tout le monde était privilégié. Il n'y avait que des privilégiés' (p.1211). He now knows for a certainty that to consider that life has no higher meaning is not equivalent to denying that it is worth living. The truth he has arrived at is 'the truth of being and feeling'.

Meursault can now accept the prospect of death because he has at last fully recognised the value of life. Facing death, and with his back against the prison wall, that wall of which 'every stone sweats sorrow'

---

83   p.1206. 'But everyone knows that life isn't worth living. And when it came down to it, I wasn't unaware of the fact that it doesn't matter very much whether you die at thirty or at seventy [...] Nothing was plainer', *OS*, p.109.
84   p.1206. 'I'd feel my heart give this terrifying leap at the thought of having another twenty years to live. [...] that burning rush of blood which would make my eyes smart and my whole body delirious with joy', *OS*, pp.109 and 110.

('toutes les pierres suent la douleur', p.1209), he is at last able, with the great onslaught of liberating words, to demolish the edifice, like Samson, and to establish a new relationship between happiness, innocence and death, beyond the futile circle of time (*Monday, Tuesday, Wednesday*, and so on, as in the *Myth*), as he freely embraces the concept of the cycle of etenity and his own reunion with the universe. The axis had swung the first time with the annihilation of a human life, it swings back again now with the rejection of an afterlife. Death it is which makes life a pearl of such price. Meursault is reconciled with his own life and death, reconciled too with his mother and with the natural world: the sea, the night; images of maternity, eternity, and death. At last he understands that silent mother, comprehends the peace which she had experienced at the end of life. He enters into the fraternity of nature and, in reaffirming the happiness of existence, he reaffirms once and for all its innocence.

Salvation achieved, his story stands nonetheless as much a warning as an example. *L'Étranger*, as Camus had affirmed (*Carnets II*, p.31), is the *point zéro*, the starting point. Death unresolved invalidates life, and if the problem of dying is not solved, there is no basis for a valid response to the challenges of human existence. Conversely, death can be accepted only if life has been a worthwhile experience, and for those who refuse a transcendental dimension, the worth of life can only consist in a measure of human happiness or at least satisfaction. We have to wait for the next novel, *La Peste*, to find a reflection upon the problems of those for whom life is not a banquet, the unfortunate, the unhappy, the incapacitated, and the working out of a scale of values in which happiness itself, even in its most generous form, can be voluntarily postponed or even sacrificed for the sake of human fraternity or solidarity, because 'Il peut y avoir de la honte à être heureux tout seul', and 'Cette histoire nous concerne tous'.[85]

Death reconciles Meursault with the sources of life, his dead mother, the earth around him, but it also consummates his estrangement from his fellow men. He has been like a child in an adult world,

---

85   TRN, *La Peste*, p.1389. 'It may be shameful to be happy by oneself [...] This business is everybody's business', *Plague*, p.199.

and several commentators have pointed out the child-like traits.[86] He is the boy who sees that the emperor has no clothes, but the refusal of any hierarchy of values has also inevitably resulted in a refusal of commitment, a failure to accept the responsibilities of maturity, most notably in the affair of Sintès and his Arab mistress (and one could extrapolate from that to other political and social disengagements). Germaine Brée makes an interesting analogy between Meursault and that other innocent, Parsifal:

> He acts in a human situation as though human relationships and therefore responsibilities do not exist. [...] Like Parsifal in the legend of the Fisher-King he fails to ask any question and thereby gravely errs.[87]

The analogy with Chrétien de Troyes's *Conte du Graal* can be pressed further: Parsifal too is an outsider, a *naïf*, and his original fault is his impatience to ride away from his mother, failing to turn back to her in her distress, leaving her to die of grief. This essential childlike egoism vitiates his ability to penetrate the mystery of suffering and redemption. His five years in the forest are a process of growing to adulthood.

Meursault is given no such timespan to put behind him the innocent self-centredness of childhood. At the end he is totally alone, and the 'cries of hate' which he hopes to hear at his execution are the only form of relationship with others left to him. How these cries may be transformed into expressions of fraternity, how the individual is to live with his ambiguous burden of innocence and guilt, how far he may seek to satisfy the 'generous desire for happiness', to achieve a happy life and a 'happy death', these are questions reserved for a dawn beyond that of the guillotine, for that early April morning in Oran when Dr Rieux will stumble over a dead rat on his landing, and the plague will come to visit a 'happy city'.

---

86 See Rey (1970), p.41: 'Sa mentalité nous paraît être la mentalité pré-morale d'un enfant de quatre ou cinq ans'; R. Champigny (1959, p.43) describes him as 'un enfant candide et réfléchi' and points to the use of childlike vocabulary such as 'gentil' and 'méchant'.
87 Brée (1959), pp.112 and 117.

Chapter III
Voices in a Time of Plague. *La Peste*

> *There's no such thing as a hero – only ordinary people asked extraordinary things in terrible circumstances – and delivering.*
> Timothy Mo, *The Redundancy of Courage*
>
> *Moi aussi, j'aimerais à croire, mais la fièvre vient de faire périr trois pauvres petits enfants chez mon voisin, ce qui me force à croire que tout n'est pas juste et beau dans ce monde.*
> Stendhal, *Promenades dans Rome*
>
> *Je ne sais si cela est simple, mais je sais que cela est vrai.*
> Tarrou in *La Peste*

The 'cycle of the Absurd' was completed in 1942, with the publicaton of *L'Étranger* in July and then *Le Mythe de Sisyphe* in December. *Caligula* would have to wait until 1945 for its first performance, but it had been written in 1938, the year in which Camus had finished *La Mort heureuse* and started to collect material and gather his thoughts for *Le Mythe* and *L'Étranger*. At the same time, ideas which would be developed in the *La Peste* had begun to appear scattered in the *Carnets*.[1]

The notion of the great pestilences as the symbol of the Absurd, the tyranny of death and universal suffering, had already taken hold of Camus's imagination. Caligula, the eponymous hero of the drama, declares plainly that he himself is the incarnation of the plague: 'Enfin, c'est moi qui remplace la peste', thus elucidating the allegorism of his

---

1   See, for example, *Carnets I* (late 1938) pp.134–8, which is the first draft of what will be Joseph Grand's story of his lost love, his wife Jeanne.

cruelties. The encounter with death (the loss of his sister and mistress Drusilla) is the moment of ultimate truth for the young and idealistic emperor, who in his mad despair closes the granaries, inflicts a famine upon the population and kills, tortures and humiliates those around him. Like the plague, he is an image of that implacable and capricious force of death and suffering to which mortal man is subject and which renders happiness precarious and life meaningless. He becomes the supreme Outsider, separated from his fellow man not only by his position of power, but by the path he has chosen, until, in the last moments of the drama, his own image in a mirror fills him with self-hatred, and he perishes surrounded by the hatred of the conspirators.

There had been curious linkages from Caligula to Meursault. The latter too looks at his own reflection and no longer recognises himself, imagines for himself a death surrounded by the cries of hatred of the spectators. The savage rage of Caligula and the stoic passivity of Meursault are the responses of outsiders for whom the notion of society, of belonging, of solidarity, does not exist, Caligula being above the social body and Meursault psychologically estranged from it. While Caligula is convinced (as Clamence will be later) that all, himself included, carry a mysterious burden of guilt, Meursault is convinced, like Sisyphus, of his own and everyone else's *innocence irréparable*. Caligula the murderous Outsider, Meursault the innocent Outsider, what in the end is guilt and what is innocence? 'Je n'ai pas pris la voie qu'il fallait', Caligula laments as the conspirators approach. 'Je n'aboutis à rien.'[2] For Meursault, there is progress insofar as he has achieved reconciliation with his own life in the solitary experience of imprisonment, but in itself his passivity has led only to his own extinction. There has to be a path leading beyond estrangement and ultimate defeat.

Camus told Gabriel d'Aubarède in 1951:

> Si on pose que rien n'a de sens, alors il faut conclure à l'absurdité du monde. Mais rien n'a-t-il de sens? Je n'ai jamais pensé qu'on puisse rester sur cette

---

2   *TRN, Caligula*, Act IV, sc.xiv. 'I have chosen the wrong path. I have achieved nothing.'

position. Déjà quand j'écrivais *le Mythe*, je songeais à l'essai sur la révolte que j'écrirais plus tard.³

There is an overlap of the maturing of ideas and different compositions in the chronology of the 'cycle of the Absurd' and *La Peste*, but the latter represents a move away from individualism, passivity and reflection to social cohesion and action, and from recognition of the Absurd to positive resistance to the forces of misery and death, be they physical, metaphysical, or political. We have now embarked upon the 'cycle of Revolt'. As early as 1938, Camus had written:

> Constater l'absurdité de la vie ne peut être une fin, mais seulement un commencement [...] Ce n'est pas cette découverte qui intéresse, mais les conséquences et les règles d'action qu'on en tire.⁴

La Peste is the collective quest for those rules of action, for the 'styles of life' adequate to our situation.

Camus had begun to work seriously on the novel in 1941, when he first had the idea for the title, reading numerous medical and historical works on the great plagues of history. It was published in 1947. In the autumn of 1942, he had thought of changing the title, and calling the work *Les Prisonniers* (*The Prisoners*).⁵ In the end he adopted as his epigraph a quotation from Daniel Defoe, which presents the same image:

---

3   *Essais*, p.1343, extract from an interview in *Les Nouvelles Littéraires*, 10 May 1951. The essay was to be *L'Homme révolté*, published in October 1951. 'If you postulate that nothing has any meaning, you have to conclude that the world is absurd. But does nothing have any meaning? I never believed that you could regard that position as final. Already when I was writing *The Myth*, I was pondering the essay on revolt that I would write later.'

4   From Camus's review of Sartre's *La Nausée* (*Alger Républicain*, 20 October 1938). Reprinted in *Essais* (pp.1417–19), see p.1419. 'The recognition of the absurdity of life cannot be an end, but only a start [...] It is not the discovery in itself which is interesting, but the consequences and rules of action which are deduced from it.'

5   *Carnets II*, p.41: 'Roman. Ne pas mettre *La Peste* dans le titre. Mais quelque chose comme *Les Prisonniers*.'

> Il est aussi raisonnable de représenter une espèce d'emprisonnement par une autre que de représenter n'importe quelle chose qui existe réellement par quelque chose qui n'existe pas.[6]

In place of the solitary prisoner in the condemned cell, we move on to a community of prisoners, and the citizens of Oran, coralled into their town and stricken by an inexplicable and irrational evil, become representative, not only, on the most obvious level, of the people living in Occupied France, but of the whole human race itself. On 23 October 1942, an entry in the *Carnets* reads: '*La Peste* a un sens social *et* un sens métaphysique. [...] Cette ambiguïté est aussi celle de *L'Étranger*.' At the end of that year another entry reads:

> Je veux exprimer au moyen de *La Peste* l'étouffement où nous avons tous souffert et l'atmosphère de menace et d'exil où nous avons vécu. Je veux du même coup étendre cette interprétation à la notion d'existence en général.[7]

After an introductory essay on Oran and its inhabitants, representative of us all, the narrative of the plague begins with Dr Rieux's discovery of the dead rat on the landing outside his surgery, and this short chapter ends with the death of the concierge. The sinister harbinger of death and disease is the introduction to a 'chronicle' which is concerned throughout with the tragic aspect of man's fate, and concludes with a melancholy reflection on the nature and fragility of human happiness.

In *L'Étranger* society is seen exclusively through Meursault's eyes and all voices in the novel come to us through his alone, the irony and the last word are always his, and the reader must decide how to read the resulting text and what faith to put in the narrator. The ambiguity is not only inter-dimensional (social and metaphysical), but

---

6   Preface to Volume III of *Robinson Crusoe*: ''Tis as reasonable to represent one kind of Imprisonment by another, as it is to represent any Thing which really exists by that which exists not.'

7   *Carnets II*, p.50 (Camus's italics), and p.72. '*The Plague* has a social *and* a metaphysical sense [...] This ambiguity is also that of *The Outsider*.' 'I want to express by means of the plague the suffocation from which we all suffered and the atmosphere of threat and exile in which we lived. At the same time, I want to extend this interpretation to the notion of existence in general', *SE*, p.231.

also intra-dimensional (the viewpoint and intentionality of the narrator). In *La Peste*, on the other hand, a number of voices are heard: the third-person narration of an observer who reveals himself only at the end of the novel to be Dr Bernard Rieux, the first-person autobiographical narrative of Tarrou, seeking how to be 'un saint sans Dieu' ('a saint without God'), the story told by Joseph Grand, the first sermon of Father Paneloux. This enrichment of narrative voices offers a more complex perception of the human predicament, and the 'styles of life' possible in response to it, than that presented by Meursault alone. It represents above all a broader reflection on the enigmas of good and evil, happiness and responsibility.

The device of a third-person narrative aims to transform what would otherwise be a subjective first-person account of events (a diary) into the (at least superficially) objective form of the chronicle. When Dr Rieux at last reveals his authorship, he affirms that his desire has been to 'prendre le ton du témoin objectif'.[8] Is this compatible with Camus's remark that, in a sense, Rieux was 'all the characters'?[9] Made in the image of the author-creator, he becomes the observer-creator of all the other characters, watching them, interpreting them. He withholds judgement, but not sympathy, even in the case of the criminal Cottard, much more victim than villain.

In *L'Étranger*, Camus had taken the laconic style of certain modern American novelists as his model for 'objective' writing. The style of *La Peste* is more reminiscent of another novel, Stendhal's deeply ironic *Le Rouge et le Noir* (*The Red and the Black*) whose sub-title was, as Camus noted, *Une Chronique de 1830* (*A Chronicle of 1830*). He also declared his admiration for the detachment of tone in the same author's *Chroniques italiennes* (*Italian Chronicles*), despite their melodramatic subject matter.[10] The ironist Stendhal is however by no means simply a neutral observer, and neither, if we look closely at his

---

8   p.1468. 'He expressly made a point of adopting the tone of an impartial observer', *Plague*, p.290.

9   'Dans un sens, il est tous les personnages.' See the *Carnet de travail, carnet rouge*, ms. quoted in Quilliot's ' Présentation' of the novel, *TRN*, p.1942.

10   *Carnets II* (1942), p.14: 'C'est dans la disproportion du ton et de l'histoire que Stendhal met son secret (à rapprocher de certains Américains).'

'chronicle', is the sympathetic and concerned Dr Bernard Rieux. Nor should we wish either of them to be so.

Roland Barthes (1972) saluted in *L'Étranger* a pioneering attempt at a 'neutral' mode of writing, a search for an ideal *absence* of style which would achieve perfect 'transparency', the direct perception of reality on the part of the reader unimpeded by the perspective of the writer. Barthes, however, concluded that such an ideal is unfortunately unattainable ('Malheureusement rien n'est plus infidèle qu'une écriture blanche', p.57). In *L'Étranger*, Camus had sought this directness through the use of the first-person narrative and the perfect tense. In *La Peste*, he seeks 'neutrality', or objectivity, through a third-person narrative, which in the end is revealed to be the work of a first-person narrator, thus avoiding Sartre's famous objection to Mauriac's fiction, that anonymous third-person narrators are, like God, omniscient, and that 'God is not an artist, neither is Monsieur Mauriac' (both propositions are debatable). Barthes makes essentially the same point, saying that the third-person narrator provides 'the security of a story-telling which is credible and yet constantly shown to be false' (p.27, tr.).

Camus's disguised narrator is not always completely successful in his striving to avoid partiality and God-like omniscience. Whether first or third-person narrative, the attempt to eliminate the writer from his writing is bound to fall short of the chimerical ideal. Dr Rieux himself, when he comes forward as the narrator, recognises that as such he must have a point of view, and declares himself on the side of the victims (p.1468). For all his precautions, he is also in fact omniscient, knowing, for example, in fine detail, the emotional state of a character such as Rambert, who is waiting, at the end of the chronicle, to be re-united with the woman he so passionately loves, yet aware that they may have become strangers, that he himself is no longer the same person:

> [Rambert] avait changé, la peste avait mis en lui une distraction que, de toutes ses forces il essayait de nier, et qui, cependant, continuait en lui comme une sourde angoisse [...] Pour le moment, il voulait faire comme tous ceux qui

avaient l'air de croire, autour de lui, que la peste peut venir et repartir sans que le coeur des hommes en soit changé.[11]

While the story of *La Peste* is that of a community, what must strike the reader is the fact that the voices we hear are those of solitaries, and indeed of men without women, whether by choice (Tarrou) or by force of circumstance (Rieux, Grand, and, for the time of the narrative, the journalist Rambert). Women's voices are not heard. But neither are the voices of siblings or kindred, with the exception of Rieux's mother. The major protagonists are united by the bonds of friendship, bonds freely chosen, not imposed by kinship or desire. Their freedom to act is untrammelled. The universe Camus creates is that masculine arena which he had described with admiration in *Le Mythe de Sisyphe*, the moral landscape of Don Juan and of 'l'homme absurde', where 'la bonté cède la place à la générosité, la tendresse au silence viril, la communion au courage solitaire'.[12] Camus's novel, seen as an allegory of the Occupation, will portray 'l'image de ceux qui dans cette guerre ont eu la part de la réflexion, du silence – et celle de la souffrance morale'.[13] Generosity, courage, and silence: the virtues of the aristocratic masculine code of French classical literature, a stoicism glorified in the great heroic dramas of Corneille in the seventeenth century.

What is new since *Le Mythe*, is that individual *solitary courage* now discovers communion and fraternity. As for relationships between the sexes, we may recall that, already in the seventeenth century, Corneille had been of the opinion that tragedy requires 'some

---

11   p.1462 and p.1463. 'He [Rambert] had changed too greatly. The plague had forced on him a detachment, which, try as he might, he couldn't think away, and which like a formless fear haunted his mind', *Plague*, pp.283; 'For the moment, he wished to behave like all those others round him, who believed, or made-believe, that plague can come and go without changing anything in men's hearts', ibid. p.284.
12   *Le Mythe de Sisyphe*, *Essais*, p.153. 'where kindness yields to generosity, affection to virile silence, and communion to solitary courage', *Myth*, p.69.
13   *Carnets II*, p.72. 'The image of those whose lot it was, in that war, to ponder, and to suffer in silence and inwardly.'

more noble and more masculine passion than love'.[14] Camus's heroes, even when they have a deep attachment, within or outside marriage, are refused the consolations of the relationship. Separation from the loved person, or final separation through the death of the latter, is their lot, intensifying their suffering. Rieux's silent heartache, Rambert's eventual renunciation of the opportunity to escape and rejoin his woman, are worthy of Corneille's heroes in their stoicism and their prioritising (in the given circumstances) of the virtues of fraternity, solidarity, or what the great dramatist had called *générosité*, over the state of happiness.

What do these values mean to different individuals with different lives and different abilities, living in different times and societies? What do they mean to the community? This is the fundamental human and social question explored in the novel. For Corneille *générosité* was the virtue of the strong, the ultimate *héros généreux* was the great soldier who sacrificed himself in defence of his country, the prince who pardoned and ruled, the martyr who died to proclaim his faith, the lover who put duty (as he perceived it) before love. Heroism is personified in Don Rodrigue in *Le Cid*, and indeed also in his beloved Doña Chimène, for Corneille was no mean admirer of female courage, but it had to conform to the masculine rules.[15] In Roman history it is represented by the martyr Polyeucte, or the Horatii and the Curiatii, or again Augustus, in *Cinna*, pardoning the conspirators and demonstrating to all that he is 'Master of [himself], as of the Universe'. The eponymous hero of *Horace* loses his status as *généreux* when he loses self-mastery and murders his sister and therein lies his tragedy. *Générosité* is inseparable from courage, from stoic self-control, from recognition of obligations to the community, from dedication to something greater than the self. It is not difficult to see how Camus is in the line of this tradition. What remains is to find how it is to be lived out by

---

14 The dignity of tragedy requires 'quelque grand intérêt d'État, ou quelque passion plus noble et plus mâle que l'amour.' *Discours de l'utilité et des parties du poème dramatique* (in H. Barnwell, ed., *Pierre Corneille. Writings on the Theatre*, Oxford, Blackwell, 1965, p.8).
15 See Longstaffe, pp.85ff.

ordinary citizens in a more egalitarian era and a time of oppression and *plague*, physical, moral, and political.

The novel opens with an essay on Oran, a description of a 'completely modern' town, defined as a very ordinary community and one whose values are commercial above all else. Its easy-going citizens have not the least nostalgia for anything deeper or more spiritual. It is a community in which *living* means earning as much money as possible during the week, and, *very sensibly* (I quote), reserving the pursuit of pleasure (women, the cinema and the beach) for the week-end (we note the exclusively masculine perspective). Living, loving, dying: in this 'completely modern' town, *loving* means either bouts of frantic sexual encounters or simply opting for the long *habit* of togetherness as a pair, while *dying* means exclusion from the company of the healthy, sequestration, a solitary end out of sight and mind of society. To sum up: 'Cette cité sans pittoresque, sans végétation et sans âme finit par sembler reposante, on s'y endort enfin'.[16] Not that the citizens are disagreeable; on the contrary, the population is 'franche, sympathique et active' ('frank-spoken, amiable and industrious') and has always inspired in the visitor 'une estime *raisonnable*' (my italics; 'a *reasonable* esteem').

One is very much reminded of the description of the little town of Verrières which opens Stendhal's *Le Rouge et le Noir*, a community where money is also the principal value and where the rules of behaviour are set, as we are told in Chapter I, by 'wise and level-headed people' ('des gens sages et modérés'). The word 'reasonable' is not a meliorative term in the vocabulary of the ironist Stendhal nor of the ironist Camus. Verrières is oblivious to its magnificent setting in the mountains of the Jura, and proud only of the mayor's hideous factory powered by the tempestuous torrent of the Doubs, while Oran turns its back on the splendid bay, and the sea can be glimpsed only by those who go in search of it.

The magnificence of nature is the domain of the spiritual, of the eternal, for Stendhal as for Camus, the revelation in which the exiled soul recognises the kingdom, an ecstatic communion to be compared

---

16   p.1221. 'Treeless, glamourless, soulless, the town of Oran ends by seeming restful and, after a while, you go complacently to sleep there', *Plague*, p.3.

only to sexual union. The poetic eroticisation of the landscape is most fully expressed in the early essay *Noces* (*Nuptials*), and in the short story entitled 'La Femme adultère' ('The Adulterous Woman'), the only fiction in which the principal protagonist is female. The heroine, Janine, leaves the marital bed to steal out of the shabby hotel, and open herself up to the immensity and beauty of the starry desert night. Woman and natural world merge. Geraldine Montgomery (2004, see p.155) remarks that the spiritual, the sacred, always resides, for Camus, in communion with the two eternally feminine elements, night and the sea, that same sea upon which the city of Oran turns its back.

The protagonists of *La Peste* are separated from their women, and so also they are separated from nature, hence from the spiritual, the enduring. The only moments of peace and communion for Rieux and Tarrou are the occasion on which they swim together in the bay. No-one else swims. The atmosphere is claustrophobically urban. Sisyphus' mountain is far away, and his boulder is replaced by a more sinister object: the dead rat over which Dr Rieux stumbles on the landing outside his surgery door on the morning of 16 April 194*. One could see in this very unpleasant phenomenon, in the midst of the most ordinary circumstances, a parallel to the experience of Kafka's hero, the unassuming commercial traveller Samsa, who, in *The Metamorphosis*, awakes one morning to find he has turned into a monstrous beetle, and yet cannot realise that his humdrum existence (the *getting up, going to work, getting home, going to bed* routine) cannot continue, that life is changed.

In sending the rats, harbingers of death and disease, does nature avenge itself on a population which has lost the connection with the sources of life and the sense of the eternal? Camus is no sentimental Romantic, for him, nature is always both magnificent and indifferent, sometimes not far removed from the unfeeling stepmother of Alfred de Vigny's pessimistic vision.[17] As the plague progresses by leaps and bounds towards its apogee, the early summer sky over Oran remains imperturbably blue and all seems serene: 'tout dans la saison invitait à la sérénité' (p.1268). Is there, in the fate which befalls the citizens of Oran, some terrible and disproportionately tragic punishment which

17 'On me dit une mère, et je suis une tombe', *La Maison du Berger.*

they have brought upon themselves? Questions of guilt and innocence are always lurking somewhere beneath the surface, even in Camus's most straightforward narratives.

The novel is simple to follow at the level of narrative: the description of the onset, progress and final disappearance of the plague in a modern urban environment, the inadequate and increasingly desperate measures taken by the authorities, initially reluctant to alarm public opinion, the bureaucratic mentality of Dr Richard, the president of the *Ordre des médecins d'Oran* (the regional General Medical Council), the role of the press and radio, the sufferings of the population, the state of emergency and quarantine which separates them from the outside world and from their absent loved ones, their collective and individual responses, the courageously altruistic efforts undertaken by a group of individuals to defeat the evil which has befallen the city, the enormous public rejoicing at the end of the state of emergency, the lifting of restrictions, the return to normality, and the reunion of those who had been separated from the ones they love. The cruel deaths of the stricken are described in stark, indeed repulsive, detail, from the death of the concierge to the agonies of those whose swollen ganglions burst open 'like a rotten fruit', pouring out a suppurating fluid (p.1244).

The tone is clinical, for this is the level of 'chronicle', of objective reporting, and to cope with his task the doctor is obliged to remain detached. But throughout the narrative, even at this 'realist' level, the anonymous voice allows itself compassionate or ironic intervention. Rambert's encounters with bureaucracy in his efforts to obtain authorisation to leave the city are recounted in a tone of black Kafkaesque comedy, while the description of the mass tipping of naked corpses into communal graves, the shallow covering of quicklime, the enforced absence of the relatives, is followed by the comment that

> le lendemain, les parents étaient invités à signer sur un registre, ce qui marquait la différence qu'il peut y avoir entre les hommes et, par exemple, les chiens: le contrôle était toujours possible.[18]

18   p.1362. 'On the following day the next-of-kin were asked to sign in the Register of Burials – which showed the distinction that can be made between men and, for example, dogs; men's deaths are checked and entered up', *Plague*, p.169.

Quilliot points to the 'macabre irony' of this whole central section of the novel. Throughout the narrative, the plague itself is constantly personified as an ultra-efficient female bureaucrat, carrying out her daily murders with precision and regularity: 'Mais il semblait [...] qu'elle apportât à ses meurtres quotidiens la précision et la régularité d'un bon fonctionnaire' (p.1412.). A fine example of personification and allegory as irony.

So we come to the second perspective: the plague as allegory of the Occupation of France and the evils of war. This dimension is not part of the original inspiration of the novel, which, as we have seen, was conceived before the outbreak of hostilities and the invasion of France. However, once the catastrophe had occurred, the aptness of the image was immediately obvious. A first idea for the title appears in Camus's notes in 1941, *Peste ou aventure*, and a first version of the novel was written in 1942.[19] The writing in its final form did not begin until 1944.

Camus was not alone in seeing the calamity in terms of the age-old disaster of a plague, for, as John Cruickshank pointed out in 1959, the Occupation was commonly referred to in France as *la peste brune* 'the brown plague'. The reader has no problem in interpreting the elements of the narrative: the initial disbelief that such an event could take place, the closing of the city, the rationing and restrictions, the oppressive atmosphere of fear among the population and at the same time their strong sense of community in the face of such undreamt-of misfortune. Clear too is the significance of the formation of resistance groups (the *formations sanitaires*, or 'health teams' in the context of the novel), the sinister walls around the isolation camps with their armed guards and their loudspeakers blaring forth, the nightmare scenario of the corpse-laden trams swaying along their rails beside the sea in the evening, on their way to the crematorium whose acrid smoke poisons the neighbourhood.

The allegorism is rich and powerful, all the more so for the level of 'realism' from which it springs. At the same time, all critics writing

---

For Rambert's encounters, see *TRN*, pp.1306–8. For Quilliot's remark, see *TRN*, p.1993 (note to p.1359).

19   *Carnets I*, p.229. See also Quilliot's 'Présentation', *TRN*, pp.1935 ff.

on this aspect of the novel have pointed out the serious inadequacy of depicting the human evil of war as a phenomenon outside the sphere of human responsibilty, a natural disaster for which man is in no way to blame. Where have the rats come from? That is the great unanswered question of the novel, and many commentators, from Sartre onwards, have pointed out the weakness of attributing all evil to a non-human source. As Cruickshank famously said, the symbol 'covers human wretchedness but ignores human wickedness' (p.177). Camus himself said, in a lecture given in a Dominican friary in 1948, that he felt like Augustine before his conversion, searching for where evil comes from, and never getting to the bottom of it.[20]

Sisyphus' boulder is a neutral object in itself, but the rats are the archetypal image of what is noxious and evil. They cannot be accepted, but must be fought. Life has to change from acceptance to resistance, from the passive to the active mode. However, the members of this resistance face no moral dilemmas about ends and means, none needs to asks himself whether the killing of one German soldier is worth the death of ten civilians which will follow as retribution, pacifists such as Tarrou do not have to agonise about the killing of the enemy (there is no human enemy). All the characters of the novel are either innocent victims or involved in the work of the resistance to some degree, with the exception of the unhappy criminal Cottard and the shadowy blackmarketeers or such *passeurs* as exploit the situation for their own gain. Camus has described man's struggle against the hostility of nature, says Sartre, but he has completely ignored man's struggle against his fellow man, an omission all the more glaring in that the rats clearly stand for the Nazis, in the context of the allegory of the Occupation.[21]

---

20 *Essais*, p.374: 'Je me sens un peu comme cet Augustin d'avant le christianisme qui disait: Je cherchais d'où vient le mal et je n'en sortais pas.'
21 'Réponse à Albert Camus', *Situations IV*, p.118: 'Vous avez pu, dans *La Peste*, faire tenir son rôle (celui de l'Allemand) par des microbes [...] Ainsi un concours de circonstances [...] vous [a] permis de vous masquer que la lutte de l'homme contre la nature est à la fois la cause et l'effet d'une autre lutte [...] la lutte de l'homme contre l'homme.' (First published in 1952, in *Les Temps Modernes*, No.82).

The case of the criminal Cottard is immensely significant, in that he is a pathetic individual, not a vicious one. We cannot pass judgement, as we are not told why he is a wanted man, what his crime or crimes may have been, except for the assurance that it was not murder (see p.1348), a crime which would be too likely to alienate the sympathy of the reader. His attempted suicide can be seen as a cry for help, it inspires pity. The theme of suicide, the Sisyphean question of whether or not life is worth living, reappears here again (as it had done in *La Mort heureuse*, with Zagreus' temptation to self-destruction), but since self-destruction is chosen by the criminal character as a result of his previous disastrously wrong choices in life, it is *ipso facto* disqualified as a valid answer to the problems of existence. We read of no other cases of suicide in the novel, despite the horrendous sufferings of the population.

The only answer to the Absurd is active revolt, which here means endurance, solidarity and the fight against the common enemy. This is the answer accepted and practised by all the leading protagonists, except only for Cottard. His complacency in the reign of terror, his happiness in the midst of his fellow-citizens' misery, seems, however, curiously innocent, a naughty child's joy at being released from the fear of punishment and accepted once more into the social group. 'Il préfère être assiégé avec tous que prisonnier tout seul', Tarrou writes in his notebooks, and when he tries to put the criminal on the right path, telling him that 'la seule façon de ne pas être séparé des autres, c'était après tout d'avoir une bonne conscience', Cottard replies that on those conditions 'personne n'est jamais avec personne.'[22] 'Use every man after his desert, and who shall 'scape whipping?', as the Prince of Denmark said.

Cottard welcomes the plague because, ironically enough, it has brought people together. His past is cancelled and he is allowed into the community. When the emergency is officially declared over and the city re-opened, fear of arrest drives him mad. He is captured by the

---

22   p.1378. 'He'd rather be one of a beleaguered crowd than a prisoner alone [...] When I suggested to him [...] that the surest way of not being cut off from others was having a clean conscience, he frowned. "If that's so, everyone's always cut off from everyone else".', *Plague*, pp.185–6.

police after a siege during which he has shot at them with a revolver and they have returned fire with machine-guns (no proportionality!). Dragging their prisoner out of the house and into the street, they proceed to beat him viciously, thus once and for all foregoing the sympathy of the reader (are policemen not to be counted among the innocent?). Social conflict and state violence take over from the previous tyranny from outside, be it metaphysical or political. Camus can be criticised for largely ignoring the ongoing reality of criminality and social division in the time of 'plague'. James Williams, for example (see p.21), notes that he does not portray the scapegoating of minority groups, especially the Jews. An allegory, however, is not social history, and in the context of the mystery of existential evil over which man has no control, the theme would be a digression. There are brief references to disorders in the city, armed attempts at escape, looting of houses, and in the end military law has to be imposed, but the cause is not human perversity or wickedness, rather the unbearable pressures resulting from the 'state of siege' in which the city finds itself (p.1358). The theme of social conflict is relegated to the background, while the metaphysical problem is foregrounded.

Cottard's fate is nonetheless emblematic of that of the collaborators after the Liberation. Rieux's final judgement on him is that '[il] avait un coeur ignorant, c'est-à-dire solitaire'. In other words, he was incapable of empathy, hence his 'only real crime', says Tarrou, was to have approved 'dans son coeur ce qui faisait mourir des enfants et des hommes'.[23] The judgement of Tarrou and Rieux here reaches heights of charity (Camus would say *générosité*) which the author himself found difficult at the time of the *épuration*, during the wave of trials and punishments (including execution) of collaborators after the Liberation. Camus, initially demanding justice (not excluding the death penalty) against notorious collaborators such as the writer Robert Brasillach, found himself ranged against François Mauriac who, like him, had worked for the Resistance, but now called for reconciliation

---

23   p.1469. 'His only real crime is that of having in his heart approved of something that killed off men, women and children [...] [He] had an ignorant, that is to say lonely, heart', *Plague*, p.291.

and mercy. Camus would later generously admit that he had come to accept that Mauriac had been right, and he himself wrong.[24]

In *La Peste*, the metaphysical and moral dimensions constitute the continuity with the themes of *L'Étranger*. It is no longer the individual, but now the whole community which is imprisoned, deprived of a future, separated from the rest of humanity, exiled from happiness, forced to contemplate evil, suffering and mortality. What values subsist? A quintet of voices expresses attitudes and answers to these questions: the narrator Rieux, on occasions when he is directly challenged (as by Father Paneloux or the journalist Rambert), or when he allows himself a personal reflection upon events and individuals, Tarrou, who recounts the story of his own life, and also commits his observations to a 'notebook', the journalist Rambert who is obliged to ponder the question of happiness and responsibility, the Jesuit Father Paneloux, who represents, in counterpoint to the non-believers, the religious *Weltanschauung*, and Joseph Grand, who represents the simple goodness of the unremarkable and humble (a hero much like Kafka's Josef K.), and who is also somewhat paradoxically charged with representing the problems of the artist and of the relationship of language, truth, and reality. We meet all five of them in the first short chapter of the narrative.

All debate on values must start from the notion of the value of life itself. Camus had given his answer to the 'fundamental question in philosophy' in *Le Mythe*. Next question: is it ever right or justifiable to take a life? It logically follows on from the basic position (the refusal of suicide) that 'The only truly serious moral problem is murder', as Camus had written in his *Carnets* in April 1946, under the mention 'Révolte'.[25] In his Introduction to *L'Homme révolté* (1951), he wrote again: 'This essay will be a continuation, in the perspective of murder and revolt, of a reflection dealing initially with suicide and the notion

---

24 In 'L'Incroyant et les chrétiens', *Essais* (p.369–75), the address given in the Dominican friary of Latour-Maubourg in 1948. On the question of the *épuration* and in particular Brasillach, see Olivier Todd, pp.509–18.

25 *Carnets II*, p.172. 'Révolte. Commencement: "Le seul problème moral vraiment sérieux c'est le meurtre. Le reste vient après. Mais de savoir si je puis tuer cet autre devant moi, ou consentir à ce qu'il soit tué [...] voilà ce qu'il faut apprendre".'

of the Absurd' (he is referring of course to *Le Mythe*).[26] 'Murder' for Camus covers both the death penalty and all forms of political 'liquidation' of enemies, from firing squads and the concentration camps to the assassination of tyrants or presidents. *L'Étranger* is, on one level, a passionate plea against capital punishment. *La Peste*, in its turn, in the narrative of Tarrou, is similarly impassioned and carries the debate forward, from the violence of the established order to the difficult moral issues raised by the use of revolutionary violence in pursuit of a new order, a new social justice.

The question of ends and means in politics, of violent revolution based on ideology, is enshrined in Tarrou's story. We are given his first-person account of his political journey, which starts when he is a seventeen-year-old adolescent onlooker in a courtroom, shocked to see his normally good-natured father transformed into a towering red-robed public prosecutor mercilessly demanding the death-sentence for the accused. The latter, a terrified little reddish-haired fellow of about thirty, nervously chewing the fingernails of his right hand, looks like a little owl terrified by the light, 'un hibou effarouché par une lumière trop vive' (p.1421). The frightened little owl, in this Kafkaesque courtroom, is about to be devoured by the 'serpents' issuing from the mouth of the nightmarish prosecutor in his scarlet robe. As in the case of Cottard, we are not told exactly what the crime has been (apart from the fact that it carries the death-penalty), so there is no danger of our sympathy being alienated from the accused. With this terrified and apparently innocuous human being, the case is powerfully made against state-sanctioned violence in the form of capital punishment.

Revolted by the episode, the young Tarrou leaves home, joins the revolutionaries fighting on various fronts throughout Europe, only to find in the end that the revolution also requires human sacrifice. He initially accepts the argument that 'ces quelques morts étaient nécessaires pour amener un monde où l'on ne tuerait plus personne', until in Hungary, he actually witnesses an execution by a revolutionary firing squad:

---

26   *Essais*, p.414. 'Cet essai se propose de poursuivre, devant le meurtre et la révolte, une réflexion commencée autour du suicide et de la notion d'absurde.'

> J'ai compris alors que moi, du moins, je n'avais pas cessé d'être un pestiféré [...] J'ai appris que j'avais indirectement souscrit à la mort de milliers d'hommes, que j'avais même provoqué cette mort en trouvant bons les actions et les principes qui l'avaient fatalement entraînée.[27]

Ideologies bring death, the heart alone is to be trusted, and it is when he *sees* the horror of the firing-squad that Tarrou rejects every form of violence and longs for inner peace, striving to become 'a saint without God'. Camus once quoted Maritain: 'La sainteté aussi est une révolte.'[28] Tarrou is the modern knight-errant, a Quixote who, disabused with the pursuit of justice through force of arms, turns to the age-old alternative route to spiritual grandeur. The question of the two vocations, of the saint and the soldier, the hardships of the spiritual life and the hardships of chivalry, is one that arises throughout Cervantes's great novel.[29] The question for Tarrou is only to know what sanctity can mean for the modern unbeliever.

Violent revolution raises the age-old moral question of ends and means. The question of the right to take life in pursuit of what the revolutionary perceives as the ultimate value, Justice, preoccupied Camus from the writing of *La Peste* onwards.[30] In a lecture given in Colombia University in 1946, he had declared that if one believes in nothing, if nothing makes any sense and we cannot find a value in anything, everything is permissible and nothing is important, so consequently there is neither good nor evil and Hitler was neither right

---

27 p.1423 and p.1424. 'I was told that these few deaths were inevitable for the building up of a new world in which murder would cease to be', *Plague*, p.240. 'And thus I came to understand that I, anyhow, had had plague through all those long years [...] I learned that I had had an indirect hand in the deaths of thousands of people; that I'd even brought about their deaths by approving of acts and principles which could only end that way', ibid. p.240–1.
28 *Carnets II*, p.298. 'Sanctity also is a revolt.'
29 In one instance, Sancho Panza urges the Don to 'turn saints as fast as we can, and that is the readiest and cheapest way to get to this same honour you talk of', to which Don Quixote replies: 'Chivalry is a religious order, and there are knights in the fraternity of saints in heaven.' *Don Quixote*, Part II, chapter VIII (Wordsworth Classics, 1993, p.54).
30 See Quilliot's footnotes to *Les Justes*, *TRN*, pp.1822ff., and to *L'Homme révolté*, *Essais*, pp.1609ff.

nor wrong.[31] But, of course, he had already said in *Le Mythe* that Ivan Karamazov's despairing cry that *everything is permissible* 'does not mean that nothing is forbidden' ('Tout est permis ne signifie pas que rien n'est défendu', p.149).

In the same lecture, attacking what he saw as the Hegelian (and Marxist) philosophy of History, the materialist ideology of Progress, he affirmed that it must lead logically to the conclusion that, if the price of 'Progress' is war, carnage and massacres, the only question is not whether all that is good or evil, but whether it is effective. If the ultimate value is not justice, but efficiency in the name of progress, then there is only one rule, to be as efficient as possible, which means the survival and domination of the fittest, and the world is no longer divided between just and unjust, but between masters and slaves. This is the denunciation made also in *L'Homme révolté*, in which he talks of Hegel as having been taken over by Marx 'and all the Hegelian Left', and providing (along with Nietzsche) 'an alibi for the masters of Dachau and Karaganda'.[32] He thereby drew down upon himself the fury of Sartre and the Left in France, who spewed him rancorously out of their midst. For a pacificist like Tarrou, however, the dilemma of how to get rid of the masters of Dachau and Karaganda remains.

Camus deals with political assassination (terrorism) in *L'Homme révolté*, in the section entitled 'Les Meurtriers délicats' ('The Fastidious Assassins'), dedicated to the Russian revolutionaries of 1905, whom he greatly admired for their self-sacrificing idealism. The text had already appeared with the same title in the review *La Table Ronde* in January 1948, and required only the addition of some supplementary historical material when included in *L'Homme révolté*. His drama, *Les Justes* (1950), was inspired by the same historical episode. The hero Kaliayev's thirst for justice springs from a deep compassion for

---

31 'La Crise de l'homme', published in *NRF*, January 1996, no.516, pp.8–29 (French translation of a speech made in English at Colombia University, 3 March 1946, under the title 'The Human Crisis', translated by Jean-Marie Laclaventine). *L'Homme révolté* would not be completed and published until 1951, but Camus was grappling with the theme from 1945 onwards, with the 'Remarque sur la révolte' (*Essais*, pp.1682–97).

32 See *Essais*, pp.544–5. Karaganda is the largest city in Kazakstan. Its development in the 1930's was achieved by the extensive use of forced labour.

the sufferings of the people. At the crucial moment he finds, however, that he is not capable of throwing the bomb into the carriage of the Grand Duke, who is accompanied by two children, two innocents, his young nephew and niece. 'Je croyais que c'était facile de tuer, que l'idée suffisait, et le courage.'[33] Kaliayev weeps, close to despair. He has learned that revolution, however just, is not *simple*. Even the Grand Duke is a human being. At a second attempt, Kaliayev carries out the assassination, and subsequently refuses to save himself from the gallows, preferring to pay with his own life for the life he has taken. Perhaps the saddest words in the play are those of the hero's mistress, Dora: 'D'autres viendront peut-être qui s'autoriseront de nous pour tuer et qui ne paieront pas de leur vie.'[34] No *perhaps* about it, we may add.

Of course, neither Kalayev's answer (the self-sacrificial revolutionary) nor Tarrou's can solve the moral dilemma. No revolution could succeed if every revolutionary paid for each life taken with his own life, nor if all followed the example of Tarrou and abandoned the struggle. Patrick McCarthy has said of the heroes of *La Peste*, Tarrou and Rieux, that, despite their professed atheism, 'their values are religious rather than practical' (1982, p.229), and this was to be even more obvious in the case of Kaliayev, who is explicitly presented as having a religious mentality and faith. What Tarrou wants to be is a Kaliayev deprived of faith.

Tarrou, like Meursault, is a man in search of values. He has found them neither in religion nor in revolutionary ideology. He belongs to no faction, and in this his philosophy could be regarded as negative. He is close to Camus himself, who, after a brief youthful adherence to the Communist party in Algiers, had adamantly refused all ideologies which justified present oppression in the name of future utopias. 'Une philosophie négative n'est pas incompatible, dans les

---

33   *TRN*, p.350, *Les Justes*, Act III. 'I had thought that it was easy to kill, that idealism and courage would suffice.'
34   ibid. p.384, Act V. 'Others will come, perhaps, who will claim us as their justification for killing, and who will not pay with their own lives.'

faits, avec une morale de la liberté et du courage', Camus affirmed.[35] Tarrou's attitude appears negative, in that he believes the most to which the individual can aspire is to *avoid doing harm*. No doubt this is what he means when he wonders whether the old bed-ridden asthmatic who passes his entire life in transferring peas from one pot to another is actually a 'saint' (p.1315). He is at any rate a character fit for Sam Beckett, a 'Sisyphus of the chickpeas', as one critic remarks (Chabot, p.153). However, to accuse Tarrou (and through him Camus) of passivity, refusal to intervene for fear of the wrong intervention, a sort of culpable abstentionism, is a misreading, as some critics, Gaeton Picon for example, have remarked. 'Through Tarrou, Camus's own ideas of commitment, dedication to the plight of others, and courageous stand against violence and injustice are made clear', writes Bernard Murchland (p.156). It is Tarrou who comes to propose to Rieux the creation of the 'voluntary health teams' (*formations sanitaires volontares*, p.1321), who recruits Grand and Paneloux, who is instrumental in Rambert's decision to stay in the stricken city and participate in the work of the health teams (p.1352), who tries to befriend Cottard and even offers him the chance to redeem himself by volunteering to work with the teams (see pp.1346–9). Tarrou's morality is, as he himself defines it, *la compréhension* (p.1325). To understand all is indeed for him to forgive all, and, as Rachel Bespaloff remarks (p.100), his 'comprehension', his path to achieving a 'holiness without God', is what the Christian tradition calls charity and ranks above all others. One could add that his total renunciation of the sword is equally evangelical. Having renounced the armed struggle, he chooses the classic pacificist option of allying himself to the doctor.

The philosophy is negative, but Tarrou has moved on from the passivity of Meursault, of whom he is an avatar. The resemblances and parallels are numerous. Like Meursault, he is a stranger, having arrived in Oran from no-one knows where only a few weeks before the onset of the plague. Meursault is condemned to death, and in another (or the same?) courtroom, Tarrou sees the accused (Meursault?) as his *alter ego*, regarding him with a 'dizzying' sense of closeness

---

35 *Combat*, September 1945; *Essais*, p.311. 'A negative philosophy is not incompatible, in fact, with an ethic of liberty and courage.'

(p.1422). Leaving the comfort of his bourgeois home at seventeen, Tarrou too has known the life of poverty, has had to forgo his studies, has seen the face of innocence and resignation in the worn features of his aged mother, who has no need of forgiveness, for

> il n'y avait rien à lui pardonner, parce qu'elle avait été pauvre toute sa vie jusqu'à son mariage et [...] la pauvreté lui avait appris la résignation.[36]

More fortunate in this than Meursault, he does not find himself obliged by circumstances to consign her to a home, but continues to care for her until she dies (p.1423).

In character as well as in circumstances, Tarrou complements Meursault. He too enjoys the pleasures of sea and sun, 'l'ami de tous les plaisirs normaux sans en être l'esclave'.[37] He even has Meursault's turns of speech: *ça m'est égal* ('I don't mind'), *dans un sens* ('in one sense'), and so on. He too finds interesting the oddities which others pass by: the old man who spits at cats from his balcony or the elderly bed-ridden asthmatic who endlessly transfers chickpeas from one pot to another, counting the hours in this way, having got rid of all his clocks. It is a strategy as good as any other for 'killing time', and perhaps that is why Tarrou finds it interesting, for, like Meursault in prison, he too ponders the baffling nature of the passage of time. He suggests strategies for reaching total awareness of it, which consist fundamentally in experiencing the weariness of complete boredom, spending whole days in a dentist's waiting-room, or all Sunday afternoon on one's balcony. We remember Meursault's Sunday afternoon on the balcony. The difference is that, while for the prisoner the object was to *kill time*, Tarrou is essentially raising the question of conferring a *value* on its meaninglessness, asking himself how to make the most of his time: 'Question: comment faire pour ne pas perdre son temps?' he writes in his notebooks (p.1237). He finds his solution and salvation in the struggle against the plague. Temporality, transience, is of the essence of the Absurd, but paradoxically time is the dimension

---

36 p.1422. 'There'd been nothing to forgive; she'd been quite poor until her marriage and poverty had taught her resignation', *Plague*, p.238.
37 p.1235; Tarrou is fond 'of all normal pleasures, without being their slave', *Plague*, pp.21–2.

through which values must be established and meaning thereby conferred upon existence.

In the Tarrou/Cottard relationship, we see that Meursault's negative refusal to judge has evolved in Tarrou into something altogether more positive, more mature, a *comprehension* of the Other which translates a negative philosophy into positive action. 'Qu'est-ce qui vous pousse à vous occuper de cela?' Rieux asks him, and he answers, 'Je ne sais pas. Ma morale, peut-être.' Rieux persists: 'Et laquelle?' Answer: 'La compréhension.'[38] Meursault becomes the friend of the unsavoury Raymond Sintès because as yet one relationship is much the same as another to him, value-free. It is only in court that his indifference is breached, and he realises that the good-hearted Céleste is *worth more than* Raymond. Tarrou, on the other hand, befriends the criminal Cottard because he sees in him an unfortunate. In this he is ahead of his time. 'Il y a des siècles on condamnait les hystériques, il viendra un temps où l'on soignera les criminels', Camus wrote in his *Carnets* in March 1942.[39]

Salvation is for Camus, as for Tarrou, neither in Marxism nor in Christianity, his affinity is with the gentle scepticism of Montaigne. In his speech at Columbia Unversity in 1946,[40] Camus recalled that certain members of the Resistance, whom he knew personally, used to read Montaigne in the train while carrying clandestine material. For him they were the living demonstration, he said, of the combination of scepticism and the sense of honour. Tarrou is the embodiment of the honourable sceptic, and with the *sense of honour* we return to the heroic ideal of an elite, not social or intellectual, but pertaining to an innate nobility of spirit. Patrick McCarthy writes (1982, p.228):

> Camus's moral thinking has never been more austere and heroic. Rieux, Tarrou and the others are an aristocracy who sacrifice their personal happiness in order to fight the plague.

---

38   p.1325. '– What on earth prompted you to take a hand in this? – I don't know. My code of morals, perhaps. – Your code of morals. What code, if I may ask? – Comprehension.', *Plague*, p.126.
39   *Carnets II*, p.17. 'In past centuries they used to pass sentence on hysterics, there will come a time when we treat criminals.'
40   'La Crise de l'homme', see above, note 31.

The aristocracy of spirit is at its noblest in fact in the humble Joseph Grand, whom Rieux proposes as the true hero of his chronicle:

> Ce héros insignifiant et effacé qui n'avait pour lui qu'un peu de bonté au coeur et un idéal apparemment ridicule.[41]

He is the Sisyphean hero, the exemplar of 'modern heroism' as Camus had defined it in *Le Mythe de Sisyphe*, on a level with Oedipus triumphing over his terrible misfortunes and judging that 'All is well' (*Essais*, p.197). Grand had not appeared in the first draft of the novel, his space being filled there by an academic named Stepan, whose wife Jeanne leaves him, and who commits suicide. Grand, his replacement, has no pretentions to any kind of social or intellectual distinction. His name is both affectionately ironic and indicative of the fact that his grandeur belongs to another sphere entirely, to that spiritual order which Pascal had placed immeasurably above the worldly or the intellectual values.

This spiritual greatness, crystallized in his apparently ridiculous ideal, his Quixotic striving after perfect truth in his notion of the writer's vocation, together with his 'goodness of heart', entitles Grand to be regarded as the true 'hero' of the novel. He is the embodiment of all the values that his creator admires: a life of poverty close to the spirit of the Beatitudes, innocence and unworldliness, concern for his neighbour (Cottard, as it happens, and his own collaboration with the 'health teams'), and the devotion to an artistic vocation (the novel he labours to write). More than one critic has pointed out that all the major characters in the novel write in some form: Rieux's 'chronicle', the 'notebooks' of Tarrou, who is revolted by the death penalty and in search of values, Rambert's journalism, Paneloux's sermons. Grand who is struggling with his writing, Rambert the crusading journalist and defender of the human right to happiness, all are projections of aspects of the author's own experience and personality.

---

41 p.1331. 'This insignificant and obscure hero who had to his credit only a little goodness of heart and a seemingly absurd ideal', *Plague*, p.133. I would prefer the literal translation and to call the ideal 'ridiculous', since 'absurd' has philosophical overtones when Camus uses it.

The forms of writing, the difficulties of expression, are a major theme of the novel. Grand lives in a permanent state of writer's block, never managing to find the words that satisfy him, whether struggling to write the opening chapter of a novel, a love-letter to his lost wife Jeanne, or simply a letter to his superior protesting at his lack of promotion. He represents on the one hand the artist and his frustrations, and on the other hand all those whose kingdom is not of this world, the innocent, the poor and humble, the excluded, the 'strangers', those who have no voice in society. Like Tarrou, he has something of Meursault in him, an older, non-hedonistic Meursault. Both are solitaries, both have problems with relationships, caused by an obsession with language and its unacceptable approximations. Meursault cannot use the word 'love' to Marie because he feels it is inexact, Grand cannot find the words which would express his love for Jeanne. Poverty has forced both to abandon their studies early and to accept a dull routine occupation, a life to which the young Camus also might have found himself condemned, and from which he always recoiled with horror.

In Grand's sparcely furnished room, lit with one bare electric light bulb, Rieux's awareness of the suffering and claustrophobia in the city outside is heightened. But Grand has another vision to offer in the midst of the plague, that of an elegant young woman riding through the sunlit Bois de Boulogne. However banal the image, however cliché-ridden the expression of this opening sentence of the novel (as its author recognises, with despair), it is still an affirmation of the light against the dark, the promise of happiness inherent in the evocation of a world of harmony and beauty. It is hope re-affirmed against despair. Unlike Stepan in the earlier draft of the novel, Grand will not commit suicide. His vision is life-affirming. The plague strikes him down, but he survives the attack.

Art is invincible. So is Grand. His personal duel with death, from which he emerges victorious despite his already precarious health, marks him out as the strongest among that band of comrades-in-arms, Rieux, Tarrou, Rambert, Dr Castel, and ultimately Paneloux and Judge Othon. After his victory, others too begin to make unexpected recoveries and the plague recedes. An underlying resemblance to the Christ-figure emerges, with this apparently miraculous 'resurrection', as Rieux/Camus expressly calls it, without being able to explain it

('Rieux ne comprenait rien à cette résurrection', p.1435). It is not only Grand's personal triumph, but the very sign of salvation. In him saint and hero are fused.

Life, Camus had indicated in his *Carnets* as early as 1936, is essentially a *jeu gratuit* (echoes of Gide's notion of the *acte gratuit*, the totally free, unconstrained act for its own sake). Those who play the game of life 'for its own sake', be they 'saint' or 'socialist', arrive either at *absurdité* or *lucidité*, or both, and must possess 'the *heroic* values' (my italics).[42] *Force et bonté*, strength and goodness, are the qualities Camus ascribes to both 'saint' and 'socialist', and Tarrou, seeking for a non-violent revolution and a non-religious holiness, possesses both. Nonetheless he does not survive the onslaught of the plague, for he is mined from within by his awareness that he carries inside himself the death-dealing 'microbe', since in his past he has mistakenly consented to it. His intellectuality is incompatible with the innocent simplicity required for the peace he seeks. That peace will be there at his deathbed, in the maternal and humble figure of Madame Rieux.

Tarrou's death nonetheless is a 'definitive defeat' (p.1458). He knows himself irremediably banished from the happiness of the state of innocence, and desires only to find peace of mind, 'or, if not, a *good death*' (my italics).[43] Not for him the euphorically *happy* death of the younger Mersault of the first novel, happiness being too positive an outcome for the professedly negative aspiration of avoiding infecting others with 'the microbe'. Rieux, on the other hand, implicitly rejects his friend's philosophy of abnegation and steadfastly affirms

---

42 See *Carnets I*, p.23: a diagram, or rather a map, shows pathways from *Saint*, or *socialisme*, combined with action, both leading via *Force et bonté*, and *Jeu gratuit*, to either *absurdité or lucidité*, but a note insists on the vital importance of having *Au fond: les valeurs héroïques*. Once again, we can go back for inspiration to the seventeenth century and the *Carte de Tendre* in Madame de Scudéry's ten-volume novel *Clélie*. It traces the amorous paths from *Nouvelle Amitié* to the destinations of *Tendre–sur–Estime*, *Tendre–sur–Reconnaissance* or *Tendre–sur–Inclination*.

43 See p.1425: 'Il faut faire ce qu'il faut pour ne plus être un pestiféré et […] c'est là ce qui peut, seul, nous faire espérer la paix, ou *une bonne mort* à son défaut' (my italics).

the nobility of the human dream of happiness, 'l'exigence généreuse du bonheur' (p.1331). In spite of the sympathy which Tarrou inspires in the reader, Camus shows us, by Tarrou's death and the survival of Rieux, that it is the latter who is in the right.

Tarrou rejects religious consolation, Rieux silences Paneloux. Camus once described *La Peste* as his most anti-Christian work,[44] but his stance is considerably more complex than the adjective would imply, or than the aversion which many critics infer from it at face value. He had little time for strident atheism, and in the next novel, *La Chute*, Clamence lampoons 'our café atheists', pious souls sent into convulsions, 'like the devil in holy water', at the merest inadvertent whisper of the word 'God' ('Dieu merci!' 'Mon Dieu!', *TRN*, p.1523). When Tarrou asks Rieux whether he believes in God, the latter replies, 'Non, mais qu'est-ce que cela veut dire? Je suis dans la nuit et j'essaie d'y voir clair.'[45] Pascal would no doubt put Dr Rieux among those who seek with a heavy heart (*qui cherchent en gémissant*). Camus himself never ceased to dialogue with Christianity, from his dissertation on Augustine to his admiration for Pascal or Simone Weil. The Christianity which he respects while rejecting it, is of the most arduous variety.

The religious debate is so fundamental to *La Peste*, and indeed to Camus's thought as a whole, that we must consider in some detail his personal attitudes and responses. His stance, like Rieux's, is a polite refusal of belief rather than a crusading atheism. He declared that:

> J'ignore s'il existe un Absolu ou non. Mais je suis convaincu que le problème n'est pas d'ordre politique. L'Absolu n'est pas l'affaire de tous, mais de chacun. Il est donc nécessaire d'organiser la vie commune de façon que chacun puisse jouir d'un espace intérieur lui permettant de s'interroger sur l'Absolu. [...] Telle est ma définition de la liberté.[46]

---

44 For a discussion of this point, see Quilliot's notes, *TRN*, pp.1986ff. (note to p.1294). Quilliot refers the reader to *L'Incroyant et le Chrétien* and *Réflexions sur le christianisme* in *La Vie intellectuelle*, 1 December 1946.

45 p.1322. 'No, but what does that mean? I'm fumbling in the dark, struggling to make something out', *Plague*, p.122.

46 'La Crise de l'homme', p.23. (op. cit.. See note 31). This is the translated French version of the lecture. The original having apparently disappeared, the following is my re-translation: 'I do not know whether there is an Absolute or

139

In fact, he endorses the French notion of the *état laïque*: belief is a private matter, an integral part of human rights, and politics are a strictly separate domain. Believers and non-believers alike had made the sacrifice in the Resistance, and Father Paneloux will in the end die along with Tarrou or Judge Othon, in the ranks of the 'health teams'.

When Camus was in Stockholm to receive the Nobel prize, he was asked by a journalist if he was about to undergo a religious conversion, to which he answered a straight 'No'. Yet he felt it necessary to add a rider in an interview with the *Figaro Littéraire*:

> J'ai conscience du sacré, du mystère qu'il y a en l'homme et je ne vois pas pourquoi je n'avouerais pas l'émotion que je ressens devant le Christ et son enseignement.[47]

He had already affirmed, in the *Interview de Stockholm*, that he had only 'respect et vénération devant la personne du Christ et devant son histoire: je ne crois pas à sa résurrection'.[48] But his real spiritual home, he felt, was with the Greeks, not classical Greece, not Plato, but the pre-Socratics, Heraclitus, Empedocles, or Parmenides (Nietzsche's influence is evident).

As regards Christianity, with great intellectual honesty Camus repeatedly gave his reasons both for respect and for non-belief. Speaking, for example, of his concept of 'revolt' against the 'absurdity' of the world, he affirmed that he had found no philosophical or other system which gives any clear justification for it, 'exception faite pour le christianisme, que tant de chrétiens nous avait découragés d'aimer'. This is a reproach which believers such as Mauriac would not have

---

    not. But I am convinced that the problem is not political. The Absolute is not a matter for the public at large, but for each individual. Society must therefore be organised in such a way that individuals can enjoy the inner freedom enabling them to ponder the Absolute. [...] This is my definition of freedom.'

47   Quoted Quilliot, *Essais*, p.1615. Interview in *Figaro littéraire*, 21 December 1957: 'I am conscious of the sacred, of the mystery within man, and I do not see why I should not confess the emotion which I feel in the presence of Christ and his teaching.'

48   Quoted Quilliot, *Essais*, p.1615 (*Interview de Stockholm*): 'I have only respect and veneration for the person of Christ and for his life: I do not believe in his resurrection.'

been slow to accept, without thereby dismissing Christianity on the grounds that it can foster a hypocritical morality or that right-wing politics can parade under its banner. Camus too has an afterthought and loyally inserts a footnote admitting that perhaps the accusation has been made a little unfairly:

> Un peu injustement d'ailleurs. Si l'on devait juger de la démocratie par les démocrates et de la liberté par ses défenseurs... Mais enfin il y avait les évêques de Franco.[49]

On a deeper level, he regarded the Christian virtue of hope in an eternal life as resignation to the ills of this one, and in his youth, in the early essays such as 'L'Ironie', or 'L'Envers et l'Endroit', he writes off Christianity itself as a faith for the old, a killjoy religion, only for those who are beyond enjoying the rapture of the world and whose hope is a measure of their despair. One critic writes:

> The hope which Camus attributes to Christians is not Christian hope, nor is the face of the God which he portrays that of the Christian God. Perhaps he was over-influenced, in fact, by the anguished and tormented Christianity which he had found in Kierkegaard or Dostoyevsky (Hermet, p.142, tr.).

The great debate about religion in *La Peste* is that between Father Paneloux and Dr Rieux. At least one critic has pointed out that this confrontation, as also the positioning of the two sermons, carefully placed at turning points during the plague (its outbreak and its peak with the death of the child), gives a central role to the religious debate (see Ellison, p.109). In his erudite homily at the onset of the calamity, Paneloux declares that the plague is the punishment for the moral laxity of the population. Camus told Quilliot that he had in mind the denunciations of French society made by certain Vichyist churchmen in 1940.[50] In such strictures, Camus saw Christianity itself as 'a doctrine of injustice' ('Ce que je reproche au Christianisme, c'est qu'il

---

49 *Essais*, p.1703, 'Défense de *L'Homme révolté*': '[–] excepting Christianity, which so many Christians had prevented us from loving.' The footnote reads: 'A bit unfair, perhaps. If one were to judge democracy by the democrats and liberty by its defenders... All the same, there were Franco's bishops.'
50 Quilliot, *TRN*, p.1986, note to p.1294.

est une doctrine de l'injustice', *Carnets II*, p.112). By that he means a faith founded upon acceptance of the suffering of the innocent, expiating the sins of others, a vicariat exemplified in the death of Christ. 'Si le Christ est mort pour certains, il n'est pas mort pour nous', he declared truculently in his dispute with Mauriac in 1945.[51] Ingrid di Meglio (p.35) points out interestingly that Camus's 'ethic of solidarity' also demands, in certain circumstances, a vicariat, D'Arrast, for example, who carries the stone for the ship's cook in the short story 'La Pierre qui pousse' ('The Growing Stone'), or Kaliayev, the hero of the drama *Les Justes*, who dies so that others may live and enjoy life more fully.

The near jubilation of Father Paneloux is hardly representative of the Christian response to misfortune, and the conflict which Camus goes on to orchestrate between priest and doctor is factitious. The miracles of the New Testament are practically all miracles of healing, the healing of the lepers, for example, also symbolising forgiveness of past sins. Interestingly, the gift of myrrh, listed in the gospel of St. Matthew along with gold and frankincense as the symbolic offerings of the Magi, had in antiquity medical usages, as well as being used for embalming, and it seems that an earlier Christian tradition than that which inteprets it as a symbol of Christ's death, saw in it the symbol of Christ the Healer.[52]

Paneloux, in his first sermon, is the antithesis of the healer, as represented in the congregation by Rieux. Even physically the balance is heavily tipped in the latter's favour. Rieux, in Tarrou's description (p.1240), is of average height, broad-shouldered, square-jawed, with regular features and dark eyes that look straight at you, a man of few words ('lips always pressed together'), a certain rugged peasant quality combined wih a touch of academic absent-mindedness, yet giving a confidence-inspiring impression of a well-informed mind. In such a man we can put our trust. Our first physical impression of Father Paneloux, on the other hand, amounts to no more than the detail of an enigmatic smile from behind a pair of round spectacles, as the priest assures Rieux that the appearance of the rats undoubtedly heralds an

---

51   *Essais*, p.287. 'If Christ died for some, he didn't die for us.'
52   See William Dalrymple, *In Xanadu* (1990) HarperCollins, p.136.

epidemic (p.1231). What makes these owlish eyes gleam? Whatever the motivation, the smile is disconcerting and far from the normal human reaction. The gleaming spectacles, the trade-mark of the intellectual, separate him from the rest of humanity, as much as his priestly garb.

Can the Jesuit's satisfaction be the detachment of the intellectual observing an interesting phenomenon? Is it anticipation of a triumphalist point-scoring which will be expressed in the opening of the famous sermon, its theme rammed home as one would land a punch ('comme on assène un coup'): 'Mes frères, vous êtes dans le malheur, mes frères, vous l'avez mérité.'[53] The stage is set for the jeremiad: in the candlelit darkness of the great cavernous cathedral, the only highlights are the huge magnified hands gripping the edge of the pulpit, like the clawed feet of some monstrous bird, and the ruddy cheeks gleaming under the round rims of the steel spectacles, all atop a squat black form. The image suggests to us, at the conscious or subconscious level, the likeness of some massive black owl. The symbolism of the owl is ambivalent in European mythology and folklore: it is both Athena's bird of wisdom (hence appropriate in that respect to the intellectual) and a screeching nocturnal bird of ill-omen, the harbinger of death. With his short arms gesticulating, and a powerful and vehement voice, Paneloux becomes a latter-day thick-set Savonarola, more skilled in the arts of oratory than any demagogue, employing in turn suspense, illustration, menace, mildness and exhortation.

The opening words of the sermon are 'vehement and hammered home', the preacher *attacks* the congregation ('Il attaqua l'assistance d'une seule phrase véhémente et martelée', p.1296). What follows is a long and terrifying disquisition on the plague as chastisement, apocalyptic in the imagery, coming to a conclusion which proposes the present misery as the instrument of salvation. Such is the force of the orator's words, that one by one, early in the sermon, the members of the congregation fall to their knees. But there is no human comfort of any kind for them, no word of solace. As the preacher reaches the climax of his discourse, the rain batters outside upon the stained glass

---

53 p.1296. 'Calamity has come upon you, my brethren, and, my brethren, you deserved it', *Plague*, p.90.

windows, the very pulpit shakes with the intense emotional trembling of his whole body, his hair hangs clammily over his forehead, the flames of the church candles bend and flicker in the cold draught which sweeps the nave. The theatrical elements, highlighted by the narrator, make of the account not a sober report of the event, but the hallucinatory depiction of a scene of mediaeval terror and superstition, from which the reader, like the congregation, is relieved to escape back into the everyday modern world, validated in its relative sanity by the end of the downpour and the reappearance of a watery sun warming the square in front of the church, together with the reassuring sounds of voices and vehicles in the streets, as the city wakes up, 'tout le langage d'une ville qui s'éveille' (p.1299). The reappearance of the sun marks the return to the *pensée solaire*, the triumph of the intelligence, the enlightenment which the Greeks had bequeathed to the Mediterranean world, and to which Camus had proclaimed his passionate allegiance at the conclusion of *L'Homme révolté*. The city is awakening indeed from a theologian's nightmare, even as it slides further into the living nightmare of the plague.

The question of narrative voice, of what Roland Barthes, in *Le Degré zéro de l'écriture*, calls the 'innocence' of the writing, comes to the fore in the treatment of Paneloux. Among the principal formal signs of a literary (non-neutral) language, Barthes lists the importance of rhythm and cadences, the use of indirect reported speech, and obviously the recourse to metaphor and other resources of rhetoric. In all these respects, Camus's writing is anything but 'innocent', and operates on two levels. The rhetorical flourishes of Paneloux's first sermon, which opens with what Rieux takes the trouble to point out as 'a clever oratorical device' ('un procédé oratoire habile', p.1296), its sonorous cadences, dramatic climaxes, and biblical metaphors are the signs at surface level of the persuasive intent of the speaker, but, beneath that, they are the vehicle of the subversive intentionality of the writer. They verge on the blatant, thus putting the wary reader on his or her guard, and in failing to bring the non-committed listener, Dr Rieux, out of his attitude of silent non-adherence to their lesson, the stratagems of persuasion and hence the message they carry are implicitly invalidated.

The disjointed style of the second sermon, the absence in it of sustained rhythmic discourse and of all but the most traditional religious metaphor, marks Paneloux's own loss of conviction in the force of his previous preaching and its presentation, in the same way as the collapse of his spiritual pride is marked by his use of the first-person plural pronoun '*nous*', which replaces the previous '*vous*' (p.1401). The indirectly reported conclusion of the first sermon, a mere résumé, suggests the final exhaustion of the reporter-listener's interest and his unaltered alienation. The second sermon is almost entirely summarised, much as the lawyers' speeches in *L'Étranger* are filtered through the summaries of Meursault. In Meursault's case indirect reported speech is used to ironic effect, while Rieux's reporting of the second sermon reflects not only the difficulty Paneloux is experiencing in his search for a coherent answer to the theological problem, but an increasing detachment on the part of the listener, whose attention wanders at certain points, as does that of the congregation in general, who start to fidget, distracted by a clanging door, or by the wind whistling draughtily down the nave. Barthes's dismissal of the possiblity of 'innocent' writing can be illustrated in any analysis of the two sermons.

From all the lengthy and at times rambling second homily, only two rhetorical challenges and the grandiloquent conclusion are given in direct speech. On each occasion, these amount to a demand for a blind leap of faith in the face of the injustice of the suffering of the innocent. The sermon is conceived in response to the anguished conversation with Rieux immediately after the atrocious death of Judge Othon's child. 'Mais peut-être devons-nous aimer ce que nous ne pouvons pas comprendre', Paneloux had said, and Rieux had replied:

> Non, mon père [...] Je me fais une autre idée de l'amour. Et je refuserai jusqu'à la mort d'aimer cette création où des enfants sont torturés.[54]

Paneloux's sermon opens by conceding his adversary's every possible point: the suffering of the innocent, of a child, is the radical problem for those who believe; such injustice cannot be counterbalanced by the

---

54   p.1397. '–But perhaps we should love what we cannot understand [...] –No, Father. I've a very different idea of love. And until my dying day I shall refuse to love a scheme of things in which children are put to torture.' *Plague*, p.208.

notion of compensation in the hereafter; no Christian can pretend that suffering does not matter, since the central mystery of Christianity is the Cross and suffering of Christ. Here Rieux reflects that the priest is 'verging on heresy', but it is difficult to see what is heretical up to this point. Is it that Rieux is somewhat astonished to hear these points repeated from the pulpit? Is it simply that Camus has a skewed notion of the breadth of theological discussion?

Unorthodoxy lies not in these questions, but in what follows: Paneloux's fatalism, his acceptance of evil (the plague) as the mysterious Divine will, his identification of the fight against such suffering as revolt against the Divinity:

> Certes, la souffrance d'un enfant était humiliante pour l'esprit et le coeur [...] Mais c'est pourquoi [...] il fallait la vouloir parce que Dieu la voulait [...] le chrétien [...] choisirait de tout croire pour ne pas être réduit à tout nier.[55]

Paneloux is asking his faithful to commit what Camus had called, in *Le Mythe*, 'le suicide philosophique', to shut down the use of reason. Perhaps, like Camus, he has been reading too much Kierkegaard. who gives his God the attributes of 'the unjust, illogical and incomprehensible Absurd', as we are told also in *Le Mythe* ('Il donne [...] à son Dieu les attributs de l'absurde injuste, inconséquent et incompréhensible', *Essais*, p.127).

Paneloux's theology could be described as 'a perverse radicalization of Paul's teaching that salvation lies not in works but in faith', as Hannah Arendt (1978, vol. II, p.106) says of Augustine's late treatise *On Grace and Free Will*, written against the followers of Pelagius, who had exalted the autonomy of the will at the expense of the role of divine Grace. Other writings of Augustine however defend the freedom of the will against the opposite heresy of the Manichaeans. The whole Jansenist controversy of the seventeenth century turned on the

---

55   p.1403. '–True, the agony of a child was humiliating to the heart and to the mind [...] And that, too, was why [...] since it was God's will, we, too, should will it [...] And [the Christian's] choice would be to believe everything so as not to be forced into denying everything.' *Plague*, p.215.

question.[56] Is the Jesuit Paneloux's sermon a paradoxically Jansenist reading of Augustine? It smacks of the pessimist doctrines of damnation, predestination and the powerlessness of human reason and effort. Paneloux is in fact much closer to Jansen than to Loyola and the Jesuit theologians who championed the ethic of energy during the Counter-Reformation.

Camus's argument with Christianity is conveyed in Rieux's suggestion that the first part of the sermon, which reflects the doctor's own preoccupations, is 'verging on heresy', while the later part, with its stark Kierkegaardian rejection of reason, is presented as the only possible Christian answer. Tarrou has the last word: Paneloux *is right*, when innocence has its eyes put out, a Christian must either lose his faith or be willing to have no eyes to see with: 'Paneloux *a raison* [...] Quand l'innocence a les yeux crevés, un chrétien doit perdre la foi ou accepter d'avoir les yeux crevés' (p.1406; my italics).

The defeat of religious belief is evident in Paneloux's tormented state of mind and in his death. The book he is writing at the time of the sermon postulates a logical incompatibility between the priest's vocation and that of the doctor. Its thesis is that if a priest consults a doctor, there is a contradiction ('Si un prêtre consulte un médecin, il y a contradiction', p.1406). The contradiction kills Paneloux. He succumbs to what may or may not be the plague, his dead face is totally expressionless (p.1410), the death certificate classifies him as a 'doubtful case'. His position is logically untenable, for if human intervention is contrary to the Divine will, why does he join the health teams?

In the first draft of Paneloux's death scene the loss of faith had been more insistently suggested. In that text, Paneloux implicitly abandons his position by calling in Rieux in his professional capacity; he does not cling to his crucifix in the last hours, and the expression

---

56   Jansen was rector of the university of Louvain from 1635, and bishop of Ypres from 1636 until his death in 1638. His work on St. Augustine, known as the *Augustinus*, was published in 1640, and condemned as heretical by Pope Innocent X in 1643. It was inspired by Augustine's writings against Pelagius, who had taught that free will was absolute and that salvation was obtained by the individual's own efforts without the need for Divine grace. Jansen held that Divine grace was given only to a small number, the 'elect', the mass of sinful humanity being doomed to perdition.

on his dead face is 'the opposite of serene'.[57] The toning-down in the published version of this defeat of religious faith is no doubt evidence of a desire on Camus's part to give more balance to the argument between priest and doctor, faith and scepticism, and to avoid any hint of triumphalism. But the debate is already irremediably skewed by the partiality of the religious voice attributed to Paneloux. In his personal refusal of any intervention against misfortune, Paneloux has turned the argument into a debate on fatality and free will. As one critic has said, 'Paneloux treads dangerously the narrow line between faith and fideism' (Gadourek, p.127, tr.). 'Fideism' can be defined as a doctrine which is opposed to rationality, maintaining that knowledge comes from faith alone, not reason.

The debate presented in *La Peste* by the opposition of priest and doctor pre-dates the Christian era. Discussing the question of human freedom and the will, Cicero had also taken the medical example, in his treatise *On Fate* (*De Fato*), which Hannah Arendt calls 'still the classical argumentation of the case'. She summarises the fatalistic argument as follows :

> When you get sick, '*it is foreordained that you will recover or not recover, whether you call a doctor or do not call a doctor*', and of course whether you call a doctor or not would also be fore-ordained. Hence the argument leads to '*infinite regress*'. Under the name of 'idle argument' it is rejected because it would obviously '*lead to the entire abolition of action from life*' (vol. II, p.36; author's italics).

In theology the problem becomes that of predestination. In Augustine's *Confessions* and in the *City of God* the question of free will is resolved through the concept of a temporality outside of which, in His eternity, stands the Divinity. Man can then resolve his own fate in the temporal dimension, within which each individual is a new beginning, directed towards a future, and endowed with a spontaneity whose 'mental organ is the Will'.[58] Each man is thus, as Camus will paradoxically and optimistically entitle his last work, *Le Premier homme*.

---

57   See Quilliot's notes, *TRN*, pp.1997–8.
58   Arendt, 1978, II, see chap. 10, 'Augustine, the first philosopher of the Will', pp.84–110. The quotations are from pp.106–7 and p.110.

The definitive verdict on Paneloux's first sermon is delivered by Tarrou, who sees in it an endorsement of collective punishment. Tarrou's attitude is fundamentally one of tolerant scepticism, and for him the week of prayer corresponds to the Chinese custom of playing on tambourines to scare off evil spirits, in other words, it is a superstitious waste of time. Like Meursault, he is unwilling to 'waste his time with God'. He has defined his morality as *la compréhension* (p.1325). It is this comprehension of others which is deficient in the intellectual Paneloux. According to Rieux, Paneloux has not seen enough human suffering and any country priest who has assisted at the deathbed of a parishioner would have the compassion which the theologian apparently lacks.[59] This analysis is confirmed by the anguish of the priest once he has witnessed the agonising death of Judge Othon's little son. Rieux's final assessment on Christians is that they are better than their doctrines, which are abstractions, out of touch with human reality (see p.1321).

Dr Rieux's own humanity is reinforced not only by the profoundly human contact which his profession entails, but by his humble origin. He mentions to Tarrou that he is the son of a workman ('fils d'ouvrier', p.1323). We have already met his mother, and know her modest background. Tarrou's mother too, before her marriage, is of humble origin, his kinship is with the poor, but his upbringing has been middle class, which no doubt separates him from the simplicity of those less fortunate. He is in fact the more mature model of the young intellectual idealist attracted to revolution, like the protagonists of Camus's drama *Les Justes*.

Neither priest nor judge, nor indeed prosecutor (Tarrou's father) is inherently wicked or cruel, but their function transforms them, in the mind of the narrator (and therefore the reader) into figures inspiring aversion or dread. The transformation is achieved by a powerful

---

59 p.1321: 'J'ai trop vécu dans les hôpitaux pour aimer l'idée de la punition collective. Mais, vous savez, les chrétiens parlent quelquefois ainsi, sans le penser jamais réellement. Ils sont meilleurs qu'ils ne paraissent.' p.1322: 'Paneloux est un homme d'études. Il n'a pas vu assez mourir, et c'est pourquoi il parle au nom d'une vérité. Mais le moindre prêtre de campagne qui administre ses paroissiens et qui a entendu la respiration d'un mourant pense comme moi. Il soignerait la misère avant de vouloir en démontrer l'excellence.'

colour-symbolism: the blood-red robe of the prosecutor in the court, the heavy black shape of the priest in the pulpit. Judge and priest both dress in black, with its connotations of death, and indeed the cadaverous figure of the magistrate could at first be mistaken for an undertaker, a *croque-mort*, to use the darkly humorous term which Camus uses to describe him (p.1226). These are the images of authority in society and of patriarchy. Othon and the elder Tarrou judge and condemn in the name of the law, Paneloux in the name of the Father Almighty.

While Tarrou and Rieux are the twin voices of humane concern, Paneloux and Othon are the voices of a dogmatic and punitive morality in the name of a paternalistic Church or State (the Jesuit is *Father* Paneloux, the judge the unbending father of two children). The judge finds the rhetoric and arguments of Paneloux's first sermon 'absolument irréfutable[s]' (p.1301). Both have a caricatural aspect, more pronounced perhaps in the case of the judge than in that of the priest, and curiously, both are, in some sinister way, owlish. With his tufts of grey hair on either side of his bald pate, his round eyes and beak of a nose above a horizontal mouth, Judge Othon looks like 'a well-bred barn owl' ('une chouette bien élevée', p.1239), and he is no less implacable for that. A judgemental father-figure like the priest, he begins by believing, like Paneloux, that 'Les hommes sont mauvais et ils ont besoin de condamnation.'[60] His certainties, like Paneloux's, crumble after the death of his child. Released from the isolation camp in which he has been confined, he chooses not to return to his profession as judge, but to go back to the camp as a volunteer, because, he says, he would feel less separated from his little boy ('Je me sentirais moins séparé de mon petit garçon', p.1431). The implications of the remark are more profoundly religious than anything it has been granted to Paneloux to pronounce, and it reflects the fundamental moral perspective of the novel, which is that love, human tenderness in all its forms, is stronger than evil, overcoming even death and separation.

---

60   'Men are wicked and need to be condemned.' (The phrase was added to the text in the edition of 1947, although omitted in the final version. See Quilliot's Notes, *TRN*, p.1991, note to p.1338.

Camus's thought, as Ingrid di Meglio remarks, is both religious and anti-Christian (I would prefer to call it non-Christian), being fed by Nietzsche as well as by Pascal or Dostoyevsky. He separates Christ from a tyrannical God. Yet, while he could not accept the idea of a life beyond the present, nor the notion of sin and culpability, nor the pursuit of spiritual perfection at the price of a rejection of the pleasures afforded by the physical world, he felt, curiously enough, the need for periods of retreat and abstinence in the name of intellectual endeavour. There is not only a pagan hedonist but also a monkish contemplative in Camus. Male icons are either Don Juan or St. Francis. Nonetheless, 'La sexualité débridée conduit à une philosophie de la non-signification du monde. La chasteté lui rend au contraire un sens (au monde)', Camus wrote in his *Carnets* after the publication of *L'Étranger*, while planning *La Peste*. Or again:

> La vie sexuelle a été donnée à l'homme pour le détourner peut-être de sa vraie voie. C'est son opium. En elle tout s'endort. [...] La sexualité ne mène à rien. Elle n'est pas immorale mais elle est improductive. [...] Mais seule la chasteté est liée à un progrès personnel.[61]

The characters of *La Peste* are remarkably chaste. Camus's Don Juan himself is no cynical woman-hater; in his debate with the Franciscan he declares himself a believer in 'courage, intelligence and women', but at the same time, in the place of Christian charity and love, he recognises only 'la tendresse et la générosité', which he defines as 'the virile forms of these female virtues' (*Carnets I*, pp.214–15). These are what endure when passion is spent. At the end of *La Peste*, when loved ones are reunited, Rieux reflects that 'S'il est une chose qu'on puisse désirer toujours et obtenir quelquefois, c'est la

---

61   *Carnets II*, p.55: 'Unbridled sexuality leads to a philosophy of the meaninglessness of the world. Chastity restores sense to it (the world).' ibid. p.49: 'The sexual life was given to man perhaps to distract him from his true path. It is his opium. Everything goes into hibernation in it.' ibid., p.51: 'Sexualiy leads to nothing. It is not immoral, but it is unproductive. [...] But only chastity is linked to a personal progress.' (This last translation in *SE*, p.265).

tendresse humaine.'[62] As to Rambert and his mistress, all Rieux can predict is that *for a while*, at least, they would be happy (*'Pour quelque temps au moins*, ils seraient heureux', p.1467, my italics). Passionate attachments can carry no guarantee of permanence, which is why Don Juan accumulates them.

La tendresse humaine is love in the widest sense, compassion, empathy, the bond uniting true friends, *agape*. It is the deep attachment of spouses grown old together, that of Dr Castel and his wife, who comes back to the stricken town to be with him and share his danger and his efforts (p.1275), it is also Rieux's tenderness for his young wife. Geraldine Montgomery (2004, p.173) sees in their relationship the Orpheus and Eurydice theme, echoed in the death on stage of the singer in the role of Orpheus, immediately after the great duet of the lovers, during the performance of *Orpheus and Eurydice* which Cottard and Tarrou go to see (p.1382). Camus had written in his *Carnets*, at the end of 1942: 'Utilisation immodérée d'Eurydice dans la littérature des années 40. C'est que jamais tant d'amants n'ont été séparés'.[63]

Camus's novels celebrate not passion, but friendship. The friendship of women is sacralised at the two critical points in *La Mort heureuse*, firstly on the balcony of the 'House above the World', on the eve of Mersault's departure, and secondly on the final ascent of the mountain in the company of his women friends, immediately preceding his last illness and death. His descent into death is eased by the friendship of Dr Bernard and Lucienne, both at his bedside, just as Rieux and old Madame Rieux are at the bedside of the dying Tarrou. The tears shed by Rieux at that supreme moment are followed by night and silence, *une veillée silencieuse* (p.1458), the setting for an elegiac reflection on *la tendresse* in friendship and in maternal love, in both cases too deep for words. Rieux knows that his mother and he will 'always love each

---

62 p.1467. 'If there is one thing that one can always yearn for, and sometimes attain, it is human love', *Plague*, p.289. I would prefer to use the literal translation of the French here: 'human tenderness.'

63 *Carnets II*, p.56. 'Excessive use of Eurydice in the literature of the forties. Because there have never been so many separated lovers', *SE*, p.267.

other in silence', just as he had 'lived alongside Tarrou', but their friendship had not had time to be 'lived to the full'.[64]

No greater tribute can be paid to the dignity and depth of friendship than this parallel, because, for Camus, mother-love is the supreme form of human tenderness. The fraternal bond existing between Rieux and Tarrou is consecrated when Tarrou finds in Madame Rieux a second mother: 'Ma mère était ainsi, j'aimais en elle le même effacement et c'est elle que j'ai toujours voulu rejoindre'.[65] He recognises in her the incarnation of love, of goodness which prevails over evil, for 'un regard où se lisait tant de bonté serait toujours plus fort que la peste'.[66] The death of Tarrou is followed the next morning by the news of the death of Rieux's wife, which he also accepts in silence, recognising in his pain the same suffering which he had known over the last months, and specifically 'in the last two days'; it is simply the continuation of the same sorrow ('C'était la même douleur qui continuait', p.1460). Maternal love, friendship, marital affection, these are the enduring bonds of *tendresse*, and prioritised by Camus in that order.

While Camus appreciated the friendship of women, in the novels there is no independent role for them. They exist in relation to the male characters. Men, on the contrary, are complete in themselves. Rieux, Rambert, even Grand, find fulfilment despite being deprived of a female presence, perhaps even because of this deprivation, which enables them to give themselves absolutely (as the writer in his period of abstinence). Could Grand devote so much of his time to the pursuit of the perfect literary and linguistic expression of his ideal if Jeanne had not left him? What if there were 'a pram in the hall'? (Camus will tackle the question in his short story *Jonas ou l'artiste au travail*). The demanding love of a wife cannot rival the unconditional love of a mother. Worse still, it culpabilises. In the hasty words of tenderness

---

64   pp.1458–9: 'Ainsi, sa mère et lui s'aimeraient toujours dans le silence [...] De la même façon, il avait vécu à côté de Tarrou et celui-ci était mort, ce soir, sans que leur amitié ait eu le temps d'être vraiment vécue.'
65   p.1446. 'She reminds me of my mother. What I loved most in mother was her self-effacement [...] and it's her I've always wanted to get back to', *Plague*, p.265.
66   p.1314. 'A gaze revealing so much goodness of heart would always triumph over plague', *Plague*, p.112.

which are Rieux's farewell to his terminally ill spouse, he acknowledges a guilt, a failure of his own love to protect her sufficiently.[67] Wives and lovers need above all the reassurance of a language of love which Grand, for example, has been unable to formulate for his young spouse Jeanne, thereby losing her. Rieux's mother replaces his wife, having no need of words, enfolding her son in her total comprehension. It is with his silent mother that Meursault, awaiting his own death, had felt himself united as he contemplated the night 'laden with signs and stars' ('cette nuit chargée de signes et d'étoiles', p.1211). Life comes from the mother and death is a return to her.

In *La Peste*, however, the deliberate aridity of Meursault's reflections on his relationship with Marie, is replaced, in the voices of Rieux, Grand, and Rambert, by new notes of tenderness, regret, and longing: the stoic tenderness of Rieux towards his wife dying alone and far from him, the tender longing of Grand for Jeanne, the desperate love of Rambert for the woman in distant Paris. Separated from the 'human warmth' of their loved ones, the plague victims had all suffered 'un exil sans remède et [...] une soif jamais contentée'.[68] The absence of women in the novel represents a tragic void which only their return at the end of the chronicle can fill. It is these absent women who lend poignancy to the situation of those who, like Rambert, must make the difficult and age-old choice between heroism and happiness (however much they refuse the vocabulary of the heroic). The old Spanish mother of the two soldiers willing to help Rambert escape from the plague-stricken city in order to rejoin the woman he loves in Paris, asks the journalist why he wishes to go in spite of the risk of infecting her. He replies that the risk is minimal, and that if he does not go he risks being separated from her for ever. Does he believe in God, the old woman asks, and when he replies in the negative, she approves his course of action: 'Il faut la rejoindre, vous avez

---

67 p.1225: 'Puis il lui dit très vite qu'il lui demandait pardon, il aurait dû veiller sur elle et il l'avait beaucoup négligée.'
68 p.1466. 'Exile without redress, thirst that was never slaked', *Plague*, p.288.

raison. Sinon, qu'est-ce qui vous resterait?'[69] The human replaces the Divine as the source of happiness, to be seized at whatever price.

The quality of the individual is measured by the quality of his or her notion of happiness, and there is a base, selfish happiness as well as a generous, self-giving happiness. The debate in *L'Étranger* had been focussed on the relationship between happiness and innocence or guilt. In *La Peste*, it is extended to encompass the choice between happiness and heroism. It is articulated in discussions between Rieux, Tarrou, and Rambert, and its complexity is not lessened by the deliberately aphoristic nature of some of the argument. Rambert is the champion of the right to happiness, which he equates with the experience of requited passionate love. He already has his credentials of physical courage, having fought with the international brigades in the Spanish civil war. However, as with Tarrou, the killing has sickened him:

> Je ne crois pas à l'héroïsme, je sais que c'est facile et j'ai appris que c'était meurtrier. Ce qui m'intéresse, c'est qu'on vive et qu'on meure de ce qu'on aime.[70]

It is not the individual capable of 'great actions' that Rambert admires, but the one capable of 'great feeling'. Is the dichotomy valid? Must we not ask if 'great feeling' is not the origin and mainspring of 'great action'?

The question of course is what Rambert means by heroism, and clearly his definition is limited to the heroism of combat. Yet if the definition is reappraised to signify not only readiness to take the ultimate physical risks (which can be motivated by evil as well as noble intent), but to sacrifice self, to give all for the Other, clearly 'living and dying for what one loves' can also become a form of heroism, indeed we have it on the best authority that there is no greater love than to lay down one's life for one's friend.

---

69   p.1385. 'You're right. You must go back to her, you are right. Or else – what would be left you?' *Plague*, p.195.

70   p.1351. 'I don't believe in heroism; I know it's easy and I've learnt it can be murderous. What interests me is living and dying for what one loves', *Plague*, p.157.

Rieux's scale of values is not different from Rambert's. In a long intervention by the narrator on the subject, we are told that heroism comes in second place, 'juste après, et jamais avant, l'exigence généreuse du bonheur'.[71] 'Il n'y a pas de honte à être heureux', Camus had written in those early essays.[72] *Généreux*, 'generous', is however the key word, that epithet so frequently bestowed upon the heroes of Corneille, signifying both courage and nobility of spirit. The happiness of Camus's heroes is incompatible with anything less, as is demonstrated when Rambert finds that after all he cannot walk away from the stricken city, and that 'il peut y avoir de la honte à être heureux tout seul'.[73]

Rieux makes no attempt to influence Rambert or prevent his going. This is strange behaviour for a doctor, given that Rambert may well risk carrying the plague to the outside world. The moral debate, which requires Rambert's total freedom of choice, here apparently takes precedence over 'realism' or psychological verisimilitude, but then we remember that Camus had always stated clearly that psychology was not his first consideration and that he was not a 'realist' novelist, whatever that may be. An American critic, Robert Brock, discusses this problem in the light of Anarchist principles, to which Camus had in fact been attracted, and which, the critic points out, have nothing to do with the popular concept of anarchy as violence, and all to do with respecting the liberty of the individual and having faith in the ability of people of good will to make informed choices which are for the good of the community. In the light of these principles, he argues, Rieux's attitude could spring from his recognition of a man of *generous* principle in Rambert, and hence his total faith in the journalist's ultimate behaviour. Altruism results from enlightenment, and Rambert will make the responsible choice.[74] 'Anarchiste chrétien n'est pas pour

---

71 p.1331. '– just after, and never before the noble claim of happiness', *Plague*, p.133.
72 'Noces à Tipasa', in *Essais*, p.58. 'There is no shame in being happy', *SE*, p.72.
73 p.1389. 'It may be shameful to be happy by oneself', *Plague*, p.199.
74 See Brock. Others who have discussed Camus's interest in Anarchist principles include Germaine Brée (1972, pp.197–8) and R. Gay-Crosier (1970).

me déplaire', Camus once wrote to the young Jean Sénac who had described himself as such.[75]

The optimistically straightforward idea of uncomplicated happiness in a world of sea and sun, of simple physical relationships between the sexes, has undergone a change since Sisyphus walked down the mountain or Meursault made love to Marie. Happiness was always threatened from outside, but now it is complicated by moral choices. Man's 'irreparable innocence' is no longer guaranteed, despite the external nature of the evil of the plague. Happiness and innocence are states of grace constantly under threat. Tarrou says to Rieux:

> Je sais de science certaine [...] que chacun la porte en soi, la peste, parce que personne, non, personne au monde n'en est indemne. Et qu'il faut se surveiller sans arrêt pour ne pas être amené, dans une minute de distraction, à respirer dans la figure d'un autre et à lui coller l'infection. Ce qui est naturel, c'est le microbe. Le reste, la santé, l'intégrité, la pureté, si vous voulez, c'est un effet de la volonté et d'une volonté qui ne doit jamais s'arrêter.[76]

Innocence can only be the innocence of victims, and Rieux, recognising that men cannot be saints, praises those who choose the alternative ideal and devote themselves to the to the service of the suffering, those who 's'efforcent cependant d'être des médecins' (p.1474).

Except for Rieux's mother, all the major characters have been found wanting in some way. Rieux reproaches himself for the inadequacies of his devotion to his wife, Grand has not found the words which would hold Jeanne, convincing her of his love, Rambert, as a journalist, has accepted limits to his ability to report the truth.[77] These

---

75   'Christian anarchist is all right by me.' Letter of 24 June 1947, in Nacer-Khodja, p.128.
76   pp.1425–6. 'I know positively [...] that each of us has the plague within him; no one, no one on earth, is free from it. And I know too that we must keep endless watch on ourselves lest in a careless moment we breathe in somebody's face and fasten the infection on him. What's natural is the microbe. All the rest – health, integrity, purity (if you like) – is a product of the human will, of a vigilance that must never falter', *Plague*, p.242.
77   p.1226: '[Rieux] voulait savoir [...] si le journaliste pouvait dire la vérité. – Certes, dit l'autre. –Je veux dire: pouvez-vous porter condamnation totale? – Totale, non, il faut bien le dire [...].'

are faults of omission, but not fatal, and each of the three survives the plague. The graver errors are those of Paneloux, Othon and Tarrou, those who have passed judgement, acquiesced in the condemnation of sinners, criminals or counter-revolutionaries, and thus 'carried the microbe' of the culture of death. They have collaborated with the plague, and it eventually kills them. It is true that each is changed by the experience of the pestilence, but the virus is unforgiving. Tarrou's early recognition of his own error has brought a total lucidity, revealing not only the 'absurdity' of creation, but undermining the conviction of Sisyphean man's 'irreparable innocence'. This is a lucidity which Meursault had not possessed, although *L'Étranger* turns upon questions of innocence and guilt, implicit not only in the story of Meursault but also of Raymond Sintès, not to mention the larger question of the relationship to the Arabs, deprived of any voice. *L'Étranger* is not a novel of innocence, but, as Cruickshank remarks (p.156), it represents a 'nostalgie de l'innocence'. 'Quand j'étais jeune, je vivais avec l'idée de mon innocence, c'est-à-dire, avec pas d'idée du tout', Tarrou remarks, a reflection which we find also in Camus's own *Carnets*.[78]

La Peste is the novel of arrival at the lucidity of maturity. The optimistic simplicity of youth is fading. Patrice Mersault in *La Mort heureuse* is younger than Meursault in *L'Étranger*, and the protagonists of *La Peste* have lived longer and seen more of life than this latter. The principal characters of the novels are ageing with their creator, Rieux is about thirty-five (p.1240), close to the age of Camus himself. He is married and has practiced for some time as a doctor. Tarrou has been active in the cause of revolution in every country in Europe (p.1423). Rambert is an investigative journalist based in Paris. Dr Castel and his wife, as also Joseph Grand, are elderly, and for the first time age is given a voice, and not represented solely by the silent mother or dismissed as sad senility. The happy innocence of the very young is replaced, at the end of *La Peste*, by Rieux's reflection upon those whom he had known, or loved and lost, and who, significantly,

---

[78] p.1420. 'When I was young, I lived with the idea of my innocence; that is to say, with no idea at all', *Plague*, p.235. See also: 'J'ai vécu toute ma jeunesse avec l'idée de mon innocence, c'est-à-dire avec pas d'idée du tout', *Carnets II*, p.154.

include Cottard, 'tous, morts ou *coupables*' (my italics).[79] Death has taken them all, the innocent and the guilty, without distinction.

At the end of the novel, the surge of joy among those reunited with their loved ones is external to the narrator. The final diapason no longer resounds with the exultation of Mersault or Meursault, but becomes an elegy:

> Pour témoigner en faveur de ces pestiférés, pour laisser du moins un souvenir de l'injustice et de la violence qui leur avaient été faites, et pour dire simplement ce qu'on apprend au milieux des fléaux, qu'il y a dans les hommes plus de choses à admirer que de choses à mépriser.[80]

The generous simplicity of the admiration is the enduring mark of Camus's humanism, but awareness of the complexity of the human predicament and of the individual's responses increases from one novel to the next. '*La Peste* est un progrès, non du zéro vers l'infini, mais vers une complexité plus profonde qui reste à définir', Camus wrote in 1942.[81] The god-like Mersault had ended his life in the garden of Eden, Meursault had been expelled from it while remaining convinced of his innocence, Oran had been the collective experience of Hell, to which the innocent victims are condemned, and with *La Chute* we come to at last to the primary question, that of the enemy within, the microbe which Tarrou had detected and Meursault had not, and which poisons the happiness and innocence of their reincarnation, Jean-Baptiste Clamence, who is both the serpent and the sinner.

---

79 p.1473. 'All alike, dead or *guilty*', Plague, p.296.
80 p.1473. 'So that he should [...] bear witness in favour of those plague-stricken people, so that some memorial of the injustice and outrage done them might endure; and to state quite simply what we learn in a time of pestilence: that there are more things to admire in men than to despise', Plague, pp.296–7.
81 *Carnets II*, p.31. '*La Peste* is a progress, not from zero to infinity, but towards a greater complexity as yet undefined.'

Chapter IV
A Sojourn in the Circles of Hell. *La Chute*

> *Car la nature est telle, qu'elle marque partout un Dieu perdu, et dans l'homme et hors de l'homme, et une nature corrompue.*
> Pascal, *Pensées*

> *Et ceux qui méprisent le plus les hommes, et les égalent aux bêtes, encore veulent-ils en être admirés.*
> Pascal, *Pensées*

> *Il a fallu d'abord que ce rire perpétuel, et les rieurs, m'apprissent à voir plus clair en moi, à découvrir enfin que je n'étais pas simple.*
> Camus, *La Chute*

> *Ah! insensé, qui crois que je ne suis pas toi!*
> Victor Hugo, Preface to *Les Contemplations*

From one work to the next Camus searches for an answer to the problem of happiness in the context of mortality and human misery. The last chord struck in each of his fictions or dramas is always an ironic or tragic evocation of one or other pole of the human condition, joy or wretchedness. The resonance alternates between the stoic optimism of the eternally happy Sisyphus, on the one hand, and, on the other, the despair of Caligula, who expires enveloped in a darkness 'as heavy as human sorrow' ('Cette nuit est lourde comme la douleur humaine', Act IV, iii). In his happy death, Patrice Mersault returns, as we have seen, 'in the joy of his heart', to those worlds where all is still, embracing his eternity as a 'stone among the stones', while the final cry of Marthe, in *Le Malentendu*, is the voice of total and bitter despair: 'Priez votre Dieu qu'il vous fasse semblable à la pierre [...] c'est le seul vrai bonheur'.¹ Patrice Mersault finds his supreme happiness in the solitude and beauty of the beach of Chenoua, while Meursault's happiness is lost forever on the beach where the Arab dies, yet both protagonists die at peace, reconciled with the natural order, and firmly convinced of their essential innocence.

Peace, innocence and reconciliation are not universally bestowed however, even upon those of the utmost goodwill. Tarrou in *La Peste*, knows himself to be a carrier of the *microbe*, the seed of all human unhappiness, and Dr Rieux cannot tell whether his friend has found in death the peace he so intensely desired. In *L'Étranger*, Meursault's aged mother experiences an interlude of liberation and tranquillity before death, and the evening of her life, like the calm evening sky, is a 'melancholy truce', but in *La Peste*, Rieux makes the sad observation that

> il n'y aurait jamais plus de paix possible pour lui-même, pas plus qu'il n'y a d'armistice pour la mère amputée de son fils ou pour l'homme qui ensevelit son ami.²

All is not rejoicing at the end of that novel, and the joy of the fortunate is ever threatened by a re-awakening of 'La Peste', who will send her rats out to die in 'a happy city'. The conclusion of the novel is an elegy for joy and innocence. It will find a mocking echo in the despairing *finale* of the next novel, *La Chute*, which marks the definitive exile from an innocent Eden:

> O jeune fille, jette-toi encore dans l'eau pour que j'aie une seconde fois la chance de nous sauver tous les deux! Une seconde fois, hein, quelle imprudence! [...] Mais rassurons-nous! Il est trop tard, maintenant, il sera toujours trop tard. *Heureusement!*³

---

1   *TRN*, Act III, ii. 'Pray to your God to turn you to stone [...] that's the only real happiness.'
2   *TRN*, p.1458. 'No peace was possible for him henceforth, any more than there can be an armistice for a mother bereaved of her son or for a man who buries his friend', *Plague*, p.278.
3   p.1551 (my italics). 'O young woman, throw yourself into the water again so that I may a second time have a chance of saving both of us. A second time, eh, what a risky suggestion! [...] But let's not worry! It's too late now. It'll always

Who is this narrator who seems to address the reader directly in the exquisitely polite opening sentence of the novel: 'Puis-je, monsieur, vous proposer mes services, sans risquer d'être importun?'?[4] Certainly a man of education and subtlety. From beginning to end of the novel an essential part of the reader's pleasure comes from piercing the riddles, detecting the signs, supplying the answers. Who is referred to as a 'gorilla'? (Answer: a barman). What and where is this 'establishment'? (Answer: a bar in Amsterdam). The pleasure is, however, a carefully laid snare, for there are deeper riddles with less obvious answers and multiple implications which the innocent reader will find more disturbing. What can we know of Jean-Baptiste Clamence, this self-confessedly most untrustworthy of all narrators ('Il est bien difficile de démêler le vrai du faux dans ce que je raconte', p.1537)? Is he joker, liar, mythomaniac, paranoid, play-actor? Brian Fitch (1970) goes so far as to suggest that he is actually the fictional creation of the anonymous fictional character, nothing but a role played by an actor, himself in turn only a creature of the imagination of the author: 'Jean-Baptiste Clamence, *comédien*',[5] in a word.

Camus, in a short prefatorial note (p.2015), points out the core question: where does confession end and accusation begin in this monologue, and is the speaker indicting himself or his times and contemporaries? At all events, concealed behind his ironic pseudonym ('Bien entendu, je ne vous ai pas dit mon vrai nom', p.1484), he lies in wait for the unwary, like some deadly spider at the centre of the web of concentric canals in the grey city of Amsterdam. Is his courteous approach to the stranger in the bar the monster's invitation to its prey? Is the whole narrative an account of an hallucination? Is it one of those waking dreams to which the narrator compares the excursion upon the Zuyderzee ('Ce n'est pas de la navigation, mais du rêve', p.1525)? Is it a nightmare, as has been suggested (Fitch, 1970, p.67)? Is it only a

---

    be too late. Fortunately!' *Fall*, p.108. For obvious reasons, given the implications of the concept of happiness in the work, I would prefer to translate this last word literally as 'Happily!'.

4   p.1477. 'May I, Monsieur, offer my services without running the risk of intruding?' *Fall*, p.5.

5   p.1500 (my italics); 'play-actor'.

gin-soaked dream filling one of Clamence's nocturnal wanderings in the city, talking interminably to himself ('Je marche des nuits durant, je rêve, ou je me parle interminablement', p.1482)? Is there an interlocutor, or is he an invention with which the narrator baits the reader? Or is the interlocutor perhaps part of the hallucination? At all events, he is listener rather than interlocutor, and his apparently monosyllabic replies can only be inferred from the uninterrupted monologue. Does the smoke-filled bar of *Mexico City* exist, or does the narrator in fact never stir from his room, wherever that may be? What does he mean by calling himself a 'judge-penitent'? What relation does this have to his claim to be in possession of the stolen panel of the Just Judges from Van Eyck's polyptych of the Adoration of the Lamb? Why is his verbal onslaught on the human race in general and himself in particular so ferociously unforgiving?

La Chute, like the previous fictions, can be read on more than one level. From one perspective, critics have insisted on the author's shocked and hurt reaction to the fierce attacks against him occasioned by the publication of *L'Homme révolté* in 1951. Clamence can be seen as a caustic parody of the hostile image of Camus drawn by his critics in the circle around Sartre, an attack all the more wounding since these were his former friends. Clamence says bitterly:

> À partir du moment où j'ai appréhendé qu'il y eût en moi quelque chose à juger, j'ai compris, en somme, qu'il y avait en eux une vocation irrésistible de jugement.[6]

It is a remark which, as Quilliot points out (*TRN*, p.2026), is probably an indirect allusion to that polemic. In 1954, the wounds were reopened by the publication of Simone de Beauvoir's *Les Mandarins*, which received the prestigieux Prix Goncourt on 6 December of that year. In one of the two principal characters of the novel (the other being transparently modelled on Sartre), Camus felt himself targeted and ridiculed as man, writer, and editor of the journal *Combat*. Olivier

---

6   p.1515. 'The moment I grasped that there was something to judge in me, I realized that, in fact, they had an irresistible vocation for judgement', *Fall*, p.58.

Todd calls the episode 'a ferocious exercise in denigration'.[7] An entry in Camus's *Carnets* on 14 December reads:

> Existentialisme. Quand ils s'accusent on peut être sûr que c'est toujours pour accabler les autres. Des juges pénitents.[8]

Clamence, the 'judge-penitent' of *La Chute*, remembers with irony the cafés 'where our professional humanists used to meet' ('les cafés spécialisés où se réunissaient nos humanistes professionnels', p.1522). No need to ask if the name of one such establishment was the Café Flore.

By virtue of his name, Jean-Baptiste Clamence is designated, or designates himself, as the twentieth-century prophet clamouring in a grey, wet urban desert (how Camus hated cold and rain, be it in Prague, Paris or Amsterdam!). In his long monologue, the erstwhile barrister and champion of 'noble causes' (p.1484) paints his self-portrait as a 'prophète vide pour temps médiocres'.[9] In his earlier life in Paris, he has been a man much admired and popular with both men and women, but one who fails the test of real courage, ignoring the cries for help of a drowning girl. His motivation, in the most secret recesses of his soul, is, in his own account, not justice or philanthropy, but a desire for power and admiration, a contempt for all around him, an arrogant determination to find a pedestal from which to dominate:

> Je gagnais ma vie en dialogant avec des gens que je méprisais [...] Le sentiment du droit, la satisfaction d'avoir raison, la joie de s'estimer soi-même, cher monsieur, sont des ressorts puissants pour nous tenir debout ou nous faire avancer.[10]

Such, as Camus perceived them, were also the charges levelled against himself in 1952 by Sartre, Jeanson and others.

---

7 p.832: 'Un exercice acharné de dénigrement.' A detailed analysis of the attack is given on pp. 827–32.
8 *Carnets III*, p.147. 'Existentialism. When they accuse themselves you can be sure it is always in order to heap blame on other people. Judge-penitents.'
9 p.1535. 'An empty prophet for shabby times', *Fall*, p.86.
10 p.1485. 'I earned my living by carrying on dialogues with people I scorned [...] The feeling for the law, the satisfaction of being right, the joy of self-esteem, *cher* Monsieur, are powerful incentives to keep us upright or make us move forward', *Fall*, p.16.

165

The self-portrait of Clamence is parody, but on two levels, for it is also a self-questioning and self-critical parody. The description of the younger Clamence could be a pen-portrait of Camus himself:

> Je n'étais pas mal fait de ma personne, je me montrais à la fois danseur infatigable et discret érudit, j'arrivais à aimer en même temps, ce qui n'est guère facile, les femmes et la justice, je pratiquais les sports et les beaux arts [...] une vie réussie [...] Mon accord avec la vie était total.[11]

The *accord avec la vie*, the very definition of happiness, as Camus had declared it to be in one of the youthful essays of *Noces*: 'Qu'est-ce que le bonheur sinon le simple accord entre un être et l'existence qu'il mène?'.[12] Yes, Clamence's happiness is complete.

Camus was not a man to evade an examination of conscience, nor could the reader of Pascal and Kierkegaard fail to ask himself what had been the role of the ego in his own behaviour. 'Me, me, me', cries Clamence:

> Moi, moi, moi, voilà le refrain de ma chère vie [...] je ne me reconnaissais pas d'égal [...] Je ne me reconnaissais que des supériorités, ce qui expliquait ma bienveillance et ma sérénité.[13]

Clamence is possessed by the cynical devil's advocate within, attributing every trace of virtue to self-interest or vanity, and seeing in every hostile criticism an echo of those reproachful 'inner voices' which Camus had described in the final paragraph of his essay 'Défense de *L'Homme révolté*' ('In Defence of *The Rebel*'):

---

11   p.1489. 'I was acceptable in appearance. I revealed myself to be both a tireless dancer and an unobtrusively learned man; I managed to love simultaneously – and this is not easy – women and justice; I indulged in sports and the fine arts [...] a successful life [...] I was altogether in harmony with life', *Fall*, p.22.
12   *Essais*, p.85. 'But what is happiness except the simple harmony between a man and the life he leads?', *SE*, p.98.
13   p.1500. 'I, I, I, is the refrain of my whole life [...] I recognized no equals [...] I found nothing but superiorities in myself and this explained my goodwill and serenity', *Fall*, p.37.

> Chaque adversaire, si répugnant soit-il, est une de nos voix intérieures que nous serions tentés de faire taire et qu'il faut que nous écoutions pour corriger, adapter, ou réaffirmer les quelques vérités que nous entrevoyons.[14]

This negative and destructive voice, the intense dislike, *la détestation méchante*, which we feel towards some part of ourselves, as he wote in the same essay, must be listened to, but made to serve a positive end, to contribute to moral strength, otherwise it will lead only to the madness and delirium into which Clamence descends. He is a human being destroyed, his goodwill obliterated, his serenity pulverised by a relentless and unforgiving introspection, a perversion of the human capacity for thinking.

'Thinking constitutes the greatness of man', wrote Pascal, but thinking is also the source of the wretchedness of man. 'Man is great in that he recognises that he is miserable. A tree is not aware of itself as miserable' (*Pasc.* p.1156, tr.). But the recognition of the human condition is only the starting point, Camus's *point zéro*. Pascal, of course, does not stop there:

> Man is manifestly made for thinking; that is all his dignity and all his worth, and all his duty is to think clearly. Now the right order of thinking is to start with oneself, and with one's creator and one's end. (*Pasc.* p.1146, tr.)

There is a thread running through the fiction of Camus, and it is the reincarnation, from one work to the next, of the thinker, the character who ponders over his past, who seeks to retrace the path he has travelled and which has led to the wreck of his happiness, to the loss of his original innocence. He is Meursault after the death of the Arab, Tarrou after his traumatic experience of revolutionary violence, or Jean-Baptiste Clamence, the indefatigable monologist of *La Chute*. They are all solitaires, not excepting the loquacious Clamence, who in Amsterdam has 'no longer any friends', but 'only accomplices' ('Je n'ai plus d'amis, je n'ai que des complices', p.1513), and like all solitaires, they are by their very nature introspective and inclined to irony.

---

14   *Essais*, p.1716. 'Every adversary, however loathsome, is one of our inner voices which we may be tempted to silence and which we must heed in order to correct, adapt or reaffirm the few truths of which we have a glimpse.'

Patrice Mersault, Meursault, Tarrou, these characters are the guinea pigs of an experiment seeking to reconcile thinking and happiness, death and felicity, experience and innocence, and to integrate the individual into the world around him, human and natural. They could even be called *extremist* thinkers, for, in response to the enigmas and problems of the human condition, they choose extreme solutions: a Nietzschean return to Nature, or silence, or holiness without God, and, in the most radical case of all, that of the 'empty prophet' for our times, Jean-Baptiste Clamence, despair and condemnation of the whole human race. The arguments swing from one extreme to the other. For Meursault everyone is innocent, sin and guilt do not exist, only *misfortune*. In Céleste's eyes, Meursault's crime is indeed a 'misfortune', *un malheur* (p.1191). For Clamence, everyone is guilty, and the concept of 'misfortune' is excusatory. Paradoxically, according to him, we can accept suffering as long as it is unjustified, what we cannot bear is to be judged and found wanting:

> La question est d'éviter le jugement. Je ne dis pas d'éviter le châtiment. Car le châtiment sans jugement est supportable. Il a un nom d'ailleurs qui garantit notre innocence: *le malheur*.[15]

If there is no excuse, no pardon, is our Fall then irremediable, our corruption incurable? Camus's frequent biblical, and specifically New Testament allusions, explicit and implicit in this short work, point to a preoccupation with an unmistakably Pascalian view of the human condition and destiny and a continuing debate with Christian apologetics. The power and poetry of Pascal's great unfinished *apologia* derive from its tragic portrayal of man's fate, from its analysis of our anxiety, of the instability of our existence and of the frailty of intellect and rationality. These ills are the result, in the theological worldview, of the loss of an original state of innocence and happiness, to which we look back with longing and a deep sense of exile. For Pascal, salvation can only lie in the reversal of this descent, this Fall, through an ascent,

---

15   p.1514 (my italics). 'The question is how to elude judgement. I'm not saying to avoid punishment, for punishment without judgement is bearable. It has a name, moreover, that guarantees our innocence: it is called *misfortune*', *Fall*, p.57 (my italics).

an upward leap into Faith: 'Wretchedness of man without God, happiness of man with God' is the ground plan of the *Pensées*. Sharing Pascal's tragic view of existence, Camus nonetheless takes issue with his excessively negative view of human nature.[16] He once made clear the dichotomy between his position and the religious concept of man's fallen nature as follows:

> Si le christianisme est pessimiste quant à l'homme, il est optimiste quant à la destinée humaine [...] Je dirai moi que, pessimiste quant à la condition humaine, je suis optimiste quant à l'homme.[17]

For Camus, who refuses the leap into faith, the whole question is to find a way to salvation without the intervention of a Saviour, and to change the 'wretchedness of man with God', as he had somewhat mischievously put it in *L'Envers et l'Endroit*, into the happiness of man *without* God.

Throughout his work, Camus is involved in debate with Pascal and Augustine about the truth of the human condition. The start of the dialogue is the 'zero point' represented by Meursault in *L'Étranger*, the negative 'truth of being and feeling' (p.1928), the simple 'physical happiness' to be found in union and harmony with the natural world around us. Meursault chooses to live in silence, since only silence is radically opposed to untruth and to judgement. Ironically, however, he himself will be the victim of language, the 'rhetorical skill of the prosecutor', as Jacqueline Lévi-Valensi writes (1970b, p.41, tr.), and his failure to make a value judgement on Sintès involves him in the affair which ends with the murder of the Arab. His attempt to live without language, which is the only tool of intellectual questioning or value judgements, leads not to fulfilment and 'simple' happiness, but to

---

16 The Jansenist denial of human freedom or free will is an extremist position, close to Calvinism, in the theological debate. Claudel once protested, in a letter to Gide (1 September 1910): 'What I reproach Pascal with, above all, is ill-treating and calumniating human nature [...] It's not Christianity, it's a sick man's ill-humour.' (tr.)

17 *Carnets II*, p.160. 'Although Christianity is pessimistic as regards mankind, it is optimistic regarding human destiny [...] As for me, I would say that, although a pessimist with regard to the human condition, I am optimistic regarding man.'

169

death. He does however, in the end, make the essential judgement on the priceless value of human existence itself, the unbelievable 'privilege' of being born into the world and experiencing its beauty. Facing his own extinction, he reaffirms, in an outpouring of passionate language, the victory of life, however brief, over death.

Camus reincarnates him in *La Peste* in order to try the experiment in other circumstances and to go farther along the road, towards the sympathy which unites the human family. Rieux and Tarrou are the two faces of one exemplary non-judgemental character, and, as we have seen, it is above all in Tarrou that Meursault is resurrected, with his desire for simplicity, his acute observation of those around him and their eccentricities, his refusal of God, his rejection of rhetoric and his choice of silence. 'C'est au moment du malheur qu'on s'habitue à la vérité, c'est-à-dire au silence', Tarrou writes in his notebooks.[18] What need is there of words, in any case, to express that 'truth of being and feeling' which Meursault and Marie, Tarrou and Rieux experience when they abandon themselves to the warm embrace of the sea? For Meursault it is 'contentment' (*contentement*, p.1162), for Rieux and Tarrou, more positively, 'happiness' (*bonheur*, p.1428).

Tarrou is older than Meursault, and his silence is qualitatively different, for it is the silence not of refusal, but of reflection. He has lived with the idea of his innocence, 'that is to say, with no idea at all' ('Je vivais avec l'idée de mon innocence, c'est-à-dire, avec pas d'idée du tout', p.1420), until the day when he is forced to reflect. Meursault, after abandoning his studies, has tried to lead a life from which reflection, and therefore judgement, is rigourously excluded. He desires to live the life before the Fall, an existence starting from 'point zero'. Clamence too, like these predecessors, has once lived with the idea of his innocence, as he declares:

> L'idée la plus naturelle à l'homme, celle qui lui vient naïvement, comme du fond de sa nature, est l'idée de son innocence.[19]

---

18 p.1314. 'It is in the thick of a calamity that one gets hardened to the truth, in other words to silence', *Plague*, p.112.
19 p.1516. 'The idea that comes most naturally to man, as if from his very nature, is the idea of his innocence', *Fall*, p.60.

But one day Meursault kills an Arab on a beach, Tarrou assents to a firing squad, Clamence fails to come to the aid of a drowning girl. We are all carriers of the plague. 'Chacun la porte en soi, la peste', says Tarrou, 'parce que personne, non, personne au monde n'en est indemne' (p.1425).

Pascal had said essentially the same thing: *La nature est corrompue*, but insisted that man's wretchedness must be counterbalanced by his greatness, the microbe of original sin overcome with the remedy of grace. While lamenting the presence of the 'microbe' lurking in every living soul, Tarrou too still believes in the goodness of the human spirit, still hopes that it is possible to achieve a 'sainthood without God', a fraternity with suffering humanity. Clamence follows on from Tarrou, but only in his pessimism, only to exploit the Fall, not seeking any palliative, human or divine. In his account of his earlier days in Paris, we glimpse in him the lawyer whom Tarrou might have become if he had followed in his father's footsteps: the altruistic champion of the underdog, the admired and successful defender of 'noble causes'. But now, 'judge and penitent', consumed with anger and despair, and desiring only to dominate, Clamence beats his breast the better to pass judgement on the rest of humanity in a stream of mercilessly ironic discourse, denying the possibility of any kind of redemption. 'Et moi, je plains sans absoudre', he cries, 'Je comprends sans pardonner.'[20]

Clamence's object is to drag us along, humiliated and despairing, in his march towards death. Ill and delirious as he is at the end of the novel, his bare cell-like room is the latest version of Pascal's prison, its sparse furnishings gleaming 'like a coffin' ('comme un cercueil'), while he himself lies prone beneath his spotless sheets, as if 'already in a shroud' ('dans un linceul déjà', p.1538). Friends have disappeared from his life, just as books have long been banished from the room (p.1537). Language, oral or written, as an exchange, as a means of fraternal communication, has been replaced by one-way discourse, words as the weapon of subjugation. Clamence's triumph is that of the demagogues, the political propagandists, the dictators, the creators and masters of the hell on earth which is the world of the concentration

---

20   p.1549. 'As for me, I pity without absolving, I understand without forgiving', *Fall*, p.105.

camps. Indeed it is an 'univers concentrationnaire' which he sees reflected all around him in the grey skies and murky waters of the canals of Amsterdam, or the cheerless waters of the Zuyderzee, 'une mer morte', a dead sea (p.1525).[21] We are in the kingdom of the dead, and the Zuyderzee itself is 'a dead sea', over which Clamence and his interlocutor seem to glide without advancing and where nothing ever changes ('Nous avançons, et rien ne change', p.1525). This is a cold, pallid world, reminiscent of Dante's frozen lake of Cocytus in the ninth and deepest circle of the *Inferno*, the place of punishment of the traitors, the abode of Judas and of Lucifer himself. Clamence too is treacherous, we can trust nothing that he says, and he aspires to Satanic power and glory.

The *univers concentrationnaire* is our epoch's version of Hell. Clamence himself evokes the analogy between the concentric canals of Amsterdam and the circles of Dante's Inferno.[22] This is the natural setting in which the Devil's Advocate, the brilliant lawyer turned 'Judge-Penitent', can pursue his calling to obtain the condemnation of the whole human race. Clamence confesses not in humility and in order to seek absolution, but to pass unforgiving judgement on human nature itself. In accusing himself, he accuses the silent interlocutor, his double, who, like himself, is a Frenchman, aged 'around' forty, has 'knocked about' the world, is 'more or less' well-dressed, can instantly spot an imperfect subjunctive and find it irritating, belongs unmistakeably to the bourgeoisie, and, in the last encounter, will not deny that he too has 'exercised the noble profession' of lawyer in Paris. In the very first encounter, Clamence classes his interlocutor as a 'Sadducee', only to concede soon afterwards that he himself has been a 'Sadducee'.[23] He designates in this way the wealthy who, despite their grand attitudes, are profoundly uncaring of those less fortunate. It is curious that he does not use the more usual term 'pharisee',

---

21 For a reading of *La Chute* as a novel of the Holocaust, see Felman.
22 p.1483: 'Avez-vous remarqué que les canaux concentriques d'Amsterdam ressemblent aux cercles de l'enfer?'
23 For the description of Clamence and his interlocutor, see p.1480 and 1551.. Also on p.1480: 'Vous êtes donc ce que j'appelle un saducéen [...] Oui, j'ai été riche, non, je n'ai rien partagé avec les autres. Qu'est-ce que cela prouve? Que j'étais aussi un saducéen.'

and that he indicates the requirement of a certain knowledge of the Scriptures for an appreciation of the full implications of the label. It is a knowledge which the interlocutor is, like Clamence again, deemed to possess. Two things, in fact, distinguish the Sadducees from the Pharisees: the former denied the immortality of the soul and they dominated the wealthy priestly caste, interpreting the Law in all its severity. In the time of Christ, Clamence would have been a Sadducee.

Clamence we know only by a pseudonym, nor do we ever have a name for his listener, but of course we do not need one, for every reader is the interlocutor before whose eyes Clamence holds up the mirror: 'Hypocrite lecteur, – mon sembable, – mon frère!', to quote the final words of Baudelaire's bitter indictment *Au Lecteur*. In a short preface, Camus himself described the novel as a 'jeu de glaces étudié' ('a studied play with mirrors', *Prière d'insérer*, p.2015). However, Clamence's ambition, his pride, is not limited to the role of mere devil's advocate, for he is only happy 'on the heights'.[24] The lover of the crests, of the moral high ground, aspires to the highest peak in Hell, displacing Satan himself. He dreams of enthronement in the fiery mouth of Etna, of all places on the planet the best from which to dominate the world lying at his feet.[25] Pride, tradition affirms, was the sin by which Lucifer/Satan fell, becoming the Enemy of humanity, the Father of Lies, the great abuser of Language. Clamence, in the monstrous pride of his psychotic dreams, takes his leave of us 'intoxicated' on toxic words ('ivre de mauvaises paroles'), deliriously jubilant, and 'Heureux', he cries, 'heureux à mourir!' (p.1549; 'Happy fit to die!').

Thus Camus's last completed novel comes full circle in ironic mode, and Clamence claims his 'Happy Death' in a mocking echo of the title of the first novel. We have had to wait for Clamence to provide a gloss to Caligula's aphorism that 'Men die and they are not

24 p.1487: 'Oui, je ne me suis jamais senti à l'aise que dans les situations élevées.' There is unmistakeably a sideswipe here at the romantic Stendhalian image of heroism, as Clamence goes on to specify that 'Selon moi, on ne méditait pas dans les caves ou les cellules des prisons (à moins qu'elles fussent situées dans une tour, avec une vue étendue)', p.1488. We recognise Julien Sorel and Fabrice del Dongo in their lofty prison towers.
25 p.1498: 'Ce que j'aime le plus au monde, c'est la Sicile [...] et encore du haut de l'Etna, dans la lumière, à condition de dominer l'île et la mer.'

173

happy', and to declare that death and happiness coincide only in madness or in the dreams of those exiled Dutch colonists (and we are all exiled colonists), for ever banished from the Eden of their former glory, for whom the sea is the highway to the fabled Cipango in the East and to the islands where men die 'crazed and happy':

> La Hollande n'est pas seulement l'Europe des marchands, mais la mer, la mer qui mène à Cipango, et à ces îles où les hommes meurent fous et heureux.[26]

Yet Meursault too had died happy, a melancholy happiness attained through his total acceptance of the human condition. Declaring that he could find interest enough in existence even if imprisoned in the trunk of a hollow tree, he had implicitly rejected the Pascalian contention that the horror of having nothing to do but contemplate our existence and our mortality is beyond our strength, driving us endlessly to seek distraction ('divertissement').[27] Camus holds to the optimism of the humanist concerning human nature, and dismisses the Christian pessimism inherent in the doctrine of original sin. But that is precisely the point at which Clamence will become the devil's advocate, espousing Pascal's very pessimistic view of a corrupted human nature, in order to deny all possibility of remedy. If Meursault is the anti-Pascal, then Clamence is the anti-Meursault. The two characters are antithetical, but also complementary.

The resemblances between Clamence and Meursault have been pointed out by a number of critics. However, the most important parallel of all is the complex of the prison. Meursault, we have seen, lives in a sort of cell even before his arrest, having shut up the other rooms of his flat after the death of his mother. Clamence too shuts himself up in his room, and admits that he has 'a bolt-the-door complex' ('le complexe du verrou', p.1541). Amsterdam also is a sort of prison; Clamence is entrapped in the concentric circles of its canals, waiting

---

26   p.1482. 'Holland is not only the Europe of merchants but also the sea, the sea that leads to Cipango and to those islands where men die mad and happy', *Fall*, p.12.

27   See the whole section 'Divertissement.' specifically *Pasc.* pp.1138–9: 'Tout le malheur des hommes vient d'une seule chose, qui est de ne savoir pas demeurer en repos dans une chambre.'

to entrap others. Van Eyck's painting of the Just Judges is locked up in Clamence's cupboard, so that Justice itself is incarcerated. For Clamence, as for Meursault, there is only one way out of the prison: Meursault imagines his own execution, the crowd acclaiming him 'with cries of hate', and Clamence, in his final ravings, sees his ultimate triumph played out on the guillotine, his head lifted high above the block to dominate the masses. The image must evoke, for the French reader, the execution of King Louis XVI or of Danton. Clamence's fevered dream is of dying like a king or a hero. Death alone, for him, is salvation. 'On me décapiterait, par exemple', he exults, 'et je n'aurais plus peur de mourir, je serais sauvé.'[28]

Victor Brombert (1975, pp.19–20) has pointed out that the image of the prisoner also portrays the situation of the writer. Meursault, Tarrou and Clamence are in fact the authors of written or verbal confessional narratives, followers of the method of Pascal or Descartes, for whom, in order to extrapolate the truth concerning the human condition, the starting point had always been an examination of the self. Clamence declares that 'Les auteurs de confession écrivent surtout pour ne pas se confesser',[29] however all reflection upon one's own life is necessarily a search for truth, even if only to conceal or disguise it once it is found, and it always results, as with Goethe, in a mixture of truth and imaginative fiction, *Dichtung und Wahrheit*. Inevitably so, for in recounting oneself, one becomes a duality, speaker and interlocutor, observer and observed, *regardant et regardé*, as Jean Rousset had put it (p.52). In his *Carnets*, Camus had already defined the intellectual as 'one who becomes double'.[30] The interlocutor is Clamence's double, his looking-glass. Both Clamence and Meursault observe their reflection, either in the mirror (p.1495), or in the prison tin dish (p.1183), and both find the image perplexing.

Where then is truth? Even memory itself, which 'is necessary for all the workings of reason' (*Pasc.* p.1115, tr.), ceaselessly deceives

---

28   p.1551. 'I'd be decapitated, for instance, and I'd have no more fear of death; I'd be saved', *Fall*, p.107.
29   p.1538. 'Authors of confessions write especially to avoid confessing', *Fall*, p.89.
30   'Intellectuel = celui qui se dédouble', *Carnets I*, p.41.

us, and this is a major theme of *La Chute*. To attain self-knowledge, Clamence has first of all to recover what is in his memory ('Il a fallu d'abord que je retrouve la mémoire', p.1500). Terry Keefe has pointed out how difficult it is to establishe a coherent chonology for the events recounted in the monologue, underlining the doubly untrustworthy role of the narrator who is above all a *remembering* narrator.[31] It is not only memory, however, which is not to be trusted. We are at the mercy of all the 'deceiving powers', under which heading Pascal groups the imagination, the senses, the effects of illnesses (no doubt he would today include our psychoses), our own interest, our vanity, the accepted opinions and customs of our society, and above all the terrible *amour-propre*, which, in the context, is both love of the self and inordinate pride in the self. There is nothing, he says, more contrary to justice and truth than this *amour-propre* which makes each *self* the centre of the universe:

> This hateful *ego* [...] injust in itself, inasmuch as it makes itself the centre of everything [...] unfair to others, since its aim is to subjugate them to itself, for each *ego* is the enemy and desires to be the tyrant of all the others. (*Pasc.* p.1171, tr.)

Clamence declares that he had loved himself exclusively for more than thirty years: 'Il y avait plus de trente ans que je m'aimais exclusivement' (p.1527).

The arduous search for truth is full of snares and difficulties. One can only 'search with a heavy heart' ('chercher en gémissant', *Pasc*, p.1171). The pain of the search is what Meursault seeks to avoid, until the moment when he pumps four bullets, after the first, into an inert body, and knows that he has rapped four times at the 'door of unhappiness' (p.1168). The truth which he seeks, and which ultimately he represents, as noted above, is 'the negative truth of being and feeling'. Stendhal, too, so admired by Camus, had taken that point of

---

31 He outlines the problems as follows (p.542): 'Time-scale A: the sequence in which Clamence *relates* events from his past; time-scale B: the sequence in which (according to Clamence) these events *took place*; time-scale C: the sequence in which such events as had been forgotten were (according to Clamence) *remembered*.'

departure, as he tells us in Chapter XXVIII of the autobiographical *Vie de Henry Brulard*:

> Mais, au fond, cher lecteur, je ne sais pas ce que je suis: bon, méchant, spirituel, sot. Ce que je sais parfaitement, ce sont les choses qui me font peine ou plaisir, que je désire ou que je hais.[32]

As we have seen, humble physical happiness satisfies Meursault, a contentment such as even the animals can experience. But if we cast an ironic and sceptical eye upon him, as would Clamence, we bcan quickly reduce him to the level of a moron. What else, other than the caricature of our friend Meursault, is this rudimentary being, deprived of language, for whom Clamence acts as interpreter, this stranger among a crowd of strangers, this 'gorilla', no doubt homesick for some primeval forest, this primate who presides over the bar of *Mexico City*? Even his way of speaking reminds us of Meursault. Like the latter, he is fond of alternatives signifying indifference: 'Take it or leave it', he grunts, and Clamence wonders, 'Que fallait-il prendre ou laisser? Sans doute, notre ami lui-même.'[33] Like Meursault in the courtroom, the 'gorilla' cannot understand the language of the place, and so can only feel uneasily that some pretty dubious business is going on in the world around him.[34] And who else, moreover, but this ape-like avatar of Meursault, the victim of a justice-system rooted in the hideous monstrosity of the death-penalty, should become the receiver of the stolen panel of Van Eyck's Just Judges, briefly enthroned over this sordid world of low-life and vice, as if to wreak a mocking vengeance upon the injustice of the law?

Here then is Meursault, forever banished from the beach where he had been happy, Meursault in *Mexico City*, transformed into the

---

32 'But, dear reader, at bottom I don't really know what I am: good, bad, witty, or stupid. What I know perfectly well are which things give me pain or pleasure, which things I desire and which things I hate.'

33 p.1477 'What did one have to take or leave? Doubtless our friend himself', *Fall*, p.6.

34 p.1478: 'À force de ne pas comprendre ce qu'on dit en sa présence, il a pris un caractère défiant […] comme s'il avait le soupçon, au moins, que quelque chose ne tourne pas rond entre les hommes.'

keeper of this antechamber of Hell (we may note that in French a *gorille* is also the colloquial term for a 'heavy', a bouncer or bodyguard). This then is his *Fall*, from the human condition he is precipitated into the brute condition of the animal. He takes his place in the zoomorphism of Clamence, for whom humanity is composed of filthy or ferocious beasts, brown bears, or gorillas. Clamence himself, like the rest of humankind, is nothing but a 'salacious ape' ('un singe salace', p.1528), who discovers at one point, that, having fallen in love with a parrot, he found himself sleeping with a serpent ('Après avoir aimé un perroquet, il me fallut coucher avec un serpent', p.1527). Like the reader who is apostrophised in Baudelaire's *Au Lecteur*, we inhabit the menagery of our vices, surrounded by 'les chacals, les panthères, les lices, / Les singes, les scorpions, les vautours, les serpents'. What a jungle, in which the very Lamb of God, whom the Just Judges of Van Eyck's painting are on their way to adore, becomes, incongruously enough, and with some derision, the 'Holy Animal' ('le saint animal', p.1542).

The bar of Mexico-City is a microcosmic Unholy City, its function and title evoking a metropolis of low-life and violence. It is set, not, like Van Eyck's Holy City, upon a sunlit hillside, but in some dank and sleazy quarter of that other metropolis, Amsterdam. It is the ironic mirror-image of the painter's representation of the Heavenly City of the Book of Revelations, the New Jerusalem to which countless multitudes from all nations are making their way. Van Eyck's throngs have passed through the 'great tribulation' and been restored to their state of innocence. In the dawn of an everlasting new day, they will drink the water of eternal life, springing from the clear fountain at the centre of the composition. The Ghent altarpiece is the ultimate icon of Christian hope and optimism. From the redeemed and unabashed Adam and Eve of the side panels to the prophets of the Old Testament, from the apostles to the hermits and the holy virgins, from the pagan Virgil to the penitent Mary Magdalen, from the Christian knights led by Saint George to the procession of the Just Judges, humanity enters into everlasting bliss, in a paradise of flowers and meadows and noble architecture.

In *Mexico-City* also they come from every nation, 'la multitude du jugement dernier'.[35] They come seeking refuge from the grey landscape and grim canals of Amsterdam, but only to fall from the dignity of humankind to the level of the brute beasts, and to quench their thirst not with the water of divine grace and everlasting life, but with the cheap gin of forgetfulness, which, *happily*, says Clamence (how he loves that adverb!), offers the 'the sole glimmer in this darkness'.[36] It is not the blessed who come to *Mexico-City* from every nation on earth, but the damned. Perdition awaits them. 'La chute se produit à l'aube', Clamence assures us,[37] for it is then, after their gin-soaked nights, that he ambushes them. Dawn, the symbol of hope, is transformed into the moment of total and irremediable despair. It was at dawn also that Meursault would be saved or destroyed. 'C'est à l'aube qu'ils venaient, je le savais', he says, and the end of every night brings anguish, for 'l'aube ou mon pourvoi était là'.[38] But there is no appeal, no mercy, in this Last Judgement presided over by Clamence. In his final delirium, he sees himself enthroned in the high heavens, receiving the adoration of the abject multitude, a new triumphant Satan, at last displacing God the Father who reigns above the happy throngs of Van Eyck's great masterpiece.[39]

The bar of *Mexico City* replaces not only the feast of the Lamb of God, but the café owned by the well-named Céleste in *L'Étranger*, a place of friendship, fellowship, and true nourishment. This small antechamber of heaven, the place where all is goodwill and fellowship, is replaced in *La Chute* by the antechamber of hell, in which dog eats dog and the only remnants of paradise are the 'paradis artificiels' of a Baudelairean dream:

---

35   p.1549. 'the multitude of the Last Judgement', *Fall*, p.105.
36   p.1481: 'Heureusement il y a le genièvre, la seule lueur dans ces ténèbres.'
37   p.1549. 'The fall occurs at dawn', *Fall*, p.105.
38   p.1205. 'Either the dawn or my appeal would still be there [...] They came at dawn, I knew that', *OS*, p.108.
39   p.1549: 'Quelle ivresse de se sentir Dieu le Père [...] Je trône parmi mes vilains anges, à la cime du ciel hollandais, je regarde monter vers moi [...] la multitude du jugement dernier.'

> Le rêve, monsieur, le rêve à peu de frais, le voyage aux Indes! Ces personnes se parfument aux épices. Vous entrez, elles tirent les rideaux et la navigation commence. Les dieux descendent sur les corps nus et les îles dérivent.[40]

Are these the gods of the lost paradise of Chenoua? The place of that beautiful young 'solitary and stubborn god', the Mersault of *La Mort heureuse*, asleep athwart his bed, is taken now by some lonely drifter in search of an illusory escape from the human condition, a brief immortality. This is the immortality, the oblivion, which Clamence seeks with his plunge into debauchery. The young woman on the Pont Royal on a November night had sought oblivion also, and plunged to her death in the murky waters of the Seine. Suicide or debauchery: Clamence has considered both, and chosen the latter, an alternative way of *falling*, of drowning in the waters of Lethe, sinking into 'un long sommeil' (p.1529; 'a long sleep'). It is another form of the 'little suicide' chosen by Meursault in prison, when he succeeds in sleeping 'sixteen or eighteen hours a day', leaving himself only 'six hours to kill' (p.1182).

The fall of Meursault and the fall of Clamence, the loss of their innocence and their happiness, are due to the same basic mistake: 'Je n'ai jamais pu croire profondément que les affaires humaines fussent choses sérieuses',[41] Clamence admits, while Meursault's stock response to everything is: 'It's all the same to me', whether talking of Raymond's offer of friendship (or complicity, rather, p.1146), or of Marie's suggestion of marriage (p.1156). They have come to the 'absurdist' view of life, but refuse to go further, to seek or create values which will confer meaning. Clamence says quite explicitly:

---

40   p.1483. 'Dream, Monsieur, cheap dream, a trip to the Indies! These persons perfume themselves with spices. You go in, they draw the curtains and the navigation begins. The gods come down on the naked bodies and the islands are set adrift', *Fall*, pp.13–14.
41   p.1519. 'I have never been really able to believe that human affairs were serious matters', *Fall*, p.64.

> Au fond, rien ne comptait. Guerre, suicide, amour, misère, j'y prêtais attention, bien sûr, quand les circonstances m'y forçaient, mais d'une manière courtoise et superficielle.[42]

Meursault and Clamence illustrate two responses to the 'absurdist' view of existence which Camus defines and rejects in his essay in defence of *L'Homme révolté*: there are those, he says, who, starting from this 'zero point', seek solace in dreams of innocence, and those who take the opposite path:

> Les uns se nourrissant des rêves d'une confortable innocence [...] les autres [...] s'enfonçant vers la servitude et la mort, jansénistes sans dieu qui restaurent le péché généralisé sans le compenser par la grâce.[43]

In one sense (to use a phrase both Meursault and Clamence love), their disengagement is a refusal to wager, as Pascal would say, to confer importance on this rather than on that, and thus to bestow meaning on one's own life. Meursault adopts an attitude of indifference, Clamence chooses play-acting. But you have to wager, says Pascal, there is no avoiding it, a refusal to choose is in itself a choice. Camus (Sartre too, of course), agrees that each serious player must place his bet. Clamence is a player of a different sort, one for whom life is a grimly ironic game and all the world a stage. 'Jean-Baptiste Clamence, *comédien*' is what the 'judge-penitent' would put on his visiting cards (p.1500). Life for him has been a show in which he has awarded himself the star role, for the pleasure of admiring his own performance. Meursault, on the other hand, knows that one must never play-act ('il ne faut jamais jouer', p.1182), but, thanks to his passivity, he becomes the plaything of circumstances, allowing himself to be embroiled in the affair of Sintès and his Arab mistress.

---

42 pp.1500–1. 'Fundamentally nothing mattered. War, suicide, love, poverty got my attention of course, when circumstances forced me, but a courteous, superficial attention', *Fall*, p.38.
43 'Défense de *L'Homme révolté*', in *Essais*, p.1714. 'Some taking refuge in dreams of a comfortable innocence [...] others [...] sinking towards servitude and death, Jansenists without God, who reinstate a general state of sinfulness without the compensating notion of grace.'

Meursault, the child of sun and sea, kills a man because he is blinded by too much light, and knows that he has shattered 'l'équilibre du jour, le silence exceptionnel d'une plage où j'avais été heureux.'[44] In the darkness of a fine Parisian night, on the Pont des Arts, Clamence, the man about town, hears laughter which puts and end to the partying where he had been happy, 'la fête où j'avais été heureux' (p.1491). Later he remarks that it was then that it all started: 'Oui, je crois bien que c'est alors que tout commença' (p.1497), echoing Meursault's melancholy statement:

> La gâchette a cédé, j'ai touché le ventre poli de la crosse, et c'est là, dans le bruit à la fois sec et assourdissant, que *tout a commencé.* [45]

They have both stumbled across a frontier and exiled themselves from the country of innocence.

It is with the heart that Meursault and Clamence recognise the loss of their happiness. As the critic Charles Baudouin has observed, the 'Pascalian heart' is first and foremost a 'purely intuitive way of knowing' ('une intuition purement connaissante', p.37). From the moment of recognition, these Pascalian pilgrims search, *en gémissant*, for the truth about themselves and the lives they have led. Clamence puts it as follows:

> À partir du soir où j'ai été appelé, car j'ai été appelé réellement, j'ai dû répondre ou du moins chercher la réponse.[46]

The laughter that he heard 'coming from nowhere, unless from the water' ('venu de nulle part, sinon des eaux', p.1495), is the laughter of Truth herself, for, says Pascal, citing Tertullien,

---

44   p.1168. 'I realized that I'd destroyed the balance of the day and the perfect silence of this beach where I'd been happy', *OS*, p.60.
45   p.1168 (my italics). 'The trigger gave, I felt the underside of the polished butt and it was there, in that sharp but deafening noise, *that it all started*', *OS*, p.60 (my italics).
46   p.1518. 'From the evening when I was called – for I was really called – I had to answer or at least seek an answer', *Fall*, p.62.

> It is Truth who has the right to laugh, because she is joyful, and to mock her enemies, for her victory is assured. (*Pasc.*, *Lettres Provinciales*, p.782, tr.)

Clamence has, until that point, been the enemy of truth, the personification of the self-centred ego, the *amour-propre*, whose nature is 'to love only itself and to consider no other than itself', as Pascal puts it (p.1125 tr.), or again: 'Man is nothing but deception, untruth and hypocrisy [...] He doesn't want to be told the truth' (p.1123 tr.).

The laugh which Clamence hears belongs to the essentially fraternal order, as Meursault would say, which underlies and sustains the natural world. It comes from the water, the life-giving element. It is an extraneous affirmation of optimism in this profoundly pessimistic monologue. Clamence says that 'il n'avait rien de mystérieux, c'était un bon rire, naturel, presque amical, qui remettait les choses en place',[47] but he reacts badly. Refusing the call of the sympathetic laughter, he throws himself into the opposite camp, that of the gibe and the jeer. To forestall the laugh, he hits upon the idea of wholeheartedly making mock of everything: 'Pour prévenir le rire, je m'imaginai donc de me jeter dans la dérision générale' (p.1522). He must admit that his efforts do not succeed in stripping the laugh of a certain good-natured kindliness which he finds *painful* ('ce qu'il avait de bienviellant, de presque tendre, et qui me faisait mal', p.1524). He declines to take truth seriously, it is a 'colossal bore' ('Mais la vérité, cher ami, est assommante', p.1527). Truth bores him because he refuses its complexity, the oppositions it contains, the greatness as well as the wretchedness of human nature, and he reduces all to one or other of these extremes. After having congratulated himself on his own excellent character and motivations, Clamence now condemns himself, as we have seen, as no more that a 'salacious ape'. We may recall Pascal's well-known aphorism: 'He who tries to act the angel finishes by acting the beast' ('Qui veut faire l'ange fait la bête').

Meursault too had heard a voice, not laughing, but singing: the voice of the Arab's flute with its three notes, the expression of a harmony with the natural world which he had been seeking and which he

---

47 p.1495. 'There was nothing mysterious about that laugh; it was a good, hearty, almost friendly laugh, which put everything properly in its place', *Fall*, p.30.

destroys. The death of the Arab is the pivotal experience for Meursault, as is the suicide of the young woman in the Seine for Clamence. Meursault's act, Clamence's failure to act, each is irreparable and life-changing. Clamence, like Meursault, must recognise that there is no way out, *il n'y a pas d'issue*, and that every choice, negative or positive, is laden with consequences:

> Supposez, après tout, que quelqu'un se jette à l'eau. De deux choses l'une, ou vous l'y suivez pour le repêcher et, dans la saison froide, vous risquez le pire! Ou vous l'y abandonnez et les plongeons rentrés laissent parfois d'étranges courbatures![48]

The dive not taken becomes the irremediable Fall.

There is no way of opting out. It is not possible to refuse to choose a path to follow, each choice entailing what Camus would call a *style de vie*. Three options are available: the Pascalian wager (choosing God), wagering on Power (Clamence's choice), or placing one's faith in essential human goodness and fraternity (this is the choice of Rieux and Tarrou). Meursault, at the end of *L'Étranger*, has yet to make this ultimate wager, to choose fraternity, nevertheless he has in fact elected to put his faith in the life-affirming qualities of innocence and happiness. Clamence, on the othe hand, stakes all his intellectual and moral capital on human culpability, focussing not on life but on death. Everything in his world is death-directed. Holland is a 'negative landscape', its dunes are 'piles of ashes', its shores pallid also, its seas pale as a corpse, the dike which must keep out these death-dealing waters is a grey line against a colourless sky.[49]

This grey, comfortless world is nothing but a vast concentration camp, all who inhabit it are to be considered guilty, degenerate beings with no hope of mercy or pardon. There is no forgiveness in such a

---

48 p.1483. 'Suppose, after all, that someone should jump in the water. One of two things – either you follow suit to fish him out and, in cold weather, that's taking a great risk! Or you forsake him there and to suppress a dive sometimes leaves one strangely aching!' *Fall*, p.13.

49 p.1512: '[...] le plus beau des paysages négatifs! [...] ce tas de cendres qu'on appelle ici une dune, la digue grise à notre droite, la grève livide à nos pieds [...] le vaste ciel où se reflètent les eaux blêmes.'

universe. The waters which surround Clamence are not those of life, but of death, full of the corpses of those who have fallen, the young woman drowned in the Seine (and that, fittingly, on a dark, damp November night, the ecclesiastical month of the dead), the debris floating on an iron-grey ocean (p.1530). People are immersed in this 'gigantic holy water font' ('ce bénitier immense', p.1531), not to be blessed, but to drown, like the dead leaves 'macerating' in the stagnant waters of the canal (p.1497). Christ himself is culpable. God no longer dies to save men, it is the Holy Innocents of Bethlehem who die in His place (p.1533).

Innocence is slaughtered in our world, and no Saviour presents himself at the Jordan for baptism, the heavenly doves find no head on which to alight.[50] No harbingers of divine grace, no iconic manifestations of the Holy Spirit wheel in the grey skies above us, nothing but commonplace seagulls, mournfully calling us to who knows what dire destiny.[51] Even the driven snow, the ultimate symbol of grace, of purity, of innocence restored, will turn to filthy sludge as soon as the city awakes,[52] for here purity has no place, neither do truth or justice. Pascal had told us that wisdom is neither in the pursuit of riches, nor even in intellectual pursuits, but in the search for *justice*.[53] But where is justice? The Just Judges of Van Eyck's Ghent altarpiece, on their way to adore the Saviour, the Lamb of God, will never find Him, for 'il n'y a plus d'agneau, ni d'innocence'.[54] Clamence's vision is not the well-ordered city of the Adoration of the Lamb, but this hell of the concentration camps. He had warned his interlocutor from the very beginning:

---

50 '[…] nulle tête où se poser.' p.1513. See Matthew, III, v.16: 'And Jesus, when he was baptized, went up straightway out of the water, and […] he saw the Spirit of God descending like a dove, and lighting upon him.'
51 p.1531. 'Écoutez! N'entendez-vous pas les cris de goélands invisibles? S'ils crient vers nous, à quoi donc nous appellent-ils?'
52 p.1550. 'Regardez, la neige tombe! […] Amsterdam endormie dans la nuit blanche […] ce sera la pureté, fugitive, avant la boue de demain.'
53 *Pasc.* p.1303: 'Il y a trois ordres de choses: la chair, l'esprit, la volonté. Les charnels sont les riches, les rois: ils ont pour objet le corps. Les curieux et les savants: ils ont pour objet l'esprit. Les sages: ils ont pour objet la justice.'
54 p.1542. 'There is no lamb or innocence any longer', *Fall*, p.95.

> Moi, j'habite le quartier juif, ou ce qui s'appelait ainsi jusqu'au moment où nos frères hitlériens y ont fait de la place. Quel lessivage! Soixante-quinze mille juifs déportés ou assassinés [...] j'habite sur les lieux d'un des plus grands crimes de l'histoire.[55]

Liquidation, purging, ethnic cleansing, to employ the hideous metaphors and euphemisms of our times, these bloodbaths are history's monstrous version of the evangelist's metaphor of 'washing clean in the Blood of the Lamb'.

Innocence restored and triumphant, this is the message of the Van Eyck polyptych. Clamence longs for such a redemption:

> Alors, la seule utilité de Dieu serait de garantir l'innocence et je verrais plutôt la religion comme une grande entreprise de blanchissage, ce qu'elle a été d'ailleurs, mais brièvement, pendant trois ans tout juste, et elle ne s'appelait pas religion.[56]

Clamence can see no other use for God, supposing He existed, than to renew our innocence, to provide a sort of spiritual laundry, washing away the stains of culpability and abolishing guilt. Suddenly we discover a deep yearning in the cynical Clamence for a state of prelapsarian innocence restored, for the message of a Christ who personifies human compassion, a Christ who accepts death because he cannot bear to know that others (the infants of Bethlehem) have died in his place, a Christ who dies despairing of the Almighty, a humanist's Christ. A Christ who is himself moreover the supreme victim of injustice, not only in his condemnation to death, but because his message has been taken over and distorted by those who claim to act in his name, who practice what Clamence, echoing Don Juan (and is there not a strange bond between Clamence and Don Juan?) regards as the cold virtue of charity instead of the noble quality of *générosité*:

---

55   p.1481. 'I live in the Jewish quarter, or what was called so until our Hitlerian brethren spaced it out a bit. What a clean-up! Seventy-five thousand Jews deported or assassinated [...] I am living on the site of one of the greatest crimes in history', *Fall*, p.10.

56   p.1532. 'God's sole usefulness would be to guarantee innocence, and I am inclined to see religion rather as a huge laundering venture – as it was once, but briefly, for exactly three years, and it wasn't called religion', *Fall*, p.82.

> Trop de gens grimpent maintenant sur la croix seulement pour qu'on les voie de plus loin [...] Trop de gens ont décidé de se passer de la générosité pour pratiquer la charité.[57]

'Christ will be in agony until the end of the world', Pascal wrote, seeing Christ in Gethsemani bearing the weight of the sins and suffering of the whole human race, past, present and to come. Clamence's Christ is also in agony, but an agony of despair: *My God, my God, why have you forsaken me?*. This is the Christ for whom Clamence, the non-believer, 'absolutely not a Christian' ('pas chrétien pour un sou', p.1545), makes an astounding confession of devotion:

> Et lui n'était pas surhumain [...] Il a crié son agonie et c'est pourquoi je l'aime, *mon ami*, qui est mort sans savoir.[58]

Since those brief three years of mercy and innocence restored, however, the false judges have been installed in the very sanctuary itself, for the copy of Van Eyck's painting in the cathedral of Ghent cannot be distinguished from the original, and the authentic Just Judges are locked up in Clamence's cupboard, inaccessible and powerless (p.1542). Pascal too had warned that our justice is no justice, that there is only 'counterfeit' justice which we put in the place of the authentic. In *La Chute*, the allegorism is clear: established religion, the Church, has betrayed the message of Christ and no longer reflects the true face of justice. In his sympathy for the person of Christ and his criticism of the Church, Clamence is unmistakably the *alter Camus*.

True justice would be the triumph of innocence, the life-giving and purifying waters of forgiveness, in a word, clemency. Critics have seen in Clamence's name an echo of the epithet of John the Baptist: *vox clamans in deserto*, but is it not equally an ironic mutilation of *clémence*, clemency? Clamence has no time for clemency or pardon:

---

57   p.1534. 'But too many people now climb on to the cross merely to be seen from a greater distance [...] Too many people have decided to do without generosity in order to practice charity', *Fall*, p.84.

58   p.1534 (my italics). 'And he was not superhuman [...] He cried aloud his agony and that's why I love him, *my friend* who died without knowing', *Fall*, p.84 (my italics).

> Pas d'excuses, jamais, pour personne [...] Je nie la bonne intention, l'erreur estimable, le faux pas, la circonstance atténuante.

Is this moral absolutism perhaps a parody of Pascal's *Lettres Provinciales* excoriating the Jesuits, whose art of casuistry was essentially the judgement of cases according to circumstance? 'With me', continues Clamence,

> on ne bénit pas, on ne distribue pas d'absolution. [...] Je suis donc pour toute théorie qui refuse l'innocence à l'homme et pour toute pratique qui le traite en coupable. Vous voyez en moi, très cher, un partisan éclairé de la servitude.[59]

For Pascal, balance is in the tension of opposite truths. Man is a mixture of sublime and grime, a 'mélange d'esprit et de boue' (*Pasc.* p.1111, note), and therefore 'true religion would have to teach both human grandeur and human wretchedness, self-esteem and contempt for the self' (*Pasc.* p.1204, tr.). The stark contemplation of our wretchedness leads to despair, whilst the unrestrained sentiment of human grandeur leads to overweening pride (*Pasc.* p.1103), the sin by which Lucifer fell. So, in the moral sphere, man is suspended between infinite Pride and infinite Despair, the two Hells of our existence. Pride is contempt for others, it begets dictatorships, tyrannies, concentration camps, for in the end it consists in making oneself God, placing oneself upon a throne above the kingdoms of the world, just as Clamence, the lover of heights, dreams of towering, Lucifer-like, over land and sea from the summit of Etna (p.1498). But the paradox is that his pride, after his Fall, is in fact a form of despair. Clamence's madness is born of a radical loss of hope, leading to self-destruction. 'Mon héros est découragé en effet', Camus said in an interview, 'et c'est pourquoi il exalte, en bon nihiliste moderne, la servitude.'[60]

---

59 p.1543. 'No excuses ever, for anyone [...] I deny the good intention, the respectable mistake, the indiscretion, the extenuating circumstance. With me there is no giving of absolution or blessing. [...] I am for any theory that refuses to grant man innocence and for any practice that treats him as guilty. You see in me, *très cher*, an enlightened advocate of slavery', *Fall*, pp.96–7.

60 Interview with Brisville, see *Essais*, p.1923. 'My hero is indeed discouraged. That is why, like any good modern nihilist, he exalts servitude.'

Clamence experiences his nothingness in all its horror that evening when he realises that he has no real friends, nobody whom he could 'punish' by doing away with himself, since nobody would really care (p.1513). In the total absence of fraternity, suicide itself is futile, his self-destruction as meaningless as all else. Relationships of friendship, of equality, having ceased to exist, the only possible route to reaffirmation of the Self is the Hegelian Master-Slave paradigm. Only in domination can Clamence impinge upon the life of the Other, thus reasserting his value in his own eyes.

Is the seed of Clamence's utter despair sown only on that night of the young woman's suicide in Paris? In our final encounter with him, fevered and unable to rise from his bed, he makes a revelation which illuminates his whole history retrospectively: he has been a prisoner in a Nazi detention camp in North Africa. In jottings in the *Carnets* in the autumn of 1954, clearly prefiguring themes incorporated in *La Chute*, Camus pens the idea which would become the story of Clamence's 'papal' episode in a *camp de concentration*.[61] Clamence is therefore not a simple prisoner of war, but a detainee in the *univers concentrationnaire*, a place of desolation, suffering, humiliation, exhaustion, and death from thirst. Where else, after this experience of hell, should he choose to live but in that bleak urban hell configured in the concentric canals of Amsterdam, and precisely on the site of 'one of the greatest crimes in history'? What else but the inhumanity of the camp and the raw struggle for survival can have made authentic and equal relationships with his fellow men (or women) for ever unattainable?

'How does one survive witnessing?' This, according to the critic Shoshana Felman (p.165), is the essential question in *La Chute*. For all his garrulousness, Clamence suffers from a terrible mutism, an inability to bear witness, to speak of what he has seen, until he is in fact *in extremis*, for we may suppose that, crazily 'happy fit to die!', delirious and alone, the bed he lies on is actually his deathbed. His strength has been ebbing in the course of these encounters, just as his feverish imaginings have increased. On the third day of the monologue, he

---

61 *Carnets III*, November 1954, p.132: 'Nouvelle. Les prisonniers d'un camp de concentration élisent un pape'.

admits that he feels out of sorts, that he is having some problem in speaking coherently and in breathing (p.1497). At the outset of the fourth day, he is fatigued and losing the thread of his conversations (p.1513). By the next day, he is too weak to rise from his bed, despite intermittent desires to do so. He is as if 'dans un linceul déjà' (p.1538; 'already in a shroud'). Death is the only adequate conclusion to this death-directed narrative. It is also, however, the moment of truth, as Clamence sardonically admits:

> Une crainte ridicule me poursuivait en effet: on ne pouvait mourir sans avoir avoué tous ses mensonges. [...] Autrement, et n'y eût-il qu'un seul mensonge de caché dans une vie, la mort le rendit définitif.[62]

He cannot die without a deathbed confession, an avowal of that moment of total abasement when he had taken the glass of water from a dying fellow-prisoner and drunk it.

When did this North African episode take place in the story of Clamence's life? Before or after the Paris episodes? There are a number of manuscript and typescript versions of the text, showing how Camus constantly filled out, re-worked, and enriched the narrative. The paragraphs recounting Clamence's experience in the camp, and his election as 'pope', only make their appearance in the second manuscript and are thus part of the thematic enrichment of the novel, the bitterly satirical Paris episodes being anterior in inspiration. This of course cannot settle the question of the fictional chronology. Terry Keefe, in his discussion of the question, inclines to think that the glittering career comes first, in which case Clamence in his Paris glory days has indeed been no better and no worse than a run-of-the-mill, self-congratulatory, bourgeois attitudinizer. But if the prison camp comes first in the chronology of Clamence's biography, while coming last in the narrative sequence, all takes on a darker hue.

The narrative is contemporaneous with the date of writing, the year 1955, since in one typescript version, referring to his relations with women, Clamence is made to remark that he is 'neither Romeo

---

62 p.1521. 'A ridiculous fear pursued me, in fact. One could not die without having confessed all one's lies. [...] Otherwise, even if there were only one lie hidden in a life, death made it definitive', *Fall*, p.66.

nor group-captain Townsend', a reference of course to Princess Margaret's ill-fated affair at that time.[63] Clamence, like his interlocutor, is at this point forty-ish ('quadragénaire', p.1480). It is hardly possible that a man in his early 40s in 1955 could have enjoyed several years of a brilliant pre-war legal career. Why then, in all the description of those years in Paris devoted to the pursuit of success and pleasure, is there no trace of any reminiscence, of any psychological aftermath, of the harrowing sojourn in the concentration camp? Clamence confesses that, after the night of the mysterious laugh behind him on the Pont des Arts, he had to 'retrouve[r] la mémoire' and that this was a gradual process, for 'jusque là, j'avais toujours été aidé par un étonnant pouvoir d'oubli'.[64] What has he forgotten? Why this frenetic pursuit of pleasure and a life lived, as he says, superficially, 'à la surface de la vie' (p.1501)? Clearly he has deliberately decided to forget the incident of the dark November night when the young woman had thrown herself from the Pont Royal. He tells no one about it and avoids reading the newspapers in the days which follow (p.1511). But the canker is within, and two or three years later, on another bridge, he will hear the laughter which will oblige him to search his conscience.[65] What else has he been deliberately forgetting or hiding from himself?

If we accept that the Paris years fall into the post-war period, the episode in the concentration camp becomes the key to the whole narrative, a darkness at the core of every episode, a memory and a culpability deliberately buried and ignored in Clamence's subconscious. It underlies the obsession with death, the insistent recall of the Holocaust in the very first encounter, the choice of the old Jewish quarter as Clamence's abode in Amsterdam, the savage Swiftian irony of the atrocity stories: the polite German officer who asks an elderly mother to choose which of her two sons to send to the firing squad, the pacifist butchered by the collaborationist French 'militia' (p.1481). It is

---

63 See Quilliot, p.2023, note to p.1505.
64 p.1500. 'First I had to recover my memory [...] Until then, I had always been aided by an extraordinary ability to forget', *Fall*, pp.37–8.
65 p.1511 (my italics): 'Cette nuit-là, en novembre, *deux ou trois ans avant le soir où je crus entendre rire* dans mon dos, je regagnais la rive gauche, et mon domicile, par le Pont Royal.'

the root of the cynicism and despair regarding friendship, human goodness, fraternity, reason itself. Clamence, the 'Cartesian Frenchman' ('le Français cartésien que je suis', p.1515), descends into delirious dreams of domination, just as Descartes's house in Amsterdam has become, in this age of murderous unreason, a lunatic asylum.[66] The shadow of the events in the camp threatens the sunlight of the Parisian years, the 'Eden', the glittering scene over which Clamence had reigned in his heyday (p.1489). Clamence, the survivor of the camp, has no right to be in Eden, he is Adam after the Fall. Hence all in him is agitation, and rotting at the core:

> J'allais de fête en fête [...] Je courais ainsi, toujours comblé, jamais rassasié, sans savoir où m'arrêter, jusqu'au jour où, jusqu'au soir plutôt où la musique s'est arrêtée, les lumières se sont éteintes.[67]

The few paragraphs of the concentration camp story contain the secret of Clamence's spiritual and psychological disaster, for it is in drinking not the water of life, but the water of another's death, the glass allocated to a dying comrade, that he has learnt the secret of the birth of tyrannies, whether of Church or State, 'les empires et les églises' (p.1541), the terrible preference of the Self in the last resort. No doubt this incident is the original sin which has destroyed his self-esteem and for which he cannot forgive himself. We get surprising glimpses every now and then of a pre-concentration camp Clamence capable of faithful friendship,[68] of affection, even of forgiving, as in his semi-burlesque anecdote of the dog in the Paris metro, which deserts him to go off after a German soldier. His comment on the episode is both unexpected and revealing: he loves dogs because 'they

---

66 See p.1535. Several critics have commented on this point. See, for example, Jones, 1980, p.56; Lévi-Valensi, 1970b, p.48.
67 pp.1490–1. 'I went from festivity to festivity [...] I ran on like that, always heaped with favours, never satiated, without knowing where to stop, until the day – until the evening rather when the music stopped and the lights went out', *Fall*, p.24.
68 See p.1492, the story of the dying friend whom Clamence visits every day until the end. The story is told in ironic mode, but the self-irony is retrospective and should not invalidate the authenticity of the friendship. As usual with Clamence, it is hard to disentangle truth from irony.

always forgive' ('Je les aime parce qu'ils pardonnent toujours', p.1538). No longer being able to forgive himself, Clamence now can forgive no-one.

The paradox is that it is precisely in the concentration camp that Clamence should have learned never to despair of the human spirit. In this spiritual and physical desert, where life-giving water is denied to body and soul, another prophet arises, not a latter-day John the Baptist preaching penance, but a frail knight-errant seeking to keep alive the spirit of fraternity, 'la communauté de nos souffrances' (p.1540), in the midst of the greatest adversity. Clamence gives him the nickname 'Du Guesclin', after the *perfect gentle* knight of France's history, the paragon of courage and generosity. In Van Eyck's altarpiece, it is the knights, under the banner of Saint George, who lead on the Just Judges, because their true role is to be the champions and defenders of Justice.

This new Du Guesclin, deeply religious ('un jeune Français, qui avait la foi', p.1539), while bitterly condemning a Church which has failed its Founder, is Camus's model of what a follower of Christ should be, the champion of the poor and the oppressed, sharing their suffering and deprivations. His inspiration for this figure is unmistakably the brilliant young Jewish philosopher Simone Weil, who died in London in 1943, at the age of thirty-four, while working for the Resistance. Camus had discovered and promoted her writings as early as 1949. Very close to Catholicism, she never actually converted, unwilling to abandon her solidarity with the Jewish people. Her early death from tuberculosis was hastened by overwork and malnutrition, as she refused to eat anything more than the scanty official rations of the population in occupied France, just as, in her earlier years of social activism on behalf of the workers (with all her intellectual qualifications, she had chosen to work on the factory floor), she had refused to eat better than her fellow-workers on outdoor relief. In like manner, Du Guesclin perishes in the camp, because he 'deprived himself too much' ('il se privait trop', p.1541). He has a precursor in the novel, the man Clamence has heard of (and significantly not actually met), who slept on the bare floorboards in order to share the hardships of his friend in prison (p.1491), clearly another avatar of Simone Weil.

This young prisoner is the only fellow-being whom Clamence has loved, the one for whom he would have resisted the temptation to love himself more than his neighbour. Christ, 'my friend', lives again in Du Guesclin. In the living hell of the concentration camp, his bare torso covered in sweat, and his ribs visible in his emaciated body, he demands that the prisoners should choose someone complete with all his faults and virtues ('un homme complet, avec ses défauts et ses vertus'), but one who will keep alive, in himself and in all of them, the vital community of suffering humanity.[69] This will be the new 'Pope', who will share the life of the unfortunate instead of praying on his throne ('Il nous déclarait qu'il fallait un nouveau pape qui vécût parmi les malheureux, au lieu de prier sur un trône'). It is Clamence who is chosen as the new saint Peter, and having accepted the role almost as a joke, he takes it more and more seriously, fulfilling the function of 'group leader or secretary of a cell' ('chef de groupe ou secrétaire de cellule'). The analogy with the Resistance is clear.

We need not suppose that Du Guesclin has made a bad choice of 'Pope'. The standard Clamence sets for Christianity is high, perhaps indeed impossibly so. 'O l'injustice, l'injustice qu'on lui a faite et qui me serre le coeur!'[70] is his impassioned indictment of the betrayal of Christ's mission. In the camp, he still answers well enough to the required profile of 'a complete man, with all his faults and virtues', neither hero nor villain. It is the horror of the camp, together with his own failure, his shameful memory of taking the water from the dying comrade, that turn him into what Camus calls a 'nihilist', but his very indignation is akin to that *saeva indignatio* which lacerated the breast of Jonathan Swift. What he excoriates is the hypocrisy of the modern industrial and commercial world (the eighteenth-century slave-trader was at least honest about his trade),[71] together with every kind of pretentiousness, and, above all, the horrors of war, tyranny, and injustice. To the end, he has the nostalgia of a state of innocence, which for him

---

69   All the quotations in this paragraph are from p.1540. See *Fall*, pp.92–3.
70   p.1534. 'Oh the injustice, the rank injustice that has been done him! It wrings my heart!' *Fall*, p.84.
71   See p.1498: 'Une enseigne. La maison appartenait à un vendeur d'esclaves. Ah! on ne cachait pas son jeu, en ce temps-là!'

had been the wonder of the theatre and the joy of the football matches in a crowded stadium on a Sunday afternoon. These reminders of his (and Camus's) youth, are, he says, 'the only places in the world' where he feels innocent.[72] Beyond the dismal waters surrounding Amsterdam, the isles of Greece are a shimmering mirage, an innocent and unattainable Eden:

> Avant de nous présenter dans les îles grecques, il faudrait nous laver longuement. L'air y est chaste, la mer et la jouissance claires.[73]

There has been no counterbalance in Clamence's life to the horror of the concentration camp, no mother-figure can be discerned, as in the case of Meursault, Rieux, or Tarrou, and friendship has perished in the concentration camp with the death of 'Du Guesclin'. He seeks to fill the void with the frenzy of the Paris years, the sexual adventures, the pursuit of pleasure and success. Truth laughs at his foolishness, but he abandons one route to self-destruction only to embark upon another, the misanthropy, the crazed dream of domination, the self-hatred and refusal to forgive himself or others, in spite of the one lesson he has learnt from his own failure as 'Pope', namely that after all we must forgive. It is not so easy to be Pope, not so easy to be a human being.

Clamence, who is convinced that 'nous avons perdu la lumière, les matins, la sainte innocence de celui qui se pardonne à lui-même',[74] sees no hope and no salvation. We cannot leave the last word to him, for his is the voice of despair. He takes leave of us with a challenge: who will dive into the freezing river to save the drowning girl? It is too late, always too late, Clamence cries derisively. But the answer is that it is only in throwing ourselves into the water, to save ourselves as

---

72 See p.1520: 'Maintenant encore, les matches du dimanche, dans un stade plein à craquer, et le théâtre, que j'ai aimé avec une passion sans égale, sont les seuls endroits du monde où je me sente innocent.'
73 pp.1525–6. 'Before appearing in the Greek islands, we should have to wash at length. There the air is chaste, the sea and sensual enjoyment transparent', *Fall*, p.73.
74 p.1550. 'Yes, we have lost track of the light, the mornings, the holy innocence of those who forgive themselves', *Fall*, p.106.

well as the young woman, that we can establish on earth a community in place of a concentration camp. Du Guesclin is dead. But his choice of 'papal' nominee is not in short supply, and will perhaps strive as heroically as he in the hour of need, the complete human being 'with his [or her] faults and virtues'. Happily.

Chapter V
The Landscapes of Solitude. *L'Exil et le Royaume*

> *Tout mon royaume est de ce monde.*
> Camus, 'L'Envers et l'endroit'
>
> *Un paysage quelconque est un état de l'âme.*
> H.-F. Amiel, *Fragments d'un journal intime*
>
> *Être pur, c'est retrouver cette patrie de l'âme où devient sensible la parenté du monde.*
> Camus, 'L'Été à Alger'

Lonely Sisyphus walks down the mountain filled with a 'silent joy' (*Essais*, p.197). He is innocent and he is happy. For the moment he is free of his burden, and life is a privilege. However, the stones which weigh heavily upon the protagonists of the short narratives of *L'Exil et le Royaume* are not the dreary daily toil from which Patrice Mersault had escaped or which Meursault had accepted, nor the plague-soaked atmosphere of Oran, nor even the manic guilt obsession of Clamence, but the terrible burden of inner loneliness, of the loss of that harmony between man and nature, that atmosphere of human warmth, of easy friendships, which youthfulness regards as a birthright. Camus wrote in 1948:

> Je suis né pauvre, sous un ciel heureux, dans une nature avec laquelle on sent un accord, non une hostilité. Je n'ai donc pas commencé par le déchirement, mais par la plénitude.[1]

For the fortunate so blessed, it is in later life that early rapture meets the shock of rupture. The simple harmony between Sisyphus

---

[1] Interview published in the *Revue du Caire*, in 1948, *Essais*, p.380. 'I was born poor, beneath a happy sky, into a natural world with which one feels harmony, not hostility. So I didn't start out in distress and division, but in plenitude.'

and his existence, his tranquil stoicism, becomes, during the years of toiling up the mountain and reflecting on the human experience on the way down, more troubled, more questioning, the certainty of man's total innocence begins to crumble. For Camus's generation, the dark years of the war, the Occupation, the concentration camps, had made faith in an innocent humanity something of an heroic virtue. 'Nous nous refusons de désespérer de l'homme', he wrote in the journal *Combat* on 11 January 1945 ('We refuse to despair of mankind'). With the loss of innocence, the earthly paradise too fades away. The ecstatic afternoon of *Noces*, the shining strand of Chenoua, the sun-drenched beach on which Meursault meets Marie, give way to the stricken urban setting of *La Peste*, to the desolate concentric canals of a grey Amsterdam, and to the arid stony deserts of the high plateaux of southern Algeria.

The collection of short stories published under the title of *L'Exil et le Royaume* appeared in 1957. *La Chute*, published in 1956, had been originally conceived as one of this set of stories, some of which had been germinating in Camus's mind since 1952. The exact date of its inspiration, whether later or earlier than the other texts, is less important, as Peter Cryle points out (pp.29–30), than the fact that Camus chose to complete it first and offer it to the public in advance of the rest. The continuity of inspiration is evident, even from the choice of title, for Exile necessarily follows the guilt of the Fall. Each of the stories of *L'Exil et le Royaume* wrestles in its own way with the double challenge issued by Clamence, who proclaims that guilt is universal and irremediable, and that none of us is capable of reaching out to another in need. 'Point d'amour sans un peu d'innocence', Camus wrote in 1953, in 'Retour à Tipasa'.[2] But is anyone innocent? Who is capable of love for neighbour? 'O young woman, throw yourself into the water again so that I may a second time have the chance of saving both of us!' Is it too late? Will it always be too late?

'Exile' we are well acquainted with in Camus's earlier work, Sisyphus toiling up his mountain in Hades, Meursault the Outsider in the condemned cell, the claustrophobic world of *La Peste*, in which all

---

2   *Essais*, p.870. 'Love cannot exist without a little innocence', *SE*, p.149.

suffer 'un exil sans remède et [...] une soif jamais contentée',³ and most despairing of all, Clamence in Amsterdam. But what is the Kingdom? Does Sisyphus behold it as he walks down the mountain, Mersault find it on the beach at Chenoua? If so, can it be known only to the solitary, the Robinson Crusoes each in exile on his island paradise? Is it to be found anywhere outside certain luminous landscapes?

'Since Dostoyevsky, we look in vain for landscapes in great European literature', Camus more than once lamented.⁴ Critics have commented on the greater 'realism' in *L'Exil et le Royaume*, in the description of environment and character. However, the role of landscape in Camus's writing has a function reaching beyond the faithful representation of reality. Pierre-Henri Simon had remarked in 1962 that Amsterdam in *La Chute* is 'not a topography but a physical climate related to the spiritual climate' (p.144, tr.). Camus had protested in *Noces* that if there are landscapes which reflect moods, they are 'the most vulgar',⁵ affirming that the landscape is outside the individual and indifferent to him or her, nonetheless his landscapes reflect the tonality of the protagonist's perception of the world. Like the stage sets which were designed by Louis Miquel for the productions of the young Camus's theatre troupe *L'Équipe*, and which, as Patrick McCarthy writes, were 'not important as a lavish display nor as a realistic setting' but 'could be used freely to emphasize a mood or a theme' (1982, p.103), the landscape is a metaphor for the metaphysical and moral climate of these narratives. From *La Mort heureuse* to *Le Premier homme*, as at least one critic has pointed out, the initial realism of Camus's landscapes is transfigured by the oneiric imagery, the suspension of time, the alienating impressions of extreme heat or cold or light (see Abdelkrim, 1999, p.62). At this level, we enter a world outside time and place.

3   *Peste*, p.1466. 'Exile withour redress, thirst that was never slaked', *Plague*, p.288.
4   *Essais*, 'L'Exil d'Hélène', p.855: 'On cherche en vain les paysages dans la grande littérature européenne depuis Dostoïevski.' Also in *Essais*, 'Le Témoin de la liberté' (1948) p.403: 'Ce n'est pas un hasard si l'on ne trouve pas de paysages dans la grande littérature européenne depuis Dostoïevski.'
5   *Essais*, p.63. 'S'il est des paysages qui sont des états d'âme, ce sont les plus vulgaires.'

The landscapes to which we are introduced in three of the six stories of *L'Exil et le Royaume* are the desert and the high plateaux of the Algerian south, the setting for 'La Femme adultère' ('The Adulterous Woman'), followed by 'Le Rénégat' ('The Renegade') and 'L'Hôte' ('The Guest'). The maternal and purifying sea, baptising all into restored innocence, the element of joy and communion, in which all men are brothers, like Rieux and Tarrou, and in which lovers, like Meursault and Marie, find each other, is inaccessible in these narratives. Even Yvars, in 'Les Muets' ('The Silent Men'), as he cycles to work along the seafront in Algiers, does not see it, obliged as he is to keep his head down in order to avoid the tramway lines, symbolic of the tyranny of the world of work in which he is imprisoned.

With the exception of the cityscape of Algiers, and of Paris in the ironically humorous 'Jonas ou l'Artiste au travail' ('The Artist at Work'), these stories introduce the reader, from their very beginning, into a hostile world of ferocious Saharan winds, the freezing cold of the high plateaux in winter, the blazing midday inferno of the desert sun, and finally the impenetrably dark and mysterious Brazilian forest in 'La Pierre qui pousse' ('The Growing Stone'). Janine, the heroine of 'La Femme adultère', shivers in the rickety bus carrying her and her husband into the desert, unable to see through the windows because of the sandstorms beating against the panes. In 'L'Hôte', Daru, the idealistic schoolmaster living alone on the high desert plateaux, watches two approaching figures, one on a horse, the other following behind tied to a rope, struggling through the snow and rocks. In Paris, winter comes, the city turns grey and cold, as the artist Jonas sinks into the depths of an artistic and moral decline. These are the landscapes of an exile more unrelenting than Sisyphus' hillside. Is there in any of them a path to the Kingdom?

Camus's first title was *Nouvelles de l'exil* (*Tales from Exile*). The emphasis was not yet on the Kingdom. But the stories were planned from 1952, when he was in his fortieth year, which he described to Quilliot as 'a sort of turning-point in my work and my life'.[6] Already in 1950, he had in mind his 'third cycle', which was to move on from the Promethean 'cycle of revolt' to the myth of Nemesis, 'the goddess

---

6   See Quilliot's 'Présentation', *TRN*, p.2037.

of measure, fatal to all excess'. She is, in Camus's mythology, the goddess of balance, of harmony, and this third cycle was to represent, as he indicated later, the ultimate stage of the human odyssey, that of (fraternal) love.[7] When all have reached that destination, the Kingdom will have come. The duality of the published title can be seen as reflecting the moment when the spiral begins to swing upwards again, after the *Fall*, from the preoccupation with darkness, death and suffering, the *Envers* of our existence, towards the light, the Kingdom, where will be found again the simplicity and joy of the beginning, the *Endroit*. Camus had once written:

> Entre cet endroit et cet envers du monde, je ne veux pas choisir [...] Le grand courage, c'est encore de tenir les yeux ouverts sur la lumière comme sur la mort.[8]

Such solitary heroism belongs to youth. The heroism of maturity is in reaching out to others, and the focus of this pivotal collection strives towards that goal, moving from exile to the rediscovery of the Kingdom.

After Sisyphus, hero of the Absurd, and Prometheus, hero-patron of the 'Cycle of Revolt', it is perhaps ironic that this collection of stories should be seen as the link to the projected 'Cycle of Nemesis', the goddess of measure, 'fatal to all excess', at the very moment when Camus's beloved Algeria was sliding into the excesses of the terrible armed struggle for independence, a conflict which would cause him the greatest inner torment and division. The political situation lurks in the background of all the narratives set in Algeria, even D'Arrast's story can be interpreted as reflecting social relationships in a colonial context. Many critics have looked in depth at the underlying political implications of the texts, but here the focus will be on the significance of the title of the collection for each of the six short tales.

In the brief foreword which he wrote for the collection ('Prière d'insérer'), Camus declared that exile was the unifying theme of the

---

7   See *Carnets II*, p.328, also *Carnets III*, editor's footnote on p.78, and p.187.
8   *Essais*, p.49. 'I do not want to choose between these two sides of the world [...] Great courage still consists in gazing steadfastly at the light as on death', *SE*, p.64.

201

stories, and as for the Kingdom, 'Il coïncide avec une certaine vie libre et nue que nous avons à retrouver, pour renaître enfin.'[9] But only those who are able to refuse both 'servitude and possession' will enter. *Servitude* and *possession*, these take many forms, but can be summed up as enslavement to the false gods of power, ideologies and riches. Camus's language has unmistakeable religious resonances, and when looking for the significance of the title, critics have perhaps not sufficiently pondered the biblical overtones. The Kingdom of Heaven as defined by the theologians, is after all two things, not only the everlasting enjoyment of the 'Beatific Vision' of Divine perfection, but also the *communion of saints*, an all-inclusive community existing in perfect harmony. How can this be translated in Camus's man-centered universe? For him, the glory of the natural world is the divinity he worships, 'le monde dont je faisais ma divinité', as he put it in the preface to *L'Envers et l'Endroit* (*Essais*, p.6). It is at Tipasa that the gods speak to him,[10] that he enters into communion with the beauty of the world. But there is also the other communion, that with our fellow human beings, and for Camus, as for Tarrou, who had desired to be 'a saint without God', this can only be attained through a morality of *comprehension*, of fraternal understanding between ordinary mortals, with all their faults and failings. Camus wrote in his *Carnets* in 1950:

> Il arrive toujours un moment où les êtres cessent de lutter et de se déchirer, acceptent enfin de s'aimer selon ce qu'ils sont. C'est le royaume des cieux.[11]

From the loss of our early state of harmony with the world around us, our *plenitude*, through the vale of our exile from happiness, to the hope of fraternal communion, such is the progression of *L'Exil et le Royaume*.

---

9   p.2039. 'It coincides with a certain free and simple life which we need to rediscover in order to be reborn.'

10   *Essais*, 'Noces à Tipasa', p.55: 'Au printemps, Tipasa est habitée par les dieux et les dieux parlent dans le soleil et l'odeur des absinthes.'

11   *Carnets II*, p.323. 'There always comes a moment when human beings give up fighting and tearing each other apart, and agree at last to love each other just as they are. That is the kingdom of heaven.'

Communion is the purest form of love and 'love is impossible without a touch of innocence'. But what is the meaning of innocence? Are lucidity and will enough to avoid incurring guilt, spreading 'the microbe' which Tarrou had declared to be natural to us ('Ce qui est naturel, c'est le microbe', p.1426)? How are we to avoid making mistaken choices, in an 'absurd' world, ruled not by reason but by chance? We do not see clearly, but as Saint Paul said, through a glass, darkly. Ambiguity is everywhere in the bitterly ironic monologue of *La Chute*, including in the title, just as it is embedded in the titles of the narratives of *L'Exil et le Royaume*. In 'La Femme adultère' no adultery in the normal sense of the word takes place; 'The Guest' could be an alternative translation for 'The Host' as the French title, 'L'Hôte', has both meanings; the original title of 'L'Artiste au travail' was prefaced by the artist's name, *Jonas*, a teasing reference to the tale of Jonah and the whale, and 'The Growing Stone' is a puzzling enough phrase, but the French title, 'La Pierre qui pousse', is still more enigmatic, since it can signify either a stone which grows or a stone which pushes or impels. This initial ambiguity provides only an enigmatic key to the final ambiguities left for the reader to ponder.

The question raised each time is always the same: is there a way out of exile and into the Kingdom? The protagonist's success or failure can be gauged only through the decoding of signs which change constantly according to perspective and light. A relentless lucidity, grounded neither in the Candide-like optimism of the artist Jonas, nor in the cynical pessimism of Clamence, is as vital in the domain of human behaviour and relationships as in the understanding of the world around us. In the end, however, no interpretation is definitive. Language is only an imperfect transmitter from one island of the mind to another, even when complexity is not compounded by irony, subterfuge or confusion. The art of Kafka's fiction, Camus had written, is that it 'obliges the reader to re-read', the endings of the narratives always necessitating new readings from fresh perspectives.[12] So too with the stories of *L'Exil et le Royaume*. They also are 'a strange writing, whose meaning has to be deciphered', like the dark, motionless

---

12   *Essais*, 'L'Espoir et l'absurde dans l'œuvre de Franz Kafka.' See p.201.

silhouettes of the desert dromedaries which appear so mysterious to Janine, the heroine of 'La Femme adultère'.[13]

Lucidity takes the form, in this collection of stories, of more constant attention to physical detail, to precise time-sequences, to the description of setting and personality, Critics have called this a greater 'realism', compared to the previous fiction. In 1954, in a preface to the collected works of Roger Martin du Gard, Camus expressed his admiration for the author's portrayal of character and expressed the desire to learn 'les secrets d'un art universal qui [...] ressusciterait les personnages dans leur chair et leur durée'.[14] He would have quibbled at the term 'realism',[15] having declared himself (as already noted in our Introduction) 'indifferent' to 'psychology, at any rate ingenious anecdotes and intriguing situations'. We should remember that he is there speaking as the author of his play, *Les Justes*, and expressing his conviction that great drama must represent not the minutiae of individual lives, but 'all of human destiny in its simplicity and its greatness'.[16] So too, for all the greater 'realism', the protagonists of *L'Exil et le Royaume* have not ceased to be representative of each of us in our human condition, hence every text is nourished with the symbols of innocence or guilt, suffering and exile, the heart's desire and the longed-for kingdom.

The first of the stories is 'La Femme adultère', the only text in which the major protagonist is a woman. The unhappy young girl of *La Chute*, who had drowned in the Seine, is now relayed by a woman in her forties living a life of quiet desperation, having married out of fear of solitude, age and death. Janine too had once been a bright young girl, straight and supple like the palm trees which herald the

---

13 The silhouettes of the dromedaries in the desert form 'les signes sombres d'une étrange écriture dont il fallait déchiffrer le sens', p.1569.
14 Camus's preface to the Pléiade edition of Roger Martin du Gard's *Œuvres complètes*, quoted Cryle, p.34. See Cryle, pp. 30–4. 'The secrets of a universal art which [...] would resurrect the characters in the flesh and in their span of life.'
15 In 1942, answering criticisms of *L'Étranger*, he had declared that the term was meaningless, 'vide de sens'. See *Carnets II*, p.32.
16 *TRN*, p.1835. Quoted already in our Introduction, note 19.

oasis village where she arrives one bitterly cold early morning,[17] with Marcel, her dullard of a husband, at the end of a wintry journey across the high stony plateaux of the south Algerian desert. At each stage of the story, as Peter Dunwoodie points out (p.32), the desert landscapes reflect the heroine's soulscape.

The opening paragraph of the narrative, describing the weary and futile circlings of a fly trapped in the rickety bus jolting along an endless bumpy road, evokes Janine's own dreary daily round. She is Sisyphus in female form, trudging round and round the same beaten path day after pointless day, never knowing the exhilaration of the mountain top, but caught instead in the same imprisoning circles which for Clamence had been the concentric canals of Amsterdam. Janine should not be written off as mediocre or unintelligent. She is of finer stuff than her husband. Marcel's limitations are encoded in his physical description in the opening paragraph: the low forehead, the coarse nose, the unlovely mouth, the fleshy hands, the heavily slumped body and inelegantly sprawling legs, the vacant bulbous eyes. Janine, however, tall and well-built rather than heavy, is still attractive enough, with her clear eyes and child-like face,[18] to catch the attention of the French soldier in the neighbouring seat. When, in the hotel, Marcel, tucking into his pork, grunts that it is forbidden in the Koran only through ignorance of good *cuisine*, his wife's silence possibly conceals a reflection on 'cette victoire des cuisiniers sur les prophètes'.[19] A certain ironic intelligence may be lurking behind the clear eyes.

Janine and Marcel are each trapped in their own solitude, unrelieved by the presence of children, and exiled in an alien world with which they cannot communicate. They too are strangers. Neither of them speaks a word of Arabic. Silence surrounds them. Not even the French soldier on the bus, who shows a passing interest in Janine, utters a word, and with his long, pointy face he resembles nothing so much as a cunning jackal (see p.1561). He thus offers no reassurance

---

17 p.1565: 'Elle rêvait aux palmiers droits et flexibles, et à la jeune fille qu'elle avait été.'
18 p.1561: 'Elle n'était pas si grosse, grande et pleine plutôt, charnelle, et encore désirable – avec son visage un peu enfantin, ses yeux frais et clairs.'
19 p.1565. 'That victory of the cooks over the prophets', *Exile*, p.17.

of the familiar, but contributes to the impression of alienation. In the bleak hotel, Janine is aware only of 'sa solitude, et le froid qui la pénétrait, et un poids plus lourd à l'endroit du coeur'.[20]

The insistence throughout the *récit* is on silence and isolation, the mysterious immensity of the desert landscape, the unknowability of its inhabitants. The implications are not political, but metaphysical, for the Kingdom is not of this world. In these early days of the Algerian fight for independence, Camus had no wish, in any case, to write a tract providing ammunition for one side or the other. Camus wrote to the young Jean Sénac on 10 February 1957, that he had decided to say nothing about Algeria, so as neither to add to the misery of the country nor to the nonsense written about it (the letter was probably never sent. See Nacer Khodja, p.155). Marcel is portrayed as narrow in his outlook, nonetheless he lives in modest circumstances in a mixed Franco-Arab district of Algiers, and Camus toned down utterances with racist overtones.[21]

The silent Arabs on the bus, who, unlike Janine and her husband, carry no luggage, the motionless shepherds by the wayside, noble and timeless in their ragged attire, only their eyes visible beneath the burnous, these are they who lead the 'free and simple life' which Camus had declared to be the way to the Kingdom. Arab pride is embodied in the tall, gloved, aquiline-faced figure sweeping arrogantly past Marcel in the street (p.1568). The supreme icons of freedom and nobility are the desert nomads whose tents Janine glimpses from the high terrace of the fort which she visits with her husband in the afternoon:

> Depuis toujours, sur la terre sèche, raclée jusqu'aux os, de ce pays démesuré, quelques hommes cheminaient sans trêve, qui ne possédaient rien mais ne servaient personne, seigneurs misérables et libres d'un étrange royaume.[22]

---

20 p.1565. 'She was aware only of her solitude, and of the penetrating cold, and of a greater weight in the region of her heart', *Exile*, p.16.
21 See on p.2042, Quilliot's note to p.1565.
22 p.1570. The two subsequent quotations are the completion of this; the overall translation reads: 'Since the beginning of time, on the dry earth of this limitless land scraped to the bone, a few men had been ceaselessly trudging, possessing nothing but serving no-one, poverty-stricken but free lords of a strange kingdom [...] She knew that this kingdom had been eternally promised her and yet

Reflecting on this vision, Jeannine

> savait seulement que ce royaume, de tout temps, lui avait été promis et que jamais, pourtant, il ne serait le sien, plus jamais, sinon à ce fugitif instant.

The eternal moment, indeed, in which it seems to her that

> le cours du monde venait alors de s'arrêter et que personne, à partir de cet instant, ne vieillirait plus ni ne mourrait.

This idealisation of the life of the desert is pure Romanticism. Realism gives way to the symbolism of the *kingdom*, not the desert itself, but the community of noble and free souls living in harmony with its vastness, its simplicity, and with each other. It is the male dream of the 'band of brothers', of the chivalry of knighthood, far removed from the circumscribed world of women in nomad society. In dreaming it, Janine invites comparisons with Emma Bovary. However, as Jean Onimus points out (p.130), her *bovarisme* is not the mere silliness which Flaubert attributes to Emma, but an awakening to profound spiritual unrest, the moment of grace when she is granted 'access to poetry'.

Critics have remarked that Janine's supreme experience of the Kingdom is ultimately described in lyrical terms of heightened female eroticism. In the night, tormented by the mind-numbing pointlessness of her life and her own dread of death, she rises from the marital bed and creeps out of the hotel. Braving the cold, the dark, and the sinister howling of the dogs of the oasis, she returns to the terrace of the fort. Her courage is rewarded, for there, in the silence, the solitude and the darkness, she opens herself to the night and the stars, her anguish ceases, the sap rises in the core of her being, and as she falls back upon the ground, the 'water of the night' fills her being and the night sky covers her. Such is Janine's adultery.

Does this experience of communion with the beauty of the world reconcile Janine with her life, as Meursault's earlier experience of the

> that it would never be hers, never again, except in this fleeting moment [...] It seemed to her that the world's course had just stopped and that, from that moment on, no one would ever age any more or die', *Exile*, p.23.

'marvellous peace' of the summer's night 'full of signs and stars' had reconciled him to his death (p.1211)? Camus does not tell us. There is no human help for her solitude. Her husband, awakened by her return, switches on the light, which slaps her full in the face ('Il se leva, donna la lumière qui la gifla en plein visage', p.1575). The world in which she must live is as hostile as ever, Marcel as uncomprehending as ever. She weeps, but we do not know whether these are tears of joy or despair. To Marcel's unspoken question, she can only answer 'Ce n'est rien, mon chéri, ce n'est rien' (p.1575; 'It's nothing, darling, nothing'). No words can convey her experience to Marcel. We can surmise that she will stay with him because, as we have been told earlier, he needs her as she needs his need of her, but also because, in their childless marriage, he is her *child*, her 'enfant faible et désarmé', (p.1572), nothing but a weak, defenceless child. Geraldine Montgomery, disagreeing with those critics who see in Janine's return to Marcel a defeat, sees it as the conquest of inner liberty, a choice freely made out of 'compassion and solidarity, two mature forms of love' (2004, p.364, tr.), and hears the note of maternal tenderness in her final words. Onimus sees her coming back to 'take possession courageously of her little mortal world' (p.129, tr.), and weeping because, after the great revelation of the starry night, she now knows that it is a prison. At all events, Janine has glimpsed the kingdom of happiness, but despite her childlike face, her innocence, she is irremediably exiled from it. Her inner solitude is unchanged, and we can only hope that she has found the strength to bear more lucidly the burden of her existence and to help Marcel bear his. *L'Exil et le Royaume* is dedicated to Camus's wife Francine (we may note the rhyming echo with the name of the heroine of this story), so we may not go far wrong in seeing in this first narrative, in some way at least, a tribute to female constancy, self-giving, and affinity to the spiritual.

The second story, 'Le Renégat', subtitled in French 'ou un esprit confus' ('or a Confused Mind') takes the reader into a nightmare world of evil and tyranny. Of all the solitaries in Camus's fiction, the Renegade is the most solitary, for from the beginning he reveals that his tongue has been torn out. All that issues from his mouth is a rattle, a gurgling, guttural 'Râ! Râ!' distorting the endless torrent of words. Language has totally failed. This Renegade is a mutilated Clamence thrust even further down into Hell, imprisoned in the nightmare kingdom of a crazed mind. The 'realism' of 'La Femme adultère' is replaced by a hallucinatory vision of evil, while landscape and plot become above all symbol and allegory in a terrifying *conte*.

The disordered stream of consciousness, to which nothing corresponds that comes out of the Renegade's mouth, contrasts with the ironic and eloquent stream of language, self-mocking, devious and derisory, which pours forth from Clamence. Owen Miller has drawn an interesting parallel between the duality of the image in the mirror in both *L'Étranger* and *La Chute* and what he calls the 'auditory' image of the voice in 'Le Renégat'. In *L'Étranger*, Meursault looks into his tin dish and sees a reflection which remains serious and does not smile back at him (p.1183), while in *La Chute* Clamence, after hearing the inexplicable laughter, sees in his bathroom mirror a reflection which persists in smiling at him (p.1495). Miller sees in each case a coming to self-awareness of a divided personality, and, in the voice over which the Renegade has no control, the total loss of unity of that personality, a division which can only be resolved in death. One could however say that in each of the first two cases the image is that of a *reflecting* self, serious in Meursault's case, sardonic and bantering in Clamence's, while the 'auditory' image is *unreflective*, the sounds issuing from the mouth as spontaneous and 'confused' as the mind of the monologuist. At the end of the story the Renegade will hear a second voice, an appeal to goodness, without knowing whether it is an inner or external voice, leaving the reader to interpret it as he may. The end of the story is as enigmatic and ambiguous as that of any fiction of Kafka.

'What pap! What pap!' (*Quelle bouillie! Quelle bouillie!*). This cry of despair and disgust heralds an unstoppable regurgitation of brutal experiences, a hideous lamentation. The brutality of the story is reflected in the harsh gutteral effects, the plethora of savage and hard images, the implacable sun, stones, rocks, metal. Victor Brombert has commented that Camus here reveals himself as 'a master of images, sounds and rhythms' (1962, p.82). The reader must ask, once again, as in Clamence's case, what faith, if any, is to be put in this first-person narrator, whose ravings become ever more horrific until silence is at last imposed with the savage comment of a mysterious (and hitherto silent) observer: 'Une poignée de sel emplit la bouche de l'esclave bavard'.[23] The unseen commentator casts his evil shadow retrospectively over the whole narrative, in which the nadir of human existence has been reached, and life is extinguished with contempt.

The monologue, over a period of time stretching from one desert dawn to the next, recounts the history of a missionary, born into a poverty-stricken background in the bleak Massif central of France, but devoured with spiritual pride and the desire for power. He travels to the most remote region of the desert hoping to achieve glory by entering the city of a ferocious tribe and converting its inhabitants. Instead he is enslaved, tortured, and in his masochistic self-abasement, himself converted to the worship of the 'fetish', the god/idol of absolute power. Abandoning love for hatred, good for evil, his madness reaches its height when he hears that his captors are about to admit into the city a new missionary, thus imperilling the supremacy of the fetish. Escaping into the desert with a rifle, he lies in wait for the newcomer and the latter's guide and kills them both, only to be recaptured by his torturers, crucified upon a 'war saddle' (*selle guerrière*) and left to become a rotting corpse upon which the jackals will feast.

What can all of this mean? As a parable about oppression, the worship of power and modern tyrannies, about the betrayal of values, the loss of self-respect and the resulting perverse self-abasement, about the drive to engulf and be engulfed in a universal culpabilisation *cum* enslavement, it is a sequel to *La Chute*, in a terrifyingly heightened register of horror fantasy. While Clamence, tortured by thirst under the ferocious sun of his North African concentration camp, had been with those who suffered (even if in the end he failed the supreme test), the Renegade serves the torturers and executioners. Clamence had dreamed of ruling the world, dethroning Satan and reigning in his place; the nameless Renegade also thirsts to convert in order to dominate. Even in the seminary he desires to outshine the rest, to be an example so as *to be seen* ('Je voulais être un exemple, moi aussi, pour qu'on me voie', p.1580). Having always worshipped power, when he meets Satan in the guise of the fetish, the evil god of absolute power, he is inevitably conquered and enslaved. This is the most Kafkaesque

23   p.1593. 'A handful of salt fills the mouth of the garrulous slave', *Exile*, p.48.

of Camus's writings, reminiscent of the equally nightmarish short narrative, 'In the Penal Colony'. There, as in Camus's text, evil and inhumanity reign supreme, justice and mercy do not exist, a killing machine, designed with clinical refinement to inflict maximum agony upon its victims, corresponds to the evil fetish of Camus's tale. An accursed island lost in the ocean, a salt basin in the inaccessible desert, such are these hellish Erewhons.

Sisyphus and this Renegade-slave are antithetical icons. Both are prisoners in some mythic Hades, both are exiles, both are solitary, but while Sisyphus' struggle is to assert the value of life and the freedom of the spirit despite the unscaleable walls of the Absurd, the Renegade collaborates with the forces of negation and envisages a 'kingdom' in which slavery is universal and the forces of oppression can rule unchallenged. Sisyphus strives towards the summit of a mountain, and thereby experiences a fulfilment and a joy, Clamence wanders in his despair through dismal streets and drifts upon grey waters, but the hell of the Renegade is of another order of the mind, a truly apocalyptic vision. Paul Fortier has analysed the allegorism of the desert setting of Clamence's North African concentration camp, but the Renegade finds himself in a desert death camp whose natural features are intensified beyond the point of madness and nightmare. The hostile face of the natural world is at its most terrifying in this desert in which no flower blooms, where the scorching sun blazes by day and the freezing cold kills by night. The extremes of inhumanity are encapsulated in the city that the Renegade enters. Here there is no population of humble Dutch Sisyphuses going about their daily tasks, but only impassive masters and faceless slaves in a Hegelian Hell.

The name of the city, Taghâsa, is a harsh and mocking echo of the paradise that had been the Tipasa of Camus's youth, 'habitée par les dieux' (*Essais*, p.55), the dwelling-place of the gods. Taghâsa is inhabited by demons, the antithesis not only of Tipasa, but also of the Heavenly City of Van Eyck's painting. It is not set high upon a sunlit hill, among groves and flower-strewn meadows, but in a deep basin hacked out of a blindingly white substratum of salt, a furnace by day, glacial by night. It is a prison, hermetically sealed above by the relentless blue sky. Dante's circles of hell appear here again, not in the form of canals as in Amsterdam, but in the concentric terraces which ring the sides of the basin (p.1584). This 'white hell' ('leur enfer blanc', p.1583), is ruled over by the fetish hidden in the recesses of his windowless house, the Lord of darkness. Evil personified, he is at once death and Satan, his face being a double axehead and his iron nose like a twisting serpent (p.1586), doubtless the serpent of Genesis. Instead of the refreshing fountain of life in the centre of the polyptych, the redeeming Lamb of God, serenaded by the angels, the throngs of happy pilgrims, apostles, virgins, martyrs, there is only a parching aridity, an impenetrable silence, a complete absence of communion and fraternity, for during the day the torrid sun makes all contact between the haughty and sinister inhabitants impossible, and the freezing cold drives them into their separate icy abodes at night.[24]

Towering, black-robed, silent, faceless, the 'lords' who inhabit this place live 'where nobody could live', thirty days' journey from all life, in some Nowhere 'à la frontière de la terre des noirs et du pays blanc, où s'élève la ville de sel'.[25] It is a land of rocks, blinding white salt, harsh metal, all that is arid, hostile, inhuman. The rays of an iron sun beat down like burning lances ('à coups de lances brûlantes', p.1582-3), the silent torturer has 'metal eyes', the grotesque sorcerer wears a mask of reeds and wire mesh, in which the two *square* holes through which he sees intensify the impression of robotic inhumanity (p.1585). These aliens are, like Janine's nomads, the 'lords of a strange kingdom', but whereas the former personify nobility, these are the incarnation of menace, cruelty, and tyranny. Having no connection with any other race or culture, they are united only in the ruthless oppression of their black slaves, whom they send to toil and die in the salt-mines (p.1583). We are back with Clamence in the concentration camp. Even the second syllable of the name of Ta*ghâ*sa is an echo of the *chambres à gaz*. As for the women, sex-slaves beaten and raped at will by the sorcerer, they serve the fetich and the 'masters'.

24   p.1583: 'Ce creux au milieu du désert, où la chaleur du plein jour interdit tout contact entre les êtres [...] où sans transition le froid de la nuit les fige un à un dans leurs coquillages de gemme [...]'
25   p.1582. 'On the confines of the white country and the land of the blacks where stands the city of salt', *Exile*, p.34.

The climax of the narration is the episode in which a woman in rags, passive, dehumanised, her face covered in tattoos to resemble the fetish, is cast at the feet of the idol and left to the mercy of the prisoner. But when he attempts to possess her, the sorcerer and torturers rush in to beat him ferociously 'where he had sinned' (castration?) and hack out his tongue. This ultimate torture and humiliation is the true moment of his apostasy, his conversion to hatred for all pertaining to his past and its values, the wild rush of fervent adoration of 'la force et la puissance' (p.1589; 'force and power').

Is there any trace of a lost heavenly 'Kingdom' in this story? Camus's exiles, when they think of the Kingdom, think of their youth, of sunlight upon a beach, of the love of a silent mother. Janine remembers her happy girlhood. Yvars ('Les Muets'), like Meursault, thinks of the warm sea, the sun, girls in their summer dresses, a happiness which 'pass[es] with youth'.[26] The mothers of Meursault, Rieux, or Tarrou all represent love, selflessness, and the poor 'in spirit' of the Beatitudes, to whom the Kingdom belongs, while Jonas's mother ('L'Artiste au travail') is nothing less than a 'lay saint' ('véritable sainte laïque', p.1630). Even Clamence, acknowledging his modest birth, can remember feeling like a prince ('J'étais d'une naissance honnête mais obscure [...] je me sentais fils de roi', p.1490). Alone among the characters of Camus's novels, the Renegade speaks rancorously of his origins, remembering only a wretched home in the chilly Massif Central, a drunken father and a near-moronic mother ('dans ce haut plateau du Massif central, mon père grossier, ma mère brute [...] et le long hiver', p.1579). This amounts to a vicious caricature of the 'two or three simple and grand images' which first were stamped upon Camus's own heart, 'the world of poverty and light', with, at its centre, 'the admirable silence of a mother'.[27] Is this the Renegade's first betrayal? A perversion of the truth in a twisted mind? Later the

---

26   p.1598. 'L'eau profonde et claire, le fort soleil, les filles, la vie du corps, il n'y avait pas d'autre bonheur dans son pays. Et ce bonheur passait avec la jeunesse.'

27   See *Essais*, Préface to *L'Envers et l'Endroit*, p.6: 'Ce monde de pauvreté et de lumière où j'ai longtemps vécu'; ibid., p.13: 'L'admirable silence d'une mère [...] les deux ou trois images simples et grandes sur lesquelles le coeur, une première fois, s'est ouvert.'

nameless monologist (the lack of a name is also a rejection of origins) will recall fresh meadows, the gentle evening rain, the soup simmering in the pot, awaiting his return, and the parents 'who occasionally smiled at me, perhaps I loved them'.[28] As he is about to die, he cries out that he wants to 'go home'('Je veux retourner chez moi', p.1593).

The Renegade has either never known love, or, more probably, turned his back on it, a renegade in that respect also. His quest for the kingdom is therefore doomed from the beginning, however justified his desire to live in the sunshine, by clear water ('dans le soleil, avec de l'eau claire' (p.1579), his longing for happiness and innocence. He converts from the cold (and, for Camus, northern) climate of Protestantism to the warm Latin promise of Catholicism, in the hope of a future in the sun ('un avenir et du soleil', p.1580). The Catholicism of St. Francis, no doubt, whose Christianity was 'un hymne à la nature et à la joie naïve', as Camus described it in his inaugural lecture for the Maison de la Culture in Algiers, in 1937.[29] But the question is, what future does the Renegade hope for? What sort of fulfilment does he desire? The kingdom of the mind is opened up for him by the *curé*, who teaches him to read, as Camus himself had found a father-figure in his primary schoolteacher, Louis Germain, whom he always held in great affection. But the sun that the Renegade finds is the hostile scorching sun of the desert, and the future of his overweening ambition will be one in which he abdicates his intellect (there is no intellectual basis to his conversion in the city of salt), and his mind is enslaved.

The origins which the Renegade disavows are not only hearth and home, but the whole heritage of the European tradition and its values, rejected as something putrid and detestable, like his drunken father whose guts are rotted. 'À bas l'Europe, la raison et l'honneur et

---

28   *Exile*, p.34. 'Frais comme les prés, comme la pluie du soir, autrefois, quand la soupe cuisait doucement, ils m'attendaient, mon père et ma mère, qui parfois me souriaient, je les aimais peut-être', p.1582.
29   *Essais*, p.1323: 'La culture indigène. La nouvelle culture méditerranéenne'. 'A hymn to nature and to naïve joy.'

la croix', is the apostate's war-cry.³⁰ The murder of the second missionary is both a parricide and the murder of the *patrie*:

> Râ, râ, tuer son père [...] il est mort depuis longtemps, le vin acide a fini par lui trouer l'estomac, alors il ne reste qu'à tuer le missionaire.³¹

Victor Brombert sees in the novel the allegory of 'the drama of the mind', and in the Renegade 'the modern intellectual, heir to a Humanist culture [...] who, in search of systems and ideologies, espouses totalitarian values that have long ago declared war [...] on the thinker and his thought' (1962, p.230). What the Renegade rejects is the Ithaca evoked at the end of *L'Homme révolté*, the 'faithful land', the inheritance of 'audacious and sober thinking' and of intellectual generosity.³² In its place he serves the *Empire idéologique*, the evil empire of absolutist ideologies, Soviet or Nazi, where servitude, terror and lies destroy the community of men, and impose 'the most terrible of silences', there being 'nothing in common between a master and a slave'.³³

To what extent does this story of a power-seeking missionary represent a blanket denunciation of a politicised Church which had, in Camus's view, dissipated its Mediterranean heritage by claiming ever greater temporal power?³⁴ Such a reading is at best incomplete, precisely because the protagonist is a *Renegade*, rejecting the evangelical turning of the other cheek, the refusal of violence which was taught in

---

30   p.1590. 'Down with Europe, reason, honour and the cross', *Exile*, p.44.
31   p.1580. 'Gra, gra, [...] to kill one's father [...] he's now long dead, the tart wine eventually cut through his stomach, so there's nothing left but to kill the missionary', *Exile*, p.31.
32   *L'Homme révolté*, in *Essais*, p.708: 'Nous choisirons Ithaque, la terre fidèle, la pensée audacieuse et frugale, l'action lucide, la générosité de l'homme qui sait.' See *The Rebel*, p.270.
33   *L'Homme révolté*, p.687: 'Il n'y a rien de commun en effet entre un maître et un esclave [...] la servitude fait régner le plus terribe des silences.' See *The Rebel*, p.247.
34   *L'Homme révolté*, p.702: 'Mais lorsque l'Église a dissipé son héritage méditerranéen, elle a mis l'accent sur l'histoire au détriment de la nature [...] et, détruisant une limite en elle-même, elle a revendiqué de plus en plus la puissance temporelle et le dynamisme historique.' See *The Rebel*, p.263.

the seminary (p.1580). Quilliot writes: 'Camus used to say provokingly, "[The Renegade] is a portrait of the Christian progressive", or, acording to Cardinal Duval, "It's the story of a Christian who adopts the Marxist ideology".'[35] Camus was still very close to the bitter controversy set alight by *L'Homme révolté*, and if we wish to look for a political message in this fable, it is the condemnation of all absolutist ideology and the tyranny to which it gives rise.

There are two missionaries in the story, the Renegade and his victim, and the second is no less significant than the first. Is he in fact a mirror-image of the first? The *Endroit* to the Renegade's *Envers*? Or simply the phantasm of a disordered mind? As with Clamence and the silent interlocutor, all interpretations are possible. By his own account, the Renegade had set out in defiance of his superiors and does not even seem to have waited for his ordination. Having transferred to a seminary in Algeria, he steals the money he requires, throws off the soutane, and leaves for the greatest challenge (which alone satisfies his spiritual pride), dreaming of 'absolute power', and telling himself that he would subjugate those savages 'like a powerful sun'.[36] What he meets, of course, and is vanquished by, is the torturing desert sun. His vocabulary is military, he wants to bring *the enemy* to his knees, to 'force[r] l'*adversaire* à capituler' (p.1581, my italics). In contrast, the second missionary will arrive unaccompanied by soldiers and without arms, to dedicate himself to the care and welfare of the children of the city. The Renegade cannot bear the thought that the newcomer will 'show off his insolent goodness' and that 'the reign of evil' will be postponed'.[37] When the other lies at his feet, the apostate rams the butt of his rifle into the dying face, exclaiming: 'Que le bruit est bon de la

---

35   See Quilliot, 'Présentation', p.2044 (*tr*). Camus was in contact with Cardinal Duval, archbishop of Algiers, for several years during the Algerian war of independence. See Todd, p.868. In *Carnets III*, p.56, Camus in fact outlines the plot of *Le Renégat* as follows: 'Le missionnaire progressiste va civiliser les barbares qui lui coupent les oreilles et la langue et le réduisent en esclavage. Il attend le prochain missionnaire et le tue avec haine.'

36   p.1581: 'Je subjuguerais ces sauvages, comme un soleil puissant [...] je rêvais du pouvoir absolu.'

37   p.1591: 'Il ferait parade de son insolente bonté [...] Le règne du mal serait retardé.'

crosse sur le visage de la bonté!'.[38] The face smiles at him, as the face in the mirror had smiled at Clamence, and this time it is the smile of goodness, of forgiveness.

There is a curious parallel between this second missionary and the historical Father Charles de Foucauld, killed by rebels in his hermitage of Tamanrasset, in the Hoggar mountains of the Sahara, in 1916. Although there seems to be no mention of him in Camus's writings, the story of his life and his work among the Tuareg, the poorest of the poor, is part of French Algerian history, and Camus must have been acquainted with it. Moreover, we know his admiration for the simple and ascetic life. There seem to be echoes here, and even the name of the fictitious town, Taghâsa, resonates with Tamanrasset.

The next question is that of colonialism and Camus's attitude to it. The second missionary's arrival is prepared by an agreement on the part of the inhabitants to accept the presence of a small French garrison outside the precincts of the town. Two points should be made. Firstly, we need to remind ourselves that perspectives have changed since this narrative was written, when, in the aftermath of two world wars, the soldier (providing always that he was on the right side!), was seen above all as the guarantor of freedom and civilisation, the incarnation of the virtues of courage and loyalty. It is the traditional image, going back to the age of chivalry and the icon of the knight errant, and reflected, for example, in the writings and poetry of Charles Péguy, who died on the battlefield in 1914. It is interesting also to recall that de Foucauld, once a young army officer himself, continued to enjoy the friendship and support of his fellow-officers during his years in the desert. Secondly, we must understand that the imminent arrival, in Camus's narrative, of the small French garrison is not a political statement, it is a part of the allegory. They are not to enter the town, but come as upholders of the values and civilisation which the Renegade has rejected, the ideals of reason and moderation inherited from Greece, a concept of honour, and the notion of fraternity which is the essence of Christianity. This is of course utopian, but that Europe may have failed to live up to these ideals, or that colonialism might be

---

38   p.1592. 'How pleasant is the sound of a rifle butt on the face of goodness!' *Exile*, p.47.

synonymous with greed and exploitation, these are truisms and debates outside the scope of the fable, and an explication of Camus's agonising political dilemma as a French Algerian has to be looked for elsewhere. What is certain is that all forms of oppression and exploitation, all totalitarian regimes, are condemned in the depiction of the master-slave 'kingdom' of the fetish, the sterile city of salt, Taghâsa.

Will the Renegade, like Clamence, persist to the end as the 'advocate of servitude'?[39] Will he continue until the end his parody of the Lord's Prayer, praying for the reign of the fetish and the coming of the 'kingdom' in which 'ruthless black-hearted tyrants' will enslave the weak?[40] Crucified, will he die as Christ or as anti-Christ? Like Meursault, *Monsieur l'Antéchrist* (p.1176), like every victim, he can paradoxically be 'the Christ that we could be'.[41] Meursault will hear only the cries of hatred that surround Calvary, but the Renegade is challenged *in extremis* to bear witness to fraternity, to the redeeming power of forgiveness and reconciliation. As he awaits death, another voice addresses him: 'Si tu consens à mourir pour la haine et la puissance, qui nous pardonnera?'. Is this an inner voice or the voice of his victim? He asks himself:

> Est-ce une autre langue en moi, ou celui-ci toujours qui ne veut pas mourir, à mes pieds, et qui répète: 'Courage, courage, courage'?[42]

Is his victim his nobler self? Is it so easy to kill the good in oneself? At all events, the values represented by the second missionary do not die. A new conversion takes place, the Renegade recognises his fellow human beings as the 'seul recours', the sole recourse of the unfortunate. Dying at dawn, like Meursault, he beseeches the Sorcerer to help him rebuild the 'city of mercy', the antithesis of the city of salt. But

---

39 *La Chute*, p.1543: 'Vous voyez en moi, très cher, un partisan éclairé de la servitude.'
40 p.1592: 'Que le royaume enfin arrive où dans une seule ville de sel et de fer de noirs tyrans asserviront et posséderont sans pitié!'
41 See Chapter II, note 11.
42 p.1593. ' "If you consent to die for hate and power, who will forgive us?' Is it another tongue in me or still that other fellow refusing to die, at my feet, and repeating "Courage! Courage! Courage!"?', *Exile*, p.48.

the hand that is stretched out stops the incoherent mouth with a fistful of salt, the symbol of the life-denying sterility that is the key image of the story.

The brutal ending of *Le Renégat* is followed by two short narratives, miniatures of the life of the French working class in Algiers on the one hand, and on the other, that of an idealistic French Algerian schoolmaster on the high plateaux of the south. Realism now takes priority over allegorism, with, for example, detailed technical descriptions of the work processes of the cooper's trade in the story of Yvars, but the tone is elegiac in both texts and the symbolism of setting and landscape is an omnipresent counterpoint. 'Les Muets' is told from the perspective of Yvars, a forty-year old employee in a cooperage in an industrial district of Algiers. Camus's own uncle Étienne Sintès, his mother's brother, was a cooper, often working a sixty-hour week. We have met him in the early essay 'L'Ironie', which opens the collection *L'Envers et l'Endroit*, and we shall meet him again in *Le Premier homme*. Yet it is possible to see, as one critic, Ray Davison, does, even in this most realist of Camus's narratives, a 'philosophical parable', a pessimistic reflection on the ontology of the group, a lament for the failure of the community of workers, the Kingdom, to overcome division and polarisation.

When the story opens, Yvars is cycling laboriously to work, his lame leg immobile on a fixed pedal. He is thus symbolically shackled. He has a wife and young son; to support them he works overtime and as an odd-job man on Sundays. He has no leisure to enjoy the nearby sea and the beaches. Camus wrote in his *Carnets*:

> Ce n'est pas la pauvreté ou le travail incessant qui font la déchéance de l'homme. Mais l'asservissement sordide de l'usine et la vie des banlieues.[43]

Times are hard in the cooper's trade; the use of traditional barrels is being replaced by oil-tankers and tanker lorries and the workforce has shrunk to about fifteen. The *patron*, Lassalle, a decent enough man, has felt unable to raise wages to meet rising costs of living, and, after

---

43 *Carnets III*, p.34. 'It is not poverty or ceaseless work which degrades, but the sordid servitude of the factory and life in the deprived city suburbs.'

an unsuccessful strike lasting twenty days, the men are returning to work, defeated. Humiliated, they obstinately ignore their employer's overtures and attempts to restore relations. But later in the day Lassalle's little daughter is taken ill, victim of some sort of stroke, and taken away in an ambulance, perhaps to die. The silence of the workers, from being a refusal to communicate, becomes an inability to communicate, a helplessness in the face of human suffering. Yvars would wish to say something to Lassalle as the latter passes through the workplace, his somewhat dishevelled hair the only sign of his distress, but the workman cannot find any word in time, and the moment is gone. *Too late, always too late!*

The underlying sense of guilt which Yvars experiences is expressed in the text only in his desire to hurry home and to wash (Meursault also, we remember, felt a compulsion to wash), then to sit outside his house and contemplate the sea in the peace of the evening. The symbolism of purification and reconciliation is patent. He cannot stop thinking of the little girl. She is for him what the young woman on the Pont des Arts had been for Clamence. His only consolation is in the tenderness of the relationship with his wife, Fernande, to whom he tells the news, as they sit side by side, he holding her hand. There is communion with this one other person, and there had been communion among the workers in the cooperage, seated on the ground, sharing out their meagre lunch packets, drinking in turn from the same glass of hot coffee, Yvars sharing his loaf of bread with his sole Arab workmate. The parallel is with the symbolism of the eucharistic bread and wine. But one other human being, Lasalle, is not included in this communion, and therefore the Kingdom has not come. The mood which concludes the story is melancholic, regret for the lost joy and innocence of youth, desire for an unattainable realm of peace and happiness somewhere else: 'Il aurait voulu être jeune, et que Fernande le fût encore, et ils seraient partis, de l'autre côté de la mer'.[44] Where is the Kingdom? Somewhere else.

The next tale takes the reader again into the inhospitable desert of the high plateaux which had been the setting for the nightmare of 'Le

44 p.1608. 'If only he were young, and Fernande too, they would have gone away, acrosss the sea', *Exile*, p.64.

Renégat'. It is winter. Daru is a schoolmaster living 'almost like a monk' ('presque en moine', p.1612) in his lonely schoolhouse, which consists of one room and a schoolroom. This harsh land is his kingdom, where he feels himself to be a *seigneur* (pp.1612). He is the ideal *seigneur*, the servant of his people, feeding and educating them (he distributes the government rations of grain to the poor families of his pupils), living their life and sharing their hardships. If Taghâsa was the kingdom of hell, this is the kingdom of the Beatitudes.

The arrival of the policeman Balducci, leading an Arab prisoner on a rope behind his horse, shatters the illusion of universal fraternity, because Daru is required to take charge of the man, who has killed his cousin, and to hand him over to justice in the neighbouring administrative centre, three hours away on foot. Judgement and retribution are no part of Daru's moral landscape: 'Le crime imbécile de cet homme le révoltait, mais le livrer était contraire à l'honneur'.[45] Nonetheless, he has to accept the assignment, but the next day, having provided the Arab with some money and provisons for a trek, he brings him to within sight of the settlement, informs him that he can either walk ahead and give himself up to the police, or walk to the south and find refuge among the nomads, a day's march away. Then he leaves him. Turning back at some distance, he sees the Arab slowly and painfully making his way towards the prison. When he returns to his schoolroom, he finds scrawled on the blackboard: 'Tu as livré notre frère. Tu paieras', and he realises that 'dans ce vaste pays qu'il avait tant aimé, il était seul'.[46]

Failure of communication, bonds of brotherhood which exclude the outsider, these are again the elements of tragedy. Daru, who speaks Arabic, has tried to reach out to the prisoner, untied his bound wrists, eaten with him, slept unarmed in the same room with him, and felt uneasily that this shared repose establishes a sort of unwelcome fraternity with a man who has committed murder. It is impossible however not to feel pity for the uncomprehending, passive and at

---

45 p.1621. 'The man's stupid crime revolted him, but to hand him over was contrary to honour', *Exile*, p.79.

46 p.1623. ' "You handed over our brother. You will pay for this." [...] In this vast landscape he had loved so much, he was alone', *Exile*, p.82.

times terrified prisoner. Thinking that the policeman will return to take him away, he utters his one plea, asking Daru not to desert him: 'Tu viens avec nous?' and again: 'Viens avec nous' (p.1619). There is an ambiguity in this last utterance. Is it again a plea to accompany the prisoner and the policeman, or an invitation to join the Arabs, wheresoever they are going? 'Come with us': we cannot after all choose who may be our brother and who not.

The Arab is in many respects a shadow image of Meursault, a more primitive, more alien Meursault. He too is a stranger, paradoxically a stranger among those who are the strangers in his own country. He does not speak their language, and although they may have some command of his, this merely increases the advantage on their side, as the lawyers in court have the advantage of Meursault. In this latter, Camus had created not so much a killer as a victim of the 'absurdity' of the universe and the prejudice of society, one with whom we can empathize and whose fate clearly demonstrates the horror of capital punishment. The case of the Arab is more difficult, we do not know why he has killed, nor does the policeman ('Ça n'est pas clair', p.1615). Daru feels only revulsion at the thought of the crime, and when he questions his 'guest', the latter can only reply, 'He ran away. I ran after him' ('Il s'est sauvé. J'ai couru derrière lui', p.1619). We are never invited into the consciousness of the Arab; his mutism seems to signify only low intelligence, as, in *La Chute*, did the mutism of the gorilla-barman. He has an 'animal mouth' and the dark and shining eyes of a trapped wild creature.[47] Yet the horror of the state-inflicted death to which he is going remains, and Daru is unwilling to send him to it.

The ending of the story is the most enigmatic of the collection, and is bound up with how we are to interpret Camus's own attitude towards the Arab population of Algeria at this stage of the independence struggle. The incomprehension between the two populations, French and Arab, is evident, as is Daru's paternalism. Nonetheless, he has something to offer, relief for the indigent (the government grain distribution), and a possibility of education. The schoolmaster serving the

47 p.1619: '[Daru] voyait seulement le regard à la fois sombre et brillant, et la bouche animale.'

poor, together with the doctor tending them, is the ultimate image of the lay saint in Camus's life and work. But Daru offers education on French terms. The chalk-drawn map on his blackboard is not a map of Algeria, but a map of France and its four rivers, and it is across this map that the message of death is scrawled, implicitly therefore politicising the text. We do not know whether the Arab's crime is political or not; it seems not to be. But his own kin, his fellow-villagers would shelter him against French justice, and the desert nomads (Janine's icons of nobility) would give him refuge.

When the Arab chooses to walk to his death at the end of the story, we do not know if this is because he simply does not understand his plight, or because of some sense of honour. One critic sees him as 'an Algerian fighting a war of liberation', the Noble Savage accepting his own death because he knows that Daru will have to pay in turn with his (Grimaud, p.180). Against this interpretation, which echoes the code of honour of the heroic Kaliayev of *Les Justes*, we might ask whether the Arab could not save both himself and Daru by simply choosing the escape route which he has been offered. Or is Daru doomed in any case? Camus leaves the reader and Daru equally perplexed as to the prisoner's motivation.

Daru and the Arab prisoner are bound together nevertheless in the brotherhood of their common humanity. The Arab may have the look of a terrified wild animal, but he is a fellow man. Only one thing is clear: the Kingdom that Daru believed in had never really existed, it has always been an accommodation between the strong and the weak. For Camus, well aware as he was of the injustices and hardships suffered by the indigenous population of Algeria, it was nonetheless never simply a case of the exploitation of the weak by the strong. Our sympathy with the tragic and idealistic Daru remains deep. His fragile kingdom has fallen apart. Loss and solitude are the final mournful notes of this lament for a vanished and noble dream of fraternity.

L'Artiste au travail is the turning point of the collection, an abrupt change in tone and style from the preceding story. It begins as a light-hearted cautionary tale reminiscent in some respects, like *L'Étranger*, of Voltaire's *Candide*. Jonas (the French form of the name of the prophet Jonah, who was swallowed up by the whale), is the innocent abroad in the predatory metropolitan jungle of art dealers, publishers, hangers-on, pseuds, landlords, *literati* and chattering classes, taking them all at face value until they come close to destroying him. Ever naïvely optimistic in the best tradition of Dr Pangloss, he is heedless of the advice or warnings of his real friend, the rather comically named Rateau (Ratty!). Friendship, marriage, even the sacrosanct mother-love, all receive an affectionately irreverent treatment. Jonas's mother is a 'lay saint' who devotes herself to the unfortunate, to such an extent that her husband declares himself fed up with her 'affair' with the poor, and divorces her ('J'en ai assez d'être trompé avec les pauvres', p.1630). The infant Jonas thereafter benefits from being spoiled by two rival parents, but grows up to be a happy-go-lucky and good-natured sort of chap:

> Gilbert Jonas, artiste peintre, croyait en son étoile. Il ne croyait d'ailleurs qu'en elle, bien qu'il sentît du respect, et même une sorte d'admiration, devant la religion des autres.[48]

The tone ranges from these whimsical opening sentences, through the gamut of irony and satire, to the caricatural humour of the children's comic strip. This last is best exemplified in the sequence describing how the well-intentioned Louise, the painter's wife, frequently makes her entry during his working day into the one decent room in their much-partitioned flat, an area which has to do duty as studio, living-room, dining-room, nursery, and also as social space for the horde of self-proclaimed friends. In she comes with exaggerated precaution, upper body thrown back, arms widespread for balance, knee raised high in front of her, toe pointed down (admirers of the comedian John Cleese will place her at once in the Ministry of Funny Walks). And of course she knocks over one of the many canvases littering the room, wakens the baby who starts to bawl, and Jonas, good-natured as ever, drops his brush, rushes to the rescue, picks up the infant, then his canvases, and at last stands listening, entranced, to

---

48   p. 1629. 'Gilbert Jonas, the painter, believed in his star. Indeed, he believed solely in it, although he felt respect, and even a sort of admiration, for other people's religion', *Exile*, p.83.

'la voix insistante et souveraine de son fils'.⁴⁹ So ends again his concentration and his day's work.

From 1950, Camus had been thinking of writing a story inspired by the problems of a writer who finds himself famous. In 1952 it became the story of an artist, and in 1953 Camus hit upon the title. It is easy to see that literary critics, at least as much as art critics, are the butt of the omniscient narrator's irony, as the bemused Jonas finds that he has an 'æsthetic' and his 'disciples' explain to him at length 'what he had painted and why'.⁵⁰ The parallel between the artist Jonas and the writer Camus had been there from the first sentence; both refuse all forms of belief other than belief in their vocation, their 'star',⁵¹ while having a certain 'admiration' for 'the religion of others'; both have responsibility for the happiness of a wife and children. They are of a similar age (around forty), since in the first paragraph we learn that Jonas is about thirty-five in the early days of his fame and popularity, when the children are tiny, and by the time of the crisis in his life they are going to school (p.1646). As the narrative progresses, confessional elements pierce through the palimpsest which is the story of Jonas, and the tone darkens. The conflicting demands of dedication to an artistic vocation and the need for human warmth and friendship, treated burlesquely at first, mask the enduring themes of imprisonment, guilt and innocence, and the loss of happiness.

Jonas's problem appears not to be solitude, but the lack of it. His good-natured gregariousness destroys his commitment to his art, and indeed his artistic integrity (he is in danger of becoming merely a fashionable society painter). He begins to disintegrate morally, feelings of guilt replace the light-hearted unconcern, dissipation, in all senses of the word, replaces effort, until finally he has to admit to his wife his casual infidelities, and sees in her face the look of a woman drowning in shock and anguish.⁵² 'A drowned woman', like the young

---

49 p.1636. 'His son's insistant and sovereign voice', *Exile*, p.92.
50 p.1638: 'Les disciples de Jonas lui expliquaient longuement ce qu'il avait peint, et pourquoi.'
51 See the entry for 10 January 1950, in *Carnets II*, p.303: 'Je n'ai jamais vu très clair en moi pour finir. Mais j'ai toujours suivi, d'instinct, une étoile invisible.'
52 p. 1650: 'Et pour la première fois, le coeur déchiré, il vit à Louise ce visage de noyée que donnent la surprise et l'excès de la douleur.'

girl whom Clamence failed to save from the Seine. Critics have pointed to Camus's own feelings of guilt towards his wife Francine, who suffered recurrent depression culminating in a very serious illness in the winter of 1953–4, during which Camus feared she was suicidal (see Todd, pp.807–19). Is there an element of pleading for forgiveness and understanding, of assurance of love for both Francine and the two children, in this story of the artist and the problems of his existence? Jonas loves his work, he loves company, but he also loves Louise and the children, he loves his faithful and honest friend Rateau, yet 'life is short, time races by, and his own energy had limits'.[53] *Apologia pro vita sua...*

Failing to place limits upon his hospitality, to restrict the numbers of those whom he admits to his frienship, Jonas's mistake, like that of Meursault, is essentially to refuse judgement, to fail to distinguish between individuals, or even between good and bad works of art, since

> exception faite pour une poignée de tableaux qui le transportaient, et pour les gribouillages évidemment grossiers, tout lui paraissait également *intéressant et indifférent* (my italics).[54]

There is an echo here of Meursault's response to Sintès, who asks him for an opinion on the story of his relationship with his Arab mistress, 'J'ai répondu que je n'en pensais rien, mais que c'était intéressant'. Meursault goes on to write the treacherous letter, to please Sintès because 'je n'avais pas de raison de ne pas le contenter'.[55] Similarly, seeing no reason *not* to please them, and having no opinions about their work, Jonas invents judgements to humour each of the crowd of would-be artists. He thus encourages them to pester him and thereby

---

53 *Exile*, p.100. 'Il aimait sa peinture, et Louise, ses enfants, Rateau, quelques-uns encore, et il avait de la sympathie pour tous. Mais la vie est brève, le temps rapide, et sa propre énergie avait des limites', p.1642.
54 p.1639. 'Except for a handful of pictures that carried him away, and for the obviously coarse daubs, everything seemed to him equally *interesting and indifferent*', *Exile*, pp.95–6 (my italics).
55 p.1147 and p.1148. 'I told him that I hadn't thought about it, but it was interesting', *OS*, p.35; 'Because I had no reason not to please him', *ibid.*, p.36.

destroys himself. In this way we can see his relationship with his importunate visitors as a transfer to the tragi-comic register of Meursault's fatal relationship with Sintès.

In this story of the artist's life, there are no landscapes. Paris is an urban jungle, unlike even Algiers, where Yvars, escaping from the confinement of the cooperage, had been able, from his terrace, to contemplate the sea, calm in the gentle evening light. Jonas's cramped flat is a prison from which he paints not mountains, desert or sea, but skies (p.1647), as Meursault had found consolation in the view of the clouds through the high prison window. However, Meursault's prison is a place of solitude, quiet and contemplation, like the prisons of the heroes of Stendhal. Jonas's space however, is invaded by the hordes of self-interested admirers and hangers-on attracted by his fame. Finally he finds himself surrounded by 'disciples' sitting on chairs placed in concentric circles around him, as Clamence had found himself caught in the concentric canals of Amsterdam. And when he escapes into the urban wastelands of Paris, he loses sight of his 'star' amid the 'dark mists' and sits alone for hours dreaming and drinking to excess in 'smoky and noisy' bars and cafés, places of casual sexual encounters which relieve his solitude, as he descends into the same hell which Clamence had entered in the period of his debauchery, also in Paris. Jonas reaches his nadir as winter sets in, a dank, piercingly cold Parisian winter which replaces the carefree atmosphere of childhood and youth (pp.1648–50).

Jonas, however, unlike Janine, or Yvars, or Daru, will not be exiled in perpetuity in the desert of solitude and quiet despair. Like Jonah emerging from the whale, he will be reborn, will find the kingdom of human love and warmth. Critics agree that his retreat into the sort of platform or cage which he constructs for himself and suspends from the high, narrow ceiling of his hallway, is a transposition of Jonah's biblical adventure in the belly of the whale. It is a place of retreat, it allows time for reflection. Like Mersault above Algiers or Rieux and Tarrou on the terrace, he is 'above the world', detached and contemplative. From his vantage point, he can both be with his friends and family and secluded from them. He can devote himself to his calling without absenting himself from the human race. The loft stands in for the prison tower or the monk's cell as a place of meditation, of the

227

finding of the self and realisation of inner freedom. The *dénouement* however leaves us, like Jonas's friend Rateau, perplexed. In his companionable solitude, Jonas has produced a blank canvas, except for a word, inscribed in very tiny letters, which could be either *solitaire* or *solidaire*. Has he solved the problem of reconciling the two states, the age-old dichotomy between the life of contemplation (or art) and the life of action (or interaction)? Is the blank canvas the symbol of the impossibility of achieving this symbiosis in our life here below?

'Chaque artiste, sans doute,' wrote Camus, 'est à la recherche de sa vérité.'[56] In his lofty retreat, Jonas tastes absolute joy, not only in the perfection and completion of his life's work ('Il se disait que maintenant il ne travaillerait plus jamais, il était heureux'), but also in the fullness of love for his family ('Il les aimait! Comme il les aimait!'),[57] and in the reappearance of his star, shining again in the darkness. Thereupon he falls into a swoon. All perfect states are transcendental, ultimate truth is ineffable, as the mystics tell us. The unconscious Jonas is carried down from these heights and will rejoin those who love him, will return to the life which is the common lot, with its humbler joys and sorrows, but, unlike Janine, he will not embark upon it with tears. Art and the commitments of social and family life appear irreconcilable, however. The burlesque morality tale which is Jonas's story leaves the reader with hope, but no guarantees of a solution, this side of death and resurrection, to the dilemma of following a lonely star without deserting those who surround us and need us, and whom we also need.

'La Pierre qui pousse', the final and longest narrative of *L'Exil et le Royaume*, opens in the dark night of an unkown country, as a car bumps its way through a dense forest whose silence is broken only by the shrill cries and unintelligible chatter of exotic birds. It comes to a halt above an immense river. The headlights pick out two miserable shacks and a wooden tower from whose summit a metal cable swings away into the mist. A 'colossal' figure emerges from the car, toils up

---

56   'L'Énigme', in *L'Été*, *Essais*, p.866. 'Each artist is undoubtedly pursuing his truth', *SE*, p.146.

57   pp.1653–4. 'He told himself that now he would never again work, he was happy. [...] He loved them! How he loved them!' *Exile*, p.114–15.

the slope ahead, appearing and disappearing until he is silhouetted against the night sky. The darkness is pierced by a distant halo of yellow light bobbing and growing with the slow approach of a sort of floating lean-to and its lantern, behind it an immense raft, and on its deck three small dark figures, naked to the waist, on their heads conical straw hats. Two tall negroes, similarly attired, are poling the craft across the river. Only now does the reader realise that this mysterious craft is a ferry come to carry the car across the river.

Not a word has been spoken. The impenetrable forest, the river, the darkness pierced by the yellow light, the silent ferrymen, the non-human chatter of the birds, the immense silhouette of the traveller, all inspire a dreamlike dread, as if the river were the Styx and Charon himself approaching. Aboard the ferry, the handful of men seem lost, adrift on this river carryng them 'towards night and the sea',[58] into darkness, the unknown, the kingdom of death. This is not the warm night and maternal sea of Meursault's longing, not the sea which is *la mère*, but the sea which is *la mort*.[59] Human voices are at last heard as the craft ties up on the far bank, and we return with relief to the land of the living, the valley of the shadow of death having been successfully crossed.

This suspenseful introduction opens a narrative in which the life-giving forces will triumph at last over the forces of darkness. We learn that we are in Brazil and that the traveller is a Frenchman by the name of D'Arrast. His chauffeur, somewhat humorously named Socrates, has a 'merry voice', D'Arrast has a hearty laugh, 'a warm hearty laugh that resembled him' ('L'homme rit, d'un bon rire, massif et chaleureux, qui lui ressemblait', p.1660). The reader is reassured. There is still strange, disorienting country to cross before the travellers reach their destination; at one point they seem to find themselves in Japan, but are actually in a colony of Japanese workers. At last they reach the town of Iguape and 'the good sea' ('la bonne mer', p.1662), the sea which is now the good mother ('la bonne mère'), the very self-same

---

58   p.1660: 'Un seul flot puissant qui coulait doucement, à travers la forêt obscure, vers la mer et la nuit […]. Entre l'océan tout proche et cette mer végétale, la poignée d'hommes qui dérivait à cette heure semblait maintenant perdue.'
59   Gassin (p.39) has pointed out the phonetic analogies.

life-bringing sea which, we shall learn later, has carried to the town the venerated statue of Jesus himself.

It is, I think, necessary to recapitulate the events of the story before considering the implications of this most exotic of Camus's tales, inspired no doubt by his own conference tour of Brazil in 1949. It was a voyage which coincided with a period of fatigue and depression, even suicidal thoughts, recorded in the travel diaries published posthumously as *Journaux de voyage*. The episodes of the story, the night journey through the tropical forest to Iguape, the disturbing and hallucinatory experience of the night of the macumba, the black girl dressed as a huntress, the religious festival in honour of the statue of Jesus found on the banks of the estuary, and the miraculous 'growing stone', the carrying of a huge stone in fulfilment of a vow after a shipwreck, all of that is in the diaries, some of it transcribed word for word into the narrative. Quilliot, in his 'Présentation', calls the story a *récit-mythe* (p.2064). In the narrative, D'Arrast is an engineer, come to construct a dyke to keep out the seasonal floods in the impoverished districts of Iguape. He has arrived during a festival celebrating the stone of the title, a 'miraculous' object reposing in a cave, beside the statue of Jesus which had been found by fishermen on the banks of the estuary. During the celebrations, the people come from far and wide, bringing hammers to chip fragments off the stone and carry them away as portents of blessings and happiness ('le bonheur béni', p.1668). The stone however always grows back to its original size.

It is at the grotto that D'Arrast meets a ship's cook, a stocky little negro who has survived a shipwreck, thanks, as he believes, to a vow made when hope seemed lost. His vow was to carry on his head a stone weighing fifty kilos during the festive procession to the church, scheduled for the next day. When pressed, D'Arrast admits that, although he has never made a vow, he too has once called desperately for help in a 'shipwreck'. What that 'shipwreck' was, he does not say, simply disclosing that it was not long ago and that 'quelqu'un allait mourir par ma faute'.[60]

A great procession is to take place the day after D'Arrast's arrival. On the eve, he is invited to attend the celebrations in the negro

---

60   p.1672. 'Someone was about to die through my fault', *Exile*, p.134.

quarter of the town, surreal and hypnotic ceremonies which fill him with such unease that he departs early, although the cook, completely possessed by the frenzied atmosphere, remains there all night long. The next day, under a blazing sun, D'Arrast, from the balcony of the judge's house, sees the start of the religious procession as, preceded by the penitents, the statue of Christ crowned with thorns is borne out of the church. Immediately behind the statue comes the cook, carrying a huge rectangulaire block on a cork board on his head. By the time the procession reaches the town hall, to which D'Arrast and the local 'notables' have in the meantime repaired, the cook is on the point of collapse. It is D'Arrast who, having rushed down from the balcony of the Town Hall in search of him, raises him up when he falls, and, taking the stone and its support upon his own head carries it, not back to the church, but down to the impoverished shacks beside the river, where he finally throws it down before the hearth in the cook's own cabin. At that moment,

> redressant toute sa taille, énorme soudain, aspirant à goulées désespérées l'odeur de misère et de cendres qu'il reconnaissait, il écouta monter en lui le flot d'une joie obscure et haletante qu'il ne pouvait pas nommer.[61]

D'Arrast/Sisyphus is not only happy, but ecstatic. The exhausted cook is helped in by his brother, then his friends crowd in, forming a circle around the stone. All is silence, no one looks at D'Arrast, until the cook's brother, still averting his gaze, invites him to 'Sit down with us' ('Assieds-toi avec nous', p.1686).

The way from solitude to solidarity is long and arduous. This oneiric journey undertaken initially by D'Arrast has mythic and symbolic resonances. After emerging from the brooding forest, where strange birds flash past the windscreen and the darkness is rent by the menacing growls of wild beasts ('un feulement étrange'), D'Arrast must make 'la longue, longue navigation à travers un désert rouge' (p.1661). Like any hero of classical myth or romantic knight-errantry,

---

61 p.1685. 'And there, straightening up until he was suddenly enormous, drinking in with desperate gulps the familiar smell of poverty and ashes, he felt rising within him a surge of obscure and panting joy that he was powerless to name', *Exile*, p.151.

he is on a perilous quest, beset by red-eyed birds, choked with red dust, scorched by the oppressive sun ('le soleil lourd'), threatened by the pale, looming mountains with their black ravines, as he undertakes the endless *navigation* across the sinister red desert with its black vultures circling the half-starved *zebus*, strange creatres resembling camels.[62] Red and black: the colours of danger, evil and death.

Conflating these alienating, dreamlike images of voyaging and desert-crossing, this story brings us back at last to within sight of 'the good sea', after all those Saharan deserts of the earlier narratives. The hero has passed the first ordeal. When he wakes up early the next morning, D'Arrast finds himself in an establishment called *Heureux Souvenir* (p.1662). The Kingdom of happiness is not forgotten, its memory is a promise. But it is clear that D'Arrast is a solitary, an exile from Europe and an exile from happiness. What has been his Fall, his shipwreck? How has he lost the kingdom? He too, like Clamence, knows that he is not innocent, that someone was going to die, and *through his fault*. Did he call out, make a vow, the cook asks, to which he replies that it seems to him that he did cry out, but made no vow, although he would have been willing to do so.[63] What are we to make of this enigmatic reply? Impossible not to sense some personal confessional element here. Does Camus have in mind Francine? Does he mean that he would have uttered a prayer and a vow *if only he could have*, if he could have believed? Quilliot sees in the cry the 'echo' of the unheeded cry of the young girl in *La Chute*. Has D'Arrast's undoing been self-satisfaction, pride, like Clamence's? 'J'étais fier', he says, 'maintenant je suis seul'.[64]

Unlike Clamence, D'Arrast will be given a second chance. But first, again like a knight on the eve of his dubbing, he has to get through a vigil. He is, after all, the descendant of the *seigneurs* of old of his own country. D'Arrast's vigil takes place during the night of the frenzied Afro-Brazilian dances, a surreal and profoundly disturbing

---

62   For all of this description, see in particular pp.1160–1, and *Exile*, pp.120–1.
63   p.1672: 'Quelqu'un allait mourir par ma faute. Il me semble que j'ai appelé. – Tu as promis? – Non, j'aurais voulu promettre. – Il y a longtemps? – Peu avant de venir ici.' See Quilliot's note, p.2068.
64   p.1672: 'I used to be proud; now I'm alone', *Exile*, p.135.

experience reminiscent of the episode of the sorcerer and his musicians and women in 'Le Renégat'. The dancers move in concentric circles, reaching climactic trance-like states in which they are convulsed from head to foot and fill the air with inarticulate cries. The red-robed sorcerer who is the master of ceremonies is an unleashed devil ('le grand diable rouge se déchaîna', p.1675), whirling a sabre above his head, dancing as if possessed, uttering a long incoherent clamour ('une longue clameur à peine phrasée', p.1675). The dominant red of his apparel (recalling the 'red desert' which has been crossed), the thunder of the drumming, the cries, the heat, the smoke from the countless cigars, give the room the coloration and atmosphere of an inferno. One after another, the young women collapse, are revived, continue dancing. D'Arrast, the appalled onlooker, at last also collapses. When he comes to, he sees the slender young girl whom he had earlier admired, now dressed as a huntress, carrying a bow and arrow upon which is impaled a multicoloured bird. She is apparently in a trance-state. Two obese female acolytes, their faces covered with raffia masks, attend her in her slow, swaying dance, until she utters a strange bird-like cry, 'shrill and yet melodious' ('Elle pouss[a] un étrange cri d'oiseau, perçant et pourtant mélodieux', p.1677). Is she priestess or sacrificial victim? Has she become the bird impaled on the arrow? At this point, the cook, utterly changed from his former good-natured self, tells D'Arrast to leave.

The episode constitutes D'Arrast's encounter with the dehumanising forces which had conquered the Renegade. The forces of the irrational are unleashed, unbearable for the searcher after 'lucidity'. A woman with an 'animal face' barks incessantly, the dancers utter a collective howl like dogs ('une sorte de rauque aboiement', p.1676), personalities change, good-nature ceases to exist. The images are all of a Hell which D'Arrast, like Christ, has to harrow before his resurrection, which begins when he re-emerges into the night, full of 'fresh aromatic scents' ('la nuit était pleine d'odeurs fraîches et aromatiques', p.1677). Nature is the great antidote, the great healer and restorer of health and sanity.

The Renegade had recanted his inheritance of rationality, moderation and fraternity, but D'Arrast resists the life-destroying madness of these possessed souls, 'who danced in order to die' ('qui dansaient pour mourir', p.1678). On the one hand, Europe fills him with shame and anger, ruled as it is now by 'policemen and merchants', while millions live in misery,[65] but here he experiences exile and solitude, and he is haunted by 'the strange cry of the wounded bird' uttered by the young girl.[66] Is it also a cry for help, the echo of the cry which Clamence had heard on a dark night in Paris? Is it the cry of the poor and oppressed? Is D'Arrast capable of answering it this time, and who exactly is he?

By birth (the aristocratic name), by profession and social status, he belongs to the privileged, and as such he is welcomed and feted by the 'notables' of the town, but in truth he is one of the 'poor in spirit' of the Beatitudes, not 'possessed' by wealth or position, but serving the poorest of the poor, using his intelligence and knowledge to contribute to improving their lives. To the evangelical spirit of poverty is added a lack of vindictiveness, a refusal to pass judgement, a spirit of forgiveness. He insists that the drunken chief-of-police, who had gate-crashed the reception and insulted him, should suffer no punishment. Ironically enough, the latter is, of course, himself the personification of retribution, whether just or unjust. D'Arrast is in the same league as teachers and doctors, as Rieux, Tarrou, Daru. It is perhaps significant that the building in which he is lodged is a former hospital. Is Camus, uneasy with the contrast between his own deprived background and his present fame and affluence, anxious to demonstrate that solidarity with those less fortunate, loyalty to them, is not impossible?

D'Arrast's silence at the sight of the extreme poverty that he sees in the cabin of the shanty town which he is taken to visit is more eloquent than any comment, it is a silence of shock. The silence of the workers and of the owner of the shack is eloquent also, expressing their injured dignity at this forced inspection, and, arising from it, a certain hostility such as Yvars and his workmates had felt towards

65   p.1669: The cook asks about Europe: 'Personne ne travaille, personne ne souffre? – Oui, des millions d'hommes. – Alors, c'est le peuple. – Comme cela oui, il y a un peuple. Mais ses maîtres sont des policiers ou des marchands.'
66   p.1678: 'Là-bas, en Europe, c'était la honte et la colère. Ici, l'exil ou la solitude [...] L'étrange cri d'oiseau blessé, poussé par la belle endormie, lui parvint encore.'

their employer. At this point, D'Arrast appears to them to be simply one of the 'seigneurs', as Socrates and the cook will call him (p.1669). But throughout the narrative, it is clear that he prefers the company of the poor to that of the mayor, the judge, and the other 'notables' of the welcome committee. These 'notables' do not speak French, as the mayor informs him (p.1663). They cannot *speak his language*, for in fact what they do not speak is the language of the poor. D'Arrast has no problem speaking with Socrates and later with the cook, with whom he speaks Spanish, for Camus the language of his mother's impoverished Spanish origins, the speech of the 'have-nots'. At the end of the story, he will leave the 'haves' on the balcony of the town hall in order to come to the aid of the humble cook, and it is to the latter's cabin that he will carry the stone, and among those who live in it that he will be accepted.

Analysing the socio-economic implications of the narrative, David Walker (1982) sees in D'Arrast the counterpart of the icon of Saint George which is worshipped, together with the little statue of a 'horned god', in the shack in which the macumba takes place. Walker sees the Christian theology of guilt, and Christian and animist superstition, together with colonialism, combining to oppress the poor. Like Saint George, D'Arrast comes as a 'champion' to deliver this people not only from the river, the dragon-like floodwaters which threaten to overwhelm them as the plague had afflicted the population of Oran, but also from their spiritual and social enslavement. Many critics however do not see the final solidarity as lasting, and point to the silence of the circle inside the cabin, the way the men avoid looking at D'Arrast, the fact that, in not carrying the stone to the church, he has done his will and not theirs, and that the cook's vow is left unfulfilled. The ending, as with each of the narratives, has a certain ambiguity.

What is positive, however, is that D'Arrast's joy is undiluted, he salutes 'life starting all over again' ('la vie qui recommençait', p.1686). Someone once was going to die through his fault, in the dark night a young girl had uttered a cry like a wounded bird, but now the human cry of distress has elicited a fraternal response, a man has been saved whom the burden would have killed, the oppressive weight of guilt has been carried and overcome, the door of the kingdom of fraternal love opened, life reaffirmed. This is no pessimistic *dénouement*.

The sound of the waters of the river fill D'Arrast with a 'tumultuous happiness' ('le bruit des eaux l'emplissaient d'un bonheur tumultueux', p.1686), for the rushing waters of this mighty Brazilian Jordan announce the washing away of his fault and the restoration of his innocence. Clamence's challenge has been met.

Who, in the end, is D'Arrast? Camus, who, in *La Peste*, had proposed the 'insignificant' Joseph Grand as the real hero, and, through the mouth of Rambert, dismissed warrior heroism as 'murderous', has been criticised for giving this hero an aristocratic name and impressive physique, and accused of elitist and racist glorification of a North European 'heroic' type (see, for example, the article of R. Theis). Peter Cryle (p.201) has ably defended Camus against such charges of fascist leanings. Indeed, the real significance of the 'colossal' stature and the aristocratic name is not that they signify muscle power and social rank, but that they symbolise moral strength and the truly noble virtue of generosity of spirit. In 1954, Camus wrote in his *Carnets* that only two sorts of aristocracy are now possible, the aristocracy of intelligence and that of work (he was in fact postulating a pact between intellectuals and workers), but that neither is authentic unless it is first and foremost the acceptance of certain duties, and unless it places the highest demands upon the self.[67] This is D'Arrast's aristocracy.

Larger than life, D'Arrast is, at the end of the narrative, an exemplary and mythic figure. Numerous critics have pointed out the parallel between his stone and that of Sisyphus. But this time Sisyphus is not toiling in isolation, it is now another's burden that he takes over, another that he saves, just as the Christ-statue of the grotto, carried in the procession, represents the Christ of the Passion, taking the burden of the world's suffering upon himself, an analogy already underlined by the critic Carina Gadourek (p.221). D'Arrast's stone is the secular counterpart of the stone in the grotto, of which all may take their portion and which never diminishes. It is eucharistic in its symbolism,

---

67 See *Carnets III*, p.105: 'Nécessité d'une aristocratie. Dans le présent, on ne peut imaginer que deux: celle de l'intelligence et celle du travail. [...] L'aristocratie n'est pas d'abord la jouissance de certains droits, mais d'abord l'acceptation de certains devoirs.' Also p.135: 'L'aristocratie [...] la vraie, est exigence à l'égard de soi-même.'

like the multiplication of the loaves and fishes, a Communion to which all are invited, the sacrament of fraternity. The mixture of races and languages represented in the narrative, encompassing the Afro-Brazilian, European, mixed-race and Asian (Japanese) populations, illustrates the universality of the message. D'Arrast is, indeed, both Sisyphus and Christ, the heroic Sisyphus asserting life and happiness against all the odds of the Absurd universe, and the Redeemer entering with all the multitudes of the disinherited into the Kingdom.

Chapter VI
Sailing to Ithaca. *Le Premier homme*

> *Nous choisirons l'Ithaque, la terre fidèle, la pensée audacieuse et frugale, l'action lucide, la générosité de l'homme qui sait.*
> Camus, *L'Homme révolté*
>
> *La pauvreté ne se choisit pas, mais elle peut se garder.*
> Camus, *Le Premier homme*
>
> *L'oeuvre est un aveu. Il me faut témoigner.*
> Camus, *Carnets II*

'I want to go home', is, as we have already seen, the last desire of the tormented soul of the Renegade. But there is no going back for him. For Clamence too, the past is a land of no return, the country of the fault, of the loss of innocence. Tarrou also bears the burden of his past, which he cannot re-visit, while D'Arrast goes forward to find a (maybe transitory) redemption in the land of his exile. For Jacques Cormery, the protagonist of Camus's unfinished last work, *Le Premier homme* (*The First Man*), however, it is precisely the return to the past, to the source, which makes possible a new beginning. In the Preface (1951) to the re-publication of *L'Envers et l'Endroit*, Camus wrote that if he did not succeed one day in re-writing those early essays, he would never have achieved anything, and that in the centre of the work to come would be

> l'admirable silence d'une mère et l'effort d'un homme pour retrouver une justice ou un amour qui équilibre ce silence [...] Une œuvre d'homme n'est rien d'autre que ce long cheminement pour retrouver par les détours de l'art les deux

ou trois images *simples* et grandes sur lesquelles le coeur, une première fois, s'est ouvert.[1]

Camus's death in the car crash on the *route nationale* on 4 January 1960, at Villeblevin, south of Fontainebleau, on his way, with his publisher Michel Gallimard, to Paris from his Provençal retreat at Lourmarin, left the work unfinished. It is perhaps best described as (lightly) fictionalised autobiography. Behind the invented names of the characters, real persons live and breathe, idealized or dramatised. Camus himself goes by the alias of Jacques Cormery (Cormery was the maiden name of his paternal grandmother). His mother is in the first pages called Lucie, and later by her actual name, Catherine, while a Freudian slip (p.189) has her learning to write her signature on her pension docket as *Vve. Camus*. His brother is sometimes Louis and sometimes Henri, his uncle is first referred to as *l'oncle Émile* and later as *l'oncle Ernest* or *l'oncle Étienne*. In another slip on page 138, the much-loved elementary schoolmaster, Monsieur Bernard, is referred to by his real name, Monsieur Germain. Corrections abound in the manuscript, as also notes in which Camus admonishes himself to rewrite, omit, add in, or reconsider, reminders which are reproduced by the editor as footnotes on the relevant printed pages.

The description of Jacques Cormery's father is consistent with what is known of Camus's father, Lucien Camus: a good height, a long face with a high, square brow, a strong jaw, blue eyes (p.12), a man of few words ('taciturne', p.65, 'pas causant', p.172). The family liked to believe its origin was Alsatian, and that they had left home and hearth rather than submit to German domination in 1871, but in fact they came from the Bordeaux region (grandfather) and the Ardèche (great-grandfather). Olivier Todd remarks that 'a poor political exile from Alsace or Lorraine had more prestige than a penniless Breton or Bordelais' (p.21, tr.). The first son, Lucien Auguste, was born in early 1911. Camus *père* was working as a *caviste* (foreman in

---

[1] *Essais*, p.13. 'I shall still place in the centre of this work the admirable silence of a mother and the effort of a man to rediscover a justice or a love which matches this silence. [...] A man's work is nothing but this slow trek to rediscover through the detours of art, those two or three great and simple images in whose presence his heart first opened', *SE*, p.26.

charge of the processing of the grapes) on the *ferme* Saint-Paul (*Saint-Apôtre* in the novel), outside the small market-town of Mondovi, connected by road to Bône, a port near the Tunisian border. The heavily pregnant Catherine and her two-year-old son arrived after eighteen hours of train from Algiers to Bône, on a *carriole* which transported them and their belongings and furniture to Mondovi, where Camus was born on 8 November 1913. All of this is reflected in the opening chapter of the novel.

We cannot know how the novel would have developed. In a letter to Georges Blin on 27 May 1959 (see Todd, p.1020), Camus said he wanted to write a novel 'd'éducation', in others words, a *Bildungsroman*. J.-C. Brisville also informed Todd (*loc.cit.*) that Camus had told him, in an interview, that he intended for the first time to write of women and his debt to them, and that they were of 'une importance capitale'. He did not live to carry out this intention. At the end of the first part of the novel, Camus writes of that 'terre de l'oubli où chacun était le premier homme' and where

> lui-même avait dû s'élever seul, sans père [...] et il lui avait fallu apprendre seul, grandir seul [...] trouver seul sa morale et sa vérité, à naître enfin comme homme pour ensuite naître encore d'une naissance plus dure, celle qui consiste à naître aux autres, aux femmes.[2]

Only the first part of this project, the growing up, was written. What we have is, however, satisfactory in itself, the story of a boy growing to adolescence, his pride in contributing his first pay packet to the household, his revolt against the iron rule of the grandmother, and his first kiss.

As it stands, the work is divided into two parts: 'Recherche du père' ('In search of the Father') and 'Le fils ou le premier homme' ('The Son, or the First Man'). The narrative switches between the past and a present situated in 1954, giving a superficial impression of lack

---

[2] p.181. 'The land of oblivion where each one is the first man, where he had to bring himself up, without a father [...] He had to learn by himself, to grow alone [...] find his own morality and truth, at last to be born as a man and then to be born in a harder childbirth, which consists in being born in relation to others, to women', *FM*, p.152.

of coherence. An outline of the events narrated may therefore not be superfluous. The first part opens with what is actually a prologue, recounting the birth of Jacques Cormery. Some forty years later, the reader accompanies Cormery on a visit to his father's grave in a war-cemetery in the bleak Breton landscape of St. Brieuc, followed by a visit to his old mentor and father-figure now retired and living in that town. On board ship on his way back to Algiers, he recalls his childhood, the boredom of the enforced siestas with the stern grandmother, the delight of playing in the streets and on the waste grounds of the *quartier pauvre*, of reaching a dingy shore and plunging into the marvellous sea. Chapter 5 is dedicated to his father, but begins with Jacques's return to Algiers and reunion with his mother, now seventy-two and still lost in her world of silence, frugality, and resignation. She can tell him nothing of his father, except that 'you are his spitting image' ('c'était toi, craché', p.63). It is from the headmaster of the primary school that Jacques has learnt of his father's time in the army, in 1905, in the war against the Moroccans, of his horror at the obscene mutilation of the corpses of the fallen, whether perpetrated by Arabs or Frenchmen. Somewhere within himself, he had been a man who kept his integrity ('refusait d'être entamé', p.67). Then the Great War, the terrible slaughter of the Algerian troops, French and Arab alike, and the telegram, delivered by the mayor in person, which his mother and grandmother cannot read, but know that it means that their son and husband is dead. The chapter ends with a brutal return to the present, to the war in Algeria, with a bomb exploding in the street outside among the crowds of Arab and French passers-by, then the chaos, the soldiers, the ambulances. Jacques asks his mother to come to France with him, but she refuses, 'Maintenant je suis trop vieille. Je veux rester chez nous.'[3]

In Chapter 6, entitled 'La Famille' ('The Family'), we learn only one thing about Jacques's father: he had gone to witness the execution of a notorious murderer, and had come home pallid and vomiting. The story made a deep inpression on the son, and is retold in *L'Étranger*, and also begins the essay 'Réflexions sur la guillotine' (*Essais*, p.1021). Tarrou too, in *La Peste*, is horrified to realise that his father is

3 p.76. 'I'm too old now. I want to stay home', *FM*, p.60.

required, as public prosecutor, to be present at executions. We become better acquainted also with other members of the family, principally the Spanish grandmother and the speech-impaired but vigourous uncle Étienne (who will become Ernest). The next section (not numbered) is devoted to Ernest, the cooper, profoundly deaf, having only a few words at his command, but generous, good-humoured, full of strength and vitality. It is on the Sunday hunting expeditions with Ernest and his friends and his dog Brillant that Jacques learns that 'la compagnie des hommes était bonne et pouvait nourrir le coeur'.[4]. Ernest has two fierce rows: the first with his close-fisted elder brother Joséphin, who thereafter ceases to come to *grand'mère*'s flat for his meals. Ernest's other memorable row is with the suitor of his widowed sister, whom he throws out of the house. Poor Catherine, who had timidly welcomed the advances of Monsieur Antoine, now retreats for ever into her solitude and poverty (p.117–18).

From these reminiscences we return to the present. *Grand'mère* is dead, the now white-haired Ernest and Catherine live together like Darby and Joan, 'non pas selon la chair mais selon le sang'.[5] Others too have disappeared. Catherine's sister Marguérite, once so young and pretty, has died of diabetes, grossly fat, ugly, totally destroyed. *Grand'mère*'s sister Jeanne and her husband Joseph are both dead, as is a whole family of neighbours. So the chapter comes to an end again on an elegiac note, and the familiar *quartier* itself takes on a strange and sinister aspect. Jacques's last recollection is of coming upon the scene of a shooting, one Christmas night, a man lying with his head in a pool of blood, his inebriated drinking companion dancing frenziedly around him. It is a scene which Camus had placed in Prague, in his first novel, *La Mort heureuse*.

Chapter 6*bis* is the story of Jacques's primary schooldays, the wisdom of Monsieur Bernard, in whom he finds a father-substitute, his success in the entrance examination to the *lycée*. It also touches upon his very scanty religious education, the 'accelerated' catechism

---

[4] p.103. 'Jacques learned that the company of men was good and could nourish the soul', *FM*, p.84.
[5] p.122. 'Like man and wife, not in the flesh but in the blood' (i.e. according to their blood-relationship), *FM*, p.100.

classes for his first communion, and the slap administered by the extremely unpleasant and younger of the two parish priests, which alienates the boy from the Church for good. Chapter 7, 'Mondovi : La colonisation et le père' ('Mondovi: The Settlement and the Father'), recounts Jacques's journey to his birthplace, in the hope of finding someone who had known his father. It becomes an apologia for the early French colonists, a plea for comprehension on both sides. The farm is now owned by a Monsieur Veillard, a man who is defending his property against the Arab insurgents and knows nothing of Cormery senior. Veillard explains that his own great-grandparents had come from Paris, a carpenter from the Faubourg-Saint-Denis and a laundress, and that they had taken part in the revolution of 1848. In the plane flying back to Algiers, Jacques thinks of his own grandfather, a refugee from the German domination of Alsace in 1871. He reflects on the fate of those impoverished early colonists, their struggles, their hardships, the hostility of the Arabs, the rains, cholera, the heat, a dozen dying every day in the camp, and the bait which had drawn so many to Algeria: 'On leur avait donné les terres des insurgés de '71 [...] persécutés-persécuteurs'.[6] The irony of the reverse injustice is patent. At the end of the journey, Jacques realises that his father, like the rest of the poor, has left no legacy, is forever lost to him, unknowable. The search for the past of previous generations is over.

The second part is a memoir of Cormery's growing-up, from the moment when, as a ten-year-old, he takes the tram and sets out in his new shoes on a new journey, leaving the family for the unknown world of the *lycée*. It ends with the bitter experience of soulless work (a summer job at the age of thirteen), the loss of the joys of long sun-filled days, and yet the pride in knowing 'that he was a man' ('Oui, il était un homme', p.252). As the first chapter was a prologue, so the final chapter is an epilogue, a reflection on what this childhood of poverty, joy, desire, and anguish, lived out against the immensity of sea and land, had given him, the forty-year-old Jacques Cormery.

The work is dedicated to Camus's mother: 'À toi, qui ne pourras jamais lire ce livre' ('To you, who will never be able to read this

---

[6] p.178. 'They were given the land of the Arab rebels of '71 [...] persecuted-persecutors [...]' *FM*, p.149.

book'). The gentle, mentally limited, silent, resigned mother presides over the book. Indeed, she is its patron saint: 'Intercesseur: Vve. Camus', as her son inscribed the work. *Intercessor*: the 'typically Catholic term' has been noted by Chabot (p.34). The narrative opens on a scene of biblical simplicity: beneath a sky swept by great rainclouds, a man and a woman are being driven at nightfall through a bleak countryside in a waggon drawn by two ponies. Soon the man, concerned for his heavily pregnant wife, takes over from the Arab driver. At last they reach the village and the sparsely furnished house, and the woman gives birth to a son. The child sleeps in a laundry-basket, the woman also sleeps. His hand in hers, the husband too drops into slumber. The flames dance in the fireplace, outside the rain has ceased. All is peace and harmony. One could say Bethlehem painted by Georges de la Tour.

The absence of proper names for much of this episode lends universality to the scene. There is a fourth presence in the early pages: the mother is holding close to herself a four-year-old child. The imagery evokes the flight into Egypt, a family seeking refuge. Later this child is eliminated from the narrative, and we are told he has been left with his grandmother in Algiers. The iconography becomes more clearly that of the Nativity. The mother's characteristic features are delineated from the outset. She is fatigued and suffering, but courageously trying to smile. She is poorly dressed, has 'a sweet and regular countenance', and occasionally a strangely absent and distracted air such as one sees always on the faces of 'certain innocents'. Her look is full of kindness, fleetingly mingled with a glimmer of 'irrational fear'.[7] The term 'innocent' is evidently used in both senses: the simple-minded and the blameless. The shadowy mother of previous fictions (*L'Étranger*, *La Peste*) is brought centre stage to receive the loving homage of her son.

This humble, resigned and gentle mother is paired with her brother, Uncle Ernest, who has the innocence of the primitive, of Adam before the Fall, an 'innocence adamique' (p.98). He lives on the

---

7   pp.12–13: 'Un visage doux et régulier […] un air d'absence et de douce distraction, comme en portent perpétuellement certains innocents, mais qui ici affleurait fugitivement sur la beauté des traits. A la bonté si frappante du regard se mêlait parfois aussi une lueur de crainte irraisonnée aussitôt éteinte.'

level of sensation ('au niveau de la sensation', p.154). He is the child of nature, followed everywhere by his faithful dog Brillant, hunting, fishing, swimming, popular with his circle of laughing friends. His outbursts of anger too are natural:

> Ces colères tout à fait semblables à un phénomène naturel. Un orage, on le voit se former, et l'on attend qu'il crève. Rien d'autre à faire.[8]

This accord with nature is, of course, Camus's definition of happiness. Both Catherine and Ernest are childlike, having only a rudimentary command of language (at least partly a result of their deafness), and limited mental horizons. Neither understands much of the world beyond their immediate surroundings. Both too are beautiful, Catherine with the beauty one sees depicted in the iconography of the saints, Ernest with the beauty of Arcady, 'avec des allures de pâtre grec endimanché'.[9] Camus seems indeed to have been dreaming at this stage of his life of some sort of fusion between the Christian and the pagan ideals:

> Le monde marche vers le paganisme mais il rejette encore les valeurs païennes. Il faut les restaurer, paganiser la croyance, gréciser le Christ et l'équilibre revient.[10]

Catherine is the incarnation of the 'female' (Christian) virtues of love and charity which Don Juan had dismissed in favour of the 'virile' qualities of 'la tendresse et la générosité' (*Carnets I*, p.215). These Ernest possesses in abundance: avuncularly tender towards the young Jacques, whom he takes swimming and hunting, he is also a man 'adoré de ses camarades pour sa bonne humeur et sa générosité'.[11] It is

---

8   p.108. 'His rages [are] like a natural phenomenon. You see a storm gathering, you wait for it to break. Nothing else to do', *FM*, p.88.

9   p.111. 'He had the look of a Greek shepherd in holiday dress', *FM*, p.90.

10   *Carnets III*, p.220 (in 1958). 'The world is moving towards paganism, but it still rejects pagan values. We must restore them, paganise belief, Hellenise Christ, and the balance will be restored.' Perhaps not far removed from what the artists of the Renaissance were trying to do.

11   p.98. 'His friends adored Ernest for his good nature and his generosity', *FM*, p.80.

he who will give Jacques the supreme accolade:'Toi, un homme' (p.252; 'You, a man'). Catherine is Jacques's mother, but Ernest is, within his limitations, a substitute father.

Catherine's inner life is simple, mysterious, and selfless, in keeping with her life in general. When the *curé* tells her to pray for her husband and the soldiers gone off to the war, she is astonished, because 'l'idée de prier ne lui serait pas venue, elle n'avait jamais voulu déranger personne'.[12] Given the 'terrible grinding-down of poverty' ('l'usure terrible de la pauvreté', p.154), there was no place for religion in the family. While Ernest sees only 'le curé et la pompe' (p.154), and makes fun of them, Catherine was

> la seule dont la douceur pût faire penser à la foi, mais justement la douceur était toute sa foi [...] Elle ne parlait jamais de Dieu.[13]

In the *Notes* for the novel (printed in appendix), Camus is more explicit. In her patience, her suffering, her acceptance, she is Christ-like: 'Sa mère *est* le Christ' (p.283, Camus's italics. 'His mother *is* the Christ.'). Other remarks insist on the parallel. She is like the protagonist of *The Idiot*:

> Maman; comme une Muichkine ignorant. Elle ne connaît pas la vie du Christ, sinon sur la croix. Et qui pourtant en est plus près?

And again:

> Christianisme de maman à la fin de sa vie. La femme pauvre, malheureuse, ignorante [...] Que la croix la soutienne!

Finally:

> Sa religion est visuelle. Elle sait ce qu'elle a vu sans pouvoir l'interpréter. Jésus c'est la souffrance, il tombe, etc.[14]

---

12   p.69. 'The idea of praying would never have entered her mind, she never wanted to bother anyone', *FM*, p.54.
13   p.154. 'Only she with her gentleness might have suggested faith, but in fact that gentleness was her faith [...] She never spoke of God', *FM*, p.129.
14   The French quotations are on pp.295, 304 and 305 respectively. '*Maman*: like an ignorant Myshkin. She does not know Christ's life except on the cross. Yet

Around her neck, on a little chain, she wears a tiny gold medal representing the Virgin Mary ('la petite médaille d'or représentant la Vierge', p.231). She is herself the patient Virgin Mother, innocent and maternal.

There is no touch of intellectual superiority or dismissal in these remarks, as in the case of the old woman in the youthful essay entitled 'L'Ironie' in *L'Envers et l'Endroit*. Camus's mother is not lost in 'the wretchedness of man in God', in the 'the disappointing tête-à-tête with God' ('la tête-à-tête décevant avec Dieu', *Essais*, p.17). The tone has changed in the intervening years. In his childhood, however, nothing in the cold, dark, ugly church moves the boy Jacques except the music of the organ, which awakens in him a sense of mystery, an extension of his wonder at the quiet smile or the silence of his mother ('le mystère quotidien du discret sourire ou du silence de sa mère', p.159), sitting in the twilight, looking down into the street below. In both cases, the child has an awareness of the spiritual. His mother is associated with the sacred and she is never mocked. In her essential goodness, Catherine is close to Rieux's quiet mother in *La Peste*, in her silence and the mystery of her inner life, she is very close to Meursault's mother in *L'Étranger*.

Grand'mère's character is summed up in a note: 'Vaillante. Non résignée' (p.93; 'Valiant. Not resigned'). Her courage is a 'masculine' quality, in contrast to the resigned courage of *maman*, with her 'beau sourire vaillant' (p.76; 'lovely valiant smile'). Even when *grand'-mère*'s dreamy, poetic husband had been alive, she it was who ruled over the household and the nine children, in a reversal of the traditional roles: 'Elle régnait, exigeant le respect pour elle et son mari'.[15] *Grand'mère* is a fighter, and to her grandchildren she is also a father-substitute.

---

    who is closer to it?' *FM*, p.239. '*Maman*'s Christianity at the end of her life. The poor, unfortunate, ignorant woman [...] May the cross sustain her!' ibid., p.245. 'Her religion is visual. She knows what she has seen without being able to interpret it. Jesus is suffering, he dies, etc', ibid., p.245.

15 p.82. 'She held sway, demanding respect for herself and her husband', *FM*, p.65.

Jacques's resentment of his grandmother has less to do with the beatings that she administers than with the fact that through him she inflicts pain on his mother, a silent and tortured witness, unable to intervene through fatigue, mental infirmity, and respect for the older woman. In the first of the essays of *L'Envers et l'Endroit*, he had described how the grandmother, when visitors came, would ask the child, in the presence of his mother, whom he loved best, his mother or his grandmother, and he would be obliged to answer 'My grandmother', with a great aching surge of love in his heart for his silent mother ('L'Ironie', *Essais*, p.20). *Maman*'s life is a long and painful trial:

> [Elle] endurait les coups pour ses enfants, comme elle endurait pour elle-même la dure journée de travail au service des autres, les parquets lavés à genoux, la vie sans homme et sans consolation.[16]

Hers is a naïve life lived in perseverance and resignation, 'une vie [...] ignorante, obstinée, résignée enfin à toutes les souffrances, les siennes comme celles des autres', Camus writes, echoing Claudel's praise of such a life, which he had thought of taking as an epigraph for *Le Premier homme*: 'Rien ne vaut contre la vie humble, ignorante, obstinée'.[17] The boy Jacques yearns for the love of this mother, so enigmatically silent,

> isolée dans sa demi-surdité, ses difficultés de langage, belle certainement mais à peu près inaccessible et d'autant plus qu'elle était plus souriante et que son coeur à lui s'élançait plus vers elle.[18]

---

16 p.61. '[She] endured those blows for her children, just as for herself she had endured the hard days of working in the service of others, washing floors on her knees, living without a man and without solace', *FM*, p.46.

17 p.61.'A life [...] unaware, persevering, a life resigned to all kinds of suffering, her own as well as that of others', *FM*, p.46. The quotation from Claudel's *L'Échange* is in the 'Notes et plans' for the novel, 'Annexes', p.275.

18 p.60. 'isolated by her semi-deafness, her difficulty in expressing herself, beautiful surely but virtually inaccessible, and never more so than when she was full of smiles and when his own heart most went out to her', *FM*, p.46.

As a forty-year-old adult, he realises that 'il ignorait tout de sa mère, sauf ce qu'il en connaissait lui-même. Et de son père'.[19] Certain critics attribute the sense of alienation in Camus's work to the inability to overcome the barrier which his mother's silence and meditative self-absorption raised between them.

The narrator's journey to visit his father's grave is undertaken, at least on one level, to please his mother. He is in search of that young father, killed in the slaughter of 1914–18, and who now lies, unsung, unknown, in a desolate cemetery in farthest Brittany. Death however does not yield up its mystery. What Jacques experiences, as he reads the headstone, is the dizzying realisation that he is now older than his father ever was. The natural order has been turned on its head, the son is older than the father, the fruits of war are madness and chaos, what he would elsewhere call the *Absurd* in all its horrible irrationality.[20] Time itself is out of joint. 'Il sent le temps se disloquer', Camus wrote in his 'Plans' (p.317). His emotions are 'l'angoisse et la pitié' (p.30), the Aristotelian emotions of tragedy. 'Il n'était plus que ce coeur angoissé, avide de vivre, révolté contre l'ordre mortel du monde.'[21] Revolt surges up in him, the self-image that he has constructed over forty years crumbles, and he now desperately desires to know the truth of his own identity, a secret bound up with this dead father. The search for the father has become a way of conquering transience, death, meaninglessness: 'Il lui semblait maintenant que ce secret avait partie liée avec ce mort, ce père cadet'.[22] But from the dead nothing is to be learned or salvaged: 'Tournant le dos à la tombe, Jacques Cormery abandonna son père'.[23]

---

19   p.62. 'He knew nothing about his mother except what he learned from his own experience. Nor about his father', *FM*, p.48.
20   p.30: 'Quelque chose ici n'était pas dans l'ordre naturel et, à vrai dire, il n'y avait pas d'ordre mais seulement folie et chaos.'
21   p.30. 'All that was left was this anguished heart, eager to live, rebelling against the deadly order of the world', *FM*, p.21.
22   p.31. 'Yet the secret he had eagerly sought to learn […] now seemed to him to be intimately linked with this dead man, this younger father', *FM*, p.21.
23   p.32. 'Turning his back on the grave, Jacques Cormery abandoned his father', *FM*, p.22.

The search for meaning, for some sense to existence, is now on. Cormery will continue to search for clues in the story of his father, as the journey to Mondovi and the questioning of his mother will show, but at heart he knows the answer is elsewhere. Before setting out on his quest, he has another visit to make. He must see Victor Malan. The initials J.G., inscribed in brackets in the chapter heading, indicate that Camus had in mind his old philosophy teacher in the *lycée*, Jean Grenier, with whom he remained in contact all his life and who had retired to his native Saint-Brieuc. 'Mon ami et mon maître', Camus calls him, in the Preface he wrote for the re-edition of *L'Envers et l'Endroit*. It was to him that Camus had dedicated these first literary compositions, and their correspondence continued until Camus's death in 1960. Grenier was himself, as well as a philosopher interested in religion and the mysticism of the East, a writer of reflective and poetic essays. 'Gr[enier], que j'ai reconnu comme père, est né là où mon vrai père est mort et est enterré', Camus wrote in his 'Notes et plans' for the novel.[24]

Cormery had decided to visit his unknown father and had even been determined to do so before visiting his old friend 'in order to feel *completely free* afterwards' (my italics).[25] Free after visiting the tomb, or after visiting Malan? It matters little, essentially both visits are the accomplishment of a duty, one which frees him to embark upon his quest, with the blessing of Malan as substitute father. 'C'est ça, *fils*', says Malan. 'Puisque vous allez voir votre mère, essayez d'apprendre quelque chose sur votre père' (my italics).[26]

Cormery assures the older man of his filial love and devotion, and receives his approval, although Malan tells him that he no longer needs a father, having brought himself up by his own efforts. This is the truth that in the end he will recognise. But the visit is depressing. Malan is a recluse, old, weary, and afraid of dying. His final words

---

24 p.293. 'Gr., whom I acknowledge as father, was born where my real father died and was buried', *FM*, p.238.
25 See pp.28–9: 'Il s'était décidé à rendre visite à ce mort inconnu et avait même tenu à le faire avant de retrouver son vieil ami *pour se sentir ensuite tout à fait libre*' (my italics).
26 p.34. 'That's it, *my son* [...] Since you're going to see your mother, try to find out something about your father', *FM*, p.23 (my italics).

are: 'Il y a en moi un vide affreux, une indifférence qui me fait mal'.[27] The parallel with the visits of Mersault to Zagreus is obvious.

Everything about northern France, between Paris and the coast, has been grey and depressing, the flat countryside, the ugly houses, the wretched little station, the fellow travellers in the train, a balding, heavy man, breathing laboriously, a peasant woman wiping the nose of a pasty-faced child. In Saint-Brieuc the ticket-collector is taciturn, the streets are narrow and miserable, the cemetery is surrounded by high forbidding walls. Northern Europe is a cold, miserable prison from which Cormery has to escape:

> C'était ainsi chaque fois qu'il quittait Paris pour l'Afrique, une jubilation sourde, le coeur s'élargissant, la satisfaction de qui vient de réussir une bonne évasion et qui rit en pensant à la tête des gardiens.[28]

On the liner taking him back to Algeria, the sun reappears. As it sinks below the horizon, he knows that Algiers awaits him 'at the end of the night' ('Il trouverait Alger au bout de la nuit', p.56). The two parts of the novel are thus divided by the Mediterranean, which separates France, the world of exile, from Algeria, the land of heart's desire. After the dark prelude, Chapter 4 sees the beginning of this 'long wayfaring', on the sun-drenched and liberating waters of the Mediterranean, as Jacques Cormery sails away from the land of the dead, of the lost father, towards the beloved land of his dearly-loved mother and the humble and happy kingdom of his childhood.

This is the only work in which a child plays any active role, and here it is central. Childhood, in all its joys and fears, sorrows and consolations, games and friendships, is lovingly depicted. Childhood's paradise, the Kingdom, is a rather dingy beach on the edge of Algiers, reached across a dreary run-down industrial landscape, and where the waves 'were not always clear' ('les premières vagues n'étaient pas toujours transparentes', p.53). But here, in the magnificent bay of Algiers, bathing naked in the warm water and the sunlight, they are

---

27 p.40. 'There is a terrible emptiness in me, an indifference that hurts', *FM*, p.29.
28 p.44. 'So it was every time he left Paris for Africa, his heart swelling with a secret exultation, with the satisfaction of one who has made good his escape and is laughing at the thought of the look on the guards' faces', *FM*, p.32.

lords of all they survey: 'Ils régnaient sur la vie et sur la mer [...] comme des seigneurs assurés de leurs richesses irremplaçables.'[29] The whole world is their Eden, even the dark cellars in the courtyard of the appartment block, regularly flooded, where they gather to play:

> Montés sur de vieilles caisses, ils jouaient aux Robinsons loin du ciel pur et des vents de la mer, triomphants dans leur royaume de misère.[30]

This is Kingdom of childhood joy, never to be recaptured. Quilliot writes, in his *Présentation* to Camus's previous publication: 'In a certain way, the short stories of *L'Exil et le Royaume* were the first steps on that pilgrimage to the sources to be undertaken in *Le Premier homme*' (*TRN*, p.2039, tr.).

The opposite of the Kingdom is the experience of imprisonment and exile. Jacques's first memories of incarceration are the enforced siestas in grandmother's bedroom and the ceaseless buzzing of a couple of bluebottles, seeking a way out (we remember the fly in the bus carrying Janine and Marcel). The enclosing bare walls of the flat are ruled over by the elderly female tyrant, wielding the strap with which she punishes the boy who has stayed too long in the kingdom and come home late for the evening meal. The *colonie de vacances*, to which the child is sent in the summer, in spite of all its attractions, is also a prison.[31] At thirteen, he becomes acquainted with yet another imprisonment: office work. His summer holidays are bartered away for work whose monotony renders the 'days too long and life too short'.[32] He has discovered the dreary round of Sisyphus, Monday through to Saturday, one day after the other. He discovers that poverty

---

29   p.54. 'They reigned over life and over the sea [..] like nobles certain that their riches were limitless', *FM*, p.41.
30   pp.50–1. 'and the children, standing on old boxes, would play Robinson Crusoe far from the open sky and the sea breezes, triumphant in their kingdom of poverty', *FM*, p.37.
31   p.138: 'Quand le soir arrivait [...] l'enfant sentait monter en lui un désespoir sans bornes et criait en silence après la pauvre maison démunie de tout de son enfance.'
32   p.248: '[Un] travail bête à pleurer dont la monotonie interminable parvient à rendre en même temps les jours trop longs et la vie trop courte.'

too is a prison: 'La misère est une fortresse sans pont-levis.'[33] It is one that allows no luxuries, not even that of truthfulness. In order to secure a holiday job with its much needed pittance, *grand'mère* obliges him, to his distress, to lie about his age and about his intention of returning to school in the autumn. As to *grand'mère* herself, in spite of all his resentment, he will come to pay tribute to her valiant struggle, her unbroken spirit in the face of poverty and adversity, she who had once been 'the young, beautiful and energetic wife', and who had borne nine children.[34] Even as a child, he realises that *grand'mère*, plunging her arm down the filthy latrine to try to retrieve the two francs which he has lied about losing, is doing so not from avarice, but from bitter necessity, for in their house, two francs mattered ('dans cette maison deux francs était une somme', p.87). *Grand'mère* is not simply the tyrannical version of a replacement father, she is also the face of courage and indomitability.

Ignorance also is a prison. For Jacques however there is an escape route: education. It is opened up for him by the substitute father *par excellence*, the schoolteacher whom he here calls Monsieur Bernard, and who was in real life Monsieur Louis Germain. Monsieur Bernard persuades the formidable grandmother to allow Jacques to sit the scholarship examination for the *lycée*. One brave fighter recognises another, and he in turn understands her fortitude, reminding the child of what he owes not only to his mother, but to her, because her life is hard ('La vie est difficile pour elle', p.151).

Doctors and teachers, Dr Bernard Rieux, Dr Bernard in *La Mort heureuse*, Monsieur Bernard, the primary schoolteacher, these are the quiet heroes of Camus's novels. For Jacques, 'À un moment précis, [Monsieur Bernard] avait su remplacer [son] père'. It is 'le seul geste paternel, à la fois réfléchi et décisif, qui fût intervenu dans sa vie d'enfance'.[35] Intensely patriotic, M. Bernard will declare to the whole

---

33 p.138. 'Poverty is a fortress without drawbridges', *FM*, p.113.
34 pp.82: 'La jeune, belle et énergique épouse', p.83: 'La pauvreté ni l'adversité ne l'avait jamais entamée.'
35 p.129. 'At a critical time he knew how to take the father's role [...] The one paternal act – both well thought out and crucial – that had affected his life as a child', *FM*, p.106.

class that he has a special place in his heart for Jacques, as for all the pupils whose fathers have died in the war, because, he tells them, 'J'essaie de remplacer ici au moins mes camarades morts'.[36] From Monsieur Bernard, Jacques accepts everything, even physical punishment, because he recognises it as just.

The *lycée* is for Jacques another life, another world:

> Ainsi, pendant des années, la vie de Jacques se partagea inégalement entre deux vies qu'il ne pouvait relier l'une à l'autre.[37]

His first departure in the tram for the new school is the start of an odyssey of exploration. He does not see his mother and grandmother waving him off, because his view is obscured by the newspaper his neighbour is reading, the world of literacy cuts him off from them. Significantly, the town library, the *bibliothèque municipale*, is halfway between the poor district where Jacques lives and the affluent suburbs and the boarding school of Sainte-Odile, the crossover point between one world and the other. When Jacques and his friend Pierre enter the library,

> ils ne voyaient pas les murs de livres noirs mais un espace et des horizons multiples qui, dès le pas de la porte, les enlevaient à la vie étroite du quartier.[38]

In the *lycée*, Jacques enters a world where he does not speak of his family, where it now appears 'different' to him, where, when told by his friend Pierre to write down on a form that his mother is a charwoman, a *domestique* (p.187), he suddenly feels ashamed, and then ashamed of being ashamed. It is a place where, bringing back an unsigned form, he tells the teacher that no-one at home can write, and realises, from the latter's surprised look, that this is not the norm (pp.189–90). And yet he loves his mother no less deeply, does not feel envy, has no desire to change his background. Simply, he learns that

---

36 p.143. 'I try at least here to take the place of my dead comrades', *FM*, p.118.
37 p.230. 'So, for years, Jacques's existence was divided unequally into two lives between which he was unable to make any connection', *FM*, p.195.
38 p.227. 'They would see not the walls of black books but multiplying horizons and expanses that, as soon as they crossed the doorstep, would take them away from the cramped life of the neighbourhood', *FM*, p.193.

others have traditions, family histories, values which he has not, which he has grown up without.

He learns this above all from his friend Georges Didier, to whom he has been drawn by a common taste for reading and literature.[39] Didier is from a middle-class family in the services, with a house in France and an attic stuffed full of family photographs and letters. He can trace his family tree back to Trafalgar. Very intelligent, patriotic and religious, he is determined to become a priest. What Jacques admires in Didier is his thirst for the absolute, his loyalty, his capacity for affection. But for Jacques there is also in Georges, so different in his background, the attraction of the exotic, 'les séductions des aventuriers basanés qui reviennent des tropiques, murés sur un secret étrange et incompréhensible'.[40] What Jacques finds exotic is not only Georges's religion or his aversion to coarse language, but his strong sense of tradition and of French patriotism. In Jacques's mind, although he recognises himself as 'French', France is an abstraction, like God, and his notions of the one are as vague as his notions of the other.

Lacking tradition, lacking an authority, Cormery's childish moral code is elementary: theft is forbidden, mothers and women are to be protected, and that is about as far as it goes (p.192). Georges's secret, Jacques's father's secret, the enigma of identity, of belonging, questions of right and wrong, all are bound up together, for, as Jacques says, much earlier in the work:

> J'ai essayé de trouver moi-même, dès le début, tout enfant, ce qui était bien et ce qui était mal – puisque personne autour de moi ne pouvait me le dire [...] J'ai besoin que quelqu'un me montre la voie et me donne blâme et louange, non selon le pouvoir mais selon l'autorité, j'ai besoin de mon père.[41]

39　Georges Didier is the actual name of Camus's friend, who became a Jesuit. Camus kept in touch until the priest was killed in a car accident in Switzerland in 1957 (see *Carnets III*, p.204). Camus intended to come back to Didier in the novel, and makes a note for himself on p.190: 'Le retrouver ensuite à sa mort.'

40　p.192. 'He had the allure [for Jacques] of some tanned adventurers who return from the tropics guarding a strange and incomprehensible secret', *FM*, p.163.

41　p.40, note. 'I tried to find out for myself, from the start, when I was a child, what was right and what was wrong – because no one around me could tell me

The present tense is interesting. Again in the 'Notes' appended to the novel, Camus wrote:

> A 40 ans, il reconnaît qu'il a besoin de quelqu'un qui lui montre la voie et lui donne blâme ou louange: un père. L'autorité et non le pouvoir.[42]

The need has been recognised in adulthood, and indeed, it is this, more than his mother's wish (which he has ignored for years, see p.28), which starts Camus (and his hero Cormery) on his pilgrimage and the visit to his father's grave. The motivation is deeper than a desire to please his mother. Jacques undertakes the visit as the starting point of a search for 'authority and not power', an authority which does not infringe the freedom of the disciple. The substitute father, Victor Malan, is consulted in Saint Brieuc, in the place of the dead father, and gives the necessary blessing to the enterprise.

It is not only the child who is fatherless in Algeria, but the whole Franco-Algerian population, this childlike people ('ce peuple enfant', as he calls them in 'L'Été à Alger') who now have to create their own tradition in 'this splendid and frightening land' to which they have come ('cette terre splendide et effrayante', p.258). One critic goes so far as to say that the central character of the novel is the land of Algeria itself.[43] But it is Algiers, not Algeria, that Camus celebrates in these memoirs, the *quartier pauvre* where the populations, European and Arab, rubbed shoulders. In the novel, Jacques's acquaintance with the countryside is restricted to the Sundays when he goes shooting with Uncle Ernest and his friends, in 'un immense plateau couvert de chênes nains et de genévriers'.[44] In his adulthood, we hear only of the journey to Mondovi, in search of the lost father. Neither of these is the desert and the life of the tribes.

[…] I need someone to show me the way and to blame me and praise me, by right not of power but of authority. I need my father', *FM*, p.29, note.

42   p.288. 'At age 40, he realizes he needs someone to show him the way and to give him censure or praise: a father. Authority and not power', *FM*, p.235.

43   Abdelkader Djemai, an Algerian novelist and journalist, in the discussions in Dubois, 1995, p.25.

44   p.104. 'A vast […] plateau wooded with dwarf oaks and junipers', *FM*, p.85.

Camus's first-hand knowledge of the 'interior' of Algeria was relatively limited, as José Lenzini observes. His experience was based largely on Algiers and his own *quartier* of Belcourt, which perhaps explains the absence of the Arabs from his work, but, as Lenzini adds, 'It would be wrong to see in that a form of rejection' (p.83, tr.). He had proved his concern for the poorest of the Arabo-Berber population very early on, with his investigative journalism into conditions in the Kabylia for *Alger Républicain* in June 1939. Published under the headline 'Misère de la Kabylie' ('Poverty in the Kabylia'), the articles were reprinted in a somewhat abbreviated version in 1958, as a response to his critics (*Actuelles III*, 'Chroniques Algériennes'). The vast land of Algeria, however, with its deserts and its tribes, Arabo-Berber Algeria, lies outside the golden vision of the city of Camus's childhood.

This final chapter of the first part of the novel, 'Mondovi: la colonisation et le père' ('Mondovi: The Settlement and the Father'), is a meditation on the odyssey of the first colonists and the hardships which awaited them, working-class makers of the revolution of 1848, now bought off with the promise of land and a place to live. When they disembark in the port of Bône, after a five-week exodus from Paris to Lyon and then down the Rhone in barges, followed by a miserable storm-tossed five-day crossing of the Mediterranean, they find themselves in an 'immense and hostile country' ('ce pays immense et hostile', p.172), surrounded by soldiers on guard, in an encampment of tents lost in the marshes, under the relentless rain, and exposed to cholera, disease and death.

This is a picture of Algeria that we have not previously seen in Camus's writing. It is of course a defence of those poverty-stricken early settlers, a plea for understanding and sympathy, but it also reflects Camus's own despair as Algeria sinks further and further into the war of independence. The bomb in the street, the jeeps 'hérissés de fusils et qui circulaient lentement',[45] which Jacques meets on his way to Mondovi, these are the sinister reminders of a tragic situation. Even the night, in the rest of Camus's work so consoling, is now full of menace. Flying back to Algiers, Jacques feels himself not liberated by

---

45 p.165; 'Slow-moving jeeps bristling with guns', *FM*, p.138.

the 'fraternal' night' in which Meursault had found peace, but doubly imprisoned by the plane and the darkness, ('cloîtré par l'avion et les ténèbres', p.171) and unable to breathe. A panic-inducing menace hangs in the air, which is full of latent violence, the plane is like 'un vis qui s'enfonçait directement dans l'épaisseur de la nuit'.[46]

Detested by the more affluent class of the French *pied-noir* population on the one hand, while on the other disowned in France by the extreme Left and those who, like Sartre, justified the terrorism of the *Front de Libération Nationale* (FLN), and regarded by the Algerian rebels as irrelevant, Camus vainly clung to the hope of a federal solution in which both populations would live together in the country in peace, and indeed he worked for it. His daughter has said, in a recent interview, that he favoured a federation such as would be achieved later in South Africa, giving equal rights to all elements of the population.[47] Herbert Lottman writes that while he 'was silent with regard to the press, he acted where he could, where he could be discreetly useful, when he was asked, often on his own' (p.592). He intervened on behalf of more than a hundred and fifty Algerian rebels standing trial for their lives. He rejected publicity, fearing it would only inflame the situation. In the case of the militant Ben Saddok, accused of having assassinated an Algerian moderate, he withdrew his letter to the court when he realised that the defence lawyer was disregarding his request not to make it public (Todd, pp.944–5). Whether this policy of silence was right and justified is still the subject of fierce debate.

'Je suis déchiré, voilà la vérité', he wrote in a letter of 1956.[48] By 1958, Patrick McCarthy sees in him a broken man (1982, p.302). He was of course swimming against the tide of history. He was anxious to point out that the 'Euro-Algerians' (as we now call them) were not in their majority an ascendancy of rich colonials or *nouveaux riches* (whom he loathed), but largely a population of the working-class poor, artisans, blue-collar and white-collar workers. These are the people of

---

46   p.171. 'like a screw driven into the thickness of the night', *FM*, p.143.
47   See the Internet interview with Russel Wilkinson for Amazon's *Spike Magazine* (s.d., Internet: http://www.spikemagazine.com/0397camu.php).
48   Letter to André Rosfelder, 26 February 1956, quoted Todd, p.874 (tr.). 'I am torn apart, that is the truth.'

his own background, the people whose obscure and humble lives are celebrated in *Le Premier homme*. The standard of living of the *pieds noirs* was 20% inferieur to that in France. There were in fact only twenty-thousand or so 'well-to-do' colonials in a population of slightly under a million. The indigenous population was however of the order of nine million.[49]

We are struck by the absence or silence of this huge population in the novels. Camus and his friends had always been passionately concerned about the situation of the Arabo-Berber people. In 1937, Camus and nine others had signed a manifesto in the monthly bulletin of the Maison de la Culture, protesting that one could not speak of culture in a country where hundreds of thousands were deprived of education, in dire poverty, and harassed by special laws and inhumane regulations.[50] In *Le Premier homme* there is compassion, but, it must be said, always from a French perspective. We get a glimpse of famished Arabs picking through the dustbins of even the poorest of the European population (p.132). They are glimpsed, but never heard. They are classified in Camus's French mind into 'good Arabs', like old Tamzal who goes on working for the *pied-noir* Veillant, and 'the bandits', those who throw the bomb among the crowds in Jacques's mother's street. 'Dis, les bandits, c'est bien?' Uncle Ernest asks anxiously, and Jacques replies, in schoolmasterly fashion: 'Non, les autres Arabes oui, les bandits non.'[51] Arab atrocities, the bomb in the street, the massacre of a father, mother, daughter and two sons on a farm next to Veillant's are foregrounded (p.167), French crimes are only obliquely mentioned, such as the disappearance of old Tamzal's son-in-law, taken away by the army and never heard of again. We do not hear of the slaughter or torture of thousands of Arab Algerians. Camus

---

49   I am indebted for these figures to Todd, pp.824–5.
50   *Essais*, p.1328: 'On ne saurait par exemple parler de culture dans un pays où 900,000 habitants sont privés d'écoles, et de civilisation, quand il s'agit d'un peuple diminué par une misère sans précédent et brimé par des lois d'exception et des codes inhumains.' Monthly bulletin of the *Maison de la Culture* of Algiers, no.2, May 1937.
51   p.123. '"Say, the bandits, that's all right?" "No," said Jacques, "the other Arabs yes, the bandits no."', *FM*, p.100.

wished to contribute to peace-making, not blood-letting. Whether justice was best served in this way is another question.

In the nativity scene which opens the novel, after the birth of the child, Jacques's father sits down on the ground beside the old Arab, who protectively holds over them both, by way of shelter, an ancient travelling holdall. Pointing to this symbolic scene, Weyemberg asks, 'How could a man born under such auspices choose between the two tutelary figures watching over his entry into the world?' (p.23, tr.). In the scene of the bomb in the street, Jacques rescues an Arab who is being threatened, bringing him into a café (pp.74–5). In the bloodshed of the war of 1914–18, we are reminded, Algerian troops, European and Arab alike, are slaughtered (p.70). But even this tragedy is not enough to establish a blood-brotherhood.

In the 'Plans' for the novel, there are several snatches of conversation and debate with an Arab interlocutor, who is evidently a militant called Saddok,[52] whom Jacques takes to his mother's flat. Saddok shows the greatest respect for the old lady: 'Elle est ma mère', dit-il. 'La mienne est morte. Je l'aime et la respecte comme si elle était ma mère.'[53] No greater bond could be created between himself and Jacques. He is an Arab version of Tarrou, but before the latter's conversion to non-violence. And Jacques recognises him as a brother, but a separated brother, saying sadly, 'Tu es mon frère, et nous sommes séparés' (p.279).

This vision of brotherhood is a dream, an aspiration. It has been pointed out (Dubois, 1995, p.73) that Camus had no knowledge of Arabic, and was completely French-educated (as of course were the few rich Arabs who managed to get a secondary education). Goodwill alone is not enough. The two cultures and traditions were too divergent, and no meeting place existed or was created. At the end of the novel, as we have it, Jacques feels himself surrounded by a people both 'attirant et inquiétant, proche et séparé', who, in spite of passing friendships or comradeships, remained alien:

---

52 We remember the militant Saddok, in whose case Camus had thought of intervening.
53 p.279. '"She is my mother," he said. "Mine is dead. I love and respect her as if she were my mother."', *FM*, p.230.

> Le soir venu, ils se retiraient pourtant dans leurs maisons inconnues, où l'on ne pénétrait jamais, barricadés aussi avec leurs femmes qu'on ne voyait jamais.[54]

When, in Jacques's childhood, the occasional street fight would break out between an Arab and a European, the gathering crowd of Arab onlookers seemed menacing in its silence and number, and the child was filled with an 'unknown anguish' ('une angoisse inconnue', p.258).

Some recent critics try hard to find an affinity between Camus and the Arabo-Berber population, also between the *pieds noirs* and the indigenous people, but the two populations in fact led separate existences, even when, as in Camus's case, they lived in mixed working-class neighbourhoods and Arab and French children played football together (p.218). Ali Yédès points out that Camus never felt at home in France, and that the hedonistic 'peuple enfant' of French Algeria had little in common with the French establishment or intelligentsia, but in fact much the same could be said of the working-class of Marseille or Nice vis-à-vis Paris. One may ask in what way the Arab population shared the hedonism of the joyful near-nudity on the beaches, or of flirtations in the cinema. 'Camus's family', says Yédès, 'like every Euro-Algerian family, was deeply influenced by Arabo-Berber family structures and values' (p.105–6, tr.). The critic doth protest too much. He is on surer ground when he writes that 'the Other' was, for Camus and his community, the Arabo-Berber on the one hand, and the metropolitan Frenchman on the other (p.259). Nacer-Khodja sees Camus in the end opting for 'his own people', the French Algerians (pp.91ff.).

The truth is that, in spite of his estrangement from the climate, literal and metaphorical, of metropolitan France, Camus saw himself as belonging to what was actually a French and European intellectual, literary and spiritual tradition. What does he mean when he says that the 'peuple enfant' of French Algeria were bereft of tradition? It seems to mean simply that, being cut off from their roots, patriotism, republicanism, or conservative moral values such as those of Georges

---

54   p.257. 'Those people, alluring yet disturbing, near and separate […] At evening they still withdrew to their closed houses, where you never entered, barricaded also with their women you never saw', *FM*, p.217.

Didier, they needed to invent their own values and tradition in those spheres. They were a new people, just as Jacques would be the 'First Man', but they were nonetheless a French people (just as the French Canadians, one could say, are a *different* French people). When asked, in an interview in Sweden, on the occasion of his receiving the Nobel prize, whether he felt that his work was 'European' in inspiration, he replied:

> Personne plus que moi n'est attaché à sa province algérienne et je n'ai pas de peine cependant à me sentir inscrit dans la tradition française [...] C'est parce que j'aime mon pays que je me sens européen. [55]

'My country': France or Algeria? Was it possible to reconcile the two, while regarding Algeria as a 'province'?

Jacques visits two cemeteries, one in Saint Brieuc and the other on his visit to Mondovi, and they symbolise for him two different worlds:

> La Méditerranée séparait en moi deux univers, l'un où dans des espaces mesurés les souvenirs et les noms étaient conservés, l'autre où le vent de sable effaçait les traces des hommes sur de grands espaces.[56]

We notice the slip: the use here of the first-person singular pronoun. The two worlds are separated 'in me', not 'in him', for it is his own tormented inner division which Camus is describing. In the following sentence he returns to the third-person pronoun. Saint Brieuc is the world of tradition and memory, Mondovi a land without a history, in which the poor, when they die, leave no legacies or names, and, like Meursault, the individual must construct his own 'mode de vie'. The 'peuple enfant' of French Algeria are happy to live simply in the sunshine, and to die and disappear without trace. The first generation of immigrants had been that of the revolution of 1848, anti-clerical,

---

55 *Essais*, p.1901. 'No-one is more attached to his Algerian province than me, and yet I have no problem with feeling myself in the line of the French tradition. It is because I love my country that I feel myself to be European.'

56 p.181. 'The Mediterranean separates two worlds in me, one where memories and names are preserved in measured spaces, the other where the wind and sand erase all trace of men on the open ranges', *FM*, pp.152–3.

disinherited, homeless foundlings in a strange land. Reflecting on those impoverished earlier French Algerians, Jacques identifies with them in a land where they had arrived

> sans passé, sans morale, sans leçon, sans religion mais heureux de l'être et de l'être dans la lumière, angoissés devant la nuit et la mort [...] tous ici enfants trouvés et perdus qui bâtissaient de fugitives cités pour mourir ensuite à jamais.[57]

Jacques's first teachers are books and Monsieur Bernard, who, in the best 'republican' and secular tradition, never breathes a word against religion or against anyone's convictions, but condemns all the more forcefully theft, tale-bearing, lack of tact, and lack of cleanliness ('le vol, la délation, l'indélicatesse, la malpropreté', p.139). Crime and social improprieties are, we note, lumped together. However he also teaches another lesson when he talks to the class about his experiences in the war of 1914–18 ('Il leur parlait [...] des souffrances des soldats, de leur courage, de leur patience', p.139). It is this stoic courage which is the basis of all Jacques's (and Camus's) morality, and he finds it also, together with the notion of honour, in the swashbuckling boys' novels which he devours, and which transport him into

> un univers comique ou héroïque qui satisfaisait en lui deux soifs essentielles, la soif de la gaieté et du courage.[58]

'Il s'exaltait à des histoires d'honneur et de courage' (p.73; 'He would thrill to tales of honour and courage.' *FM*, p.58). 'Valiant' is a word that Jacques applies both to his mother and his grandmother. His father's epitaph is pronounced in four words by the nurse who had watched over him: 'Il était bien courageux' (p.72. 'He was very courageous.'). Jacques himself earns the same accolade on the day when, despite his revulsion and horror, he fetches a chicken for *grand'mère*

---

57   pp.178–9: 'With no past, without ethics, without guidance, without religion, but glad to be so and to be in the light, fearful in the face of night and death', *FM*, p.150. 'All these found and lost children who built transient towns in order to die for ever in themselves and in others', *FM*, p.151.
58   p.225. 'A world of comedy or heroism, where his two basic appetites, for joy and for courage, were satisfied', *FM*, p.190.

to slaughter. Uncle Ernest pronounces him courageous, and his mother echoes the verdict (p.216). What he admires in the poor, as in the early settlers, is this same quality, for the necessity of toiling to make a living is a 'leçon de courage, non de morale' (p.86. 'A lesson of courage, not of morality'). They live now, as earlier, in a hostile land, and, like Janine, in *La Femme adultère*, he admires the courage in their daily lives ('courage à vivre', *TRN*, p.1560).

Camus endows Jacques with a thirst for gaiety and for courage. The comic was important to him, as he notes in his 'Plans' ('Important aussi le thème de la comédie', p.272), and more so here than anywhere else, except perhaps in the short story 'Jonas ou l'Artiste au travail'. Here we have the young Jacques suffering agonies of embarrassment as he escorts his grandmother to the cinema to see the silent cliffhanging serials that she loves, and having to read out the subtitles to her, above the noise of the piano accompaniment and the enthusiastic audience participation, without broadcasting to all and sundry that she is illiterate (pp.92–3). Here is grandmother again, the only woman coming to the school prize-day wearing the old Spanish peasant headscarf, and causing her grandson agonies once more as she apostrophizes those next to her (p.232). Or here is Uncle Michel, hugely dignified, a 'veritable peasant patriarch', who occasionally releases a loud fart, 'a sonorous incongruity', as Camus puts it, for which he politely apologises to his wife ('une sonore incongruité dont il s'excusait courtoisement auprès de sa femme', p.126). Here is miserly Uncle Joséphin, managing to marry a pretty young wife, who brings him furniture and bourgeois happiness. However, 'il est vrai que Joséphin pour finir devait garder les meubles et non la femme'.[59]

Realism and humour merge in descriptions rich in vivid and detailed impressions of sounds, sights and smells. On his way to school, Jacques remembers, among the different tramdrivers, the Arab 'brown bear' who always stares straight ahead, the old Italian who will stop the tram to save a dog, the 'big sausage' they call Zorro, Douglas Fairbanks's double, with his little moustache (pp.194–5). Then the street Bab-Azoun, down which the youngsters hurry on their way from the

---

59 p.114. 'It is true that Josephin ended up keeping the furniture and not the wife', *FM*, p.92.

tram-stop to the *lycée*, with its teeming arcades and bazaars, the hideous pottery for tourists, the grocers' shops, flower shops, Arab merchants' stalls, cloth merchants, the air again heavy with the scent of spices, flowers, coffee and pastries, and the Arab doughnut-maker with his delicious doughnuts (pp.197–200).

The realism frequently has an earthy ring. Smells in particular are remembered with astonishing clarity, the odour of the dog Brillant, of the *garrigue* (scrubland) on the days of the hunters, of the biscuits called *oreillettes*, smelling of vanilla, and also, in the stables of Uncle Michel, 'la bonne odeur de poils, de paille et de crottin'.[60] There are the 'appetising' horse droppings, the horseshoes striking sparks, the bells jangling on the nodding horses (p.125). The smell of the oranges lingers in the mind, too, from the liqueur factory on the way to school (p.135), and, at school, the smell of the wooden rulers and the inkwells. Jacques remembers the taste of the strap of his schoolbag which he chewed, the smooth, cold feel of the pages of certain books (p.137), the different smell of the pages of the Nelson and Fasquelle editions of children's books (p.228). The scent of seringa and magnolia wafts through the classroom window (p.207). The cargo boats from the different countries docked in the port of Algiers have each their individual smell, which Jacques breathes in, when, still at school, he works for a ship-broker (p.249).

Le Premier homme was to be a vast fresco of the history of French Algeria in parallel with the destiny of Jacques Cormery. The style of the novel would range over an equally large diapason, from 'realism' to the lyrical, the elegiac, the ironic, the comical, and the aphoristic. The third and final part was to have been entitled *La Mère*, and in it Jacques was to explain to his mother everything from the Arab question to the ultimate destiny of Western civilization: 'la question arabe, la civilisation créole, le destin de l'Occident' (p.307, 'Notes et Plans'). This would have been the *dénouement* of the work.

Underlying Camus's major fiction is always the structure of drama, but what is missing in *Le Premier homme* is the restraint of the classical theatre, so elegantly mirrored in *L'Étranger*. The power of that novel lies in the balance between its two parallel parts, in the

---

60   p.124. 'The good smell of horsehair, of straw and manure', *FM*, p.101.

careful neutrality of tone which rises to metaphor or poetry only at the points of climax and resolution, which are the pistol shots on the beach and the final passionate rejection of the chaplain, followed by the lyrical dénouement. As for *La Peste*, critics have pointed out the broad parallel with the five acts of French tragedy: the plague reaches its climax precisely in the central (third) part of the novel, in the sweltering heat of summer ('ce sommet de la chaleur et de la maladie', p.1355), and fades out at the end of winter, in the fifth and final part. At these points, the narrator's deliberately objective tone gives way to melancholy or irony. As for *La Chute*, it is a dramatic monologue delivered by 'Jean-Baptiste Clamence, *comédien*'. One can discern the classical structure within *Le Premier homme* also, the prologue which is the nativity scene, the parallelism between childhood and adulthood, and the lyrical outpourings which form the epilogues to each part. The problem is that Camus was never able to prune and strip the work where needed.

'La véritable œuvre d'art est celle qui dit moins', he had written in 1938 in his first *Carnets*.[61] In 1957, he had quoted Gide's maxim that 'Art lives on constraint and dies of liberty' (*Essais*, p.1093). Art, he said, must impose its own restraints on itself. However, in *Le Premier homme* he seems in places to have indulged the compulsion to write 'more' rather than 'less'. The final chapters of each section of the novel, which are the epilogues, so to speak, of the two parts as we have them, lose the reader with their marathon and sonorous Proustian periods. 'Le temps perdu ne se retrouve que chez les riches',[62] Camus wrote aphoristically earlier in the novel, Proust being evidently at the back of his mind. The influence cannot be said to have been happy. Talking of the first drafts of certain passages in *La Peste*, Quilliot deplores a 'certain heaviness of style, repetitions, convoluted phrases', and comments that Camus had to suppress a tendency to lyricism and eliminate 'the parasites which naturally battened on his sentences' (*TRN*, p.1939, tr.). Doubtless given time, Camus would have subdued and disciplined these outpourings which are so much less successful than the rare and climactic lyricism of *L'Étranger* or the equally rare

---

61 *Carnets I*, p.127: 'The true work of art is that which says less.'
62 p.79. 'Remembrance of things past is just for the rich', *FM*, p.62.

elegiac passages of *La Peste*. Going from one extreme to the other, he also thought of writing alternating chapters, in which the mother would comment on the events in the four hundred or so words at her command, a feat which would have tested the laconism of Meursault himself (see 'Plans', p.312).

The range of registers is comprehensive, but irony is much less evident here than in *L'Étranger* or *La Chute*. The more subtle form of irony, indirect reported speech, is not in evidence, for the ironies are not directed at individuals. The shafts of ironic remarks are generally reserved for the class of Parisian intellectuals with their scorn for such *pieds-noirs* as Veillard's elderly father. Ploughing up his vineyards before leaving, the old man remarks sarcastically to the young lieutenant overseeing the evacuation: 'Jeune homme, puisque ce que nous avons fait ici est un crime, il faut l'effacer.'[63] Such barbs are rare.

The novel was to end with Cormery's confession to his mother and a plea for pardon. Like Meursault, like Camus too, he is haunted by an obscure sense of guilt. At the end of the first part of the novel, he reproaches himself with seeking escape from the poor, persevering and simple life which he admired in his mother and those around her, 'la vie pauvre, ignorante, obstinée' (p.181). Is there here also, as Germaine Brée (1959) had suggested in the case of Meursault, a Parsifal-complex, a guilt incurred when the son rides away from the mother, out into the wider world, leaving her to her isolation and grief? Does the seed of Jacques's guilt-complex reside in some obscure sentiment of betrayal?

'Confession à la mère pour finir', Camus wrote in his 'Plans'. She alone could forgive:

> Tu seule peux le faire, mais tu ne me comprends pas et ne peux pas me lire. Aussi je te parle, je t'écris à toi, à toi seule, et, quand ce sera fini, je demanderai pardon sans autre explication et tu me souriras.[64]

---

63   p.168. 'Young man, since what we made here is a crime, it has to be wiped out', *FM*, p.141.
64   p.319. 'You alone can do it, but you do not understand me and cannot read me. And I am speaking to you, I am writing to you, to you alone, and when it is finished, I will ask forgiveness without further explanation and you will smile on me', *FM*, p.254.

These echoes of guilt had become louder from Meursault to Rieux and Tarrou and finally Clamence. We see in the 'Plans' how they would have appeared in the completed novel. Jacques is made to say:

> J'ai commencé à croire à mon innocence. J'étais tzar. Je régnais sur tout et sur tous [...] Puis j'ai appris que je n'avais pas assez de coeur pour aimer vraiment et j'ai cru mourir de mépris pour moi-même.[65]

Clamence lives again. Again in the 'Plans', Jacques's friend Pierre is cast in the role of Tarrou, but an active and expiating Tarrou. He is to be a lawyer (not an artist, as at first planned, significantly enough, p.280), and 'the defence counsel of Yveton' ('Pierre avocat. Et avocat d'Yveton', p.281). A note tells us that Yveton was a communist militant who had placed a bomb in a factory during the Algerian war and was guillotined. Pierre redeems Tarrou. Jacques, who is in fact the artist, the writer, finds no other redemption, no other absolution from the burden of guilt which he so obscurely carries, than in seeking the forgiveness of his mother, his father's blessing having been transmitted already vicariously by Victor Malan. '*The First Man* is, in equal parts, the story of a boy's liberation from his mother and the story of a man's return to her', writes Rizzuto (1998, p.136).

The dread of mortality, the anxiety about the irrational, the Absurd, the effort to overcome these fears, reflected in Meursault's inner debates in the condemned cell, are the central preoccupations of all of Camus's work and appear here already in childhood. In the evening *Grand'mère* carefully and ceremoniously lights the oil-lamp, its glow bathing the faces of the woman and the boy, whose anxious unspoken fear of 'the unknown and death' ('cette angoisse devant l'inconnu et la mort', p.211) fades away as the consoling and reassuring light grows and spreads. It is a calming scene painted by Georges de la Tour once again.

The narrative does not end on that note, however. The last word is always elegiac. As Rieux had remarked, amid the rejoicing at the end of *La Peste*, the microbe never dies, and the day may well come

---

65   p.283. 'I began to believe in my innocence. I was Tsar. I reigned over everyone and everything [...] Then I found out I didn't have enough heart truly to love and I thought I would die of contempt for myself', *FM*, p.233.

again when, for our misfortune and a lesson for all of us, the rats will be sent forth 'to die in a happy city'.[66] After the opening chapter of the nativity, and until the penultimate chapter, where the young Jacques asserts himself against his grandmother, every chapter ends on a note of sadness or menace. In Saint Brieuc, Jacques turns his back on his father's grave, and later takes his leave of a dejected Victor Malan. On board the ship taking him to Algiers, his memories end with his recall of tears at his mother's few words of consolation for the punishment meted out by *grand'mère*. The homecoming finishes with the bomb in the street. The comic episode of *grand'mère* at the cinema ends on a melancholy note, as the silent mother sits by the window, looking out into the street which she has spent half her life contemplating, excluded by her deafness and poverty from the joyful life passing her by. The chapter devoted to Uncle Ernest closes on a meditation on old age and death, and its final image is that of the corpse in a pool of blood in the street. Jacques's triumph in the entrance exam for the *lycée* ends with a regret for the loss of the 'innocent and warm' life of the poor which he is leaving behind (p.163). The visit to Mondovi closes with Jacques's reflections on his own life and the meaning of his future death, 'acceptant avec une sorte d'étrange joie que la mort le ramène dans sa vraie patrie'.[67] The account of his days in the *lycée* ends again on the image of his mother sitting in the darkness and looking out into the street, the boy watching her, 'plein d'une angoisse obscure devant un malheur qu'il ne pouvait pas comprendre'.[68] This last is the master-image of the whole work.

After the revolt against *grand'mère*, and Uncle Ernest's accolade ('Toi, un homme'), the substance of the final chapter is a celebration of what life has taught the boy and the man, his strivings to formulate a code of conduct and a tradition for himself, in the 'immense country around him', the sea, the mountains, the plateaux, the desert, and the

---

66   *TRN*, p.1474: 'Le jour viendrait où, pour le malheur et l'enseignement des hommes, la peste réveillerait ses rats et les enverrait mourir dans une cité heureuse.'
67   p.182. 'acknowledging with a strange sort of pleasure that death would return him to his true homeland', *FM*, p.153.
68   p.209. 'filled with an obscure anxiety in the presence of adversity he could not understand', *FM*, p.178.

'constant danger', this 'pays où, précisement, il se sentait jeté, comme s'il était le premier habitant ou le premier conquérant', a country in which 'seul le courage permettait d'y vivre'.[69] But at the end there is the 'le sentiment soudain que le temps de la jeunesse s'enfuyait',[70] and the recollection of a passionate affair (no doubt to be recounted in a later episode), a woman who 'refused the world as it is' and desired only to

> fuir vers un pays où personne ne vieillirait ni ne mourrait, où la beauté serait impérissable, la vie serait toujours sauvage et éclatante, et qui n'existait pas.[71]

The unattainable kingdom. For himself, he hopes only that the obscure inner strength which has given him reasons for living, will enable him in the end to accept old age and death, giving him 'des raisons de vieillir et de mourir sans révolte' (p.261). Sisyphus accepts his stone, the absurdity of the world is irremediable, and Camus's last work offers us the noble Stoic message of courage and acceptance.

---

69   pp.257 and p.258. 'This was the very country into which he felt he had been tossed, as if he were the first inhabitant, or the first conqueror', *FM*, p.217; 'and only with courage could you live here', ibid., p.218.
70   p.260. 'The sudden terrible feeling that the time of his youth was slipping away', *FM*, p.219.
71   p.261. 'She wanted to flee, flee to a country where no one would grow old or die, where beauty was imperishable, where life would always be wild and radiant, and that did not exist', *FM*, p.220.

Conclusion
Adam's Tale Retold

> *Le grand fait humain est le désir du bonheur et de la joie [...] et nous n'avons pas plus de raison de ne pas nous y fier qu'à notre appétit qui nous indique qu'il faut manger.*
> Paul Claudel, in a letter to Jacques Rivière

> *Ulysse peut choisir chez Calypso entre l'immortalité et la terre de la patrie. Il choisit la terre, et la mort avec elle.*
> Camus, 'L'Exil d'Hélène', in *Essais*

'Quant à moi', Camus said in 1952,

> Je ne crois pas, en ce qui me concerne, aux livres isolés. Chez certains écrivains, il me semble que leurs œuvres forment un tout, où chacune s'éclaire par les autres, et où toutes se regardent.'[1]

He himself conceived of his work as a totality, organised in cycles, and the same preoccupations and themes recur from one work to another, with however a certain progression. The absurdity of our human condition, born only to die, the problem of happiness in the context of mortality and contingency, its relationship to innocence or culpability, its fragility, the search for a rule of conduct, a *mode de vie*, these themes preoccupy him from *La Mort heureuse* to *Le Premier homme*, from the dissertation on Saint Augustine and *Le Mythe de Sisyphe* to *La Chute*. How are we to reconcile death and joy, thinking and happiness, experience and innocence? By what values are we to live, where

---

1   Interview in *La Gazette des Lettres*, February 1952. Quoted in Todd, p.770. 'I do not believe in isolated works. With certain writers, it seems to me that their works form a whole, each one shedding light upon the others, and all looking to each other.'

can we find an authority based on love, not power; does such a thing even exist? Adam finds himself alone in the universe, without earthly or heavenly Father, in search of his identity and of a meaning to his existence. *Dans un sens*, all is simple, we live, we love, we die; but, in another sense, nothing is simple.

A search for values and a search for love, a search for the father and a return to the mother, and in all a desire to make meaningful our 'absurd' existence in a universe devoid of meaning. The first search starts with the contemplation of death, in the graveyard of Saint Brieuc, as *Le Mythe de Sisyphe* too had started with a reflection on mortality. The second ends with Jacques Cormery's prayer for the strength to 'grow old and die without revolt', to accept death in the way Patrice Mersault had gracefully returned to Mother Earth, or as Meursault had been united with his mother at last in the marvellous peace of the starry night.

But first our innocence has to be restored, some guilt, mysterious and unspecified as that of Sisyphus, has to be washed away. The final section of *Le Premier homme* was to end with a confession and a plea for forgiveness to the mother, through whom alone reconciliation and redemption are possible. Without innocence there can be no happiness, and who is innocent? Tarrou proclaims that everyone carries the plague within themselves ('Chacun la porte en soi, la peste'). But what was the mother to forgive?

> Tu ne me comprends pas, et pourtant tu es la seule qui puisse me pardonner [...] Simplement cela, pardonner, et non pas vous demander de mériter le pardon, d'attendre [...] Un seul être pouvait me pardonner [...] mais il est mort et je suis seul.[2]

The father being dead (and God the Father dead also), the return to the mother is a quest for unconditional absolution, for the restitution of the primal state of innocence. She is the source of love. The humble mother, poor and patient, is an important element in the psychological

---

2   *PH*, p.319. 'You do not understand me, and yet you are the only one who can forgive me [...] Just that, to forgive, and not to ask you to deserve forgiveness, to wait [...] One person alone could have forgiven me [...] but he is dead and I am alone', *FM*, p.254.

profiling of most of Camus's major characters. Patrice Mersault, Meursault, Rieux, Tarrou, all hold the saintly maternal image in their hearts. Poverty and maternity are the emblems of simplicity and love. The ideal mother passes on to her children a kinship with the poor and the unfortunate. Father Paneloux and Judge Othon have no such iconic figure in their background. They come from middle-class stock, and no mention is made in either case of the indispensible mother personifying goodness. They can only learn humility and compassion from bitter experience. Similarly the aristocratic D'Arrast in 'La Pierre qui pousse' can only earn acceptance among the poor through ordeal, while the cynical Clamence of *La Chute*, who finds that contempt for his fellow man comes naturally to him, is solidly middle class, not only by education and profession but by origin (his father, he tells us, was 'an officer', presumably military: 'J'étais d'une naissance honnête mais obscure, mon père était officier', *TNR*, p.1490). No mention of a mother to whom he could turn for forgiveness.

Happiness is 'le simple accord entre un être et l'existence qu'il mène', Camus had written in 'Noces'.[3] But how to maintain that 'simple' harmonious existence is a question that must be addressed. It is compatible only with a state of innocence. Does each of us carry the microbe, as Tarrou affirms? Is all human behaviour motivated by the ego, as Clamence believes? 'Moi, moi, moi!' The refrain of his precious life, as he says, 'Me, me, me!'. And try as we may, how are we to avoid tripping over some stumbling block and thereby injuring ourselves and our neighbour, like Meursault? How can we be happy while contemplating decrepitude and mortality? Whether the humble happiness of Meursault in *L'Étranger* or the hedonistic happiness of the people of Oran, the state of contentment is bound up with the prelapsarian innocence of those who have not yet felt the shock of the encounter with death. For Meursault this is the murder of the Arab, following so close upon his mother's death, for Clamence (although it takes him two or three years to face up to it), only the suicide of the young woman in the Seine shatters the cocoon of refusal of awareness which he has woven tightly around himself. Once he has consciously

---

3   *Essais*, p.85; 'But what is happiness except the simple harmony between a man and the life he leads?' *SE*, p.98. Already quoted in chapter IV.

acknowledged the experience, 'la pensée de la mort fit irruption dans [sa] vie quotidienne'.[4]

There is no father, in heaven or on earth, to dispense forgiveness. The loss of the father is irremediable, none of the substitute fathers can do more than point a way forward. The hero in the end is always alone, for the silence of the dead father is mirrored in the silence of the humble mother. Meursault's search starts here, his laconism and 'indifference' arise out of this silence. They are the deliberate negation of the emotional, and represent an effort to live by the intellect alone, to discover a *mode de vie* from the 'zero' starting point. He is in fact the intellectual hero, and his valiant attempt to live in innocence and 'indifference' ends in defeat, for it is impossible to live without value judgements, which are ultimately intuitive. The communication of emotion will be a problem for all Camus's characters: Meursault and Marie, Rieux and his wife, Joseph Grand and Jeanne, Clamence ironically perorating to his double, Janine and Marcel, the workmen in 'Les Muets', the Renegade whose tongue has been cut out, Daru and the Arab, the solitary D'Arrast, Jacques Cormery and his mother.

All that is given is the capacity of the human heart for love and the appetite for happiness, and one is not satisfied without the other. Patrice Mersault remembers that

> la pauvreté près de sa mère avait une douceur. Lorsqu'ils se retrouvaient le soir et mangeaient en silence autour de la lampe à pétrole, il y avait un bonheur secret dans cette simplicité et ce retranchement [...] Maintenant, au contraire, la pauvreté dans la solitude était une affreuse misère.[5]

Now that she is gone, poverty and loneliness are well-nigh unbearable. Happiness is not dependent upon optimism, 'il est lié à l'amour – ce qui n'est pas la même chose', Camus wrote in *Noces*, in 1939.[6]

---

4   *TRN*, p.1521. 'The thought of death burst into my daily life', *Fall*, p.66.
5   *MH*, p.40–1. 'The poverty they shared had a certain sweetness about it: when the end of the day came and they would eat their dinner in silence with the oil-lamp between them, there was a secret joy in such simplicity, such retrenchment. [...] But now the poverty in solitude was misery', *HD*, p.20.
6   p.86, *Essais*. 'It is linked with love – which is not the same thing', *SE*, p.99.

The question of happiness is far from simple. 'Votre seul devoir est de vivre et d'être heureux', Zagreus tells his disciple. However Mersault, the young god with a divine right to slay, becomes Meursault the innocent nature-worshipper who commits murder and falls victim to the sun-god. If happiness is indeed 'the simple harmony between a being and the life he leads', a single wrong note, played accidentally, can introduce a calamitous dissonance. Clamence, the hero who aspires to dethrone the Almighty, tells us:

> Oui, peu d'êtres ont été plus naturels que moi. Mon accord avec la vie était total [...] En vérité, à force d'être homme, avec tant de plénitude et de simplicité, je me trouvais un peu surhomme.[7]

The trajectory of the fallen superman is that of Lucifer, and Clamence ends in the hell which he has created around himself in his dream of domination, having turned a deaf ear to the call of unhappiness and despair. Rambert had realised that there is a selfish happiness. As he put it, 'Il peut y avoir de la honte à être heureux tout seul'. The harmony between a being and his existence is very fragile, the line between such happiness and egoism very fine. In certain circumstances courage and the notion of honour must take precedence, and happiness must become generosity. Only Cottard can be happy doing nothing at all when all around are dying.

Happiness is in loving and being loved, it is also in living life and accepting the end of life. It is blithely taken for granted by the crowds of young people on the beaches of Algeria. But it is an emotional state, not something directed by the will, which alone forges the virtues. It may well be the first of the values, if indeed it includes relationships of love and friendship, but the first of the virtues, for Camus at least, is courage, which, since virtue arises out of the perception of a value, comes in second place, 'juste après, et jamais avant, l'exigence généreuse du bonheur', as Rieux had made clear. Courage, intelligence and generosity are Don Juan's virtues, and these natural 'pagan'

---

7   TRN, pp.1489–90. 'Yes, few creatures were more natural than I. I was altogether in harmony with life [...] To tell the truth, just from being so fully and simply a man, I looked upon myself as something of a superman', *Fall*, pp.22–3.

virtues, as the old Church Fathers (approvingly) called them, are the alpha and omega of Camus's *mode de vie*. The redeeming feature of the orphaned Franco-Algerian people is their *courage à vivre*, as Janine remarks, and the highest praise that Jacques's mother and Uncle Ernest can give the boy is that 'He has courage' ('Il a le courage', 'Tu es courageux', p.216).

At the end of *La Peste*, when the city gates are opened, there is an explosion of joy as those who were separated are reunited. The citizens find their *vraie patrie*, the hills, the sea, and the *weight of love* ('le poids de l'amour', p.1466), the only counterweight to Sisyphus' stone. It is in women that this weight of love is greatest, as Camus, so often accused of ignoring women or dismissing them, freely admits:

> Une femme qui aime vraiment, de toute l'âme, dans le don total [...] grandit alors si démesurément qu'il n'est pas un homme qui ne devienne, en comparaison, médiocre, misérable, et sans générosité.[8]

Why then are there so few female characters, and only one principal one (Janine) in his work? Like the Arabs, they are conspicious by their absence. What are we to make of the sallies in the *Notebooks*, in which Camus decides to free himself from the tyranny of feminine attractions, finds women boring outside love-making, or regrets that marriage and love are conflated? On the other hand, he also makes the comment that 'Ceux qui aiment la vérité doivent chercher l'amour dans le mariage, c'est-à-dire l'amour sans illusions'.[9] Is this merely an ironic sally? Or is it a perception of the nature of married love?

If we look at the works rather than at the petulant outbursts in the *Carnets*, we find, as early as in *La Mort heureuse*, bonds of friendship and equality between Mersault and his young women friends, even in

---

8   *Carnets III*, p.25. 'A woman who loves truly, with all her soul, in total self-giving, grows in stature so immeasurably that there is no man who in comparison does not become mediocre, miserable, and lacking in generosity.'
9   *Carnets II*, p.101. 'Those who love truth should seek love in marriage, that is, love without illusions.' Other remarks are as follows: *Carnets I*, p.227: 'Renoncer à cette servitude qu'est l'attirance féminine'; *Carnets II*, p.58: 'La femme, hors de l'amour, est ennuyeuse'; *Carnets II*, p.290: 'On s'obstine à confondre le mariage et l'amour'.

the strange marriage to Lucienne, who, after all, instigates the arrangement. We should remember that, when interviewed by J.-C. Brisville not long before his untimely death, Camus declared that his favourite characters were Marie and Céleste in *L'Étranger*, and also Dora in *Les Justes*. Out of the three characters, two are women, one humble, simple, and not very good at expressing herself, the other an intellectual and revolutionary, but who proclaims also, in Act I, 'Mon coeur est simple' ('My heart is simple'). Simplicity (which does not mean stupidity) is the common quality of all three, and Camus finds it most often in women, from his mother onwards. The only true simplicity is the simplicity of the heart.

In *L'Étranger*, Meursault's relationship with Marie is deeper than he is willing to admit. After *L'Étranger*, there is an underlying guilt-complex with regard to women, and specifically in the husband-wife relationship, with Rieux's regrets, Joseph Grand's sadness, and Jonas's repentance. The concept of marriage as fulfilment is however problematic: Meursault discounts it; Rieux fulfils his vocation as a doctor, but at the cost of neglecting his wife; Jonas, in the later short story, will find the conflicting demands of art and matrimony irreconcilable. On the other hand, do we not glimpse in Rieux and his wife the tragic lovers Orpheus and Eurydice, as Geraldine Montgomery suggests (p.173)? The analogy is strengthened by the episode in which the tenor singing Orpheus collapses and dies on stage in the middle of his great love-duet with Eurydice. Love and tenderness are celebrated also in Rambert and his ardent desire to be re-united with his beloved, in the marriage of Dr Castell and his wife, in Yvars, at the end of the story, sitting hand in hand with Fernande, 'comme aux premiers temps de leur mariage' ('as in the early days of their marriage'), in Jonas's declarations of repentance and love, even in Janine's return to Marcel.

Men without women generally cut a sorry figure, except when, as in the case of Tarrou, they are in fact only one half of an idealised self-projection of Camus (Tarrou/Rieux being the composite ideal figure). They are Rambert the criminal, Clamence, who has only known debauchery, the tortured Renegade, Daru, isolated on his high plateau, D'Arrast, expiating some grievous past error. In praise of women, Camus gives us Mersault's farewell to Catherine, in *La Mort heureuse*:

> Ne renonce jamais, Catherine. Tu as tant de choses en toi, et la plus noble de toutes, le sens du bonheur. N'attends pas seulement la vie d'un homme. C'est pour cela que tant de femmes se trompent. Mais attends-la de toi-même.[10]

Geraldine Montgomery comments that these remarks imply a fundamentally open and friendly attitude to women from the very beginning of the work. The same critic also highlights the mystique of night and the sea in Camus's fiction, the indwelling of the sacred in the two feminine elements. We cannot dismiss Camus as a nothing but a die-hard macho.

The Arabs, like the women, are missing from the work as we have it. Camus no doubt intended to represent them, as he intended to portray women, much more fully in the final version of *Le Premier homme*. How successful he would have been in either endeavour we can only speculate. Certainly he could only have portrayed the Arabs from the standpoint of a sympathetic onlooker. While it is not clear whether the young man and his aged mother, who gaze so intently and wordlessly at each other in the episode of Marie's prison visit in *L'Étranger*, are in fact an Arab couple, it seems likely that this was Camus's intention. Marie is surrounded by Arab women ('entourée de Mauresques'), and, in contrast to the shouting of the Europeans, the Arabs around her manage to communicate quietly, almost without words.[11] The ethnicity of the two figures, mother and son, is no doubt deliberately unclear, highlighting the universality of the relationship, but in creating the impression of an Arab context for these ideal figures, Camus is paying the highest possible tribute to Arab spirituality. In any case, as we have seen, the Arab Saddok, in the Appendices to *Le Premier homme*, declares that he loves and respects Jacques's mother as if she were his own. No greater symbol of brotherhood could be conceived.

---

10 *MH*, pp.155–6. 'Never give up, Catherine. You have so much inside you, and the noblest sense of happiness of all [*sic*]. Don't just wait for a man to come along. That's the mistake so many women make. Find your happiness in yourself', *HD*, p.113.

11 *TRN*, p.1178: 'Malgré le tumulte, ils [les Arabes] parvenaient à s'entendre en parlant très bas.'

What Camus has given us in his fiction, however, is a picture of French Algeria and the life of the most humble of its inhabitants. Where the Arabs appear, they are victims, as is the Arab girl who is beaten by Sintès or the Arab murdered by Meursault. They are secret, silent, unfathomable; the keepers of some sacred mystery whose echoes are heard in the three notes of the flute on the beach in *L'Étranger*, and glimpsed in the noble figures of the nomads in 'La Femme adultère' who represent the Kingdom of the free. They are proud too, like the Arab officer who sweeps past the two French travellers. Janine and Marcel know themselves uncomfortably to be strangers and intruders in this land. And in the end, the Arabo-Berbers seem menacing, threatening some sort of revolt, leaving their message on Daru's blackboard, gathering silently at the scene of a street fight. In the worst nightmares, somewhere deep in the subconscious, they are transformed into the terrifyingly alien figures of 'Le Renégat'. Camus's goodwill struggles with Camus's fears. In the final pages of *Le Premier homme*, Jacques's mother sees two street combatants, a Frenchman and an Arab, arrested and bundled off by the police. She utters two words of compassion. 'Les pauvres', she says (p.258; 'Poor things'). It is a lament for the two peoples of Algeria.

Happiness, innocence, guilt, imprisonment, exile: these are the preoccupations of Camus's allegorising fictions. On a hot summer's day, on a beach in North Africa, a young man, whom we know only by the name of Meursault, kills a nameless Arab, pumping into his recumbent body a total of five bullets. At that instant he becomes an exile from the kingdom of happiness, even before society expels him from the ranks of the innocent and propels him into the cell which is the antechamber of death. Michel le Guern (p.176) has observed that since Tertullien, spiritual literature has frequently compared the human condition to that of a condemned prisoner. Prisons are everywhere in Camus's fiction, the prison of Meursault, the imprisonment of the population in Oran in *La Peste*, the *malconfort*, the 'cell of spittle' in *La Chute*, Clamence's own shrinking universe which finally imprisons him in his room, the imprisonment of the Renegade, the imprisonment which awaits the Arab in 'L'Hôte', the prison-like hotel room which Janine and Marcel occupy, and the imprisonment of poverty, to escape which Mersault kills, and from which Jacques Cormery climbs out, up the ladder of education.

In 1956, the year of *La Chute*, the year when his friend Jean de Maisonseul was arrested in Algiers, the year when Guy Mollet threatened total war, Camus wrote in his *Carnets*:

> Jeanne la folle est restée quarante-quatre ans dans une petite chambre sans fenêtre, éclairée jour et nuit par une lampe, d'où elle ne sortait que pour passer dans le couvent voisin et contempler le tombeau de son mari. Peut-être est-ce cela la vraie vie.[12]

Jeanne takes up Pascal's challenge: she is capable of sitting in a room and doing nothing other than contemplate the human condition. But of course she is *mad*. The refusal of life, the mere shutting out of the world, is a destructive temptation. There is a different cell, one that is liberating: Jonas's retreat, or the monk's cell, a place where distractions are kept at bay and creativity becomes possible. Camus wrote to Jean Grenier:

> Les conditions de travail pour moi ont toujours été celles de la vie monastique: la solitude et la frugalité.[13]

Solitude on the one hand, solidarity on the other, the artist is pulled in opposite directions by these two poles. He (or she) needs solitude to create, empathy with his (or her) fellow human beings in order to create humanely. And in the end, all the protagonists of Camus's novels are in some sense artists. As Germaine Brée remarks, 'The introducing of the figure of Zagreus [in *La Mort heureuse*] is the clear indicator that the myth Camus has in mind is the Dionysian myth of the artist' (1972, p.66). Mersault, in that early novel, wishes to make a work of art out of his own life. In *L'Étranger*, Meursault has the gifts of a writer and an ironic eye. In Rieux's chronicle we have a

---

12 *Carnets III*, p.199. 'Joan the Mad [Queen of Spain] remained forty-four years in a little room with no window, lit day and night by a lamp, which she left only for the neighbouring convent, to contemplate her husband's tomb. Perhaps that is true life.'

13 Quoted in Todd, p.1022. 'My working conditions have always been those of the monastic life, solitude and frugality.'

masterpiece of humane writing, Clamence is both actor and consummate ironic story-teller, Jacques Cormery too is a writer, and a successful one. But we should remember that the efforts of the artist Jonas are in the end reduced to the blank canvas, which is to say, to silence, ultimate truth being beyond words.

Sisyphus' journey is from the simplicity of innocence to the complexity of experience. Like Sisyphus, Camus's heroes view the world from a height and a distance, Patrice from the terrace of the House above the World or the terrace of the house in Chenoua, Rieux also contemplates from a terrace, and Janine ascends to the fort. Geraldine Montgomery has pointed out this association of height with the sacred. But the ascension is not always towards a (humanist) sanctity. There is also a link with the diabolical, and the view from the top of the mountain is not that from its foot. There is a parody of Sisyphus on his mountain, and it is Clamence, with his taste for airy summits ('mon goût des sommets aérés', p.1539), seeing himself perched on his Satanic peak. Camus's mistrust of heights and heroism grows throughout his work. In the end, it is the embrace of the sea and the simplicity of the humble which he holds in his heart.

The duality of characters runs through the work from one fiction to another. Human beings too are composed of *L'Envers et l'Endroit*, light and darkness. Over the course of the work ironically distorting mirrors are held up to them all, not only Meursault and the 'gorilla' of *La Chute*, not only the noble tribesmen of 'La Femme adultère', who are the 'lords of a strange kingdom', and the inhuman 'lords' of Taghâsa, the Kingdom of salt, not only the Renegade and his victim, but also benevolent Uncle Étienne, who had made an early appearance in the guise of the wretched cooper Cardona in *La Mort heureuse*; Zagreus is reflected negatively in Raymond Sintès, Tarrou is satirised in Clamence, and *grand'mère* is both valiant and tyrannical. Nature also has a double face: never simply beautiful, positive or healthful, she is always also 'overwhelmingly powerful, threatening, at times even dangerously hostile, as is evident above all in *L'Étranger*', writes a German critic (Schlette, p.91, tr.). The sun can drive men mad, even homicidal, not only Meursault, but the Arab hairdresser who, in *Le Premier homme*, cuts the throat of his customer (p.239). All of Camus's fiction reposes on these antitheses and ambivalences,

L'Envers et l'Endroit, the life-giving and life-threatening sun, happiness and its fragility, innocence and guilt, solitude and fraternity, the friendly maternal sea, and the cold waters of the Zuyderzee.

Certain exemplary figures nonetheless stand out throughout Camus's work, and are not subjected to irony. From Dr Bernard in *La Mort heureuse* onwards, the figure of the doctor would evolve in Camus's work, together with that of the teacher, idealised in Monsieur Bernard, the *instituteur* (we notice the identical names of doctor and schoolmaster), and in Daru, devoting his life to the education of the children of the desert tribes. To them is added the figure of the artist, always in palimpsest behind the major figures, and not exempt from a certain good-natured raillery when he takes the foreground, as in *Jonas ou l'Artiste au travail*, since he is in fact Camus himself. The doctor, the teacher, the committed artist whom Camus praises in his Nobel prize speeches in 1957, all three are pitted against the injustices of our condition: malady, suffering, ignorance, oppression. Together with the poor, including the 'poor in spirit', they personify the values and ideals, human and spiritual, by which Camus seeks the path to the Kingdom.

In the *styles de vie*, Camus proposes two exemplars, Sisyphus and Christ. Nor indeed are they irreconcilable, both being examples of suffering patiently and indomitably endured, and death defied. Of all the figures drawn from classical mythology, Camus's Sisyphus provides a uniquely Christ-like icon. Sisyphus' stone is the weight of living day after dreary day, but there is also the heavy burden that must be carried in the search for the Kingdom. These two are the same burden in the end, that which is carried by D'Arrast, who comes as the Saviour. The mother too is always, and most obviously in *Le Premier homme*, a patient Sisyphus and a suffering Christ-figure. Viggiani (p.872) notes a predilection for certain names in the novels and plays: Jean, Jan, Yanek, Jeanne, Marie, Maria, Martha, Joseph Grand, Céleste, Emmanuel, with their New Testament associations. They are the people of the Beatitudes, the 'poor in spirit', the humble. Old Pérez the fisherman, in *La Mort heureuse*, combines both traditions, for he is an avatar of Charon, ferrying the dead to their true home, re-uniting them with their mother, but is he not also Peter the Fisherman, Pérez, Pierre, fishing for men, a father (*père*) solicitous for his children, offering the refuge of his boat, the traditional image of the Church? 'Is it not Christ – an absurd Christ, it is true – and not Sisyphus, who is hidden behind the developing hero of Camus's fictions?' asks Viggiani (p.887). Seen from a certain angle, the two profiles merge. Meursault begins as Sisyphus in his innocence and ends as 'le seul Christ que nous méritons' ('the only Christ we deserve').

Between Classical and Christian Europe, Camus opts for the first. This does not mean that he dismisses the second. He doesn't fit in well with a post-Christian Europe, which in fact he pre-dates, the secularised and science-based West, the world in which the human being is largely regarded as a biological and chemical phenomenon which can be unravelled, reproduced or manipulated psychologically as well as physically, a world in which metaphysics have no place and such questions as whether life is worth living ('si la vie vaut ou ne vaut pas la peine d'être vécue?') are no longer asked.

'Le livre *doit être* inachevé', Camus wrote in his 'Plans' for *Le Premier homme*.[14] His work is indeed unfinished, but it could never be finished. There is no last word to the questions he raises. Alain Robbe-Grillet recalls that for himself, and for all his generation, *L'Étranger* was a beacon and a landmark, and that each time he re-opens it 'its power, intact, works again'.[15] Each succeeding work renewed the questioning and re-formulated the enigma. Camus leaves us something better than an answer: a call to 'think through' and to act, a challenge for each one of us and for our times.

---

14 *PH*, p.288 (Camus's italics). 'The book *must be* unfinished', *FM*, p.235.
15 In Pingaud, p.203.

Bibliography

Camus

In the Pléiade collection:

Essais, Paris, Gallimard, 1965 (achevé d'imprimer 2000)
Théâtre, Récits, Nouvelles, Paris, Gallimard,1962 (achevé d'imprimer 1999)

Other works:

Albert Camus / Jean Grenier: Correspondance 1932–1960. Avertissement et notes par Marguerite Dobrenn, Paris, NRF, Gallimard, 1981
Cahiers Albert Camus I: La Mort heureuse. Introduction et notes de Jean Sarocchi, Paris, NRF, Gallimard, 1971
Carnets mai 1935 – février 1942, Paris, Gallimard, 1962
Carnets janvier 1942 – mars 1951, Paris, Gallimard, 1964
Carnets III mars 1951 – décembre 1959, Paris, Gallimard, 1989
Le Premier homme, Paris, Gallimard, 1994

English translations appearing in the footnotes are taken from the following Penguin editions:

Exile and the Kingdom, trans. by Justin O'Brien, Harmondsworth, Penguin Modern Classics, 1983 (reprint)
The Fall, trans. by Justin O'Brien and with an introduction by Olivier Todd, London, Penguin Books, 2000 (reprint)
The First Man, trans. by David Hapgood, London, Penguin Books, 1996
A Happy Death. Cahiers Albert Camus I. Afterword and Notes by Jean Sarocchi, trans. by Richard Howard, London, Hamish Hamilton. 1971

The Myth of Sisyphus, trans. by Justin O'Brien with an introduction by James Wood, London, Penguin Modern Classics, 2005 (reprint)
The Outsider, trans. by Joseph Laredo, London, Penguin Books, 2000 (reprint)
The Plague, trans. by Stewart Gilbert, London, Penguin Books, 2001 (reprint)
The Rebel, trans. by Antony Bower. With a foreword by Sir Herbert Reid, Harmondsworth, Penguin Books (Peregrine), 1962
Selected Essays and Notebooks, ed. and trans. by Philip Thody, Harmondsworth, Penguin Books, 1979

Critical Works Cited

Multiple entries for an author are arranged in chronological order of publication

Abdelkrim, Zedgiga (1999) 'Le dit du corps et du silence', in *Europe. Revue littéraire mensuelle*, 77e année, no.846, octobre 1999 (issue entitled *Albert Camus*), pp.59–66
Arendt, Hannah (2002) *'Qu'est-ce que la philosophie de l'existence?', suivi de 'L'Existentialisme français' et de 'Heidegger le renard'*, Paris, Payot et Rivages
Arendt, Hannah (1978) *The Life of the Mind. Volume I. Thinking*, London, Secker and Warburg
—— (1978) *The Life of the Mind. Volume 2: Willing*, New York and London, Harcourt Brace Jovanovich
Baranger, W. (1959): see Pichon-Rivière
Barrier, M. G. (1962) *L'Art du récit dans 'L'Étranger' de Camus*, Paris, Nizet
Barthes, Roland (1970) *'L'Étranger, roman solaire'*, in *Les critiques de notre temps et Camus* (ed. Lévi-Valensi, below), pp.60–4
—— (1972) *Le degré zéro de l'écriture. Suivi de Nouveaux Essais Critiques*, Paris, Éditions du Seuil (first published 1953)
Baudouin, Charles (1969) *Blaise Pascal*, Paris, Éditions Universitaires
Bespaloff, Rachel (1962) 'The World of the Man Condemned to Death', in *Camus. A Collection of Critical Essays* (ed. Brée, below), pp.92–107

Also in French in *Les Critiques de notre temps et Camus* (ed. Lévi-Valensi, below, 1970a), pp.136–47
Bloom, Harold (ed., 1989) *Albert Camus. Edited and with an Introduction by Harold Bloom*, New York, Chelsea House Publishers
Brée, Germaine (1959) *Camus*, New Brunswick, Rutgers University Press
—— (ed., 1962) *Camus. A Collection of Critical Essays*, New Jersey, Englewood Cliffs
—— (1972) *Camus and Sartre*, New York, Dell Publishing Co.
Brock, Robert R. (1985) 'Crime and the Anarchist in *The Plague*', in *Approaches to Teaching Camus's 'The Plague'* (ed. Kellman, below), MLA (Modern Language Association of America), pp.158–63
Brombert, V. (1962) *The Intellectual Hero. Studies in the French Novel, 1880–1955*, London, Faber & Faber
—— (1975) *La Prison romantique*, Paris, Corti
Castex, P. (1965) *Albert Camus et 'L'Étranger'*, Paris, Corti
Chabot, J. (2002) *Albert Camus.'La pensée de midi'*, Aix-en-Provence, Édisud
Champigny, R. (1959) *Sur un héros païen*, Paris, Gallimard
Chestov, Leo: see Shestov
Crochet, M. (1973) *Les Mythes dans l'œuvre de Camus*, Paris, Éds. Universitaires
Cruickshank, J. (1959) *Albert Camus and the Literature of Revolt*, London, Oxford University Press
Cryle, Peter (1973) *Bilan critique: 'L'Exil et le Royaume' d'Albert Camus. Essai d'analyse*, Paris, Minard, Lettres Modernes
Cunningham, Jesse G. (ed., 2001) *Readings on 'The Plague'*, San Diego, C.A., Greenhaven Press, Inc.
Davison, Ray (1994) 'L'éloquence philosophique des *Muets*', in *Albert Camus. Les extrêmes et l'équilibre* (ed. Walker, below), pp.188–96
Deguy, J. (1995) 'Sartre lecteur de *L'Étranger*', in *Albert Camus 16* (ed. Gay-Crosier, below), pp.63–83
Di Meglio, Ingrid (1982) 'Camus et la religion. Antireligiosité et crypto-théologie', in *Albert Camus 11. Camus et la religion*, Paris, Revue des Lettres Modernes, pp.7–48
Dubois, Lionel (1995) *Les Trois Guerres d'Albert Camus. Actes du Colloque International de Poitiers 4–5–6 mai 1995*, Poitiers, Les Éditions du Pont Neuf
—— (1997) *Albert Camus. Entre la misère et le soleil. Actes du 2ème Colloque International de Poitiers. 29–30–31 mai 1997*, Poitiers, Les Éditions du Pont-Neuf

Dunwoodie, Peter (1985) *'L'Envers et l'Endroit'* and *'L'Exil et le Royaume'*, London, Grant and Cutler

Eisenzweig, Uri (1983) *Les Jeux de l'écriture dans 'L'Étranger' de Camus*, Archives des Lettres Modernes 211, Paris, Lettres Modernes

Ellison, David R. (1990) *Understanding Albert Camus*, Columbia, South Carolina, University of S. Carolina Press

Favre, Frantz (1995) 'L'Étranger et les ambiguïtés de l'absurde', in *Albert Camus 16* (ed. Gay-Crosier, below), pp.137–47

Felman, Shoshana (1992) 'Camus' *The Fall*, or the Betrayal of the Witness', in *Testimony. Crises of Witnessing in Literature, Psychoanalysis, and History*, by S. Felman and D. Laub, New York and London, Routledge, pp.165–203

Fitch, Brian T. (ed., 1970a) *Albert Camus 3 (1970). Sur 'La Chute'. Textes réunis par Brian Fitch. Revue des Lettres Modernes*, no.238–44, 1970 (4), Paris, Lettres Modernes

—— (1970b) 'Une voix qui se parle, qui nous parle, que nous parlons, ou l'espace théâtral de *La Chute*'. In *Albert Camus 3* (ed. Fitch), pp.59–79

—— (ed., 1982a) *Albert Camus 10. Textes réunis par Brian T. Fitch*, Paris, Lettres Modernes

—— (1982b) *The Narcissistic Text. A Reading of Camus' Fiction*, Toronto, University of Toronto Press

Fortier, Paul A. (1977) *Une Lecture de Camus. La valeur des éléments descriptifs dans l'œuvre romanesque*, Paris, Klincksieck

Gadourek, Carina (1963) *Les Innocents et les Coupables. Essai d'exégèse de l'œuvre d'Albert Camus*, The Hague, Mouton et Cie.

Gassin, Jean (1981) *L'univers symbolique d'Albert Camus. Essai d'interprétation psychanalytique*, Paris, Minard

Gay-Crosier, Raymond (1970) 'L'Anarchisme mesuré de Camus', in *Symposium*, Fall 1970, pp.243–53

—— (ed., 1980) *Albert Camus 1980: Second International Conference*, Gainesville, University Press of Florida

—— (ed., 1995) *Albert Camus 16: 'L'Étranger' cinquante ans après. Actes du colloque d'Amiens, 11–12 décembre 1992. Sous la direction de J. Lévi-Valensi. Textes réunis par Raymond Gay-Crosier*, Paris, Lettres Modernes

—— (ed., 1996) *Albert Camus 17. Toujours autour de 'L'Étranger'. Textes réunis par Raymond Gay-Crosier*, Paris, Lettres Modernes

Girard, René (1964) 'Camus's Stranger Retried', in *PMLA (Publications of the Modern Language Association)* no.79, pp.519–33

Grimaud, Michel (1992) 'Humanism and the "White Man's Burden": Camus, Daru, Meursault and the Arabs', in *Camus's 'L'Étranger'. Fifty Years On*, (ed. King, below), pp.170–82, London, Macmillan Press Ltd.

Guérin, Jeanyves (1993) *Camus, portrait de l'artiste en citoyen*, Paris, François Bourin

Hargreaves, Alec G. (1992) 'History and Ethnicity in the Reception of *L'Étranger*', in *Camus's 'L'Étranger'. Fifty Years On* (ed. King, below), pp.101–12

Hermet, Joseph (1976) *Albert Camus et le Christianisme. L'espérance en procès*, Paris, Éditions Beauchesne

Imbert, H.F. (1967) *Les Métamorphoses de la liberté, ou Stendhal devant la Restauration et le Risorgimento*, Paris, Corti

Isaac, Jeffrey C. (1992) *Arendt, Camus, and Modern Rebellion*, New Haven and London, Yale University Press

Jones, Rosemary (1980) *Camus. 'L'Étranger' and 'La Chute'*, London, Grant and Cutler

—— (1992) 'Telling Stories: Narrative Reflexions in *L'Étranger*', in *Camus's 'L'Étranger'. Fifty Years On* (ed. King, below), pp.114–24

Jung, C. G. (1968–9) *Collected Works*, trans. R. F. C. Hull, 12 vols. London, Routledge and Kegan Paul. See vol. II and vol. VIII

Keefe, Terry ((1974) 'Camus' *La Chute*. Some outstanding problems of interpretation concerning Clamence's past', in *Modern Language Review*, vol. 69, 1974, pp. 541–55

Kellman, Steven G. (ed., 1985), *Approaches to Teaching Camus's 'The Plague'*, MLA (Modern Language Association of America)

Kierkegaard, Søren (2000) *The Essential Kierkegaard*, ed. Howard V. Hong and Edna H. Hong, New Jersey, Princeton University Press

King, Adele (ed., 1992) *Camus's 'L'Étranger'. Fifty Years On*, London, Macmillan

Le Guern, Michel (1969) *L'Image dans l'œuvre de Pascal*, Paris, Armand Colin

Le Hir, Jeanne (1982) 'De Mersault à Meursault', in *Albert Camus 10: Nouvelles approches*, Paris, Minard, pp.29–52

Leites, N. (1963) 'The Stranger', in *Art and Psychoanalysis*, ed. William Phillips, New York, Meridian Books, pp.247–67

Lenzini, José (1987) *L'Algérie de Camus*, La Calade, Aix-en-Provence, Édisud

Lévi-Valensi, Jacqueline (ed., 1970a) *Les Critiques de notre temps et Camus*, Paris, Éditions Garnier Frères

—— (1970 b) 'La Chute ou la parole en procès', in *Albert Camus 3* (ed. Fitch, 1970a, above), pp.33–57

—— (1996) *Jacqueline Lévi-Valensi commente 'La Chute' d'Albert Camus*, Paris, Gallimard, Collection Folio

Longstaffe, M. (1999) *Metamorphoses of Passion and the Heroic in French Literature. Corneille, Stendhal, Claudel*, Lampeter, Edwin Mellen

Lottman, H. R. (1981) *Albert Camus. A Biography*, London, Picador

McBride, Joseph (1993) *Albert Camus. Philosopher and Littérateur*, New York, St. Martin's Press

McCann, J. (1990) 'The Verdict on Meursault', in *Nottingham French Studies*, vol. 29, Spring 1990, pp.51–63

McCarthy, Patrick (1982) *Camus: A Critical Study of His Life and Work*, London, Hamilton

—— (1988) *Camus' 'The Stranger'*, Cambridge, Cambridge University Press

Miller, Owen J. (1970) 'L'Image du miroir dans l'œuvre romanesque de Camus', in *Albert Camus 3* (ed. Fitch, 1970a, above), Paris, Lettres Modernes, pp.129–50

Montgomery, Geraldine (1997) 'De la dernière femme au Premier homme: Intermittences du féminin dans l'œuvre de Camus', in *Albert Camus. Entre la misère et le soleil* (ed. Dubois, above) pp.143–58

—— (2004) *Noces pour femme seule. Le féminin et le sacré dans l'œuvre d'Albert Camus*, Amsterdam, Rodopi

Morot-Sir, É. (1996) 'Actualité de *L'Étranger*', in *Albert Camus 17* (ed.Gay-Crosier, above), Paris, Lettres Modernes, pp.7–26

Mounier, Emmanuel (1953) *Malraux Camus Sartre Bernanos. L'espoir des désespérés*, Paris, Seuil

Murchland, Bernard C. (2001) 'Dark Night and the Coming of Grace', in *Readings on 'The Plague'* (ed. Cunningham, above) pp.153–7. (From 'Albert Camus: Rebel', first published in *The Catholic World*, vol. CLXXXVIII, no. 1126, January 1959)

Nacer-Khodja, Hamid (2004) *Albert Camus. Jean Sénac ou le fils rebelle*, Paris, Éditions Paris-Méditerranée

Noyer-Weidner, A. (1980) 'Structure et sens de *L'Étranger*', in *Albert Camus 1980* (ed.Gay-Crosier, above) pp.72–86

O'Brien, Conor Cruise (1970) *Albert Camus*, New York, Viking Press

Onimus, Jean (1980) 'Camus, "The Adulterous Woman" and the Starry Sky', in *Essays on Camus's 'Exile and the Kingdom'* (ed. Suther, below) pp.121–31. First published in French in *Cahiers Universitaires Catholiques*, no. 10 (July 1960)

Parker, Emmet (1966) *The Artist in the Arena*, Madison, University of Wisconsin Press

Pascal, Blaise. *Les Pensées*, in the Pléiade edition of the *Œuvres complètes*, Paris, Gallimard (achevé d'imprimer 1969)

Peyre, Henri (1962) 'Camus the Pagan', in *Camus. A Collection of Critical Essays* (ed. Brée, above) pp.65–70

Pichon-Rivière, A. de, and Baranger, W. (1959) 'Notes sur *L'Étranger* de Camus', in *Revue Française de Psychanalyse*, XXIII, mai–juin 1959, pp.409–20

Picon, Gaëton (1962) 'Notes on *La Peste*' (from *L'Usage de la lecture*, 1960), in *Camus. A Collection of Critical Essays* (ed. Brée, above) pp.145–51

Pieper, Annemarie (ed., 1994) *Die Gegenwart des Absurden. Studien zu Albert Camus*, Tübingen & Basel, A. Franke Verlag

Pilkington, A. E. (1969) 'Sartre's Existentialist Ethic', in *French Studies*, vol. XXIII, no. 1, January 1969, pp.38–48

Pingaud, Bernard (1992) *Bernard Pingaud présente 'L'Étranger' d'Albert Camus*, Paris, Gallimard, Collection Folio

Pratt, B. (1980) *L'Évangile selon Albert Camus*, Paris, J. Corti

Quilliot, Roger (1970) *La Mer et les Prisons*, Paris, Gallimard (first published 1956)

Rabaté, D. (1995) 'L'Économie de la mort dans *L'Étranger*', in *Albert Camus 16* (ed. Gay-Crosier, above), pp.93–107

Reichelberg, Ruth (1983) *Albert Camus: Une approche du sacré*, Paris, Nizet

Rey, P. L. (1970) *Camus: 'L'Étranger'*, Paris, Hatier

Rigaud, Jan (1992) 'The Depiction of Arabs in *L'Étranger*', in *Camus's 'L'Étranger'. Fifty Years On* (ed. King, above), pp.183–92

Rizzuto, Antony (1981) *Camus' Imperial Vision*, Carbondale, Southern Illinois University Press.

—— (1998) *Camus. Love and Sexuality*, University Press of Florida

Robbe-Grillet, Alain (1963) 'Nature, Humanisme, Tragédie', reprinted in *Pour un nouveau Roman* (first published 1958), Paris, Les Éditions de Minuit, pp.45–67

—— (1984) *Le Miroir qui revient*, Paris, Les Éditions de Minuit (extract reproduced in Pingaud, pp.203–8)

Rousset, J. (1963) *Forme et signification. Essai sur les structures littéraires de Corneille à Claudel*, Paris, Corti

Said, Edward W. (1994) *Culture and Imperialism*, London, Vintage Books. (On Camus, see pp. 207–25)

Sarang, Vilas (1992) 'A Brother to the Stranger', in *Camus's 'L'Étranger'. Fifty Years On* (ed. King, above), pp.51–8

Sarocchi, Jean (1995) *Le dernier Camus, ou 'Le Premier homme'*, Paris, Nizet

Sarraute, N. (1956) *L'Ère du soupçon*, Paris, Gallimard

Sartre, J. P. (1947) 'Explication de *L'Étranger*', in *Situations I*, Paris, Gallimard, pp.92–112

—— (1960) *L'Existentialisme est un humanisme*, Paris, Éditions Nagel

—— (1964) 'Réponse à Albert Camus', in *Situations IV*, Paris, Gallimard, pp.90–125

Schlette, Heinz Robert (1994) 'Zur Interpretation der Natur bei Camus', in *Die Gegenwart des Absurden. Studien zu Albert Camus* (ed. Pieper, above), pp.87–102

Shestov, Leo (Chestov, in publications in French) (1923) *La Nuit de Gethsémani. Essai sur la philosophie de Pascal*, in the series *Les Cahiers Verts*, ed. Daniel Halevy, no.23, pp.i–xi, and 1–161, Paris, Grasset

—— (1969) *Kierkegaard and the Existential Philosophy*, trans. by Elinor Hewitt, Ohio University Press

Simon, P.-H. (1962) *Présence de Camus*, Paris, La Renaissance du Livre

Sjursen, N. (1995) 'Meursault, un Job de notre temps? Une lecture girardienne', in *Albert Camus 16* (ed. Gay-Crosier, above), pp.123–35

Suther, Judith D. (ed., 1980) *Essays on Camus's 'Exile and the Kingdom'*, University of Mississippi, Romance Monographs, Inc. No. 41

Tacca, O. (1980) 'L'Étranger comme récit d'auteur-transcripteur', *in Albert Camus 1980* (ed. Gay-Crosier, above), pp.87–100

Theis, Raymund (1980) 'Albert Camus's Return to Sisyphus', in *Essays on Camus's 'Exile and the Kingdom'* (ed. Suther, above) pp.21–43. Originally in German in *Romanische Forschungen*, no. 70 (1958), pp. 66–90

Todd, Olivier (1996) *Albert Camus. Une vie*, Paris, Gallimard, Collection Folio

Van Huy, Nguyen (1961) *La métaphysique du bonheur chez Albert Camus*, Neuchâtel, Imprimerie Centrale

Viggiani, Carl A. (1956) 'Camus' *L'Étranger*', in *PMLA* (*Publications of the Modern Languages Association*), December 1956, pp.865–87

Walker, David H. (1982) 'Image, symbole et signification dans "La Pierre qui pousse",' in *Albert Camus 11. Camus et la Religion, Revue des Lettres Modernes*, Paris, Lettres Modernes, pp.77–104

—— (ed., 1994) *Albert Camus. Les extrêmes et l'équilibre. Actes du colloque de Keele, 25–27 mars 1993. Réunis et présentés par David H. Walker*, Amsterdam, Rodopi

Weyembergh, Maurice (1998) *Albert Camus ou la mémoire des origines*, Paris, De Boek & Larcier

Williams, James S. (2000) *'La Peste'*, London, Grant & Cutler

Yedes, Ali (2003) *Camus l'Algérien*, Paris, L'Harmattan

Index

Abdelkrim, Z., 199
Arendt, H., 21–2, 30, 86n, 146, 148
Augustine (St.), 30, 36–7, 45, 74, 125, 139, 146–8, 169, 273

Baranger, W., 98
Barrier, M., 82
Barthes, R., 92, 108, 118, 144, 145
Baudouin, Ch., 182
Bespaloff, R., 76, 133
Bloom, H., 16
Brée, G., 23, 49n, 51n, 73, 96, 111, 156n, 268, 282
Brisville, J.-Cl., 37, 92, 188n, 241, 279
Brock, R., 156n
Brombert, V., 51n, 175, 209, 215

Camus, Albert,
  Texts (drama)
    Caligula, 15, 37–8, 75, 113–14, 161
    Justes (Les), 15, 19, 66, 92, 131, 132
    Malentendu (Le), 15, 17, 18, 104, 161
  Texts (fiction)
    Chute (La), 15, 16, 29, 31, 32, 42, 64, 84, 93, 95, 139, 159, 161–96, 198–9, 203–4, 209–10, 218, 222, 232, 267–8, 273, 275, 281–3
    Étranger (L'), 15–18, 29, 32–3, 37, 39, 43, 49, 50–1, 55–6, 62–3, 65, 68–71, 74–111, 116–18, 128–9, 145, 151, 155, 158, 162, 169, 179, 184, 204, 209, 223, 242, 245, 248, 266–8, 275, 279, 280–3, 285
    Exil et le Royaume (L'), 16, 29, 197–237, 253
    Mort heureuse (La), 18, 29, 32, 37, 39, 41, 47–71, 73, 75–6, 80, 82, 92, 113, 126, 152, 158, 180, 199, 243, 254, 273, 278, 279, 282–4
    Peste (La), 15–16, 18–19, 26, 29, 33, 55–6, 93, 110, 113–60, 162, 170, 198, 236, 242, 245, 248, 267, 269, 278, 281
    Premier Homme (Le), 16, 18, 29, 44, 59, 63, 65, 71, 148, 199, 219, 239–71, 273–4, 280–1, 283–5
  Texts (other writings)
    Carnets, 15–18, 20–1, 26, 28n–31, 33–5, 37n–8, 41–2, 44, 46, 50, 51, 54, 56–8, 63, 69, 70n, 77, 79n, 81–2, 88n, 110, 113n, 115n, 116, 117n, 119, 124n–5, 128n, 130, 135, 138, 142, 151, 152, 158n–9, 165, 169, 175, 189n, 201n–2, 204n, 216n, 219, 225n, 236n, 246, 256n, 267, 278, 282
    Envers et l'endroit (L'), 34–37n, 57, 141, 169, 202, 213, 219, 239, 248–9, 251, 283
    Homme révolté (L'), 14, 66, 115n, 128, 131, 141, 144, 164, 166, 181, 215, 216, 239
    Journaux de voyage, 230
    Mythe de Sisyphe (Le), 17–19, 22–3, 24n, 25n, 28, 31n, 34, 37, 39n, 41, 44, 49, 56, 73, 75, 78, 90, 91n, 93, 103, 113, 119, 131, 136, 146, 273–4
    Noces, 37n, 38n, 42, 43n, 55n, 62, 122, 156n, 166, 198, 199, 202n, 275, 276
  Texts (short essays, dissertation, etc.,)

'Crise de l'homme' (La), 131n, 135n, 139
'Énigme' (L'), 26n, 39n, 228n
'Été à Alger' (L'), 58n, 257
'Exil d'Hélène' (L'), 24, 199n
'Intelligence et l'échafaud' (L'), 16n, 17n, 46n
'Métaphysique chrétienne et néo-platonisme', 30n
'Noces à Tipasa', 62, 156, 202n
'Sur l'avenir de la tragédie', 19n
'Vent à Djémila' (Le), 38, 53–4
Attitudes to
Algeria and Arabs, 43, 65, 68, 76, 78–9, 95–9, 102, 111, 162, 167, 169, 171, 181, 183, 206, 220, 221–3, 226, 242, 244, 245, 252, 257–63, 266, 280, 281
Existentialism and the Absurd, 17, 21, 23–4, 26–9, 39n, 44–5, 47–8n,, 50, 75, 79, 89–90, 94, 96, 115, 138, 165, 203
Greece and pagan antiquity, 25, 30, 34–5, 36n, 37n, 42, 44–5, 49, 51, 62, 91n, 140, 246, 277–8
Religion, 24–5, 30–1, 33–7, 39, 42, 44–5, 49, 70, 73–9, 85, 88–90, 93, 107, 130, 132–3, 135, 139–151, 155, 168–9, 171, 174, 185–8, 193–4, 202, 215–18, 225, 235–7, 243–4, 246–8, 256, 274, 284–5
Women, 29, 43, 57, 61, 92, 119–22, 152–5, 208, 241, 278–80
Concept of
Happiness, 31–2, 37–8, 40–4, 47–71, 73–6, 78, 80, 91–3, 100, 105, 110–1, 120, 138–9, 152, 154–7, 161–2, 166–70, 173–4, 177, 182, 184, 197, 232, 236, 246, 273, 275–7, 281, 284

Innocence and guilt, 29, 30–3, 37, 66–7, 69–70, 74–6, 93–4, 100, 102, 104, 110–111, 114, 123, 134, 138, 147, 154, 157, 158, 159, 162, 168, 170, 180, 181, 184–8, 194–5, 198, 203, 245, 274–5, 281
Castex, P., 81n, 82, 87
Chabot, J., 80n, 133, 245
Chamfort, Nicolas de, 13
Champigny, R., 91n, 111n
Claudel, P., 47, 169n, 249, 273
Corneille, P., 119, 120, 156
Crochet, M., 85n
Cruickshank, J., 80n, 124–5, 158
Cryle, P., 198, 204n, 236

Davison, R., 219
Deguy, J., 84n
Descartes, René, 39, 175, 192
Di Meglio, I., 77n, 142, 151
Djemai, A., 16, 257n
Dostoyevsky, F., 23, 24, 25, 26, 141
Dubois, L., 18n, 261
Dunwoodie, P., 205

Eisenzweig, U., 83, 94
Ellison, D., 141

Favre, F., 89
Felman, S., 172n, 189
Fitch, B.T., 83, 163
Flaubert, G., 18, 207
Fortier, P., 211
Foucauld, Ch. de, 217

Gadourek, C., 148, 236
Gassin, J., 38, 80n, 96, 103n, 229n
Gay-Crosier, R., 156n
Gide, A., 24, 56, 138, 169, 267
Girard, R., 77n

Goethe, J.W. von, 34, 107–8, 175
Grenier, J., 56, 251, 282
Grimaud, M., 223
Guérin, J., 16

Hargreaves, A., 97n
Heidegger, M., 21, 22n, 24
Hermet, J., 141
Imbert, H., 17n

Isaac, J., 15n, 21n

Jones, R., 97n, 192n
Jung, C.G., 76n, 78, 106

Kafka, F., 24, 94, 122, 128, 203, 209
Keefe, T., 176, 190
Kierkegaard, S., 23, 24, 27, 141, 146, 166

Lafayette, Madame de, 14, 16, 17n, 18
Le Guern, M., 281
Le Hir, J., 80n , 96
Leites, N., 85
Lenzini, J., 258
Lévi-Valensi, J., 169, 192
Longstaffe, M., 120n
Lottman, H., 49, 259

Maritain, J., 33, 130
Martin du Gard, R., 204
Mauriac, F., 118, 127–8, 140, 142
McBride, J., 28, 30n, 74n
McCann, J., 108
McCarthy, P., 78, 82–3, 89, 96, 101, 103, 132, 135, 199, 259
Miller, O., 209
Montgomery, G., 79, 91n, 122, 152, 208, 279–80, 283
Morot-Sir, É., 77n, 81, 83
Mounier, E., 34, 45, 91n
Murchland, B., 133

Nacer-Khodja, H., 157n, 206, 262
Nietzsche, F., 21, 24–5, 29–30, 38, 41, 52, 54–6, 60–1, 131, 140, 151
Noyer-Weidner, A., 79n, 81

O'Brien, C.C., 96, 97n
Onimus, J., 207, 208

Parker, E., 96
Peyre, H., 34, 36
Pichon-Rivière, A., 98n
Picon, G., 133
Pilkington, A., 26n
Pingaud, B., 15n, 18n, 69, 87, 93, 95
Plotinus, 30, 36, 91
Pratt, B., 82, 91n, 96
Proust, M., 17, 267
Pullman, P., 13

Quilliot, R., 21, 23n, 25n, 36n, 45, 48n, 51n, 54, 55n, 80n, 85, 124, 130n, 139n, 141, 148n, 150n, 164, 191n, 200, 206n, 216, 230, 232, 253, 267

Rabaté, D., 82n
Reichelberg, R., 49, 84, 96
Rey, P.L., 111n
Rigaud, J., 99
Rizzuto, A., 40, 42n, 43n, 80n, 81, 91n, 96, 269
Robbe-Grillet, A., 15, 39, 285
Rousset, J., 81, 175

Sade (Marquis de), 17
Said, E., 16, 96
Sarang, V., 49
Sarocchi, J., 59n, 82
Sarraute, N., 15, 85
Sartre, J.-P., 14, 20–3, 26, 50–1, 75, 84, 118, 125, 131, 164–5, 181, 259
Schlette, H., 283
Sénac, J., 157, 206

Shestov, L. (Chestov), 23–5
Simon, P.-H., 199
Sjursen, N., 85n
Stendhal (Henri Beyle), 17–20, 28–9, 31, 41, 52, 56, 113, 117, 121, 176, 227
Swift, J., 20, 194

Tacca, O., 82n
Theis, R., 236
Todd, O., 128n, 165, 216n, 226, 240, 241, 259, 260, 273, 282

Van Huy, N., 91
Viggiani, C., 80, 85n, 284–5

Walker, D., 235
Weil, S., 139, 193–4
Weyembergh, M., 16, 21–2, 54, 60, 61n, 67, 261
Williams, J., 127

Yédès, A., 262

Modern French Identities
Edited by Peter Collier

This series aims to publish monographs, editions or collections of papers based on recent research into modern French Literature. It welcomes contributions from academics, researchers and writers in British and Irish universities in particular.

Modern French Identities focuses on the French and Francophone writing of the twentieth century, whose formal experiments and revisions of genre have combined to create an entirely new set of literary forms, from the thematic autobiographies of Michel Leiris and Bernard Noël to the magic realism of French Caribbean writers.

The idea that identities are constructed rather than found, and that the self is an area to explore rather than a given pretext, runs through much of modern French literature, from Proust, Gide and Apollinaire to Kristeva, Barthes, Duras, Germain and Roubaud.

This series reflects a concern to explore the turn-of-the-century turmoil in ideas and values that is expressed in the works of theorists like Lacan, Irigaray and Bourdieu and to follow through the impact of current ideologies such as feminism and postmodernism on the literary and cultural interpretation and presentation of the self, whether in terms of psychoanalytic theory, gender, autobiography, cinema, fiction and poetry, or in newer forms like performance art.

The series publishes studies of individual authors and artists, comparative studies, and interdisciplinary projects, including those where art and cinema intersect with literature.

Volume 1   Victoria Best & Peter Collier (eds.): Powerful Bodies.
            Performance in French Cultural Studies.
            220 pages. 1999. ISBN 3-906762-56-4 / US-ISBN 0-8204-4239-9

Volume 2   Julia Waters: Intersexual Rivalry.
            A 'Reading in Pairs' of Marguerite Duras and Alain Robbe-Grillet.
            228 pages. 2000. ISBN 3-906763-74-9 / US-ISBN 0-8204-4626-2

Volume 3   Sarah Cooper: Relating to Queer Theory.
            Rereading Sexual Self-Definition with Irigaray, Kristeva, Wittig
            and Cixous.
            231 pages. 2000. ISBN 3-906764-46-X / US-ISBN 0-8204-4636-X

Volume 4   Julia Prest & Hannah Thompson (eds.): Corporeal Practices.
            (Re)figuring the Body in French Studies.
            166 pages. 2000. ISBN 3-906764-53-2 / US-ISBN 0-8204-4639-4

Volume 5   Victoria Best: Critical Subjectivities.
            Identity and Narrative in the Work
            of Colette and Marguerite Duras.
            243 pages. 2000. ISBN 3-906763-89-7 / US-ISBN 0-8204-4631-9

Volume 6   David Houston Jones: The Body Abject: Self and Text in
            Jean Genet and Samuel Beckett.
            213 pages. 2000. ISBN 3-906765-07-5 / US-ISBN 0-8204-5058-8

Volume 7   Robin MacKenzie: The Unconscious in Proust's *A la recherche
            du temps perdu.*
            270 pages. 2000. ISBN 3-906758-38-9 / US-ISBN 0-8204-5070-7

Volume 8   Rosemary Chapman: Siting the Quebec Novel.
            The Representation of Space in Francophone Writing in Quebec.
            282 pages. 2000. ISBN 3-906758-85-0 / US-ISBN 0-8204-5090-1

Volume 9   Gill Rye: Reading for Change.
            Interactions between Text Identity in Contemporary French
            Women's Writing (Baroche, Cixous, Constant).
            223 pages. 2001. ISBN 3-906765-97-0 / US-ISBN 0-8204-5315-3

Volume 10   Jonathan Paul Murphy: Proust's Art.
            Painting, Sculpture and Writing in *A la recherche du temps perdu.*
            248 pages. 2001. ISBN 3-906766-17-9 / US-ISBN 0-8204-5319-6

Volume 11   Julia Dobson: Hélène Cixous and the Theatre.
            The Scene of Writing.
            166 pages. 2002. ISBN 3-906766-20-9 / US-ISBN 0-8204-5322-6

Volume 12   Emily Butterworth & Kathryn Robson (eds.): Shifting Borders.
            Theory and Identity in French Literature.
            VIII + 208 pages. 2001.
            ISBN 3-906766-86-1 / US-ISBN 0-8204-5602-0

Volume 13   Victoria Korzeniowska: The Heroine as Social Redeemer in
            the Plays of Jean Giraudoux.
            144 pages. 2001. ISBN 3-906766-92-6 / US-ISBN 0-8204-5608-X

Volume 14　Kay Chadwick: Alphonse de Châteaubriant:
　　　　　　Catholic Collaborator.
　　　　　　327 pages. 2002. ISBN 3-906766-94-2 / US-ISBN 0-8204-5610-1

Volume 15　Nina Bastin: Queneau's Fictional Worlds.
　　　　　　291 pages. 2002. ISBN 3-906768-32-5 / US-ISBN 0-8204-5620-9

Volume 16　Sarah Fishwick: The Body in the Work of Simone de Beauvoir.
　　　　　　284 pages. 2002. ISBN 3-906768-33-3 / US-ISBN 0-8204-5621-7

Volume 17　Simon Kemp & Libby Saxton (eds.): Seeing Things.
　　　　　　Vision, Perception and Interpretation in French Studies.
　　　　　　287 pages. 2002. ISBN 3-906768-46-5 / US-ISBN 0-8204-5858-9

Volume 18　Kamal Salhi (ed.): French in and out of France.
　　　　　　Language Policies, Intercultural Antagonisms and Dialogue.
　　　　　　487 pages. 2002. ISBN 3-906768-47-3 / US-ISBN 0-8204-5859-7

Volume 19　Genevieve Shepherd: Simone de Beauvoir's Fiction.
　　　　　　A Psychoanalytic Rereading.
　　　　　　262 pages. 2003. ISBN 3-906768-55-4 / US-ISBN 0-8204-5867-8

Volume 20　Lucille Cairns (ed.): Gay and Lesbian Cultures in France.
　　　　　　290 pages. 2002. ISBN 3-906769-66-6 / US-ISBN 0-8204-5903-8

Volume 21　Wendy Goolcharan-Kumeta: My Mother, My Country.
　　　　　　Reconstructing the Female Self in Guadeloupean Women's Writing.
　　　　　　236 pages. 2003. ISBN 3-906769-76-3 / US-ISBN 0-8204-5913-5

Volume 22　Patricia O'Flaherty: Henry de Montherlant (1895–1972).
　　　　　　A Philosophy of Failure.
　　　　　　256 pages. 2003. ISBN 3-03910-013-0 / US-ISBN 0-8204-6282-9

Volume 23　Katherine Ashley (ed.): Prix Goncourt, 1903–2003: essais critiques.
　　　　　　205 pages. 2004. ISBN 3-03910-018-1 / US-ISBN 0-8204-6287-X

Volume 24　Julia Horn & Lynsey Russell-Watts (eds): Possessions.
　　　　　　Essays in French Literature, Cinema and Theory.
　　　　　　223 pages. 2003. ISBN 3-03910-005-X / US-ISBN 0-8204-5924-0

Volume 25　Steve Wharton: Screening Reality.
　　　　　　French Documentary Film during the German Occupation.
　　　　　　252 pages. 2006. ISBN 3-03910-066-1 / US-ISBN 0-8204-6882-7

Volume 26　Frédéric Royall (ed.): Contemporary French Cultures and Societies.
　　　　　　421 pages. 2004. ISBN 3-03910-074-2 / US-ISBN 0-8204-6890-8

Volume 27   Tom Genrich: Authentic Fictions.
            Cosmopolitan Writing of the Troisième République, 1908–1940.
            288 pages. ISBN 3-03910-285-0 / US-ISBN 0-8204-7212-3

Volume 28   Forthcoming.

Volume 29   Kathryn Banks & Joseph Harris (eds): Exposure.
            Revealing Bodies, Unveiling Representations.
            194 pages. 2004. ISBN 3-03910-163-3 / US-ISBN 0-8204-6973-4

Volume 30   Emma Gilby & Katja Haustein (eds): Space.
            New Dimensions in French Studies.
            169 pages. 2005. ISBN 3-03910-178-1 / US-ISBN 0-8204-6988-2

Volume 31   Rachel Killick (ed.): Uncertain Relations.
            Some Configurations of the 'Third Space' in Francophone Writings
            of the Americas and of Europe.
            258 pages. 2005. ISBN 3-03910-189-7 / US-ISBN 0-8204-6999-8

Volume 32   Sarah F. Donachie & Kim Harrison (eds): Love and Sexuality.
            New Approaches in French Studies.
            194 pages. 2005. ISBN 3-03910-249-4 / US-ISBN 0-8204-7178-X

Volume 33   Michaël Abecassis: The Representation of Parisian Speech in
            the Cinema of the 1930s.
            409 pages. 2005. ISBN 3-03910-260-5 / US-ISBN 0-8204-7189-5

Volume 34   Benedict O'Donohoe: Sartre's Theatre: Acts for Life.
            301 pages. 2005. ISBN 3-03910-250-X / US-ISBN 0-8204-7207-7

Volume 35   Moya Longstaffe: The Fiction of Albert Camus. A Complex Simplicity.
            300 pages. 2007. ISBN 3-03910-304-0 / US-ISBN 0-8204-7229-8

Volume 36: Forthcoming.

Volume 37   Shirley Ann Jordan: Contemporary French Women's Writing:
            Women's Visions, Women's Voices, Women's Lives.
            308 pages. 2005. ISBN 3-03910-315-6 / US-ISBN 0-8204-7240-9

Volume 38   Forthcoming.

Volume 39   Michael O'Dwyer & Michèle Raclot: Le Journal de Julien Green:
            Miroir d'une âme, miroir d'un siècle.
            289 pages. 2005. ISBN 3-03910-319-9

Volume 40   Thomas Baldwin: The Material Object in the Work of Marcel Proust.
            188 pages. 2005. ISBN 3-03910-323-7 / US-ISBN 0-8204-7247-6

Volume 41   Charles Forsdick & Andrew Stafford (eds.): The Modern Essay
            in French: Genre, Sociology, Performance.
            296 pages. 2005. ISBN 3-03910-514-0 / US-ISBN 0-8204-7520-3

Volume 42   Peter Dunwoodie: Francophone Writing in Transition.
            Algeria 1900–1945.
            339 pages. 2005. ISBN 3-03910-294-X / US-ISBN 0-8204-7220-4

Volume 43   Emma Webb (ed.): Marie Cardinal: New Perspectives.
            260 pages. 2006. ISBN 3-03910-544-2 / US-ISBN 0-8204-7547-5

Volume 44   Forthcoming.

Volume 45   David Gascoigne: The Games of Fiction: Georges Perec and Modern
            French Ludic Narrative.
            327 pages. 2006. ISBN 3-03910-697-X / US-ISBN 0-8204-7962-4

Volume 46–53 Forthcoming.

Volume 54   Nicole Thatcher & Ethel Tolansky (eds.): Six Authors in Captivity.
            Literary Responses to the Occupation of France during World War II.
            205 pages. 2006. ISBN 3-03910-520-5 / US-ISBN 0-8204-7526-2